CHALLENGING THINKING ABOUT TEACHING AND LEARNING

CHALLENGING THINKING ABOUT TEACHING AND LEARNING

CHRISTINE M. RUBIE-DAVIES
AND CATHERINE RAWLINSON
EDITORS

Nova Science Publishers, Inc.
New York

NOTICE TO THE READER

The Publisher has taken reasonable care in the preparation of this book, but makes no expressed or implied warranty of any kind and assumes no responsibility for any errors or omissions. No liability is assumed for incidental or consequential damages in connection with or arising out of information contained in this book. The Publisher shall not be liable for any special, consequential, or exemplary damages resulting, in whole or in part, from the readers' use of, or reliance upon, this material.

Independent verification should be sought for any data, advice or recommendations contained in this book. In addition, no responsibility is assumed by the publisher for any injury and/or damage to persons or property arising from any methods, products, instructions, ideas or otherwise contained in this publication.

This publication is designed to provide accurate and authoritative information with regard to the subject matter covered herein. It is sold with the clear understanding that the Publisher is not engaged in rendering legal or any other professional services. If legal or any other expert assistance is required, the services of a competent person should be sought. FROM A DECLARATION OF PARTICIPANTS JOINTLY ADOPTED BY A COMMITTEE OF THE AMERICAN BAR ASSOCIATION AND A COMMITTEE OF PUBLISHERS.

LIBRARY OF CONGRESS CATALOGING-IN-PUBLICATION DATA

Challenging thinking about teaching and learning / Christine M. Rubie-Davies and Catherine Rawlinson, editors.
    p. cm.
 ISBN 978-1-60456-744-1 (hardcover)
 1. Teaching. 2. Learning, Psychology of. 3. Teachers--In-service training. I. Rubie-Davies, Christine M. II. Rawlinson, Catherine.
 LB1025.3.C397 2008
 371.102--dc22
                          2008023103

Published by Nova Science Publishers, Inc. — New York

CONTENTS

PREFACE

This book is designed to stimulate and challenge thinking about pedagogy and learning. It includes recent research but is also strongly practitioner-based, i.e., all chapters and sections show how the findings might be implemented in classrooms. It comprises a collection of research papers and brief reports related to teaching and learning.

The book includes articles that cover all levels of schooling: early childhood, elementary, middle school, secondary and tertiary as well as articles that have direct relevance for teacher education and teacher professional development, including reports that use sociological or psychological frameworks.

FOREWORD

Frances Langdon

The value of this book, *Challenging Thinking about Teaching and Learning*, is that the contributions draw on diverse educational fields—psychology, sociology, and teacher and special education. The intention is to generate cross-talk among educationalists of different theoretical research traditions and practice affiliations, and to challenge compartmentalisation. The desire to address theoretical and methodological segregation was not a whimsical disregard of the importance of individual disciplines. It was instead recognition of the complexity of teaching and learning and the educational context, and an acknowledgement of the understandings to be gained from critical appraisal of research findings presented from multiple perspectives. Writing in 1959 in *A Room of One's Own*, Virginia Woolf, when prohibited from entering the university library, observed that while it is "unpleasant to be locked out . . . it is worse perhaps to be locked in". It is not a viable option for teachers to be locked into thinking about teaching and learning from one frame of reference given the complexity of teaching and the challenges associated with an imperative to cater for the learning of increasingly diverse populations.

A credible future for education hinges upon teachers' and scholars' engagement in the search for meaning to advance practice and the professional community of education. I agree with the distinguished educational psychologist and researcher Lee Shulman, who, in his 1992 essay *Research on Teaching: A Historical and Personal Perspective*, argued that this moral purpose is dependent upon the accommodation of a schizophrenic stance by both being "impassioned and dispassionate, deeply committed and objectively accurate". He predicted the focus of educators' and scholars' work will "grow increasingly cognitive, substantive, contextual, and—in several senses—local", and that disciplinary boundaries will blur. Quite rightly, the quest for generalizations to inform our understanding about teaching, learning, and professional development will continue but we will increasingly see teachers become agents of research, rather than subjects—with the purpose of advancing teaching, learning, and the education profession.

The methodologically varied contributions in this volume reflect the blurring of disciplinary boundaries and a moral commitment to the enhancement of practice. They provide insight into a range of research findings on student and teacher learning and achievement from preschool to the tertiary level. They address a range of topics including the gifted and talented, boys, special education, students presenting with behavioural challenges, and the diverse needs associated with identity, as well as matters relating to assessment, critical thinking skills, and pedagogical challenges for teacher education and professional development. Those engaged in teaching and learning in whatever capacity should have their interest triggered as both theoretical and practical questions related to learning and teaching are interrogated. Questions examined in this volume include: What do teachers need to know about teaching in order to promote learning and raise student achievement? What kinds of evidence are required to know that learning has occurred? How important is it for the teacher to recognize the needs of diverse student groups in terms of their ability to teach? How do teachers challenge their own practice to advance both student and teacher learning?

The genesis for this book was the establishment of the School of Teaching, Learning and Development at the University of Auckland, which brought together more than 50 educational academics—educational theorists and teacher educators. In my role as Head of School, I was intent upon supporting collaborative endeavours that would show-case research activity and expertise, and promote the opportunity to engage in review, critique, and discussion of thought and practice in the field of education. Like many good ideas, this one was sparked by a conversation among colleagues, which, once ignited, was fuelled by the research committee and the sterling work of the editors, contributors, and reviewers. Professor Deborah Butler, who provided the link with the University of British Columbia, and her colleagues have contributed to the rigour of the publication.

It is anticipated that the reader will have ideas and practices confirmed or, in some instances, disconfirmed. In the latter case it is hoped that this will be a catalyst for examination and questioning of theory and experiences anew and for engaging in a quest for further understanding and the advancement of practice. I hope this first edition of the School of Teaching Learning and Development's monograph will be widely read, provoke debate, and contribute in a meaningful way to educational practice and the profession.

Frances Langdon
Head of School
Teaching, Learning and Development

Te Kura Whakawhanake Akoranga
Faculty of Education
University of Auckland

INTRODUCTION

Christine Rubie-Davies and Catherine Rawlinson

This book is designed to stimulate and challenge thinking about teaching and learning. It is a collection of research papers and brief reports on recent research, but it is also strongly practitioner-based, with suggestions on how the research findings might be implemented in classrooms and early childhood centres.

The chapters have been organized into four major themes: raising achievement, recognizing diversity, challenging pedagogy, and enhancing pedagogy. The various studies were conducted mainly in New Zealand but also in the United States and Singapore. Various methodologies are used—some of the studies are qualitative, others quantitative; some incorporate a psychological perspective and others are sociological. But whatever the context or methodology, the information presented and the issues raised are those that are currently engaging the interest of educators internationally. We hope the studies will contribute to educational debate and understandings globally.

Unlike many education books with a narrow focus on one specialist topic, this book is broad ranging in that it covers and combines the theoretical or academic with the practical. For this reason, it is aimed at a wide readership—the intended audience includes all education professionals, from practising and preservice teachers to teacher educators, education researchers, and other educationalists.

It is essential for professional educators, whatever the area in which they work, to continually examine their practice critically in order that all students receive high quality education. We envisage the book will be useful across a variety of courses. For example, it offers a powerful resource for postgraduate students, giving them access to current research in a wide range of education areas and raising possible topics for their own research. It will stimulate debate on pedagogy among teacher educators and teachers, and challenge teachers' thinking about pedagogy, whether at the early childhood, elementary, secondary, or tertiary levels. It also provides some innovative ideas to introduce to teaching practice in early childhood centres and schools. For the academic, it will extend current thinking and sow the seeds for future research.

There has been much discussion internationally on our first theme, raising student achievement. For example, the United States has introduced the "No child left behind" (NCLB) policy, and there is a similar trend in the United Kingdom aimed at improving literacy and numeracy. New Zealand likewise has a raft of initiatives to support the national goal of enhancing student achievement: for example, Starpath (an initiative to investigate the reasons for underparticipation by certain population groups in tertiary education, and to determine practical solutions to this problem); Te Kotahitanga (a collaborative response to underachievement among Maori students in which researchers work alongside teachers to introduce more collaborative and co-operative forms of teaching) and the Talent Development Initiative for gifted students. Such a focus on raising achievement is important because for many groups in western societies, particularly minority groups, large numbers of students are underachieving in our school systems. It is important that any changes designed to raise achievement take account of what the research evidence indicates will work. The chapters in this section provide studies that we expect will promote debate about enhancing student performance.

One aspect of raising achievement is ensuring that the wide range of students in the classroom and early childhood centres is catered for—hence our second theme, recognizing diversity. The concept of diversity includes ethnicity, gender, language, cultural background, and having special education needs or particular gifts. New Zealand, as with all Western countries, is characterized by an increasing diversity in the population, and this is reflected in the children we teach. It is important that teachers are well equipped to cater for the range of student needs.

If all students are to be successful within education, we need to focus on teachers rather than students; holding the student or the student's background or environment as primarily responsible for underachievement should be an anathema to the teaching profession. Effective teaching can make a difference to student achievement, which leads to our third theme of challenging pedagogy—if students are not being successful, it is time to examine teaching practice and the pedagogy that supports it. We also need to make sure that, when we are examining teacher implementation of pedagogy, we do so in a way that is evidence-based— when new programmes or methods are introduced, it is important to have clear baseline data and then to measure actual student outcomes to show whether the new pedagogy has led to improvements.

However, challenging our thinking about pedagogy is still only part of the equation; we must also change our pedagogy and practice based on what we learn from our critique, and this is the theme of the final section—enhancing pedagogy (that is, advancing what we do as teachers and teacher educators). The chapters in this section provide some detailed and specific examples, from early childhood through to teacher education and adult education, of how a change in pedagogy can lead to enhanced student learning.

While the four themes in our book are set out in linear form, the process of reflective professional inquiry that the book aims to stimulate is an iterative process, more cyclic than linear. Any debates raised by the themes in the latter parts of the book (challenging and enhancing pedagogy to improve student learning) should inevitably lead back to the themes in the first sections (raising achievement and respecting diversity) and to the effects of any changes in practice on students and their learning. As educators, we all need to be engaged constantly in this reflective cycle of professional inquiry that draws on research evidence to help us improve our practice and raise the achievement of all students.

We now describe each part, and its constituent chapters, in more detail.

PART 1. RAISING ACHIEVEMENT

The book opens with two chapters that present contrasting debates relating to underachievement—the first discusses the issues in relation to ethnic minority groups forming a "tail" of underachievement and the second chapter reminds us that concentrating solely on the lower end of the achievement scale can draw attention away from the underperforming individuals in the higher achieving groups. Teacher beliefs and expectations can also contribute significantly to student learning and hence achievement—a topic also explored in this section. Other chapters explore achievement from a curriculum perspective—in particular, science, mathematics, and literacy. There is also a chapter on New Zealand's asTTle programme (the collection of student data for formative assessment) and data on students' higher order thinking skills. The section concludes with a chapter on the role of students' critical thinking skills in raising student achievement.

PART 2. RECOGNIZING DIVERSITY

Part 2 explores in some detail the reasons some specific groups may be achieving or underachieving within education, with chapters that examine specific marginalized groups: the gifted, children with special education needs, children with behaviour difficulties, and ethnic minorities. The part begins with a chapter that analyses the way that identity is constructed for students with a dual heritage—in this instance, Maori and Pakeha (New Zealand Europeans). This is followed by two chapters relating to gifted students, the first of which explores factors that may contribute to gifted student underachievement and the second which examines influences that can affect young gifted and talented writers achieving their potential. The other chapters, respectively, discuss research on teacher and parent perceptions of young boys with behavioural difficulties, the learning difficulties experienced by older students in mainstream education who were in foster care, and quality indicators for alternative education programmes operating outside the mainstream school. The final chapter highlights the experience of a group of students with special educational needs, as voiced by the students.

PART 3. CHALLENGING PEDAGOGY

The chapters in this part examine and challenge aspects of pedagogy, and include some specific recommendations and implications for teacher education programmes. When students are not successful within the education system, it is important that, rather than "blaming" the student, we scrutinize those aspects of teaching that may be contributing to student underachievement. Teacher education has a major responsibility to continually develop and enhance the pedagogy of its learners, be they preservice or practising teachers.

The opening chapter gives an example of an innovative means for teachers to reflect on and enhance their pedagogy through the use of drama in the teacher education classroom. The theme of innovative pedagogy is picked up in another chapter, which examines how web-based tools can contribute to learning. The marginalization of gifted education within teacher education is concerning to many educators in New Zealand and one of the middle chapters analyzes this issue. Another chapter examines the extent to which a cohort of teachers on a specialized training programme for teaching deaf students remain in this specialist field once they graduate. Finally, there are two chapters which discuss the role of the practicum in challenging and developing the pedagogy of preservice teachers. One examines the role of the associate teacher while the other discusses aspects of the practicum that make it a successful learning experience for preservice teachers.

PART 4. ENHANCING PEDAGOGY

Having challenged current pedagogy, the debates then move to an in-depth exploration of ways in which pedagogy may be fostered to improve student learning. The opening chapter provides an example of the type of ethical issues that may surface when government agencies sponsor research; researchers may produce findings that do not "suit" the outcomes their funding agency may have expected, for example. That type of dilemma arises outside the classroom—within the classroom or early childhood centre, it may be teacher beliefs that need to be confronted. This is discussed in the chapter on how teachers' conceptions of assessment can affect the efficacy of any professional development. Teachers undertook education designed to enhance their understanding of appropriate assessment practices but its effective implementation was overshadowed by teachers' existing conceptions. Student beliefs, too, can affect learning outcomes, as discussed in a chapter on how students' beliefs about internal and external locus of control affect their approach to learning. Two other chapters focus specifically on the individual teacher. One looks at the use of video-recording as a form of professional development, in which teachers record their own practice to develop a deeper understanding of their pedagogical decision making. The other examines the literature related to teacher questioning and its role in developing higher order thinking among students.

SUMMARY

We hope, then, that this book will inspire researchers and teachers to question their pedagogy and to closely examine how students are learning in their early childhood centre, classroom, or lecture theatre. The debates encompassed by this book should encourage and stimulate us to question our beliefs about pedagogy. The book aims to make us all— preservice and practising teachers, teacher educators, and education researchers—think about our instructional practices and whether our actions are having a positive influence on student learning and achievement, particularly in relation to groups that commonly underachieve. If any group, or individual, is underachieving, our pedagogy is not wholly effective.

We would like to thank the authors for their thoughtful and considered contributions to this book. Every chapter underwent peer review by at least two reviewers. This was a significant commitment for the reviewers, most of whom read and reflected upon four chapters each. We are extremely grateful to the reviewers for their generous donation of time and the calibre of their feedback, which has contributed to the high quality of this publication.

Special thanks go to our colleagues from the University of British Columbia: Deborah Butler, Marilyn Chapman, Anthony Clarke, Kadriye Ercikan, Victor Glickman, Lee Gunderson, and Lisa Loutzenheiser; and to and our colleagues from the University of Auckland, Faculty of Education: Airini, Gavin Brown, Lexie Grudnoff, Susan Farruggia, Mavis Haigh, Richard Hamilton, John Hattie, Eleanor Hawe, Helen Hedges, Mary Hill, Frances Langdon, Deidre Le Fevre, Pam Millward, Catherine Rawlinson, and Christine Rubie-Davies.

Finally we wish to thank Janet Rivers who has provided us with outstanding manuscript preparation assistance and who has worked extremely hard on this book.

PART 1. RAISING ACHIEVEMENT

In: Challenging Thinking about Teaching and Learning
Editors: C. M. Rubie-Davies and C. Rawlinson

ISBN: 978-1-60456-744-1
© 2008 Nova Science Publishers, Inc.

Chapter 1

A TAIL OF UNDERACHIEVEMENT

Pam Millward

ABSTRACT

International research has documented that although some New Zealand students' achievement in reading is equal to the best in the world, there is wide disparity of achievement. The performance of students at the lower end of the dispersion has been referred to as "a tail of underachievement". Of concern is the over-representation of Maori and Pacific Island students in that "tail". Of even more concern is that no change in literacy achievement has been identified over a period of 15 years, despite 16 years of significant educational reform and increased government expenditure on education. The chapter discusses explanations for the "tail", including factors external to the education system and those related to the system. It concludes that a complex interaction of home-based and school-based factors needs to be taken into account.

INTRODUCTION

New Zealand education policy, as stated in the National Administration Guidelines (NAGS) (Ministry of Education, 2001b), requires that all students be provided with opportunities to achieve and demonstrate progress. Despite such worthy goals, significant disparities in New Zealand students' achievements have been identified by a number of international research studies over a period of 15 years. The International Education Assessment's (IEA) 1990 reading literacy study (Elley, 1994) initially identified the wide variance in achievement. These findings have been replicated in subsequent international studies including the Programme for International Student Assessment Studies (PISA) (Organisation for Economic Co-operation and Development, 2001, 2005) and the Progress in International Reading Literacy Study (PIRLS) (Mullis, Martin, Gonzalez, & Kennedy, 2003). Not surprisingly, these findings have generated considerable concern among educators and policymakers. A major cause of this concern is that the ethnic groups over-represented in the so-called "tail of underachievement" have been identified as the fastest growing sectors of the population and are predicted to comprise the majority of the New Zealand school population by the year 2040 (Statistics New Zealand, 2001).

INTERNATIONAL LITERACY ACHIEVEMENT STUDIES

The IEA reading literacy study was a cross-national, comparative examination of reading literacy of 9- and 14-year-olds in 32 countries. This study established that high performing New Zealand students achieved at a level equivalent to high performing students from the United States, France, Sweden, Hungary, Iceland, Switzerland, and Hong Kong. Low performing students from New Zealand, however, achieved at a lower level than students from other participating countries, indicating a wide disparity of achievement for New Zealand students. Maori and Pacific Island students were over-represented in the low performance group compared to those of other ethnicities.

The PISA 2000 study analyzed the mathematics, science, and reading literacy achievement of students from 32 countries (Organisation for Economic Co-operation and Development, 2001). Students aged 15 years formed the target group regardless of the school grade in which they were enrolled. Between 4,000 and 10,000 students from each country were involved in the study and sampling procedures ensured that a representative sample of the target population was included. Each subject was tested using a broad sample of tasks with differing levels of difficulty.

The main focus of PISA 2000 was reading literacy. The reading literacy assessment exposed students to a range of written texts including a short story, a letter on the internet, and information presented in a diagram. Students were assessed on their ability to retrieve, interpret, and evaluate specified information. Scores from the three tasks were combined to produce an overall reading performance score and students were assigned a reading competency level. Students proficient at level one were able to complete only the least complex reading tasks while students proficient at level five were able to complete sophisticated and complex reading tasks. Proficiency at level five meant students were able to manage information that was difficult to find in unfamiliar texts, demonstrate detailed understanding of texts by inferring which information was relevant to a set task, and to evaluate critically and build hypotheses by drawing on specialized knowledge while accommodating contrary concepts. Students and school principals completed background questionnaires providing information on students' personal characteristics, family backgrounds, school resources, and institutional settings.

While the findings from the PISA 2000 study supported findings from other international research that poverty and limited resources had a negative effect on student achievement, it was also noted that differences between schools accounted for only 16% of the variation in achievement of the New Zealand Year 11 students in reading literacy (Ministry of Education, 2001a). This PISA study identified New Zealand as having the highest within-school variance of any of the 32 countries studied and comparatively low between-school variance (Organisation for Economic Co-operation and Development, 2001). Further analysis of the PISA 2000 data revealed that despite the high within-school variance, only 11% of that variance was explained by the socioeconomic status of students' families, "suggesting a strong effect for teaching" (Alton-Lee, 2003 p. 3). This would suggest that socioeconomic status is only one of the factors affecting students' achievement levels, and that school-based factors have a major effect.

The PISA 2000 identification of wide variations in the achievement levels of New Zealand students was confirmed a year later in the findings of the Progress in International Reading Literacy Study (PIRLS). The PIRLS 2001 research project involved 34 countries, including New Zealand. Almost 2,500 New Zealand students, aged between 9 and 10 years who were in their fifth year at school, had their reading literacy skills assessed. A total of 156 schools participated in the New Zealand study. The key findings from this study identified that the mean score for New Zealand students was significantly higher than the international mean, but New Zealand's mean was significantly lower than 11 other countries. The PIRLS research identified the spread of scores for New Zealand students was wider than for most other countries (Ministry of Education, 2003).

The PISA and PIRLS studies described above were snapshots in time that identified a recurring theme of wide-ranging achievement levels in New Zealand schools. The occurrence of these findings over a significant period of time was reaffirmed by the Trends study—a study that partly replicated the 1990–91 IEA reading literacy study and provided data that enabled the participating countries to compare their reading literacy achievement in 2001 with that of the 1990–1991 study (Martin, Mullis, Gonzalez, & Kennedy, 2003). New Zealand was one of nine countries that participated in the Trends study in the latter part of 2001. This study assessed the reading literacy skills of middle primary level students (Year 5 students, approximately 9-years-old), but drew from a different sample of Year 5 students from that used in the PIRLS study. Approximately 1,200 Year 5 students from 73 schools participated. The key findings from the Trends study established that the overall performance of New Zealand students in reading literacy was virtually unchanged since 1990 and that the wide disparity of achievement remained (Ministry of Education, 2003).

The PISA 2000 and PIRLS 2001 findings are confirmed by the National Education Monitoring Programme (NEMP), which has tracked New Zealand students' achievement at Year 4 and Year 8 on a regular basis. NEMP has repeatedly described a wide gap in performance and achievement between Maori and Pacific Island students compared to European and other ethnic groups of students. More recent NEMP studies have noted reading gains for Maori students, particularly in oral reading fluency, but substantial diversity of achievement remains, particularly for reading comprehension (National Education Monitoring Project, 2000).

Thus, a wide dispersion of achievement in which Maori and Pacific Island students are over-represented at the underachieving end has been clearly documented since 1990. It is of concern that this situation has continued unchanged for at least 15 years, and it raises the question of how such a situation has occurred.

Explanations for the unsatisfactory achievement of a significant minority of students that make up New Zealand's so called "tail" of low achievement are reviewed in the next sections of this chapter. First, the role of factors external to the education system, such as ethnic and social factors, is considered. This includes a review of two recent school-based studies that show that, notwithstanding the role of social factors, schools and teachers can make a difference to the achievement of students in low socioeconomic areas, and of the debate engendered by those studies. Secondly, factors related to the education system are reviewed.

POSSIBLE REASONS FOR THE "TAIL"

Factors External to the Education System

The first explanation that is examined focuses on factors external to the school environment, such as poverty, ethnicity, and limited quality preschool experience, because these factors have been identified as limiting students' academic achievements (Fuchs & Wobmann, 2004; Harker, 2003; Nash, 1993).

Poverty has been identified as the most significant risk factor for student underachievement. This conclusion was reached through the identification of high numbers of underachieving students attending schools located in the lowest socioeconomic areas while high achieving students were found to more frequently attend schools in middle and upper socioeconomic areas (Martin et al., 2003; Mullis, Martin, Gonzalez, Gregory, & Garten, 2000; Sturrock & May, 2002). Not all evidence, however, leads to this conclusion, as further studies have identified that it is possible for students from low socioeconomic areas to attain reading levels closer to age-appropriate bands of achievement than had previously been attained (McNaughton, Lai, MacDonald, & Farry, 2004; Phillips, McNaughton, & MacDonald, 2003; Timperley & Lam, 2002).

Ethnicity has been identified as a compounding factor because of the high incidence of underachievement of Maori students as well as of students from the Pacific nations compared to students of other ethnicities (Fuchs & Wobmann, 2004; Gilmore, 1998; McNaughton, 2002; Nash, 1982). Ethnicity and poverty issues are difficult to isolate from one another, however, as Maori and Pacific Island families are over-represented in low socioeconomic groups, making it difficult to attribute causality (Statistics New Zealand, 2001).

Limited high quality preschool educational experience has also been suggested as a limiting factor. Data from Wylie's Competent Children study in Wellington, New Zealand indicated that students from middle and high income families were more likely to have accessed quality preschool education than students of low socioeconomic status (Wylie, 2001). Again, it is difficult to isolate the influence of preschool experience from poverty and ethnicity factors because children living in low socioeconomic areas are far less likely to have experienced quality preschool education (Alton-Lee, 2003).

Nash has considered the influence of ethnicity and poverty on student achievement for more than 20 years (Nash, 1982, 1993, 2002, 2003). The Access and Opportunity in Education project studied 500 randomly selected families from three different areas of the North Island of New Zealand in 1989 (Nash, 1993). Oral questionnaires were administered and willing families were followed up with an in-depth interview. Progress and Achievement Test (Reid & Elley, 1990) reading comprehension scores of 987 students were also analyzed. Nash noted that the mean reading comprehension scores of Maori students were below all other groups and that, on average, students from the upper socioeconomic groups achieved at half to one standard deviation above other groups. Analysis based on 1,393 completed interviews led Nash to propose that the best predictor of a student's educational performance was the degree of wealth, education, and social connection enjoyed by their parents (Nash, 1993). Nash found that working class students were much less likely to learn to decode and comprehend text at an age-appropriate level than students from middle class families. He also found that the families of higher achieving students owned more books. The findings led

Nash to identify that the number of books in the home was one of the best predictors of educational achievement and that reading ability was influenced by the literacy environment to which children were exposed. He maintained that competency in reading is learnt in literacy environments where children are continuously involved in rich literacy opportunities. Nash explained this by stating that the number and types of text students were exposed to influenced their vocabulary development, their ability to discuss texts, and consequently the development of higher order abstract thinking skills. Analysis of the PISA 2000 data also identified a link between higher achievement levels and higher numbers of books in homes (Organisation for Economic Co-operation and Development, 2001). While he did not wish to blame poorly educated low income families for the achievement levels of their children, Nash maintained that it was extremely difficult for schools to compensate for the advantages that resulted from being brought up in a well-educated, affluent environment (Nash, 2002).

An additional compounding factor Nash identified from his interview data was that working class parents depended on schools to inform them of the achievement levels of their children (Nash, 1993). When a school did not give precise information about a student's underachievement, parents tended to assume that satisfactory progress was being made. Nash observed that middle and upper class parents were far more likely to question professionals about their children's achievement and seek remedial intervention when necessary (Nash, 1993). He also noted that working class students were capable of achieving well if supported by parents and sympathetic teachers but that external factors such as poverty all too often limited this achievement.

Moderating the Effects of Poverty

However, while it has been widely accepted that poverty is a significant predictor of future underachievement, evidence has emerged over recent years that, under certain conditions, the performance of students attending schools in low socioeconomic areas can be enhanced and they can attain achievement levels that are closer to national levels of expectation.

Two New Zealand school-based studies, Picking up the Pace (Phillips et al., 2003) and Analysis and Use of Student Achievement Data (AUSAD) (Timperley & Lam, 2002), identified that moving students' achievement in reading closer to national levels of expectation was possible despite the effects of external factors commonly linked to underachievement.

Picking up the Pace was a three-phase research study that was designed specifically to address the learning needs of Maori and Pacific Island students educated in 12 schools located in the lowest socioeconomic areas in South Auckland (Phillips et al., 2003). The study provided specific professional development in literacy teaching to teachers of early childhood and Year 1 students in order to evaluate if such an intervention could enhance the achievement of these disadvantaged students by the time they turned 6 years of age. The professional development programme was entitled the Early Childhood Primary Link (ECPL) initiative. Groups of intervention and non-intervention students were tracked at six-monthly intervals from 4½ years to 6 years of age. The professional development for their teachers took place on 10 half-days spread over two terms and involved discussing and addressing literacy teaching issues as well as viewing demonstrations of alternative practice. The professional development for the primary teachers was aimed at challenging their previously held beliefs about literacy learning as well as providing very specific guidance on managing students' early literacy instruction. A teaching and learning analysis was carried out and the results demonstrated that, despite low early language levels, substantial learning gains in literacy skills were achieved for the intervention group after one year at school. The researchers also noted that their primary intervention had a powerful effect on teachers' attitudes, expectations, and understanding of literacy acquisition for students in their first year at school. An increased awareness of how to teach early literacy strategies and how to identify and respond to children's reading behaviours gave these teachers greater confidence in accepting responsibility for students' learning outcomes (Phillips et al., 2003).

In the AUSAD study, Timperley and colleagues examined school-based factors associated with the sustainability of the ECPL intervention described in the Picking up the Pace project. The AUSAD study involved seven schools located in low socioeconomic suburbs of South Auckland, New Zealand (Timperley & Lam, 2002; Timperley & Wiseman, 2003).

Timperley and colleagues established that while all seven schools demonstrated reading gains for their 6-year-old students across the three years of the study, two of the schools achieved significantly higher reading levels. The researchers sought to establish why these two schools achieved statistically higher levels of success than the other five schools when all seven had received the same quantity and quality of professional development and all were enthusiastic about the programme. The only difference that Timperley and colleagues were able to identify was in the way in which two of the schools used their student achievement data.

Specifically, the key difference was the way the two high performing schools used student achievement data to inform their teaching practice. Running record data were collected and graphed, identifying not only students' reading levels but also the number of weeks they had been attending school. The graphed results clearly demonstrated whether or not students were achieving at national levels of expectation. In the two high performing schools, these data were regularly discussed by groups of teachers at meetings where the majority of the meeting time focused on discussing the achievement data. The teachers identified specific students who were not progressing satisfactorily and made possible suggestions to move these particular students towards expected levels of achievement. The literacy leaders, who were also the associate principals of these schools, worked with the teachers to support and guide them to change their teaching practice in order to enhance the learning outcomes of the students. The junior class teachers in these two schools constantly reflected on their teaching practice in order to improve the reading achievement levels of the students in their classes. There developed a constant cycle of teaching, assessing, and reviewing of achievement data followed by the review and refinement of learning programmes. The teachers in the two high achieving schools realized that their teaching was facilitating improved learning outcomes for their Maori and Pacific Island students despite the constraining influences of external factors such as poverty and limited preschool experience. These external factors had previously limited teachers' expectations of their own practice.

The researchers were able to rule out the effects of many external factors because, while the seven schools shared these factors, the effects on student achievement varied among the seven schools. All the schools were located in the lowest socioeconomic areas of South Auckland, all had high numbers of Maori and Pacific Island students, and all expressed satisfaction with the ECPL programme—yet only two schools reflected on and used the student achievement data generated to inform and refine their teaching practice. The teachers in these two schools did not work in isolation but in collaborative groups co-ordinated by experienced school leaders who were also literacy experts and who facilitated the teachers' critique of each other's practice in a trusting and supportive environment.

On the completion of the first AUSAD research project, the findings were shared with all seven participating schools. The five lower achieving schools changed their practices after being made aware of the research results. These five schools began to review and use data on a regular basis in ways similar to that used by the two high performing schools in the first stage of the project (Timperley & Wiseman, 2003). All of the schools recorded improved reading levels for most of the children after their first year at school, and Timperley and Wiseman concluded that this indicated that professional development or the implementation of a programme on its own was not enough to lift student achievement; teachers also needed to take part in collaborative professional discussions of their students' achievement and progress—that is, be part of professional learning communities. The teachers had not previously discussed student achievement in this way, but revealed during semi-structured interviews that although they might have initially found it intimidating to discuss their students' progress with other teachers, they became used to it, saw the benefit of participating, and now valued the practice. The discussions that occurred between groups of professionals who were prepared to learn from each other were identified as being highly significant in changing the learning outcomes for the students. Timperley and Wiseman (2003) referred to these groups of educators as a "professional learning community" (Timperley & Wiseman, 2003, p. 124).

Critique of the Studies

Both the Picking up the Pace research and the AUSAD research have been critiqued by New Zealand educational researchers (Harker, 2003; Nash, 2003). Nash interpreted that the Picking up the Pace researchers claimed the students involved in the study achieved at national levels of expectation, and found it difficult to agree that the intervention was able to lift the reading levels of Pacific Island children from predominantly working class backgrounds to age-appropriate levels after one year at school. He commented:

> It is one thing to be convinced that literacy standards can, in principle, be improved in this way, but it is quite another to show that it has been done. Any programme able to demonstrate that Polynesian children from predominantly working class backgrounds can achieve—and within a year of entering school-levels of reading attainment at the national average would have accomplished something quite extraordinary. (Nash, 2003, p. 249)

Given his extensive research identifying clear links between poverty and underachievement, it is understandable that Nash may be sceptical about these results. Phillips et al. (2003) did not, however, disagree that poverty was a significant risk factor, nor did they state that all, or even on average, students in the study achieved at age-appropriate reading levels. When the Picking up the Pace researchers compared their data for phase one, two, and three of the study across all 12 schools with their baseline data, they found there had been significant changes in achievement across all indicators (Phillips et. al, 2003). They identified a reduction in the risk of underachievement because the distribution curve in the participating schools had moved towards expected levels of achievement:

The reduction of risk indicates that the actual distribution curve in these schools had shifted towards the expected (normal) distribution across a range of measures and an increased number of students were achieving within the expected range for their age at six. (Phillips et al., 2003, p. 140)

In his own studies, Nash had noted that individual teachers had the power to have a positive effect on students' learning and that students were capable of achieving well if supported by parents and sympathetic teachers (Nash, 1993). The Picking up the Pace research findings validate that claim and also encourage educators to pursue similar outcomes for at-risk students. Phillips et al. concluded that the "interventions show that low progress is neither inevitable nor immutable" (Phillips et al., 2003, p. 191).

They do not say that all children attending low socioeconomic early childhood or Year 1 classrooms will achieve at national levels of expectation. Instead, they provide evidence to indicate that it is possible to shift the distribution of achievement closer to "normal" levels if the pace of literacy instruction is "picked up" for the specific purpose of accelerating progress in reading and writing for at-risk students.

In order to "pick up the pace" of instruction, though, the teachers had to first question and sometimes reject their previous teaching literacy practices. This process required the teachers to critically inquire into their established practice and question the adequacy of previously held theories of teaching reading and writing.

Thus, this review of the evidence indicates schools can moderate the effects of external factors for the significant minority of students underachieving in the New Zealand education system. This is supported by a best evidence synthesis compiled by Alton-Lee (2003) that concluded that at least 59% of the difference in student achievement could be attributed to within-classroom effects resulting from quality teaching in quality learning environments.

The next section explores in more detail factors related to the education system that might help to explain the underachievement problem, including how the system might have reinforced it.

Factors Related to the New Zealand Education System

Unresponsiveness of the Education System
One explanation for New Zealand's tail of underachievement focuses on the unresponsiveness of the education system to the needs of ethnic minority groups. While it has been frequently reported both nationally and internationally that Maori and Pacific Island students attending schools in low socioeconomic areas are at the highest risk of underachieving (Nash, 2003; Organisation for Economic Co-operation and Development, 2001), Maori and Pacific Island educators and researchers do not recognize factors external to the education system as the exclusive reason for this underachievement (Hall & Bishop, 2001; Bishop & Glynn, 1999). Notwithstanding the accelerated expansion of New Zealand's social and cultural diversity, a critique by Hall and Bishop (2001) describes the evolution of a monocultural education system based on a New Zealand European culture that does not cater for diversity.

In the case of indigenous Maori, ethnic disadvantage was embedded in the education system in New Zealand from its colonial history. Simon and Smith (2001) have provided historical evidence from the Native School system of an education system that was set up for European success, and Simon (1998) has also shown it was a system where the intellectual development of Maori students was given a relatively low priority by both the state and the missionary teachers.

Simon and Smith (2001) examined perceptions and representations of the Native School system through the collection of oral testimonies of teachers and students. These were supplemented with data gathered from archival and other documentary sources to develop a comprehensive critique of the Native School system as a site of struggle. The authors critically assessed a nineteenth-century system which was established in order to "civilize" or Europeanise the indigenous Maori population. They noted that in gathering the oral histories, the resulting testimonies could not be considered as "truths" about the native schools but rather perceptions of them. They saw a belief emerging that the Native School system was set up to reinforce the dominance of European culture over the Maori culture and maintain unequal social relations.

A number of researchers maintain the education system has continued to disadvantage ethnic minority groups (Bishop & Glynn, 1999; Coxon, Jenkins, Marshall, & Massey, 1994; Hall & Bishop, 2001; Simon, 1998; Simon & Smith, 2001). Some Maori and Pacific Island educators claim that ethnic minority groups are disadvantaged when the curriculum and pedagogy is focused on meeting the needs of a single dominant culture (Hall & Bishop, 2001). Hall and Bishop believe that, under these circumstances, students who belong to a different ethnicity to those who make up the dominant group might inadvertently, but persistently, be sent messages of inferiority in a number of ways, which might affect the ultimate outcome of their educational experience.

> How polyethnic schools deal with cultural diversity has important implications for the life chances of those students who are seen as "culturally different" by the dominant cultural group. (Hall & Bishop, 2001, p. 191)

At the same time, Maori and Pacific Island educators recognize that New Zealand's Maori and Pacific Island students no longer live in remote or isolated communities. They are members of a rich and vibrant multi-ethnic community exposed to the global influences which provide opportunities and create demands for all sectors living in the twenty-first century. In the information-focused world of today, all students require advanced literacy, analytical, and referential research skills because the everyday world we live in and the education system these students operate in demand it. The over-representation of Maori and Pacific Island students in New Zealand's tail of underachievement, however, does indicate that the current education system is not catering adequately for all students' needs. The New Zealand education system, according to Hall and Bishop, has developed as a monocultural system that meets the needs of the dominant European culture to the exclusion of other ethnic groups and they claim it must become more responsive to the needs of diverse cultures (Hall & Bishop, 2001).

Te Kotahitanga (Bishop, Berryman, Taikiwai, & Richardson, 2003) was a research project that sought to investigate what was involved in improving educational achievement for Maori students. The research was designed over three phases. In the first phase, the researchers collected and analyzed oral narratives from Maori students attending four different secondary schools. The second phase involved the development of a professional development programme to implement change in classroom relationships and interactions. The third phase involved the measurement of changes in student achievement. Bishop et al. identified that the most important influence on Maori educational achievement was the quality of students' daily in-class interactions with their teachers. The researchers identified deficit theorizing (i.e., teachers assuming that factors outside of school, such as social background, affected learning) by teachers as a major impediment to Maori students' academic achievement. They concluded a key to improving Maori students' educational achievement was to enable teachers to critically reflect on their own theorizing and on the effect this might have on Maori students' learning outcomes. Their research indicated that when such professional development resulted in positive classroom relationships and interactions, then Maori students achieved at appropriate levels along with their non-Maori peers (Bishop et al., 2003).

Findings from the PISA 2000 study (Organisation for Economic Co-operation and Development, 2001), described earlier, identified relatively low between-school variance in achievement, but high within-school variance. These data indicated that there was relatively little difference in the achievement levels attained in schools located in low, middle, or high socioeconomic areas, but significant variation of students' achievement within individual schools, regardless of the socioeconomic area in which they were situated. These findings have prompted a closer examination of other factors that might have affected students' achievement levels.

School and Teacher Effects

The literature reviewed so far in this chapter indicates that school, or more specifically teacher, effects may provide an additional explanation for the wide variation in student achievement. As noted earlier, a Ministry of Education analysis of the PISA 2000 reading literacy results identified that only 16% of the variance in student achievement was accounted for by differences between schools. The Ministry of Education concluded that most of the variation of New Zealand students' achievement was explained by differences in performance within individual schools (Ministry of Education, 2001a). These data indicate that teacher effects, or the effects that individual teachers have on the learning outcomes of students, within a single school setting vary significantly more than any between-school effects. Alton-Lee (2003) pointed out that very little New Zealand research had been carried out into within-school effects.

Scheerens, Vermeulen, and Pelgrum (1989) identified evidence that these effects have been apparent in New Zealand for at least two decades. Their multi-level analysis of the Second International Mathematics Study (SIMS) using the 1981 data identified a 42% variance in the achievement of Year 9 students between classes but an undetectable variation between schools. It was thought that the lack of variation between schools may have been explained by the fact that students had spent less than one year at their secondary school. This explanation could not, however, account for the very wide variation in achievement between classes. A longitudinal study was carried out and identified that many of the students from classes who had made the biggest gains started with very low pretest scores. It was also shown that students from 5 out of the 199 classes either made no learning gains or, in some cases, their learning declined. These data indicated a very strong teacher effect regardless of the background or prior knowledge of the students.

It may well be that New Zealand research has not focused in the past on either school or teacher effects, which may have disguised the very significant effect of students' educational experience.

Nash and Harker used standardized national examination data gathered at Year 11 to measure variance of achievement in English, science, and mathematics. They attributed relatively small effects on students' achievement to school effects with just 5%–10% in mathematics, 5%–7% in science and 9%–10% in English (Nash & Harker, 1997). Higher percentages for school effects, however, were observed in the final phase of another New Zealand study known as the Smithfield project (Hughes et al., 2000).This study also investigated the relationship between secondary school performance and student learning outcomes. The Smithfield project researchers attributed almost 21% of the variance in mathematics and 16% in both English and science to school effects (Hughes et al., 2000). It was thought that these results may have been higher than the Nash and Harker results because the Smithfield study included the results of some lower performing students who were held back until the end of the sixth form before being allowed to sit national fifth form examinations. When Nash and Harker reviewed their own data and used the Smithfield approach, their percentages rose to 18.2% variance in mathematics, 14.3% in science and 14.6% in English (Nash & Harker, 1997). These results demonstrate a greater variance of performance being attributed to school-based factors.

International research has identified a much higher impact of teacher effects on students' learning outcomes. Cuttance reviewed the quality assurance reviews of schools in Australia and identified an 8%–9% variance of student learning outcomes between schools. Of significance was the observation of a further 55% variance in individual learning between classrooms within individual schools. These data demonstrate individual teachers within a single school having a much greater effect on student learning than was observed for collated achievement data between schools (Cuttance, 1998).

Similarly, a study by Wright, Horn, and Sanders (1997) involved analyzing the achievement of more than 10,000 students in the United States. Wright et al. demonstrated a wide variation in the effectiveness of the teachers involved in the study and concluded that the teacher was the most important factor affecting student achievement. They concluded that:

> The immediate and clear implications of this finding is that seemingly more can be done to improve education by improving the effectiveness of teachers than by any other single factor. (Wright et al., 1997, p. 63)

These data from two international studies indicate that, for developed countries with education systems like New Zealand's, student achievement is more likely to be affected by the class the student is in and the teacher who teaches them rather than the particular school they attend. Alton-Lee in her synthesis of best evidence research (2003) identified that quality teaching was a key influence on high quality learning outcomes for diverse students.

CONCLUSION

The reviewed studies indicate that rather than one simple explanation for student underachievement, a complex interaction of home-based and school-based factors may need to be taken into account. Evidence from the PIRLs study indicates that some Maori and Pacific Island students are represented among New Zealand's high achieving students, indicating that positive learning outcomes are possible for students traditionally identified as being at risk of underachieving (Ministry of Education, 2003). Further evidence has been sought to identify factors that might temper the pessimistic achievement expectations associated with Maori and Pacific Island students educated in low decile schools. Encouragingly, there is an evidence base emerging that, despite some children's home circumstances not being conducive to educational achievement, some at-risk children do achieve at the highest level (Alton-Lee, 2003; Biddulph, Biddulph, & Biddulph, 2003; Bishop et al., 2003; Phillips et al., 2003; Timperley & Lam, 2002). Of particular interest are the findings from the previously cited PISA 2000 research which highlight the within-school variance of achievement across all socioeconomic categories. These findings indicate that individual teachers may be moderating achievement to a greater extent than had previously been considered possible. The research evidence reviewed indicates that rather than focusing on external factors, a focus on school-based factors, particularly within-school factors which might moderate the variance of teacher effects, could provide the greatest point of leverage in improving student learning outcomes (Alton-Lee, 2003; Hattie, 2003).

REFERENCES

Alton-Lee, A. (2003). *Quality teaching for diverse students in schooling: Best evidence synthesis*. Wellington, New Zealand: Ministry of Education.

Biddulph, F., Biddulph, J., & Biddulph, C. (2003). The complexity of community and family influences on children's achievement in New Zealand: Best evidence synthesis. Wellington. New Zealand: Ministry of Education.

Bishop, R., Berryman, M., Taikiwai, S., & Richardson, C. (2003). *Te Kotahitanga: The experiences of Year 9 and 10 Maori students in mainstream classrooms*. Wellington, New Zealand: Ministry of Education.

Bishop, R., & Glynn, T. (1999). *Culture counts: Changing power relations in education*. Palmerston North, New Zealand: Dunmore Press.

Coxon, E., Jenkins, K., Marshall, J., & Massey, L. (1994). *The politics of learning and teaching in Aotearoa–New Zealand*. Palmerston North, New Zealand: Dunmore Press.

Cuttance, P. (1998). Quality assurance reviews as a catalyst for school improvement in Australia. In A. Hargreaves, M. Lieberman, M. Fullan, & D. Hopkins (Eds.), *International handbook of educational change (part two)* (pp. 1135–1162). Dordrecht, Netherlands: Kluwer.

Elley, W. (1994). *The IEA study of reading literacy: Achievement and instruction in thirty-two school systems*. Oxford: Pergamon Press.

Fuchs, T., & Wobmann, L. (2004). *What accounts for international difference in student performance? A re-examination using PISA data*. Munich, Germany.

Gilmore, A. (1998). *School entry assessment: The first national picture July 1997–May 1998.* Wellington, New Zealand: Ministry of Education.

Hall, A., & Bishop, R. (2001). Teacher ethics, professionalism and cultural diversity. *New Zealand Journal of Educational Studies, 36*(2), 187–202.

Harker, R. (2003). External validity and the Pace research. *New Zealand Journal of Educational Studies, 38*(2), 245–247.

Hattie, J. (2003, February). *New Zealand education snapshot with specific reference to the Years 1–13.* Paper presented to the Knowledge Wave 2003 leadership forum, Auckland, New Zealand.

Hughes, D., Lauder, H., Watson, S., Strathdee, R., Simiyu, I., Robinson, T. et al. (2000). *Do schools make a difference? Hierarchical linear modelling of school certificate results in 23 schools the Smithfield project – Phase 3. Eight report to the Ministry of Education (The Smithfield Project).* Wellington, New Zealand: Ministry of Education.

Martin, M. O., Mullis, I. V. S., Gonzalez, E. J., & Kennedy, A. M. (2003). *Trends in children's reading literacy achievement 1991–2001: IEA's repeat in nine countries of the 1991 Reading Literacy Study.* Chestnut Hill, MA: Boston College.

McNaughton, S. (2002). *Meeting of minds.* Wellington, New Zealand: Learning Media.

McNaughton, S., Lai, M., MacDonald, S., & Farry, S. (2004). Designing more effective teaching of comprehension in culturally and linguistically diverse classrooms in New Zealand. *Australian Journal of Language and Literacy, 27*(3), 184–197.

Mullis, I. V. S., Martin, M. O., Gonzalez, E. J., Gregory, K. D., & Garten, R. A. (2000). *TIMSS 1999 International Mathematics Report: Findings from IEA's repeat of the Third International Mathematics and Science Study at the eighth grade.* Boston, MA: Boston College.

Mullis, I. V. S., Martin, M. O., Gonzalez, E. J., & Kennedy, A. M. (2003). *PIRLS 2001 International Report: IEA's study of reading literacy achievement in primary schools.* Chestnut Hill, MA: Boston College.

Ministry of Education. (2001a). *Assessing knowledge and skills for life: First results from the Programme for International Student Assessment (PISA 2000) New Zealand summary report.* Wellington, New Zealand: Ministry of Education.

Ministry of Education. (2001b, April 05). *The national administration guidelines.* Retrieved 27 June, 2001, from http://www.tki.org.nz/e/governance/negs/guidelines/nags.php.

Ministry of Education. (2003). *Reading literacy in New Zealand. The results from the Progress in International Reading Literacy Study (PIRLS) and the Repeat of the 1990-1991 Reading Literacy Study (10-Year Trends Study) for Year 5 students.* Wellington, New Zealand: Ministry of Education.

Nash, R. (1982). *Schools can't make jobs.* Palmerston North, New Zealand: Dunmore Press.

Nash, R. (1993). *Succeeding generations.* Auckland, New Zealand: Oxford University Press.

Nash, R. (2002). Family resources and reading: Literacy practices, cognition and school success. In P. Adams and H. Ryan (Eds.), *Learning to read in Aotearoa New Zealand* (pp. 243–255). Palmerston North, New Zealand: Dunmore Press.

Nash, R. (2003). One pace forwards two steps backwards. *New Zealand Journal of Educational Studies, 38*(2), 249–254.

Nash, R., & Harker, R. K. (1997). *Progress at school: Final report to the Ministry of Education.* Palmerston North, New Zealand: Massey University, Educational Research and Development Centre.

National Education Monitoring Project. (2000). *Forum comment*. Dunedin, New Zealand: Educational Assessment Research Unit, University of Otago.

Organisation for Economic Co-operation and Development. (2001). *Knowledge and skills for life: First results from PISA 2000. Programme for International Student Assessment*. Paris: Author.

Organisation for Economic Co-operation and Development. (2005). *PISA 2003 Technical Report*. Paris: Author.

Phillips, G., McNaughton, S., & MacDonald, S. (2003). *Picking up the pace: Effective literacy interventions for accelerated progress over the transition into decile 1 schools* (Final report on the professional development associated with the Early Childhood Primary Links via Literacy (ECPL) project). Wellington, New Zealand: Ministry of Education.

Reid, J., & Elley, W. (1990). *Progressive Achievement Test: Reading comprehension and vocabulary* (revised). Wellington, New Zealand: New Zealand Council for Educational Research.

Scheerens, J., Vermeulen, C., & Pelgrum, W. J. (1989). Generalizability of instructional and school effectiveness indicators across nations. *International Journal of Educational Research, 13*(7), 789–799.

Simon, J. (Ed.). (1998). *Nga kura Maori: The native school system 1867–1969*. Auckland, New Zealand: Auckland University Press.

Simon, J., & Smith, L. (Eds.). (2001). *A civilising mission? Perceptions and representations of the New Zealand native schools system*. Auckland, New Zealand: Auckland University Press.

Statistics New Zealand. (2001). *2001 Census: Snapshot 3 (Work education and income), 4 (Maori) 6 (Pacific peoples)*. Wellington, New Zealand.

Sturrock, F., & May, S. (2002). PISA 2000: T*he New Zealand context – the reading, mathematical and scientific literacy of 15 year-olds: Results from the Programme for International Student Assessment*. Wellington, New Zealand: Ministry of Education.

Timperley, H., & Lam, P. (2002). *Analysis and use of student achievement data: Baseline report to the schools in Mangere and Otara and the Ministry of Education*. Wellington, New Zealand: Ministry of Education.

Timperley, H., and Wiseman, J. (2003). *The sustainability of professional development in literacy. Part two, school-based factors associated with high student achievement*. Wellington, New Zealand: Ministry of Education.

Wright, S. P., Horn, S. P., & Sanders, W. L. (1997). Teacher and classroom context effects on student achievement implications for teacher evaluation. *Journal of Personnel Evaluation in Education*, 57–67.

Wylie, C. (2001). *Ten years old and competent – the fourth stage of the competent children project: A summary of the main findings*. Wellington, New Zealand: New Zealand Council for Educational Research.

AUTHOR NOTE

Pam Millward is a Senior Lecturer in the Faculty of Education, University of Auckland, New Zealand. She is the co-ordinator of the University of Auckland's Bachelor of Education programme located at Manukau Institute of Technology. This chapter was developed from her thesis for her EdD.

The author would like to acknowledge the significant contribution made to this piece of work by her supervisors Professor Viviane Robinson and Professor Helen Timperley.

Correspondence concerning this chapter should be addressed by email to: pam.millward@manukau.ac.nz

In: Challenging Thinking about Teaching and Learning   ISBN: 978-1-60456-744-1
Editors: C. M. Rubie-Davies and C. Rawlinson   © 2008 Nova Science Publishers, Inc.

Chapter 2

Narrow the Gap, Fix the Tail, or Close the Curves: The Power of Words

John Hattie

Abstract

This chapter presents the case for using metaphors other than "the tail of underachievement" for describing New Zealand's distribution of student achievement. The aim is to enhance achievement over all points of the distribution for Maori and Pacific Island students.

Introduction

A common claim is that New Zealand has an educational problem with the "tail" of underachieving students and we must "narrow the gap", particularly for Maori and Pacific Island underachievement problems. However, these metaphors conjure pictures that are misleading—and lead to seeking solutions to the wrong problem. Too often the "tail" is interpreted as more Maori and Pacific Island than European New Zealand students performing at the lower end of the achievement distribution (Figure 2.1), or that we have to close or narrow the gap by pouring more resources into helping these lower achieving students, who are disproportionately Maori and Pacific Island students (Figure 2.2). In fact, neither of these metaphors depicts the complete situation.

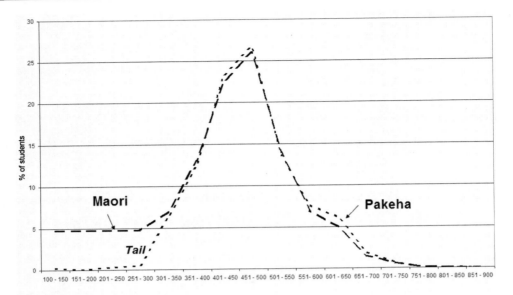

Note. Pakeha = New Zealand European.

Figure 2.1. The Tail.

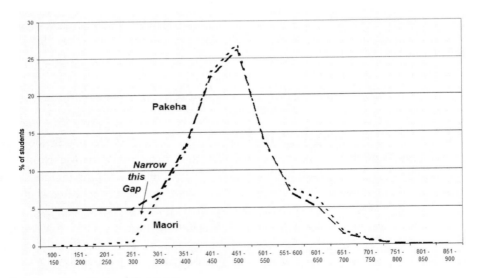

Note. Pakeha = New Zealand European.

Figure 2.2. Narrowing the Gap.

THE CASE FOR CHANGING THE UNDERACHIEVEMENT METAPHOR

New Zealand has one of the largest "spreads" or dispersions of student reading scores in the world. That is, we have a *flatter* reading achievement curve compared to many other countries. This greater dispersion is often presented as a "tail"—and in one sense it is—but the correct meaning is that there is a greater *spread* of scores or a flatter distribution and not necessarily more Maori or Pacific Island students clustered in the left hand tail than anywhere else.

Using asTTle norming data (see chapter 7), Figures 2.3 and 2.4 depict the distribution of scores for Maori, Pacific Island, New Zealand European, and Asian students in reading and mathematics. It is the case that there are greater proportions of New Zealand European and Asian than Maori and Pacific Island students above the overall median (55% vs. 39% for reading and 59% vs. 33% for mathematics). The major message, however, is that there are two gaps (above and below the median)—the tail is less of a problem than the gaps on either side of the middle.

READING

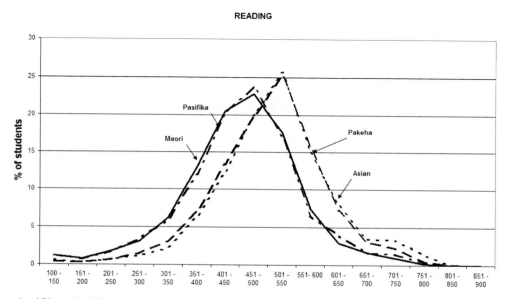

Note. Pasifika = Pacific Island; Pakeha = New Zealand European.

Figure 2.3. asTTle Norming Data for Reading.

Rather than pulling up the bottom, we need to pull the curves together, and reduce the disparity everywhere—that is, move the two distributions together so that they are superimposed one on top of the other. We need a metaphor that points to moving up those Maori and Pacific Island students who are *above* the middle so they are even further up than they are now as well as moving those *below* the middle upwards: that is, we need to move up *both* groups. The wrong metaphors (i.e., gap, tails) mean that we focus on the bottom students and ignore the major group of students whom we need to move up.

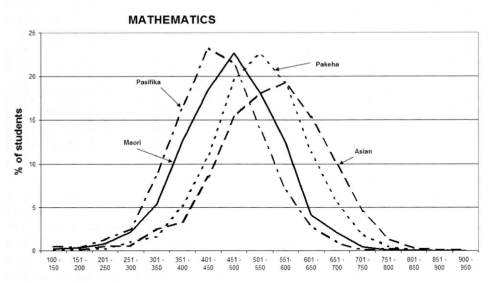

Note. Pasifika = Pacific Island; Pakeha = New Zealand European.

Figure 2.4. asTTle Norming Data for Mathematics.

CONCLUSION

A metaphor more along the lines of a seismic shift to align the plates, or of closing the waves, is needed to accurately address the nature of achievement differences between Maori and Pacific Island students and New Zealand European or Asian students. Perhaps a difference in our language will lead to a difference in our practices such that all Maori and Pacific Island students benefit. This is not to say that we owe no responsibility to the tail—rather the suggestion is that the data on academic achievement clearly indicate that we have neglected the majority of underperforming students—those who are around the middle and whose performance needs "pulling up"—by using the wrong language and metaphors.

REFERENCE

Hattie, J. A. C. (2008). *Correlates of academic performance in New Zealand schools: The asTTle database.* (See chapter 7 of this volume).

AUTHOR NOTE

John Hattie is a Professor in the Faculty of Education, University of Auckland, New Zealand, and Director of Project asTTle (Assessment Tools for Teaching and Learning). His areas of research include measurement models and their application to educational problems, meta-analysis, and models of teaching and learning. Over the past five years, he has headed a team introducing a model of assessment for teachers in all schools in New Zealand, and thus providing schools with evidence-based information about the teaching and learning. He is editor of the International Journal of Testing, and an associate editor of the British Journal of Educational Psychology

Correspondence concerning this chapter should be addressed by email to: j.hattie@auckland.ac.nz

In: Challenging Thinking about Teaching and Learning   ISBN: 978-1-60456-744-1
Editors: C. M. Rubie-Davies and C. Rawlinson   © 2008 Nova Science Publishers, Inc.

Chapter 3

TEACHER BELIEFS AND EXPECTATIONS: RELATIONSHIPS WITH STUDENT LEARNING

Christine M. Rubie-Davies

ABSTRACT

There have been many calls for teachers to have high expectations for all students, with an assumption that this will lead to improved academic achievement. However, teacher expectation research has concentrated on expectations for individuals rather than for classes of students. This is despite contentions by researchers (Blatchford, Burke, Farquhar, Plewis, & Tizard, 1989; Brophy, 1985) two decades ago that class-level expectations are more likely to have greater effects on student outcomes than expectations for individual students. The current study aimed to address this gap in the literature. Teachers with high or low expectations for all students in their classes were identified and then interviewed about their pedagogical beliefs and instructional practices. There were substantial differences in the beliefs of high and low expectation teachers. High expectation teachers adopted a facilitative approach to teaching while low expectation teachers adopted a directive approach. This study points to a need for further investigations into teachers' expectations for their classes of students. Implications for practising teachers and for teacher education programmes are discussed.

INTRODUCTION

In recent years, policymakers, government agencies, and school management personnel have called for teachers to have high expectations for all students. It is assumed that if teachers have such expectations these will translate into improved progress and academic achievement for students. The phenomenon of class-level teacher expectations has, however, been sparsely investigated. Although it was suggested two decades ago that class-level expectations may have far more import for students than individual teacher–student interactions (Blatchford, Burke, Farquhar, Plewis, & Tizard, 1989; Brophy, 1985), researchers have instead concentrated on teacher expectations for individual students. In particular, the research has focused on the differing behaviours that teachers display towards students depending on whether they hold high or low expectations of the students, and the student characteristics that may influence teacher expectations.

Teacher expectation research began with the work of Rosenthal and Jacobson (1968). Rosenthal proposed that when teachers had high or low expectations for particular students, they interacted with them in ways that conveyed their expectations. With regular similar interactions, eventually students fulfilled teachers' expectations. This came to be known as the self-fulfilling prophecy effect. Though fraught with controversy related largely to the methodology used in the study, Rosenthal's seminal work established a productive area of psychological research.

Rosenthal's findings led researchers working in the field of teacher expectations to concentrate on trying to uncover the teacher behaviours that provided students with salient and more subtle messages about their teachers' expectations of them (Brophy & Good, 1974; Cooper & Good, 1983). Brophy (1983) identified 17 ways in which students for whom teachers had high expectations were treated differently from students for whom teachers had low expectations. He reported, for example, that teachers accepted poor performances from students for whom they had low expectations but not from those for whom their expectations were high; they provided feedback on learning more often to students for whom they had high expectations than they did for students for whom their expectations were low; and they criticized students for whom they had low expectations more frequently than they criticized students for whom they had high expectations when students gave incorrect answers to questions. Cooper and Good (1983) showed teachers interacted more often in public with students for whom they held high expectations but more often in private with students for whom expectations were low—students they had high expectations for were chosen to answer questions directed to the class, while students for whom they held low expectations were questioned and supported in private.

Harris and Rosenthal (1985) later conducted a meta-analysis of 136 studies that reported a total of 31 teacher behaviours that differed depending on whether the teachers held high or low expectations of particular students. Their synthesis of the data showed the effect sizes for commonly identified behaviours such as criticizing students for whom they held low expectations ($r = .04$), praising students for whom they held high expectations ($r = .12$), and wait time ($r = .18$) were less important to student outcomes than behaviours such as creating a positive classroom climate ($r = .40$), providing students for whom they held high expectations with more challenging learning opportunities ($r = .33$), and having extended interactions with students ($r = .47$). This analysis suggested whole-class factors may have more implications for student outcomes than the individual student–teacher interactions that had been the main focus of research.

Brattesani, Weinstein, and Marshall (1984) showed that differences in the way teachers behaved towards students for whom they held high expectations and those for whom they held low expectations was more marked in some teachers than others. The researchers referred to these teachers as high and low differentiating teachers. High differentiating teachers provided students with explicit information about who in the class they expected to perform at high levels and who they anticipated would not make good academic progress. In contrast, low differentiating teachers did not provide their students with such obvious messages. Learning opportunities for all students were much more similar in these classrooms than they were in the classes of high differentiating teachers.

Similarly, in an experimental study, Babad and his colleagues identified what they termed high and low bias teachers (Babad, Inbar, & Rosenthal, 1982). High bias teachers were those who, when provided with false data about prior student performance, interacted with students according to expectations they formed from the given information, rather than placing credence in current student performance. They were readily swayed by portfolio information. On the other hand, low bias teachers planned student work in keeping with current student performance and were not readily influenced by inaccurate information provided about some students. Babad later videotaped high bias teachers interacting with students for whom they held high expectations and with students for whom they held low expectations (Babad, Bernieri, & Rosenthal, 1991; Babad & Taylor, 1992). Fourth-grade students viewed 10-second video clips of the teachers (they could not see the student being spoken to) and from subtle differences in facial expressions and other body language could readily determine whether the teacher was interacting with a low or high expectation student.

Brophy (1985) suggested two decades ago that individual teacher characteristics could result in some teachers having much greater self-fulfilling prophecy effects on students than others. He suggested teachers' expectations for their classes would have greater self-fulfilling prophecy effects on student outcomes than the individual teacher–student interactions that had provided the main impetus for teacher expectation research. Yet, until recently, no investigations have explored any effects of expectations at the class level.

Rubie-Davies (2006) identified two groups of teachers, one she called high expectation teachers and another named the low expectation group. At the beginning of a school year, teachers completed a survey where they indicated on a 1–7 Likert scale (where, for example, 1 = very much below average, 4 = average, 6 = moderately above average) how well they expected each student to perform in reading by the end of the year. In order to improve consistency of judgement, teachers were provided with reading levels that would align with the points on the Likert scale. Expectations for end-of-year achievement were then compared with the students' actual beginning-of-year performance. Of the original group of teachers (N = 21), six were identified whose expectations for their class's achievement were significantly above the students' actual performance (high expectation teachers) and three teachers had expectations that were well below where their students were operating (low expectation teachers). In order to determine the teachers' expectations were indeed for all students rather than exceptionally high or low for some, the students in each class were then divided into above average, average, and below average groups, and the teachers' expectations compared for each group. This analysis showed, indeed, that high expectation teachers had high expectations for all students and that conversely low expectation teachers' expectations were low for all students (Rubie-Davies, 2007).

At the end of the year, data were gathered for students' reading achievement and compared with results from the beginning of the year. The students of high expectation teachers made considerably more progress than students with low expectation teachers. Cohen's d was used to determine relative effect size gains in reading across all nine classrooms. In the classes of high expectation teachers, mean effect size gains in each class were: 1.44, 1.28, 1.27, .86, .73, .50. Gains in low expectation classrooms were: .20, -.02, -.03 (Rubie-Davies, 2007). The differential progress of students in the classes of the two groups of teachers proffered an opportunity to further investigate other disparities that could be contributing to student achievement.

The pedagogical beliefs that teachers hold can translate into variations in classroom practices, in how concepts are taught, and in the opportunities to learn with which students are provided. Zohar, Degani, and Vaaknin (2001) interviewed teachers about use of higher order questions with low ability students. They reported almost half of the teachers thought these questions were unsuitable for low ability students and approximately one third stated they never used questions requiring higher order thinking with such students. The researchers showed the outcome of such beliefs was that distinct learning opportunities, varying substantially in quality, were being offered to high and low expectation students. When teachers alter their instructional practices as a consequence of particular pedagogical beliefs, they may constrain (or enhance) students' learning simply by reducing or extending the opportunities to learn that they provide.

The current study aimed to investigate pedagogical beliefs and self-reported practices of high and low expectation teachers to ascertain whether any differences might offer an explanation for contrasting rates of progress among students. Did low expectation teachers report instructional practices that could be constraining student progress? If so, what were these practices and how did they differ from those described by high expectation teachers?

METHOD

Participants

The nine participants in this study had taken part in the initial study which identified high and low expectation teachers. They worked in schools in the Auckland area of New Zealand. Table 3.1 provides further details about each teacher. In New Zealand, all schools are given a 1–10 decile ranking which broadly indicates the socioeconomic level of the school. Schools with a decile ranking of 1–5 were classed as low socioeconomic; those 6–10 as high. Junior classes were Years 1 and 2 (aged 5–6 years); senior were Years 5 and 6 (aged 9–10 years). Six teachers were New Zealand European, two were Maori, and one was other European. As can be seen from Table 3.1, both high expectation and low expectation teachers could be found in high and low socioeconomic areas and in junior and senior classes. Interestingly, the two teachers with most years of teaching experience (25 years each) had high expectations for their students and were both working in low socioeconomic schools.

Table 3.1. Demographic Details for High and Low Expectation Teachers

Teacher group	Socioeconomic area	Class level	Teaching service	Ethnicity	Gender
HiEx	Low	Junior	25	NZ	F
HiEx	High	Senior	1	NZ	F
HiEx	High	Junior	5	NZ	F
HiEx	High	Junior	7	NZ	F
HiEx	High	Senior	6	M	F
HiEx	Low	Junior	25	NZ	F
LoEx	Low	Senior	4	M	M
LoEx	High	Senior	8	E	F
LoEx	High	Junior	7	NZ	F

Note. HiEx = high expectation teachers; LoEx = low expectation teachers; NZ = New Zealand European; M = Maori; E = other European.

Materials

All teachers were provided with a standard interview schedule one week before their interview in order to give them time to reflect on their beliefs and practices. It was expected this would contribute to thoughtful responses and enrich the data collected. All teachers agreed to be audiotaped and were asked questions pertaining to the ways in which they planned and delivered reading lessons. For example: "How do you determine the learning outcomes for your students?", "How do you decide on the learning experiences for your students?", "How do you ensure the cognitive engagement of your students?", and "What factors contribute to the success of your students?"

Analyses

Initially the data were coded manually and then separately into QSR NUD*IST, a software application for coding qualitative data. Coding was then cross-validated and any discrepancies resolved. Finally an independent researcher coded the data according to the themes that emerged from the original coding. An agreement rate of 94% was reached, which was considered acceptable. The program's pattern search facilities were used to search for suitable words and word patterns, their context was located, and they were then matched to high and low expectation teachers. Disconfirming data were sought as well.

This chapter reports on the results from two of the themes that emerged from the analyses: (a) grouping students homogeneously by ability and (b) planning, teaching, and learning for homogeneous ability groups.

Because the study compares the frequencies with which the high and low expectation teachers used particular descriptors, it was prudent to ascertain comparative lengths of transcripts for each teacher (Table 3.2). The table shows that while there are some variations among individual teachers, the mean number of words for each group is similar. In order to facilitate readability, pseudonyms allocated to high expectation teachers begin with "H" while those for low expectation teachers begin with "L".

**Table 3.2. Word Count for Interview Transcripts
for Each Teacher by Teacher Group**

HiEx teachers	Transcript word Count	LoEx teachers	Transcript word count
Helen	2,440	Luke	2,544
Heidi	2,643	Lauren	3,083
Hannah	2,568	Lana	2,314
Heather	2,946		
Holly	3,687		
Hayley	1,012		
Mean	2,549.33	Mean	2,647

Note. HiEx = high expectation teachers; LoEx = low expectation teachers.

RESULTS AND DISCUSSION

Grouping Students Homogeneously by Ability

Generally in primary (elementary) school classrooms in New Zealand, teachers group their students for reading, mathematics, spelling, and sometimes written language. Wilkinson and Townsend (2000) reported that New Zealand teachers had the highest grouping rate of all OECD countries. Therefore it was not surprising that all teachers reported grouping students by ability for instructional reading. When teachers were questioned further, however, some differences between the high expectation and low expectation teacher groups were found. The three low expectation teachers maintained ability groupings for instruction as well as learning experiences. Lana explained how this benefited her low ability students:

> They wouldn't be able to cope with a task that I had set for the high ability so I do that to cater for where they are at.

The responses of the high expectation teachers were quite different, however. Only one of these teachers, Hayley, maintained ability grouping for both instruction and learning activities but frequently her students were assigned whole-class or individual activities. Hannah, Holly, and Heather all allowed students to choose the activities they completed. Although there was variation in the skills required to complete differing activities, the teachers did not place any restrictions on students. Holly stated:

> The children can choose the activities they do so they are not grouped for actual activities.

Hannah and Heidi ran individualized programmes where students were only grouped if they had common needs at the time. Heidi's students completed similar activities with some variation for ability:

> Like if we are making a booklet, they are all making a book. Some of them are making it for themselves. Some of them are making it to teach others with and things like that. I try to get them all to do roughly the same sort of activity but try not to make it obvious that they're doing—well trying to differ the parts within that activity for each group rather than them all doing totally different work.

The final teacher in this group, Helen, grouped her students for instruction but learning experiences were completed in quite different socially based groupings. In addition, Heather paired her students so the first and third quartile were matched, as were those in the second and fourth quartile; these pairs read together daily.

This analysis showed the high expectation and low expectation teachers appeared to structure their students' learning experiences differently. Low expectation teachers provided quite discrete learning activities for high and low ability students, which meant students in these groupings were given differing learning opportunities. High expectation teachers, however, offered all students similar activities—certainly the discrimination between high and low ability students would not be as evident as in low expectation teachers' classes; students with high expectation teachers would all have similar opportunities to learn.

Planning, Teaching, and Learning for Homogeneous Ability Groups

The following sections will explore more closely how the two groups of teachers planned and designed students' activities, monitored student progress, provided opportunities for student autonomy, used goal setting in classroom programmes, and used motivation to promote student learning. Table 3.3 provides the input words for the pattern searches and the results of those searches.

Plan and Design of Student Learning Experiences

Table 3.3 shows that high expectation teachers reported differentiation between learning opportunities for high and low ability students less frequently than low expectation teachers. This was most evident when teachers spoke about learning opportunities they provided for low ability students. Three high expectation teachers made statements including phrases associated with the teaching of low ability students whereas all low expectation teachers used such expressions. Hayley (the only high expectation teacher who on occasion did ability group her students for learning experiences) reported: "The low ability children require more activities using concrete materials". Similarly Luke stated when referring to low ability students: "A lot of repetition, every day . . . until they can start recalling their basic number facts". One interesting finding was that there were four responses from high expectation teachers who, when referring to low ability students, used the words: "problem solving", "research" and "independent". No low expectation teachers used such expressions when referring to low ability students. Hannah stated:

> They need activities that are challenging so they are motivated. If I don't make them independent as well [as the high ability students] they won't learn to run by themselves. They'll always need the teacher.

The pattern of teacher references to learning opportunities for high ability students was similar for both high expectation and low expectation teachers (see Table 3.3). Five high expectation teachers referred to providing extension, research, or independent activities for high ability students and all low expectation teachers made such statements. A crucial difference was that low expectation teachers confined such activities only to high ability students. This did not appear to occur in classes of high expectation teachers. Hannah reported:

> For the high ability . . . to develop independence in their learning, the children can go to the learning centre and do the problem solution chart and really think about what they have read and things like that.

But she did not confine these activities only to high ability children. In contrast, Lauren said:

> I would be looking at more independent type activities for my high ability children compared to the low ability children. Yes, I think just for my high ability group I would be looking at more complex tasks, tasks that they would have to work on in a more independent way.

Monitoring Student Learning

There was a contrasting pattern for high expectation and low expectation teachers when speaking about forms of assessment. High expectation teachers far more frequently referred to ongoing monitoring and feedback for students while low expectation teachers were more likely to talk about assessment in terms of pretesting student achievement and a later summative assessment (see Table 3.3). All spoke about using running records to group students by ability and conducting further such assessments later to see how students were progressing. The only comment from a low expectation teacher that refers to ongoing monitoring is the following from Lauren: "My students do a lot of self-assessment and peer assessment. At the end of the day they give me the thumbs up or thumbs inside of how they worked". In contrast, the following comment from Heather is characteristic of comments made by high expectation teachers:

> The lessons are needs-based in that I give a lot of feedback to children and in the talking you know about them, and the watching, the observing, that's the time when I actually identify their learning or lack of learning and what skill they need to sharpen next, so then I weave that into whatever I am doing.

It appears assessment may have played a differing role in high expectation and low expectation teachers' classes. Low expectation teachers appeared to monitor students' learning needs less closely on a daily basis and more typically used summative forms of assessment. High expectation teachers, on the other hand, appeared to be engaged in ongoing monitoring of students' progress and regarded assessment as informing their design of student learning programmes.

Student Autonomy and Motivation

The following section will further explore the degree of autonomy students were given with learning activities in the classes of high expectation and low expectation teachers. Interview transcripts were also analyzed to explore how teachers created interest and facilitated engagement in learning experiences.

High expectation teachers made more comments related to providing students with choices than did low expectation teachers (see Table 3.3). Four high expectation teachers spoke about choices they offered students. For example, Helen reported: "There are activities that they can go to by choice. There are computer activities . . ." and she went on to list activities she provided for students in several curriculum areas, including reading. The following comments from Holly show she also presented her students with choices: "I basically give them a choice to a point and as long as they are going in the right direction that I want them to be going in. . . . So often I try and let them decide on their own learning experiences". Hannah articulated a similar belief: "I might give them a range and say we could work on this, or we could work on that, what would you like to work on? So that they have got to take ownership of it".

In contrast, the only low expectation teacher who spoke about giving students any choices was Laura who, when speaking about her high ability students, said:

> I just sort of give them an idea of where we are going, how we are going to get there but I actually let them take some ownership of the process. How do you want to do it? Do

we want to use overheads? Do we want to make a video of what we are doing? . . . but I actually let them take some ownership of the process.

High expectation teachers appeared to be offering all students some choices in types of learning activities they undertook whereas this did not appear to be a feature of low expectation teachers' classrooms. Any choices provided by low expectation teachers were only offered to high ability students. This presents a picture of contrasting opportunities to learn, especially for less able students in classes of high expectation teachers. All students in these classes—high and low ability students—had access to challenging learning opportunities that were reserved for able students only in other classes. Less able students in high expectation classes were less often presented with the low level, repetitive activities that researchers have previously reported such students are frequently exposed to (Barr & Dreeben, 1991; Davenport, 1993; Gamoran, 1992; Good & Brophy, 2003; Hacker, Rowe, & Evans, 1992). A further implication of providing students with choices is they are more likely to have occasion to work with a variety of peers and hence may enjoy advantages of positive peer modelling.

Goal Setting

However, offering students a selection of activities was not the only means by which high expectation teachers seemed to promote student autonomy. Teachers who developed clear learning steps with students through goal setting described how this gave students achievable learning targets, motivated them to learn, and facilitated self-determination. Of four teachers who spoke about the significance of goal setting in their classrooms, three were high expectation teachers. Heather's statement is representative of their views:

> Well I think they have to know what they can do. We talk about goal setting, and resetting goals and going forward again, and then coming back and reflecting on it. . . . Actually knowing what it is that they are learning to do is really powerful and potent. So it's easy for the children to know what they are working on and I try to always be specific about why we are doing it because I just think that's educationally sound. I think they need to know when they have made personal progress.

Lauren, the only low expectation teacher to speak about goal setting, said: "They write their own goals at the beginning of the year, and go back to the goals and I say 'How have you done in your goals?'". She did not, however, talk about refining or altering student goals as they progressed. It would appear for high expectation teachers that goal setting (as with monitoring) was an ongoing process, whereas this was not apparent from Lauren's comment. High expectation teachers more commonly spoke about goal setting (see Table 3.3) and used this to motivate students and develop independence.

Another strategy used by teachers to increase student engagement was to include activities and topics centred on student interests. Five high expectation teachers spoke about the importance they felt could be attached to incorporating students' interests into classroom activities and one low expectation teacher also mentioned using student interests in his planning. As Table 3.3 shows, however, using student interests as part of teacher planning was repeatedly mentioned by high expectation teachers but not by low expectation teachers. Helen said: "I'm always looking to see what interests children". Holly appeared to use student interest to increase student engagement and motivation:

I have a couple of really low kids who aren't interested in math and just don't like it, but they love cricket so we found some batting averages activities and they just loved it and they worked on that problem for 40 minutes until they worked it out. . . . Sometimes it's finding activities that they are interested in, rather than just doing something they are not into.

Table 3.3. Number of Teacher Utterances Containing Descriptors Related to Each Subheading

	HiEx Group ($n = 6$)	LoEx Group ($n = 3$)
Providing Learning Opportunities		
Descriptors related to high ability students:		
[extension|independent|research|problem solving|complex]	12	9
[higher order thinking|beyond the text|thinking outside the square|inferential]	1	5
Descriptors related to low ability students:		
[repetitive|repetition|structured|simple|easy|reinforcing| reinforcement|simplified]	3	5
[hands on|concrete|kinaesthetic|games]	4	5
[short concentration|lack concentration]	0	2
Assessing and Monitoring Students		
Descriptors:		
[monitoring|monitor|pretest|diagnostic|identify their learning|what they can do]	17	3
[assess|assessment|assessments|assessing|assessed]	17	9
[feedback about their learning|feedback]	6	2
Student Choice		
Descriptors:		
[choice|choose|pick|they choose|they decide|ownership]	17	2
Descriptors related to high ability students only:		
[choice|choose|pick|they choose|they decide|ownership]	6	0
Using Student Interests and Motivation in Planning		
Descriptors:		
[setting up goals|the next goal|small achieveable goals|achieve their goals|goal setting|goals]	10	4
[motivation|motivate|motivated|motivates|motivating]	5	1
[enjoy|enjoyment|enjoying|excited|exciting|keen]	12	8
[interest|their interest|interested|interests|student interest|interesting]	28	2

Note. HiEx = high expectation teachers; LoEx = low expectation teachers.

Similarly, Heather, who gave her students a lot of autonomy, seemed to think student motivation could be enhanced when students were interested in learning activities. Having spoken about offering students choices she said:

I just think that having mixed ability with the ability is really important so that they have all got a contribution to make and their skills, their particular skills are valued this way because if you have a pecking order in the class, motivation can go out the window and you won't see star charts and stuff like that in my room. I am more interested in intrinsic motivation than extrinsic so I don't have them.

Luke also took student interests into account:

When I had that first lot of parent interviews, that was one of the questions I got my parents to answer. What are their interests at home? So I base my topics around their interests. So that motivates them to put that extra effort in.

One important difference between Luke and the high expectation teachers, however, was that the high expectation teachers were considering ways to incorporate student interests into the core curriculum areas of mathematics and reading whereas Luke only did this for topic studies (i.e., social studies, science, and health). Luke's activities for his student ability groups in reading were quite discrete and teacher-selected.

The importance of fostering student motivation, particularly intrinsic motivation, has been well-documented (Dweck, Mangels, & Good, 2004). The reported practices of high expectation teachers suggest they recognize the salience of intrinsic motivation for student learning more so than low expectation teachers. They have also developed useful strategies for enhancing student motivation and interest in learning. They recognize the role of student autonomy and interest in improving learning (Hidi, Renninger, & Krapp, 2004; Reeve & Jang, 2006) and can clearly articulate reasons for teaching decisions.

CONCLUSION

Overall, high expectation teachers adopted a facilitative approach to teaching whereas low expectation teachers were more directive. This had a number of implications in terms of the pedagogy each group of teachers reported implementing and the beliefs they held. High expectation teachers mostly did not identify learning experiences available in the classroom as specifically for completion by high or by low ability students. Instead they facilitated student learning by having all students complete similar activities. These teachers articulated the importance of offering low ability students challenging learning experiences to foster progress. Their students often made choices about which learning tasks they would complete so student responsibility for learning was encouraged and student autonomy developed. On the other hand, low expectation teachers structured students' learning experiences quite differently. They provided activities for high and low ability students that were quite distinct and students worked on these in separate ability groups. They emphasized the importance of low ability students repetitively practising basic skills in order to improve. In these classrooms, teachers decided who completed what, when, and how. They directed all student learning experiences. There were few opportunities for student input.

There were differences, too, in ways high and low expectation teachers monitored student learning. The high expectation teachers appeared to be assessing students in an ongoing manner and constantly moving students forward. They discussed progress with students and together set clear goals for students to reach. These were frequently re-evaluated and adjusted to current student needs. Assessment information was used in a formative manner and students played an active role in directing learning. Teachers were monitoring student learning as facilitators. Low expectation teachers did not appear to be monitoring student learning so regularly; certainly they spoke infrequently about assessment. Their discussion of monitoring related mostly to summative assessments where they tested students at intervals. They did not speak about using the information to design programmes and learning experiences for students to direct learning. There did not appear to be the ongoing evaluation and re-designing of student programmes in order to meet current needs. They did not appear to provide students with regular feedback about learning or set clear learning goals with them.

High expectation teachers also recognized that including exciting and challenging learning opportunities helped increase student motivation. This was one reason given for providing students with choices, and it was also why these teachers tried to regularly include activities centred on student interests. Low expectation teachers did not give student motivation so much credence, especially with regard to activities in reading. For these teachers, the learning opportunities provided were what students needed, but perhaps not what they wanted. There was some evidence that low expectation teachers did take student interest into account during topic studies (i.e., science, social studies, health). Perhaps these subjects were regarded as less important than core subjects, where teachers made all decisions.

In classes of high expectation teachers, one consequence of students being given choices of learning opportunities and of all students completing similar activities was students were encouraged to work with a range of peers, not just those of similar ability. Teachers appeared to believe such interactions were beneficial for all students but particularly low ability students. Linchevski and Kutscher (1998) showed students working in mixed ability groupings made much greater progress than those working in homogeneous ability groups. When students are separated into distinct ability groups, they will inevitably be given differing opportunities to learn, as was the case in the classes of low expectation students in the current study. Several researchers have argued that designing differing learning opportunities for high and low expectation students is the cornerstone of the self-fulfilling prophecy effect (Timperley & Robinson, 2001; Warren, 2002; Zohar et al., 2001). Students will learn what they are given the opportunity to learn.

Following earlier research where Weinstein and her colleagues identified high and low differentiating teachers (Brattesani et al., 1984), Weinstein interviewed teachers and observed in their classrooms with the aim of identifying differences in the instructional and socioemotional environments of such teachers (Weinstein, 2002). She reported high differentiating teachers (those who clearly differentiated between high and low ability students) espoused a fixed view of ability, placed students in largely inflexible ability groups, clearly differentiated between instructional activities of high and low ability students, emphasized performance goals, and used largely negative behaviour management techniques. Low differentiating teachers (those who did not differentiate between high and low ability students), on the other hand, held incremental notions of intelligence, mainly used interest-based grouping, emphasized task-mastery goals, and created positive relationships with students. It is interesting that where the same teacher characteristics were explored in the current study, such as using ability groups versus using flexible mixed ability groupings, findings for high and low expectation teachers were similar to those for high and low differentiating teachers identified by Weinstein (2002). This is an area that could be explored further in future research.

It has been argued that teacher expectation effects are small (Brophy, 1998) but that conclusion is based on effects of teacher expectations on individuals within a classroom, and the evidence is equivocal. Blatchford and his colleagues (Blatchford et al., 1989), for example, found large expectation effects in some classrooms. This suggests such effects may be teacher-centred and further implies, therefore, that whole-class effects are likely to be more important than any expectation effects based on individual teacher–student interactions. At a time where there are constant calls for teachers to have high expectations for all students, it seems ironic there are few studies that have actually investigated whole-class effects or teacher beliefs and practices associated with high expectations, since it those that make the difference to student learning. Expectations do not exist in a vacuum. The results of the current study and those of Weinstein suggest a need for future investigations to examine not only expectations at the class level but also the mechanisms of such expectations.

One finding in the current study was there were high and low expectation teachers in both high and low socioeconomic schools. It has often been argued teachers with low expectations are to be found in low socioeconomic schools (Oakes, Gamoran, & Page, 1992), with the converse assumed for high expectation teachers. This study questions that supposition, certainly in New Zealand where the study took place. In New Zealand, there is no stigma attached to teaching in low socioeconomic schools and many experienced teachers make a conscious decision to teach in such schools, where they feel they can make a difference to children's learning.

All the high expectation teachers could readily articulate beliefs about why they practised as they did but it needs emphasizing they sat outside the conventional New Zealand framework. In New Zealand, teachers have traditionally ability-grouped students for both instruction and learning experiences, but the high expectation teachers did not operate like that. They had developed strong arguments for practising differently from convention. The high expectation teachers in low socioeconomic schools each had 25 years' experience and could clearly articulate ideas for practising as they did. Soodak and Podell (1998) reported teachers with more than 16 years' teaching experience have greater teaching self-efficacy than teachers with fewer years' experience. Such teachers have strong beliefs in their abilities to make a difference to student learning and it would seem likely teachers with high self-efficacy would also have high expectations for students. Future research should investigate the relationship between teacher self-efficacy and class-based expectations.

In this study, there were more junior school than senior school teachers who had high expectations for students; the opposite was found for low expectation teachers. The number of participants, however, precludes any generalizations being made about class-level expectations by student age group. This is an area in teacher expectation research that has not yet been investigated: Do junior school primary teachers have higher expectations for students than senior school teachers? Future research including larger numbers of high and low expectation teachers could begin to unravel the importance of the diverse range of variables.

This study has shown pedagogical beliefs and self-reported practices of teachers having uniformly high or low expectations for classes vary in substantial ways. Given differences found between beliefs and self-reported practices of high and low expectation teachers, it would seem possible that teacher beliefs are one mechanism of teacher expectations through which differing learning opportunities are provided to students. Such divergent pedagogical beliefs may have important implications for student learning as they result in children being exposed to quite disparate learning opportunities depending on the types of teachers with whom they are placed. This has implications for both professional development of practising teachers as well as for initial teacher education courses. If all students are to achieve their learning potential, they deserve to be given the utmost opportunity to do so.

REFERENCES

Babad, E., Bernieri, F., & Rosenthal, R. (1991). Students as judges of teachers' verbal and nonverbal behavior. *American Educational Research Journal, 28*, 211–234.

Babad, E., Inbar, J., & Rosenthal, R. (1982). Pygmalion, Galatea and the Golem: Investigations of biased and unbiased teachers. *Journal of Educational Psychology, 74*, 459–474.

Babad, E., & Taylor, P. B. (1992). Transparency of teacher expectancies across language, cultural boundaries. *Journal of Educational Research, 86*, 120–125.

Barr, R., & Dreeben, R. (1991). Grouping students for reading instruction. In R. Barr, M. L. Kamil, P. B. Mosenthal, & P. D. Pearson (Eds.), *Handbook of Reading Research* (Vol. II, pp. 885–910). White Plains, NY: Longman.

Blatchford, P., Burke, J., Farquhar, C., Plewis, I., & Tizard, B. (1989). Teacher expectations in infant school: Associations with attainment and progress, curriculum coverage and classroom interaction. *British Journal of Educational Psychology, 59*, 19–30.

Brattesani, K. A., Weinstein, R. S., & Marshall, H. H. (1984). Student perceptions of differential teacher treatment as moderators of teacher expectation effects. *Journal of Educational Psychology, 76*, 236–247.

Brophy, J. E. (1983). Research on the self-fulfilling prophecy and teacher expectations. *Journal of Educational Psychology, 75*, 631–661.

Brophy, J. E. (1985). Teacher-student interaction. In J. B. Dusek (Ed.), *Teacher expectancies* (pp. 303–328). Hillsdale, NJ: Lawrence Erlbaum.

Brophy, J. E. (1998). Introduction. In J. E. Brophy (Ed.), *Advances in Research on Teaching* (Vol. 7, pp. ix–xvii). Greenwich, Connecticut: JAI Press.

Brophy, J. E., & Good, T. (1974). *Teacher-Student Relationships: Causes and Consequences.* New York : Holt, Rinehart & Winston.

Cooper, H., and Good, T. (1983). *Pygmalion grows up: Studies in the expectation communication process.* New York: Longman.

Davenport, L. R. (1993). *The effects of homogeneous groupings in mathematics* (ERIC Digest). Columbus: ERIC Clearinghouse for Science, Mathematics and Environmental Education.

Dweck, C. S., Mangels, J. A., & Good, C. (2004). Motivational effects on attention, cognition, and performance. In D. Y. Dai & R. J. Sternberg (Eds.), *Motivation, emotion, and cognition: integrative perspectives on intellectual functioning and development* (pp. 41–56). Mahwah, NJ: Lawrence Erlbaum.

Gamoran, A. (1992). Is ability grouping equitable? *Educational Leadership, 50*(2), 11–17.

Good, T. L., & Brophy, J. E. (2003). *Looking in classrooms* (9th ed.). Boston, MA: Allyn & Bacon.

Hacker, R. G., Rowe, M. J., & Evans, R. D. (1992). The influences of ability groupings for secondary science lessons upon classroom processes. Part 2. *School Science Review, 73*(264), 119–123.

Harris, M. J., & Rosenthal, R. (1985). Mediation of interpersonal expectancy effects: 31 meta-analyses. *Psychological Bulletin, 97*, 363–386.

Hidi, S., Renninger, K. A., & Krapp, A. (2004). Interest, a motivational variable that combines affective and cognitive functioning. In D. Y. Dai & R. J. Sternberg (Eds.),

Motivation, emotion and cognition: Integrative perspectives on intellectual functioning and development (pp. 89–115). Mahwah, NJ: Lawrence Erlbaum.

Linchevski, L., & Kutscher, B. (1998). Tell me with whom you're learning, and I'll tell you how much you've learned: Mixed ability versus same-ability grouping in mathematics. *Journal for Research in Mathematics Education, 29*(5), 533–554.

Oakes, J., Gamoran, A., & Page, R. N. (1992). Curriculum differentiation, opportunities, outcomes and meanings. In P. Jackson (Ed.), *Handbook of Research on Curriculum* (pp. 570–608). New York : McMillan.

Reeve, J., & Jang, H. (2006). What teachers say and do to support students' autonomy during a learning activity. *Journal of Educational Psychology, 98,* 209–218.

Rosenthal, R., & Jacobson, L. (1968). *Pygmalion in the classroom: Teacher expectation and pupils' intellectual development.* New York: Holt, Rinehart & Winston.

Rubie-Davies, C. M. (2006). Teacher expectations and student self-perceptions: Exploring relationships. *Psychology in the Schools, 43,* 537–552.

Rubie-Davies, C. M. (2007). Classroom interactions: Exploring the practices of high and low expectation teachers. *British Journal of Educational Psychology, 77,* 289–306.

Soodak, L. C., & Podell, D. M. (1998). Teacher efficacy and the vulnerability of the difficult-to-teach student. In J. Brophy (Ed.), *Advances in Research on Teaching. Expectations in the Classroom* (Vol. 7, pp. 75–110). Greenwich, Connecticut: JAI Press.

Timperley, H. S., & Robinson, V. M. J. (2001). Achieving school improvement through challenging and changing teachers' schema. *Journal of Educational Change, 2,* 281–300.

Warren, S. R. (2002). Stories from the classrooms: How expectations and efficacy of diverse teachers affect the academic performance of children in poor urban schools. *Educational Horizons, 80*(3), 109–116.

Weinstein, R. S. (2002). *Reaching higher: The power of expectations in schooling.* Cambridge, MA: Harvard University Press.

Wilkinson, I. G., & Townsend, M. A. R. (2000). From Rata to Rimu: Grouping for instruction in best practice New Zealand classrooms. *The Reading Teacher, 53*(6), 460–471.

Zohar, A., Degani, A., & Vaaknin, E. (2001). Teachers' beliefs about low-achieving students and higher order thinking. *Teaching and Teacher Education, 17,* 469–485.

AUTHOR NOTE

Christine Rubie-Davies is a Senior Lecturer in the Faculty of Education, University of Auckland, New Zealand. She is a recent recipient of a National Tertiary Teaching Award for Sustained Excellence in Teaching. She had an extensive primary teaching background before moving into the tertiary sector in 1998. Her research interests include teacher expectations and beliefs, student self-esteem, the instructional and socioemotional environment of the classroom, and ethnic issues.

This research was conducted as part of the author's thesis for a PhD in Education at the University of Auckland. The author would like to acknowledge the outstanding supervision of Professors John Hattie and Michael Townsend and Dr Richard Hamilton.

Correspondence concerning this chapter should be addressed by email to: c.rubie@auckland.ac.nz

In: Challenging Thinking about Teaching and Learning   ISBN: 978-1-60456-744-1
Editors: C. M. Rubie-Davies and C. Rawlinson   © 2008 Nova Science Publishers, Inc.

Chapter 4

IMPROVING MOTIVATION AND PERFORMANCE IN SECONDARY SCHOOL SCIENCE

Wendell M. Jackman, Michael Townsend and Richard Hamilton

ABSTRACT

Successful students of science are characterized by an adaptive or proactive approach to learning science. Such students approach science with a positive attitude and engage with their learning in ways that enhance their mastery of scientific concepts. Less successful students often adopt learning and motivational practices that make less use of effective cognitive strategies in their learning, and are maladaptive with regard to their engagement in studying science, the value they hold for science, and their self-beliefs about their ability to learn science. This chapter outlines the rationale, methodology, and brief results of a school-based intervention designed to foster an adaptive approach to studying science in low achieving Year 10 students at a secondary (high) school in New Zealand. Students with a maladaptive approach to learning showed positive improvements in motivation but not achievement. Students with an adaptive approach to learning showed positive improvements in achievement but not motivation.

INTRODUCTION

Science achievement is hailed around the world as an important indicator of individual as well as societal development and as a foundation for innovation and scientific enterprise. Generally, students who succeed at science have an adaptive motivational pattern that includes high levels of academic self-efficacy (a belief in personal competence to learn science), a mastery achievement goal orientation (a desire to understand science) and place a high value on science as an academic activity. They set appropriate short-, medium-, and long-term learning goals and constantly revise these goals in the light of their learning success. They also use study and revision techniques that involve meaningful engagement with the scientific concepts. On the other hand, students who are less successful at science frequently hold a maladaptive motivational pattern. They view themselves as having limited capacity to learn science, are disinclined to want to understand science, and may view science as unimportant or irrelevant in their lives. Not surprisingly, they often use learning and revision strategies such as rehearsal or copying that may not lead to deeper understanding of the material.

There is reason to be concerned about achievement in science among students in New Zealand. The recent Trends in International Mathematics and Science Study (TIMSS) survey of national differences in educational achievement (Martin, Mullis, Gonzales, & Chrostowski, 2004) indicated that New Zealand students at age 14 years had average achievement lower than students in countries such as Australia, England, Hong Kong, Korea, Netherlands, Singapore, Sweden, Taiwan, and the United States. But, perhaps more importantly, the survey revealed that New Zealand had a relatively high proportion of low achieving students and that these students were markedly lower in motivation for science, both in their self-efficacy for science and in the value they placed on science, than their overseas counterparts. When seen alongside teachers' reports that such students are often disinterested, disruptive, and absent from science classes, it is evident that there is an urgent need for instructional practices that address these issues.

These concerns about the motivation and achievement of students studying science in New Zealand mirrored the first author's experiences of difficulties in teaching high school science to students in Trinidad. This chapter discusses a school-based intervention designed to improve the motivation and achievement of low-achieving science students by having them adopt a more adaptive, mastery-oriented approach to studying science. The intervention was conducted at one secondary (high) school where senior teachers were concerned about the students' progress in science. A summary of the results is included, but the major focus here is to explain the conceptual framework and the procedures adopted in attempting to improve motivation and achievement in science. An understanding of this framework provides teachers with a useful tool that may be applied with similar students in other learning situations. In brief, the intervention addressed three motivational elements (self-efficacy, task value, and goal orientation) and two cognitive strategies (goal setting and the use of annotated diagrams) which, according to international research, underlie successful learning in science. Because of their importance to this study, and to teachers in classrooms, each of the elements and strategies is now briefly reviewed.

Academic self-efficacy, according to Bandura (1997), is the belief that one is capable of competence or mastery of domain-specific academic tasks. Self-efficacy in a particular subject has been linked to explanations for and predictions of improvements and declines in achievement (Pastorelli, Vittori, Barbaranelli, Jarek, & Bandura, 2001). Consequently, individuals with high self-efficacy tend to visualize success which, in turn, leads to academic engagement. On the other hand, those with low self-efficacy are generally less engaged with learning (Schunk, 2003). This is because low self-efficacy prompts individuals to see themselves as failing, and this is associated with maladaptive behaviours such as self-doubt, negative thoughts, avoidance of difficult problems, lower resilience to failure, lower persistence in learning and revision, and lowering of academic goals (Bandura, 2000).

Academic self-efficacy is influenced by a number of factors including prior performance on academic tasks, classroom influences (e.g., classroom climate, teacher feedback), social modelling (e.g., positive peer role models), and social persuasion (e.g., verbal encouragement from a teacher). In terms of past performances, mastery of structured tasks (where the emphasis is on increased learning and understanding) helps to maintain and increase academic self-efficacy as it emphasizes self-referent progress and improvement. On the other hand, tasks that emphasize performance and which measure competence in socially comparative terms (i.e., doing better than others) can lower self-efficacy, especially among the weaker students (Schunk, 2003). In a similar vein, a co-operative classroom climate, often associated with a mastery approach to learning (that is, aiming to understand the content or master a task), can have a positive effect on academic self-efficacy, while a climate that highlights competition or a performance-based reward system can undermine it (Schunk & Pajares, 2002). Students can also experience a boost in academic self-efficacy when they observe a social model, especially a respected class peer, competently performing academic tasks (Schunk, 2003). Finally, "social persuasion" can also influence academic self-efficacy (Bandura, 2004). During social persuasion students are verbally inspired by a significant other (friend, teacher, parent, coach) to attempt challenging tasks; such motivating words can improve self-efficacy and empower students if they believe the source to be credible. Because self-efficacy is a powerful predictor of student achievement, regardless of ability and skill level (Bandura, 1997), it formed a central component to the intervention described here.

Academic task-value is the importance that students place on the academic content and tasks in a particular domain or subject (Pintrich & Zusho, 2002). It is thought to consist of three related aspects: intrinsic value ("How much do I enjoy this?"), attainment value ("How important is this to me?"), and utility value ("How useful is this for me?") (Eccles & Wigfield, 1995). Students who hold high levels of academic task-value are generally more engaged with learning and show more positive behavioural and motivational attitudes during learning. As a result, researchers have found that higher academic task-value ratings are associated with better school grades and the choice of more challenging academic tasks and deeper cognitive processing (Jacobs & Eccles, 2000). However, it is important to note that, unless students are taught how to maintain or improve it, academic task-value shows a tendency to decline during the secondary school years (Jacobs & Eccles, 2000). In addition, science students who hold low levels of academic task-value may engage in maladaptive behaviours (e.g., time-wasting in class, copying) or try to escape challenging academic situations in order to avoid having their weaknesses or incompetencies exposed (Pajares, Britner, & Valiante, 2000). Such behaviours reduce opportunities to learn and inevitably result in lower achievement.

Achievement goal orientation refers, in simple terms, to the way that a learner approaches a learning task. In the original work on achievement goal orientation (see Ames & Archer, 1988), researchers recognized that some students seem to approach classroom learning with a goal of understanding the material to be learned. Because such students seem to have a goal of mastering the learning, they are said to have a mastery goal orientation. But other students seem to approach classroom learning with a goal to perform well, relative to others, on the tasks used to assess learning. Such students may be attempting, for example, to achieve the highest test score in the class, to get an A-grade on an assignment, to be first finished, or just to obtain a higher grade than a rival classmate. These latter students are said to have a performance goal orientation to learning. On the surface it might not seem important to achievement whether a student is trying to understand the material or be the best in the class on the assessment activity. But mastery-oriented students may engage in different, more effective learning behaviours than students with a performance goal orientation. A performance-oriented learner may not read beyond the given learning material in order to avoid confusion from the other material or to reduce learning overload, or they may engage in lower-level learning strategies (such as rehearsal) if they believe the test is not going to assess deeper learning, or they may engage in activities that give them an advantage on the assessment task (e.g., removing critical classroom or library information to prevent others from using it). Mastery- and performance-oriented learners may also differ in their response to failure. Failure to understand something typically strengthens the resolve of the mastery-oriented person to Figure out what else they need to know. A performance-oriented learner, on the other hand, may actually reduce subsequent effort to learn (and may even make this public) or set lower performance goals, in order to avoid the shame of failure. Thus, a student's achievement goal orientation is directly related to their engagement or disengagement during the learning process (Anderman, Austin, & Johnson, 2002; Elliot & Dweck, 1988; Midgley, 2002).

More recently, however, the mastery–performance distinction has been combined with an approach–avoidance distinction (Elliot, 1999; Pintrich 2000). Some performance-oriented students might focus on demonstrating their superiority and thus seek out opportunities to perform better than others (i.e., have an "approach" focus). Alternatively, some performance-oriented students might focus on avoiding failure or looking incompetent (i.e., have an "avoidance" focus). Teachers will recognize these latter students as those who avoid eye contact by looking earnestly at their textbook when a class question is asked, or who raise their hand when they do not know the answer to a question, hoping that the teacher will not call on them to answer. The latter strategy, if successful, not only avoids failure but gives the appearance of being smart. But students with a mastery orientation may also adopt either an approach focus or an avoidance focus. The mastery–approach student is easily recognized as the person whose focus is to search for deep understanding and to make progress in their own learning. The concept of mastery–avoidance refers to students whose focus is on avoiding misunderstanding or ensuring that they do not fail on the task. Put simply, such students are often perfectionists who do not want to make mistakes. Some authors (e.g., Pintrich & Schunk, 1996) have questioned the utility of this concept in the context of classrooms because it seems counterintuitive to pursue mastery yet focus on not misunderstanding. The concept might be more easily understood in the context of sport where older athletes are no longer capable of meeting the outstanding standards of their youth and hence may adopt a mastery–avoidance focus in which they avoid those activities they could achieve earlier even though they still value mastery of them.

As may be seen, the combination of two types of orientation goals (mastery and performance) with two types of focus (approach and avoidance) creates four types of goal orientation that a student might hold: mastery–approach, mastery–avoidance, performance–approach and performance–avoidance (Elliot, 1999; Pintrich 2000). These classifications can be used to understand how students become engaged or disengaged from academic tasks in unique ways. In this system, mastery goals, where students seek to increase their understanding, are generally considered to engender the most adaptive engagement processes with learning. Performance–approach goals, where students compare their performance with the performance of others, can be either positive or negative depending on other features of the learning situation. However, performance–avoidance goals are unlikely to promote adaptive engagement and usually prompt superficial engagement processes or even disengagement (Elliot, 1999). To complicate matters, researchers have further speculated that, for the same academic task, students may simultaneously hold varying levels of *both* mastery–avoidance and performance–avoidance goals based on different previous learning experiences (Elliot & Church, 2003; Pintrich, 2003). This suggests that actual learning behaviour for a particular learning task may be a function of the strength of the varying levels of different achievement goals, expressed as a ratio (Harackiewicz, Barron, Tauer, Carter, & Elliot, 2000; Pintrich, 2003). Although it is important to understand that students may adopt different goals and different approaches to different learning tasks, the study reported here focused on a more general distinction between an adaptive approach to learning (i.e., a mastery orientation) and a maladaptive approach to learning (i.e., a performance–avoidance orientation).

The three motivational elements of self-efficacy, task value, and goal orientation were included in the intervention discussed in this chapter because they are known to affect the way that students engage with learning tasks. The intervention also included training in two specific cognitive strategies—academic goal setting and the use of annotated diagrams—designed to directly assist the learning of low-achieving students.

Academic goal setting is a cognitive strategy that directs and prompts positive, achievement-related behaviour (Schunk, 2003). It assists students in remaining task-focused during different stages of achieving the goal, and stimulates higher levels of motivation and self-efficacy (Locke, 1996; Locke & Latham, 2002). For poorly motivated, underachieving science students, the continued setting and achieving of reasonable, achievable goals enhances a sense of self-efficacy, encouraging heightened academic commitment, greater effort, and increased persistence in the face of inevitable, and often desirable, error (Foesterling, 1985). This recursive process also encourages self-assessments and adjustment to strategy and effort, and encourages the setting of more challenging goals when initial goals are accomplished (Zimmerman, 1998; 2000). While academic goal setting is related to a variety of positive motivational and behavioural consequences, it does not come naturally to some learners and so needs to be encouraged. In the absence of strategic goal setting, less able students are unlikely to remain engaged with a task over long periods of time (Pressley, 1995).

Self-generated annotated diagrams are diagrams or other pictorial representations (e.g., mind maps) of subject matter with explanatory notes (Vekiri, 2002). By its very nature, science is an appropriate subject for the application and use of annotated diagrams to aid and enhance understanding because of its numerous logical, sequential, abstract, and image-laden concepts and phenomena. Indeed, science textbooks make frequent use of such diagrams to convey information to students. Creating personally annotated diagrams or restructuring existing diagrams demands a level of engagement with the concepts and ideas which enhances learning, particularly for low-achieving students (Lowe, 1991). Diagrams provide a store of visual memories that are often more easily accessible than text information, Further, the combination of visual and text information may also enhance both initial learning and long-term recall (Paivio & Caspo, 1973).

As noted earlier, not all students possess these strategies or orientations to learning. The intervention described below was designed to help students with low motivation and poor cognitive strategies to take a more positive and successful approach to science.

A SCHOOL-BASED INTERVENTION IN SCIENCE

The study involved an evidence-based school intervention of 9 weeks that was intended to enhance the three motivational elements of academic self-efficacy, academic task-value, and a mastery goal orientation. It was also designed to introduce the students to the two cognitive strategies of academic goal setting and the use of self-generated annotated diagrams. Thus, the intervention catered for students with low motivation or cognition, or both (Lau & Roeser, 2002).

The participants in the study were 94 low-achieving Year 10 students (mean age 14.4 years) from four science classrooms of a suburban secondary school in a relatively low socioeconomic area of Auckland, New Zealand. Three classrooms (64 students) served as the intervention group, while one classroom (30 students) was assigned as a non-intervention group. The classes represented the lower achieving science students of the cohort year. Scores on internally assessed science tests and examinations for the year were converted to a 10-point scale which paralleled the reporting system used for the National Certificate in Educational Achievement (the national school qualification), where "Not Achieved" was rated 3, "Achieved" was rated 6.5, "Merit" was rated 8, and "Excellent" was rated 9.5. The mean score (and standard deviation) for the students was 4.72 (1.17), confirming that students had relatively low achievement in science.

The intervention was explained to the students in a single interactive workshop of approximately one hour. The motivational and cognitive concepts, together with associated strategies, were introduced through examples drawn from popular sports figures in New Zealand who served as role models. In brief, the *self-efficacy* enhancement strategy taught students how to create self-motivating statements (e.g., "I will be able to do this if I work through to the end"), whether silent or spoken aloud, to boost flagging commitment or low self-efficacy. The academic *task-value* strategy required students to reflect on and record the personal value of each science topic as they approached it during the term. The *mastery goal* training involved helping students to use verbal statements directed at mastering a task that would satisfy their curiosity, or deepen their understanding, or improve their competence about each science topic; students were also encouraged to strive for good grades or marks but as hallmarks of personal progress not for socially comparative or competitive reasons. Students were also taught how to set and achieve short-term and medium-term academic goals, the need for regular and systematic reflection about progress toward these goals, how to readjust goals when necessary, how to deal with failure or error, and to predict and prepare for potential obstacles to learning. In all of this training, students were encouraged to think about ability as an ever-expanding pool of skills and competencies rather than a fixed, unchanging entity (Dweck & Leggett, 1988; Grant & Dweck, 2003). Finally, students were shown the value of annotative diagrams, how to generate their own diagrams for each science topic, and how to use them for revision.

At the workshop, each student received an intervention booklet that included an age-appropriate explanation of each strategy and examples of its application for science. Science teachers of the intervention classes were present during these workshops, as they were required to reinforce these strategies during their science classes and facilitate application of the strategies—in particular, by providing time to use the annotated diagram drawing strategy and giving scaffolding as needed.

Assessments of self-efficacy, task value, and goal orientation were made before, midway through, and at the end of the 9-week intervention using relevant subscales of the Pattern of Adaptive Learning Scales (PALS) used in previous research (Midgley, Maehr, Hicks, Roeser, Urdan, Anderman, et al., 2000). Additionally, students kept weekly journals in which they responded to scaled questions about the frequency, circumstances, and value of using each of the five major strategies during their science work in the past week.

As already noted, one of the four classrooms was randomly assigned to a non-intervention condition. Preliminary analyses indicated no significant differences in initial motivation or achievement scores between the intervention and non-intervention classrooms. Each student was then classified as having an adaptive or a maladaptive motivation orientation based on the ratio of mastery to performance–avoidance that they endorsed in the first administration of the PALS. Those with an adaptive motivation structure held a dominant mastery orientation and low performance–avoidance profile; these students were focused on personal progress toward understanding the science topics. Those with a maladaptive motivation structure held a dominant performance–avoidance goal orientation and a low mastery goal orientation profile; these students were focused on reducing the likelihood that they would appear as poor learners to their peers.

RESULTS

Data from this study were examined using both quantitative and qualitative procedures. The major statistical analyses examined differences in students' motivational, cognitive strategy, and achievement scores at three times (pre-intervention, mid-intervention, and post-intervention), in both the intervention and non-intervention groups, and for those initially classified as having an adaptive or maladaptive motivation orientation. The major thematic analyses were based on entries in the students' weekly journal reports, particularly in relation to their reported use and perceived benefits of the strategies and concepts. An overview of the main findings is presented here. A full account of these analyses and results can be found in Jackman (2007).

Students with a maladaptive motivation orientation who received the intervention made significant, positive gains in their motivation for science. They improved in academic self-efficacy, academic task-value, and achievement goal orientation. These results suggest that science students can, even with a relatively long history of low achievement, have greater confidence in their ability to learn science, increase their value for science, and develop a greater focus on improving their understanding of science. Given that the intervention workshop was approximately one hour, these findings indicate that a student-oriented, specifically focused intervention does not have to be lengthy, so long as the ideas are reinforced during regular teaching.

However, students with a maladaptive motivation orientation did not make a parallel significant gain in science achievement. Analyses of the test and examination achievement results indicated that achievement scores for students in the intervention group increased slightly over the course of the intervention, while students in the non-intervention decreased slightly, but these changes were not statistically significant. Further research is needed to determine whether a more elaborate intervention, more follow-up support, or simply more time is needed to bring about positive gains in achievement for students with a maladaptive orientation.

Students with an adaptive achievement goal orientation did not differ significantly from their non-intervention peers on the three motivation elements during the intervention. This was not unexpected, although it had been thought that the intervention might strengthen their adaptive orientation. The lack of improvement across the intervention could not be attributed to "ceiling effects" associated with the tests since all measures showed room for improvement, even at the end of the intervention. Somewhat surprisingly, however, although students with an adaptive motivation orientation did not improve in motivation over the time of the intervention, they showed a significant increase in achievement. It was unexpected that the intervention would facilitate learning for students with adaptive motivation but not for students with maladaptive motivation. Given that students with adaptive motivation did not increase in their motivation it seems likely that their increase in achievement was attributable to the cognitive skills training in goal setting and using annotated diagrams, a result consistent with previous research on the effectiveness of these strategies. If this is so, further research is needed on why the cognitive skills activities do not lead to similar gains in achievement in the students with a maladaptive orientation. Perhaps the positive engagement associated with an adaptive motivation orientation is a necessary prerequisite to the adoption of the cognitive skills. These findings suggest that students with adaptive motivation can be trained in the classroom to maintain their motivational levels while improving the application of their cognitive skills. While it is tempting to think that low achieving students who are adaptively motivated only need strategies to improve their cognitive competence, it is important to remember that, as noted earlier, academic motivation tends to decline both within and across school years if it is not fostered.

CONCLUSION

Although teachers are generally well aware of the importance and benefits of a mastery orientation in their students, this chapter reinforces the need to simultaneously consider the complexity of different motivational orientations that directly influence the ways that students engage or disengage with science. These complexities can be captured in a general distinction between students who hold an adaptive approach to science learning and those who hold a maladaptive approach. An adaptive approach is characterized by a positive attitude toward the self as a learner, science is a valued activity, and there is a desire to understand science. A maladaptive approach is characterized by a high level of concern about personal accomplishments relative to other students and a focus on minimizing engagement in activities that carry a risk of failure. In this study, a distinction was made between students who have an adaptive approach to learning science and those who have a maladaptive approach. A 9-week intervention to encourage a more adaptive approach to learning science was successful in increasing positive motivation, but not achievement, for students with a maladaptive approach, and for increasing achievement, but not motivation, for students with an adaptive approach. Careful articulation of concepts that make up what is commonly referred to as "motivation" is critical to the successful application of such concepts in educational settings. Further, attempts to improve motivation need to be accompanied by strategies that increase cognitive engagement with the learning. While some students will always have lower achievement in science than others, it is not inevitable that New Zealand has a sizeable minority of students with low science achievement.

REFERENCES

Ames, C., & Archer, J. (1988). Achievement goals in the classroom: Students' learning strategies and motivation processes. *Journal of Educational Psychology, 71,* 260–267.

Anderman, E. M., Austin, C. C., & Johnson, D. M. (2002). The development of goal orientation. In A. Wigfield & J. S. Eccles (Eds.), *Development of achievement motivation* (pp. 197–220). San Diego, CA: Academic Press.

Bandura, A. (1997). *Self-efficacy: The exercise of control.* New York : Freeman.

Bandura, A. (2000). Social-cognitive theory. In A. E. Kazdin (Ed.), *Encyclopedia of psychology* (Vol. 7, pp. 329–332). Washington, DC: American Psychological Association.

Bandura, A. (2004). Swimming against the mainstream: The early years from chilly tributary to transformative mainstream. *Behaviour Research and Therapy, 42*(6), 613–630.

Dweck, C. S., & Leggett, E. L. (1988). A social cognitive approach to motivation and personality. *Psychological Review, 95,* 256–273.

Eccles, J. S., & Wigfield, A. (1995). In the mind of the actor: The structure of adolescents' achievement task values and expectancy-related beliefs. *Personality and Social Psychology Bulletin, 21*(3), 215–225.

Elliot, A. J. (1999). Approach and avoidance motivation and achievement goals. *Educational Psychologist, 34*(3), 169–189.

Elliot, A. J., & Church, M. A. (2003). A motivational analysis of defensive pessimism and self-handicapping. *Journal of Personality, 71*(3), 369–396.

Elliot, E. S., & Dweck, C. S. (1988). Goals: An approach to motivation and achievement. *Journal of Personality and Social Psychology, 54,* 5–12.

Foesterling, F. (1985). Attributional retraining: A review. *Psychological Bulletin, 98,* 495–512.

Grant, H., & Dweck, C. S. (2003). Clarifying achievement goals and their impact. *Journal of Personality and Social Psychology, 85,* 541–553.

Harackiewicz, J. M., Barron, K. E., Tauer, J. M., Carter, S. M., & Elliot, A. J. (2000). Short-term and long-term consequences of achievement goals: Predicting interest and performance over time. *Journal of Educational Psychology, 92*(2), 316–330.

Jackman, W. M. (2007). *The effects of a learning strategies intervention on academic motivation and science achievement.* Unpublished doctoral dissertation, University of Auckland, New Zealand.

Jacobs, J. E., & Eccles, J. S. (2000). Parents, task values, and real-life achievement-related choices. In C. Sansone & J. M. Harackiewicz (Eds.), *Intrinsic and extrinsic motivation: The search for optimal motivation and performance* (pp. 405–439). San Diego, CA: Academic Press.

Lau, S., & Roeser, R. W. (2002). Cognitive abilities and motivational processes in high school students' situational engagement and achievement in science. *Educational Assessment, 8*(2), 139–162.

Locke, E. (1996). Motivation through conscious goal setting. *Applied and Preventive Psychology, 5*, 117–124.

Locke, E., & Latham, G. P. (2002). Building a practically useful theory of goal setting and task motivation. *American Psychologist, 57*(9), 705–717.

Lowe, R. (1991). Expository illustrations: A new challenge for reading instruction. *Australian Journal of Reading, 14*, 215–226.

Martin, M. O., Mullis, I. V. S., Gonzales, E. J., & Chrostowski, S. J. (2004). *TIMSS 2003 international science report*. IEA, Boston College.

Midgley, C. (Ed.). (2002). *Goals, goal structures and patterns of adaptive learning*. Mahwah, NJ: Lawrence Erlbaum.

Midgley, C., Maehr, M. L., Hruda, L. Z., Anderman, E., Anderman, L., Freeman, K., et al. (2000). *Manual for the Patterns of Adaptive Learning Survey (PALS)*. (Revised ed.). Ann Arbor, MI: University of Michigan.

Paivio, A., & Caspo, K. (1973). Picture superiority in free recall: Imagery or dual coding? *Cognitive Psychology, 5*(2), 176–206.

Pajares, F., Britner, S. L., & Valiante, G. (2000). Relation between achievement goals and self-beliefs of middle school students in writing and science. *Contemporary Educational Psychology, 25*(4), 406–422.

Pastorelli, C., Gian Vittori, C., Barbaranelli, C., Jarek, R., & Bandura, A. (2001). The structure of children's perceived self-efficacy: A cross-national study. *European Journal of Psychologica Assessment, 17*(2), 87–97.

Pintrich, P. (2000). An achievement goal theory perspective on issues in motivation terminology, theory, and research. *Contemporary Educational Psychology, 25*, 92–104.

Pintrich, P. R. (2003). A motivational science perspective on the role of student motivation in learning and teaching contexts. *Journal of Educational Psychology, 95*(4), 667–686.

Pintrich, P. R., & Schunk, D.H., (1996). *Motivation in education: Theory, research and applications*. Englewood Cliffs, NJ: Prentice-Hall.

Pintrich, P. R., & Zusho, A. (2002). The development of academic self-regulation: The role of cognitive and motivational factors. In A. Wigfield & J. Eccles (Eds.), *Development of achievement motivation* (pp. 250–284). San Diego, CA, Academic Press.

Pressley, M. (1995). More about the development of self-regulation: Complex, long-term, and thoroughly social. *Educational Psychologist, 30*(4), 201–212.

Schunk, D. H. (2003). Self-efficacy for reading and writing: Influence of modeling, goal setting, and self-evaluation. *Reading and Writing Quarterly: Overcoming Learning Difficulties, 19*(2), 159–172.

Schunk, D. H., & Pajares, F. (2002). The development of academic self-efficacy. In A. Wigfield & J. S. Eccles (Eds.), *Development of Achievement Motivation* (pp. 15–31). San Diego, CA: Academic Press.

Vekiri, I. (2002). What is the value of graphical displays in learning? *Educational Psychology Review, 14*(3), 261–312.

Zimmerman, B. J. (1998). Academic studying and the development of personal skill: A self-regulatory perspective. *Educational Psychologist, 33*(2–3), 73–86.

Zimmerman, B. J. (2000). Attaining self-regulation: A social cognitive perspective. In M. Boekaerts, P. Pintrich & M. Zeidner (Eds.), *The handbook of self-regulation* (pp. 13– 39). San Diego: Academic Press.

AUTHOR NOTE

Wendell M. Jackman is an Assistant Professor in the School for Studies in Learning, Cognition and Education at the University of Trinidad & Tobago. Michael Townsend is Professor of Educational Psychology, School of Education, Massey University at Auckland. Richard Hamilton is a Senior Lecturer in the Faculty of Education, University of Auckland, New Zealand.

This chapter is based on a PhD thesis completed by the first author in 2007 at the University of Auckland.

Correspondence concerning this chapter should be addressed by email to: M.Townsend@massey.ac.nz

In: Challenging Thinking about Teaching and Learning   ISBN: 978-1-60456-744-1
Editors: C. M. Rubie-Davies and C. Rawlinson   © 2008 Nova Science Publishers, Inc.

Chapter 5

WHAT CHILDREN SEE AS MATHEMATICS BEYOND THE SCHOOL GATE

Mark R. Kilpatrick

ABSTRACT

This chapter discusses beliefs about mathematics beyond the school gate held by a group of Year 5 children. These children's beliefs about mathematics, explored through questionnaires, indicated that the mathematics beyond the school gate they saw was either computation mathematics or mathematics that solved everyday problems. However, it appeared that the children did not see other aspects of mathematics. This raised a concern in light of connection making between the mathematics of the classroom and of the world beyond the school gate. This concern is briefly discussed and possible solutions are suggested.

INTRODUCTION

This chapter reports an investigation of the beliefs about mathematics beyond the school gate held by 16 Year 5 children (aged 9 or 10 years) from Reliant Street School (a pseudonym), a large metropolitan city school in New Zealand. The children were asked questions that explored their beliefs about the existence of mathematics beyond the school gate and what that mathematics might look like to them. The children's beliefs are reported in two parts: the mathematics they saw themselves using beyond the school gate and the mathematics they saw others using beyond the school gate. The chapter discusses the responses, identifies an area of concern in relation to curriculum requirements, and considers the possible implications of this concern for primary school teachers.

WHY BELIEFS?

A belief can be described as an individually constructed perception (McDonough, 1995b, 1998), a personal construct (Leder & Forgasz, 2002), or the way people see or perceive something (Op't Eydne, De Corte, & Verschaffel, 2002). In the current study, the concept of belief was explained to the children as what they saw as ("I see . . .") or believed to be ("I believe . . .") mathematics. This explanation was based on Rokeach's defined belief (1968, cited McDonough, 1995a, 1995b), which McDonough (1995a) expressed as "any simple proposition, conscious or unconscious, inferred from what a person says or does, capable of being preceded by the phrase, 'I believe that'" (p. 483).

LITERATURE REVIEW

The literature (e.g., Civil, 1990, 2002a, 2002b; Kloosterman, Raymond, & Emenaker, 1996; McDonough, 1998, 1999; Nunes, Schliemann, & Carraher, 1993) has suggested that primary school children hold beliefs about mathematics that place mathematics as two distinct entities: one that is confined to the school classroom and the other that is used in the world beyond the school gate. However, it is not clear if children see connections between these two forms of mathematics.

American elementary school children seemed to hold the belief that mathematics was "two distinct behaviours, one inside the school and one outside" (Civil, 1990, p. 8). Civil suggested that children's beliefs about mathematics out of school were about problems to be solved. Another group of American elementary school children also reported believing mathematics to be two entities: formal and informal (Nunes, Schliemann, & Carraher, 1993). The children described mathematics as formal in-school mathematics and informal out-of-school mathematics. Some of these children expressed the opinion that they felt more proficient and comfortable with the informal out-of-school mathematics than the formal in-school mathematics. Other American elementary school children have described mathematics beyond the school gate as mathematics used when shopping, cooking and doing sports, and in other family contexts (Kloosterman, Raymond, & Emenaker, 1996). Although these children described their beliefs about mathematics beyond the school gate, there was no discussion as to whether they, or any of the children, saw connections between mathematics of the classroom and mathematics beyond the school gate.

Nearly 10 years later, Civil (2002a, 2002b), writing about other American elementary school children's beliefs about mathematics, reported that children's beliefs about mathematics beyond the school gate focused on mathematics of an everyday nature which solved everyday problems. Civil stated that children made little, if any, connection between formal in-school mathematics and the informal everyday mathematics of the world beyond the school gate. Civil believed this was because children in her study saw little or no relevance between the two mathematics.

Specific beliefs about mathematics held by Australian lower primary school children were investigated by McDonough (1998, 1999). McDonough reported that the children's beliefs about mathematics placed mathematics, again, in two distinct categories: mathematics which McDonough described as a set of procedures which led to correct answers (in-school mathematics) and mathematics of real-life, non-school situations.

When 9-year-olds from a New Zealand provincial centre were interviewed about their beliefs about mathematics, they perceived mathematics as mainly arithmetic (computation) (Young-Loveridge, 1992). However, when they were asked about the importance of mathematics, they described real-life situations in which mathematics played an important part. These situations included both at-home and away-from-home contexts, but Young-Loveridge did not discuss whether the children made connections between their in-school mathematics and mathematics of the world beyond the school gate. In a more recent project (Kilpatrick, 2002), a group of Year 5 children indicated that mathematics is more than number (computation). Kilpatrick's participants saw mathematics being used away from the school context, either by themselves or others, in several ways. Some children saw mathematics in a home setting, when they counted their saved pocket money, helped a younger sibling to count toys as they put them away, or when telling the time. Other children told of seeing mathematics when parents paid bills or brought work such as accounts (bookkeeping) home. In a setting away from home, children told of seeing mathematics to do with money when in shops or paying bus fares, and seeing mathematics to do with aspects of measurement when helping a relative cook or watching a builder building a house.

The above literature suggests that children hold beliefs about mathematics in which mathematics is seen as comprising two distinct entities. The first entity is of an in-school formal mathematics that provides children with answers to the mathematical problems posed by their teachers. The second entity is an out-of-school informal mathematics that is used by children and others to solve mathematical problems of an everyday nature. However the above literature, apart from Civil (2002a, 2002b) and Kilpatrick (2002), does not make it clear if children see connections between these two entities, although for New Zealand teachers such connection making is required by the national curriculum (Ministry of Education, 2007).

METHOD

The current study used a qualitative methodology, which provided opportunities for exploring and clarifying understanding of the children's beliefs about mathematics. This approach allowed for children to explain their beliefs about mathematics in a natural setting—their school (Davidson & Tolich, 1999; Denzin & Lincoln, 1994). The data gathering was by questionnaire, as questionnaires have proved to be useful when seeking information from children (Kloosterman & Stage, 1992). The questionnaire sought answers to how children saw mathematics beyond the school gate.

Within the "mathematics beyond the school gate" section—the focus of this chapter—the questions sought answers to what the children believed to be mathematics seen and used, by themselves and others, away from the school setting. Particular questions asked were: "If I am doing or using maths away from school, this is what I do" and "When other people do/use maths away from school, this is what they do". Analysis of the children's answers was undertaken by collating their answers on a grid for each question. Collation of data took the form of listing all 16 children's answers as statements. These statements were then themed according to whether the mathematics described was computation or topic (non-computation) mathematics, or of another nature. Computation mathematics is an umbrella term to describe the four computation functions of addition, subtraction, multiplication, and division, and the basic facts for each function. Topic mathematics is an umbrella term for other areas of mathematics: algebra, geometry, measurement, number (excluding computation), and statistics and graphs. As an example, Table 5.1 shows the statements and themes generated in response to question 15, "If I am doing/using maths away from school, this is what I do".

**Table 5.1. Responses to Q15—"If I Am Doing/Using Maths
Away From School, This Is What I Do"**

Statements	Themes
Practising basic facts (add/subt/multi/div)	Homework—basic facts, drawing graphs, counting money for homework
Homework—computation practice	Ditto
Homework— drawing graphs	Ditto
Counting money, practising school mathematics	Ditto
Money—shopping	Money—shops and bank, counting money
Money—going to the bank	Ditto
Measuring when making clothes and sewing	Measurement—linear

All 16 children (11 girls and 5 boys) completed the questionnaire, which could be answered with both written and visual responses. The visual responses allowed for children who felt less able to express their thoughts in written form to use drawings or diagrams (McDonough, 2002; Wetton & McWhirter, 1998).

In this chapter, only the "beyond the school gate" beliefs about mathematics of the 16 children are discussed.

RESULTS

Mathematics Used by the Children

Half (8) of the children said "Yes" they used mathematics beyond the school gate, and over a third (6) said they "Sometimes" used mathematics. Only two children said "No" they did not use mathematics beyond the school gate.

Of the 14 children who reported using mathematics beyond the school gate, the mathematics they used was primarily computation mathematics in the form of basic facts practice for homework, or addition and subtraction of money, whether for homework or when shopping.

Rani and Rajni, (all names are pseudonyms) referred to mathematics homework, one as "calculation and whatever I do at school" (Rani) and the other as "practise what we do at school" (Rajni). For both these boys, mathematics beyond the school gate was directly linked to the mathematics of the classroom and was seen as practice of that classroom mathematics. But Rose told of seeing mathematics that was not homework. She told of both computation and topic mathematics used beyond the school gate and wrote: "When I'm doing shopping, I help Mum and Dad do the counting. When I go to the bank, I practise my maths. When I help my Mum to measure the cloth, I practise my measuring".

However, many other children only reported seeing money as mathematics beyond the school gate and predominately when shopping—counting money and checking change. For one child, Ryme, money was almost an invisible form of mathematics beyond the school gate. She wrote: "I look at the price and see if I have enough money. I don't need to count it and I get some money back, so I don't need to do maths". However, it is likely she did do some form of mental computation mathematics even though Ryme did not appear to be aware of this mathematics. Rosslyn saw mathematics in everyday life and commented that: "We can't live without it. We use maths without knowing it, everyday". However, Rosslyn did not distinguish between computation and topic mathematics beyond the school gate.

Mathematics Used by Others

When telling of whether they saw others using mathematics beyond the school gate, 3 said "Yes" and 11 said "Sometimes". Again, only two children said "No", they saw no mathematics being used by others beyond the school gate.

Of the 14 children who saw others use mathematics beyond the school gate, the mathematics they reported was mainly money-related computation mathematics or mathematics related to homework. There was only one instance of topic mathematics, which was associated with telling the time. For example, Ryme and Ruth both wrote of seeing others using mathematics associated with money, such as "counting how much money they have, but only when shopping" (Ryme) and "count money and work out their finances" (Ruth). Rataro told of seeing family members doing mathematical homework or being helped with mathematical homework by other family members and wrote that others were "practising their x, -, +, ÷, >, <, and other things". Rani also wrote that "my brother [secondary school student] asks my Dad [a mathematics teacher in their home country] about the question that he doesn't know". Rajni suggested that others were studying for a mathematics test. Ronnie reported his one instance of topic mathematics when he told of seeing others using a watch to tell the time because they were waiting for a television programme to begin. Again, Rosslyn made an observation about others using mental mathematics to undertake computation: "People usually use maths inside their head, not at the grocery store counting on their fingers".

DISCUSSION

The findings reported from the Reliant Street school children about mathematics beyond the school gate were similar to and supported findings reported previously by primary (elementary) school children both overseas (America and Australia) and from New Zealand about mathematics beyond the school gate.

The Reliant Street children saw what they believed to be mathematics used away from the school—beyond the school gate—as primarily computation mathematics dealing with money. This mathematics described by the Reliant Street children is of an everyday nature, used to solve everyday problems, as described by Civil (2002a, 2002b). The Reliant Street children reported using what they believed to be mathematics that was used to solve mathematical problems in family contexts. These family contexts were similar to those described by Kloostermann, Raymond, and Emenaker (1996).

Findings from Australian (McDonough, 1998, 1999) and New Zealand (Young-Loveridge, 1992) primary school children have reported that children saw mathematics away from school as mathematics that solves problems of an everyday nature—the same as described by the Reliant Street children.

However, the Reliant Street results raise a concern when considered in the light of the clear requirement within the mathematics and statistics learning area of *The New Zealand Curriculum* (Ministry of Education, 2007) for connection making. This states that children need to recognize relationships that help them to make "sense of the world in which they live" (p. 26). Such relationships within the mathematics and statistics learning area are highlighted as providing "a broad range of practical applications in everyday life, in other learning areas, and in workplaces" (Ministry of Education, 2007, p. 26). Connection making is clearly expressed in the section on effective pedagogy where teachers are urged to "help students to make connections across learning areas as well as connections to home practices and to the wider world" (Ministry of Education, 2007, p. 34).

With no more than half the children reporting seeing what they believe to be mathematics beyond the school gate, then is the requirement of the curriculum document being fulfilled? Is 50% an adequate pass rate? I would suggest not.

It is apparent that for these Reliant Street children there was little connection making between in-school and out-of-school mathematics other than for computation mathematics. However, McDonough (1999) and Kilpatrick (2002) suggest that connection making is easier for children who have experienced classroom activities that encourage discovery of and discussion about the connections between in-class and beyond-the-school-gate mathematics. McDonough (1998, 1999) considers that children's beliefs are influenced by both recent classroom mathematical experiences as well as real-life situations.

Such connection making may have influenced Kilpatrick's (2002) children's beliefs about mathematics beyond the school. These children had had deliberate and proactive connection making, by their class teacher, between the mathematics of the classroom and the world beyond the school gate.

Civil (2002a, 2002b), writing about American elementary school children's perceptions of mathematics, stated that children in her study appeared to make few, if any, connections between "proper", or in-school, mathematics and the everyday mathematics of the world beyond the school gate. Civil believed this was because the children saw no relevance between the two forms of mathematics. New Zealand school children have also reported seeing no relevance between their school mathematics and that of the world beyond the school gate (Young-Loveridge, 1992). Earlier, Civil (1990) had questioned the reality of the problems presented in school mathematics and suggested that if in-school problems failed to reflect the reality of the outside world then children were less likely to make connections between the two mathematical entities. The relevance of in-school mathematical problems to the mathematical problems of the world out of school appear to be important aspects of the classroom mathematics programme if children are to be encouraged and supported to make connections between the two mathematical entities (Ministry of Education, 2007).

Although many of the Reliant Street children saw themselves and others using mathematics beyond the school gate, the mathematics they identified was limited. Why did the Reliant Street children make so few connections between their in-school mathematics and that of the mathematics of the world beyond the school gate? Other researchers (e.g., Barnes & Horne, 1996; Taylor & Biddulph, 1994) have argued that both prior classroom experiences and observation of the real world are strong influences on children's connection making. If such connection making had not occurred at Reliant Street, then it is less likely the children would make the connections for themselves.

Another possible explanation could be societal or familial views of mathematics. Such views could position mathematics as an in-school activity only. If this is the situation, then this could have influenced the Reliant Street children's beliefs about mathematics. Such positioning of mathematics as an in-school activity only has been discussed by both Civil (2002a) and Leder (1995), who suggested that, influenced by their parents' beliefs, children do not see any relevance between in-school mathematics and the mathematics of the everyday world. If this is so, then children are not likely to bring into the class setting everyday experiences that they believe to be a form of mathematics or, conversely, take their classroom mathematics experiences out in to the world beyond the school gate.

If, as this research suggests, children see computation mathematics beyond the school gate, but little topic mathematics, then children need to be assisted to see topic mathematics. Absolum (2006) strongly suggests that classroom learning must have explicit connections to real world examples. With this in mind, mathematics of the classroom should be related to the mathematics of the real world. Teachers need to make clear to children why something is to be learnt and the relevance of that learning.

The New Zealand Curriculum (Ministry of Education, 2007) states children need to be confident users of mathematics and statistics in a broad range of practical applications in everyday life (p. 26) and that "connections to home practices and to the wider world" (p. 34) be made relevant for children. If pedagogy influences the way children see their world in the classroom setting and beyond the school gate, then pedagogical changes may assist children to make connections between in-school and out-of-school mathematics (Leder, 1992; Ministry of Education, 2007).

One such pedagogical change could be to highlight mathematics beyond the classroom. Children possibly do not see topic mathematics beyond the classroom because that mathematics has not been highlighted in some way for them. Mansfield, Scott, and Burgess (1994) have argued that if children only see use for mathematical concepts in a school setting then children are less likely to take ownership of those concepts and transfer them to the real world setting. Highlighting of mathematics beyond the school gate through discussions between teachers and children may help children see the relevance of classroom topic mathematics to topic mathematics beyond the school gate. Discussing aspects of authentic task topic mathematics in a classroom could be a method to help children see and make connections (McNaught, 2005). This would draw on the children's experiences of the everyday world to make relevant the curriculum to the children's everyday life.

McDonough (2002) argues that this connection making is the responsibility of both the school and family. Children may see topic mathematics beyond the classroom door if guided to them, either by their teachers or by their family. This connection making could enhance the children's ability to make connections for themselves. In order to include families in this process, schools must communicate with them (Absolum, 2006). Communicating with and providing parents with information about their child's mathematics programme may assist parents to support the school programme and extend their child's perceptions of mathematics (Absolum, 2006; Greenhough et al., 2005; McDonough, 2002; Onslow, 1992; Tranter, 2002). Such a communication method could be newsletters from the school or class teacher. In these newsletters, parents could read about their child's mathematics programme for that week and suggestions for possible activities that could support their child's mathematical understanding. Outlining mathematics activities in such a way provides support for parents and possible encouragement to discuss, with their child, their child's mathematics programme (Absolum, 2006; Greenhough et al., 2005; McDonough, 2002; Onslow, 1992; Tranter, 2002).

For example, if a child's mathematics programme includes fractions and fractional work, the newsletter could suggest to parents ways they could show their child fractions in everyday life, such as cutting a pizza or cake, the half-full milk bottle, or quarter-full petrol tank as indicated on the petrol gauge. The newsletter could suggest appropriate questions for parents to ask their children that may extend understanding, such as "How much milk is left in the bottle?" As well, the newsletter could ask the parents to share their expertise, experiences, and knowledge with their children. Such actions and questions may help children to see connections between in-school and everyday mathematics beyond the school gate.

CONCLUSION

This research indicates that children's beliefs about mathematics, as described by the children, place mathematics as two separate entities: an in-school mathematics that solves school mathematics and an out-of-school mathematics that solves everyday mathematics. However, the mathematics the children see out of school is primarily computation, with little topic mathematics seen. The findings suggest that connection making or translation of understanding, particularly of topic mathematics, may not necessarily happen. Consequently teachers need to actively encourage children to make connections in this area. Connection making can be achieved through the use of discussion in class and communication with parents.

REFERENCES

Absolum, M. (2006). Clarity in the classroom: Using formative assessment-building learning-focused relationships. Auckland, New Zealand: Hodder Education

Barnes, M., & Horne, M. (1996). Gender and mathematics. In B. Atweh, K. Owens, & P. Sullivan (Eds.), *Research in mathematics education in Australasia 1992–1995* (pp. 51–87). Sydney, Australia: Mathematics Education Research Group of Australasia.

Civil, M. (1990). You only do math in math: A look at four prospective teachers' views about mathematics. *For the Learning of Mathematics, 10*(1), 7–9.

Civil, M. (2002a). Culture and mathematics: A community approach. *Journal of Intercultural Studies, 23*(2), 133–149.

Civil, M. (2002b). Everyday mathematics, mathematicians' mathematics, and school mathematics: Can we bring them together? In M. Brenner & J. Moschkovich (Eds.),

Everyday and academic mathematics in the classroom: Journal of Research in Mathematics Education monograph 11 (pp. 40–62). Reston, VA: National Council of Teachers of Mathematics.

Davidson, C., & Tolich, M. (Eds.). (1999). *Social science research in New Zealand.* Auckland, New Zealand: Longman.

Denzin, N., & Lincoln, Y. (1994). Introduction: Entering the field of qualitative research. In N. Denzin, & Y. Lincoln (Eds.), *Handbook of qualitative research* (pp. 1–18). Thousand Oaks, CA: Sage.

Greenhough, P., Scanlan, M., Feiler, A., Johnson, D., Yee, W., Andrews, J., et al. (2005). Boxing clever: Using shoeboxes to support home-school knowledge exchange. *Literacy, 39*(2), 97–103.

Kilpatrick, M. (2002). *Something used everyday in all sorts of ways: Some children's beliefs about mathematics.* Unpublished manuscript, Auckland College of Education. (Available from author).

Kloosterman, P., Raymond, A., & Emenaker, C. (1996). Students' beliefs about mathematics: A three-year study. *The Elementary School Journal, 97*(1), 39–56.

Kloosterman, P., & Stage, F. (1992). Measuring beliefs about mathematical problems. *School Science and Mathematics, 92*(3), 109–115.

Leder, G. (1992). Mathematics and gender: Changing perspectives. In D. Grouws (Ed.), *Handbook of research on mathematics teaching and learning* (pp. 597–622). New York: MacMillan.

Leder, G. (1995). Learning mathematics: The importance of (social) content. *The New Zealand Mathematics Magazine, 32*(3), 27–40.

Leder, G., & Forgasz, H. (2002). Measuring mathematical beliefs and their impact on the learning of mathematics: A new approach. In G. Leder, E. Pehkonen, & G. Törner (Eds.), *Beliefs: A hidden variable in mathematics education?* (pp. 95–113). Dordrecht, Netherlands: Kluwer.

McDonough, A. (1995a). Expanding the repertoire of assessment strategies: Some approaches for accessing student beliefs about their learning of mathematics. In R. Hunting, G. Fitzsimons, D. Clarkson, & A. Bishop (Eds.), *Regional collaboration in mathematics education* (pp. 481–490). Melbourne, Australia: Monash University.

McDonough, A. (1995b). Using multiple methods to access student beliefs to inform teaching. In A. Richards (Ed.), *Proceedings of the 15th biennial conference of the Australian Association of Mathematics Teachers: FLAIR forging links and integrating resources* (pp. 271–277). Adelaide: Australian Association of Mathematics Teachers.

McDonough, A. (1998). Young children's beliefs about the nature of mathematics. In A. Olivier, & K. Newstead (Eds.), *Proceedings of the 22nd conference of the International Group for the Psychology of Mathematics Education* (pp. 263–270) Stellenbosch, South Africa: Psychology for Mathematics Education.

McDonough, A. (1999). Teaching the big ideas in mathematics. In Department of Education, Employment and Training (Ed.), *Proceedings of the conference of Early Years of Schooling P–4: Targeting excellence: Continuing the journey* (pp. 47–54). Melbourne: Department of Education, Employment and Training.

McDonough, A. (2002). Measurement and its relationship to mathematics: Complexity within young children's beliefs. In B. Barton, K. Irwin, M. Pfannkuch, & M. Thomas (Eds.), *Proceedings of the 25th annual conference of the Mathematics Education Research*

Group of Australasia: Mathematics education in the South Pacific (pp. 449–456). Auckland, New Zealand: Mathematics Education Research Group of Australasia.

McNaught, K. (2005). Text as resources, not programs. *Australian Primary Mathematics Classroom, 10*(1), 9–11.

Mansfield, H., Scott, J., & Burgess, Y. (1994). Teacher education students helping primary pupils re-construct mathematics. In J. Ponte, & J. Matos (Eds.), *Proceedings of the 18th annual conference of the International Group for the Psychology of Mathematics in Education* (pp. 224–231). Lisbon, Spain: International Group for the Psychology of Mathematics Education.

Ministry of Education, (2007). *The New Zealand curriculum.* Wellington, New Zealand: Learning Media.

Nunes, T., Schliemann, A., & Carraher, D. (1993). *Street mathematics and school mathematics.* Cambridge, UK: Cambridge University Press.

Onslow, B. (1992). Improving the attitude of students and parents through family involvement in mathematics. *Mathematics Education Research Journal, 4*(3), 24–31.

Op't Eydne, P., De Corte, E., & Verschaffel, L. (2002). Framing students' mathematics-related beliefs. In G. Leder, E. Pehkonen, & G. Törner (Eds.), *Beliefs: A hidden variable in mathematics education?* (pp. 13–37). Dordrecht, Netherlands: Kluwer.

Taylor, M., & Biddulph, F. (1994). "Context" in probability learning at the primary school level. *SAMEPapers 1994,* 96–111.

Tranter, D. (2002). What is it about homework? In J. Loughran, I. Mitchell, & J. Mitchell (Eds.), *Learning from teacher research* (pp. 37–56). St. Leonards, Australia: Allen & Unwin.

Wetton, N., & McWhirter, J. (1998). Images and curriculum development in health education. In J. Prosser (Ed.), *Image-based research: A sourcebook for qualitative researchers* (pp. 263–283). London, UK: Falmer Press.

Young-Loveridge, J. (1992). Attitudes towards mathematics: Insights into the thoughts and feelings of nine-year-olds. *SAMEPapers 1992,* 90–116.

AUTHOR NOTE

Mark Kilpatrick is a Lecturer in the Faculty of Education, University of Auckland, New Zealand. He teaches learning theories and assessment practice for the BEd (Teaching) degree. Mark has an interest in connection-making between the mathematics of the classroom and that of the world beyond the classroom, with a focus on the use of homework/home study worksheets.

This chapter is adapted from, and reports a part of, research undertaken for an MEd thesis.

Correspondence concerning this chapter should be addressed by email to: m.kilpatrick@auckland.ac.nz

In: Challenging Thinking about Teaching and Learning   ISBN: 978-1-60456-744-1
Editors: C. M. Rubie-Davies and C. Rawlinson   © 2008 Nova Science Publishers, Inc.

Chapter 6

EXPLANATIONS AND YOUNG CHILDREN'S VOCABULARY ACQUISITION

Sandra Kunalan and Dennis Rose

ABSTRACT

We assessed the effects on the vocabulary knowledge of 46 Singaporean preschoolers of providing brief explanations while reading stories to them. Two texts were selected and 11 words from each text were designated as target words. We developed receptive vocabulary tests, modelled on the Peabody Picture Vocabulary Tests, for these words. All of the children were exposed to reading with explanations for one book and reading without explanations for another book. This was counterbalanced so that half of the children heard explanations with one text and half of them heard explanations with the other text. The pretest–posttest design with follow-up testing after four weeks assessed both acquisition of vocabulary and maintenance of that vocabulary under both conditions. The results demonstrated that Singaporean preschool children learned new vocabulary from listening to stories with and without explanations, but that hearing brief explanations of words more than doubled their acquisition and that they remembered this newly acquired vocabulary four weeks later, independently of the method used in acquisition. Children who had a richer vocabulary before the investigation started tended to learn more.

INTRODUCTION

Vocabulary learning is widely acknowledged as being important to developing literacy and learning new subject matter in school (Nagy & Scott, 2000). Hart and Risley (2003) studied children in their homes during their first three years and found that the amount of language they experienced through interactions, especially with their parents, was a strong predictor of their immediate language learning and of their language skills and achievement in other academic domains such as reading comprehension at ages 9 and 10. Further, the amount of language that these children experienced was predicted by the socioeconomic status of their families. The average child from a family on welfare had about half as much exposure to language (616 words per hour) as the average child from a working class home (1,251 words per hour), which in turn was substantially less than that experienced by the average child from a professional family (2,153 words per hour).

Research such as Hart and Risley's has strengthened beliefs that hearing language is both important and necessary for children to learn vocabulary. This includes children hearing stories read to them. Numerous publications exhort or instruct parents to read to their children (e.g., Beck, McKeown, & Kucan, 2003; Butler & Clay, 1979) but there is rather less published research about the effects of doing this.

Children's vocabulary learning in Singapore is complicated by their bilingual or multilingual status. Most Singaporean children do not learn English as a first language. Rose (2001) studied 94 student teachers who were enrolled in a two-year Diploma of Education. These student teachers may be regarded as among the better educated school leavers as they needed to have A Level passes in the Cambridge examinations to gain entry to the diploma programme. Rose found that most student teachers did not consider English to be their first language. English was the main language used at home for only 28% of them, while 12% stated that English was not used in their homes at all when they were school age. However, English is the main language of instruction in Singapore's schools and children are expected to have adequate instructional levels of reading and spoken English before they enter school at 6 years of age. Most children attend a kindergarten programme in which they are instructed and taught to read in English.

The research that does exist provides strong evidence that both independent reading and shared reading (i.e., reading aloud to children) are effective ways to increase children's vocabulary knowledge (Robins & Ehri, 1994; Sénéchal & Cornell, 1993). Active participation (Sénéchal, Thomas, & Monker, 1995), joint book reading (Ard & Beverly, 2004), prior teaching (Jenkins, Stein, & Wysocki, 1984), and explanations of some words (Brett, Rothlein, & Hurley, 1996; Elley, 1989; Justice, Meier, & Walpole, 2005) all boost children's vocabulary acquisition. Elley reported that children aged 7 and 8 years old learned new vocabulary incidentally when they listened to stories at school, but that they learned almost twice as much when their teachers briefly explained the meanings of some words during the readings.

The current study replicates Elley's (1989) study with kindergarten-level children (aged 5 to 6 years) whose language histories were bilingual or multilingual. Its purpose was to determine whether those children's English vocabulary could be expanded more rapidly with explanations while listening to stories than by listening without explanations.

METHOD

Participants and Settings

Forty-six children from four Singaporean childcare centres participated in the study. Thirty-nine of them (85%) were aged 6 years and the remaining seven children were aged 5 years. There were 25 boys (54%) and 21 girls. Eighty-seven per cent of the children were Chinese, 11% were Indian, and 2% were Malay. This distribution differed a little from that reported from census data, with Malays being under-represented (14% in census data) and

Chinese and Indians being over-represented (77% and 7% respectively in census data) (Cheng & Tay, 1996). Malays in Singapore tend to not have as high a socioeconomic status as other ethnic groups so the relatively lower proportion of Malays in the sample may be because of economic factors as the centres were fee charging. All of the children were bilingual although it was not possible to determine the language used predominantly by each individual child. Some children were multilingual as they also spoke dialect in addition to their official mother tongue language and English. Two centres were located in a residential area surrounded by private landed property. The other two centres were located in a satellite town surrounded by public housing. The centres were private day-care facilities and all participants attended them on a full-day, fee-paying basis. Lessons typically included English, mother tongue language, mathematics, science, and art and craft.

Materials

Two texts were selected because of their interesting story lines, familiar themes, and colourful and clear illustrations, and because they had a number of words that were likely to be unfamiliar to preschool children. The texts were *Oscar's Spots* (Robertson, 1993) and *Beryl's Box* (Dann, 1993). Some words were changed to fit experimental requirements and some parts of the text of *Beryl's Box* were excluded to reduce its length. Words were added to utilize the illustrations. In *Oscar's Spots*, "Mr. Wizard" was used instead of "Mr. Wobble" throughout the text, "washing up" was added to the text (p. 3), "furious" replaced "angry" (p. 5), "and scrubbed" was added (p. 15), and "delighted" replaced "pleased" (p. 18). The words chosen for explanations and the pages on which they were explained were "fur" (p. 1), "spots" (p. 2), "washing up" (p. 3), "make up" and "sneeze" (p. 6), "furious" (p. 7), "wizard" (p. 11), "ingredients" (p. 13), "scrubbed" (p. 15), "delighted" (p. 17), and "chuckled" (p. 24).

In *Beryl's Box*, "lots of toys" replaced "five teddies, two pairs of roller skates, ten pots of luminous paint, three world cup footballs and a bike with special wheels for mountain climbing" (p. 3), "toys" replaced "teddies and her roller skates and her luminous paints and her world cup footballs and her bike with special wheels for mountain climbing" (p. 7), "TV" replaced "telly" (p. 8), "Penelope jumped on top of the box" replaced "Beryl did one of her best bendy-legged jumps, but the fruits were too high up. So Penelope tipped the box on its side and leap-frogged on to the top of it" (p. 15), "leaving the monster far behind" replaced "until the monster was just a slippery speck in the distance" (p. 19), "and still they went on climbing—up and over the moon, then on past the stars which glittered cold and blue and looked like icicles in the sky" was omitted (p. 20), and "cuddled" replaced "hugged" (p.21). The words chosen for explanations and the pages on which they were explained were "freckles" and "bendy" (p. 4), "slurped" (p. 6), "booted" (p. 8), "fireplace" (p. 9), "ocean liner" (p. 11), "paddle" (p. 13), "whirlpool", "reached" (p. 14), "on top" (p. 15), and "cuddled" (p. 21).

Measures

Pre-existing vocabulary knowledge was assessed using Form IIIA of the third edition of the *Peabody Picture Vocabulary Test* (PPVT-III) (Dunn & Dunn, 1997) and extracts of both texts were used as an informal measure of reading accuracy in an untimed session. This was administered by asking the children to read the passages aloud, recording the number of errors and total words read, and then calculating the percentage accuracy from the results. Responses were only scored as correct if they were pronounced correctly. Tests were administered in a standardized fashion and scored on standard sheets. Scoring was re-checked by the experimenter and an independent person. Calculations were double-checked by the experimenter and then checked again by the independent person.

Two 15-word multiple choice vocabulary tests, based on words encountered in the texts, were developed to measure gains in vocabulary. The vocabulary tests were constructed so that they had the same format as the PPVT-III; that is, children heard a stimulus word and pointed to a page containing four pictures, one of which matched the stimulus word. Instructions for the vocabulary tests were identical to the instructions given for the PPVT-III. Of the 30 words, two were practice items and six were control words that did not appear in either story. The control words were included as a check against learning which may have occurred from exposure to the pretest or incidental learning. The remaining 22 words were selected from the stories for explanation during shared reading.

The vocabulary tests were piloted with 10 children from a separate childcare centre. Changes were made to the instruments in the light of the pilot results, as a high percentage of children already knew some words at pretest. The words were also balanced by parts of speech as Elley (1989) had found higher gains on nouns and lower gains on verbs and adjectives. The vocabulary chosen for *Oscar's Spots* consisted of five nouns, four verbs, and two adjectives. Vocabulary for *Beryl's Box* consisted of five nouns, four verbs, one adjective, and one preposition.

The words in the vocabulary tests were selected because of their perceived difficulty and to ensure balance in terms of parts of speech. There were 33 potential target words and 10 potential control words. Final selections were made in the light of the results. The number of target words in the tests was reduced to 22 (11 in each) to achieve equivalent word difficulty between the two tests.

Of the 30 words used in the two final vocabulary tests, two were practice items and six were control words that did not appear in either story. The control words were included as a check against learning that may have occurred from exposure to the pretest, incidental learning opportunities, or children independently seeking explanations outside of the experimental conditions. The remaining 22 words were selected from the stories.

Experimental Treatments

There were two experimental conditions: explanations and no explanations. Children were assigned to one condition during the second week and to the other condition during the third week. Children in the no explanations groups heard unembellished readings of the story. Children in the explanations groups heard brief explanations of the target words as they occurred in the text. Explanations were given by pointing to a relevant illustration (where applicable) and providing a definition. These explanations were predetermined and were therefore identical for all readings.

Research Design

A counterbalanced pretest–posttest design with follow-up measures was used to assess acquisition and maintenance of children's vocabulary. Pretesting was conducted in the first week. In the second week, some groups of children heard *Oscar's Spots* with explanations and the other groups of children heard it without explanations. Other groups of children heard *Beryl's Box*, some with explanations and some without. In the third week, both the texts and the experimental conditions were reversed. For example, a group of children who heard *Oscar's Spots* without explanations during the second week heard *Beryl's Box* with explanations during the third week. This counterbalancing resulted in each child being exposed to both conditions and each text was used for both conditions. Posttesting was conducted on the last day of the week each book was read and a follow-up test was conducted four weeks after the posttest. This design provided a measure of acquisition of vocabulary through a comparison of the pretest and posttest scores and a measure of maintenance of vocabulary learning through the comparison of the posttest scores and the follow-up scores.

Procedure

All children were individually tested in a standardized fashion. Scoring was re-checked by the first author and an independent person. The PPVT-III and reading accuracy tests were administered over the first two days of pretesting. The vocabulary tests were administered on the third day.

Children were randomly assigned within a centre to groups of three to six children, resulting in nine groups in total. All children in a particular centre were read the same story during the second week, then the other story during the third week. This was to prevent children of different groups discussing the stories and sensitizing one another to unheard stories.

The reading sessions started on the week following the pretests. On the first day, all groups heard the story read once. On the second day, those in the explanations groups heard brief explanations of 50% of the target words (every other target word as they occurred in the text). On the third day the explanations groups heard brief explanations of the remaining 50% of the words. On the fourth day, explanations of all the target words were provided once more. Words were explained only on their first occurrence in the text. The posttest was administered on the fifth day and further follow-up tests were conducted four weeks after the initial posttests.

RESULTS

The results are in three sections. The first section addresses the two main research questions: Did Singaporean preschool children acquire the target vocabulary through the shared reading programme, and was the learning that took place increased by the provision of brief explanations of the target words? The second section addresses the question of maintenance. The third section examines the effects of other factors such as children's pre-existing vocabulary knowledge and parts of speech. Two-tailed *t*-tests were conducted to assess whether differences in raw scores were significant and effect sizes were calculated on the raw scores using Cohen's *d* (Cohen, 1992).

Acquisition Results

Six children's data were removed before the analysis because of the child's absence during some of the tests, absence of more than one day during the story readings, or because families moved house. The experimental design provided an assessment of whether gains in vocabulary acquisition could be directly attributed to one or both of the experimental treatments or whether they occurred incidentally through maturation and accidental exposure. The use of control words in the vocabulary test was a means of assessing growth in vocabulary not presented through the treatments but presented at the same frequency as other words in the test.

Vocabulary acquisition under the two experimental conditions and for the control condition was assessed by comparing the pretest mean raw scores to the posttest mean raw scores. Table 6.1 displays separate results for the two texts and for the texts combined in each of the experimental conditions and for the control words. Standard deviations are shown in parentheses.

Table 6.1. Mean Vocabulary Acquisition Raw Scores, Gains and Effect Sizes by Condition and Text

Condition	Pretest	Posttest	Gain	*d*
Control Words	1.03 (0.77)	1.09 (0.78)	0.06 (0.92)	0.08
No explanations condition				
Beryl's Box	3.82 (1.42)	4.88 (1.54)	1.06 (1.68)*	0.71
Oscar's Spots	5.48 (1.56)	6.61 (2.02)	1.13 (1.94)*	0.63
Both books combined	4.78 (1.70)	5.88 (2.00)	1.10 (1.81)**	0.59
Explanations condition				
Beryl's Box (n=45)	3.53 (0.87)	6.65 (1.84)	3.12 (1.90)***	2.10
Oscar's Spots (n=41)	6.00 (1.31)	8.17 (1.56)	2.17 (1.59)***	1.51
Both books combined	4.95 (1.68)	7.53 (1.83)	2.58 (1.77)***	1.47

Note. Of the 48 children, 3 were excluded from the analysis of Beryl's Box and 2 were excluded from the analysis of Oscar's Spots, as they had failed to attend enough sessions to hear all target vocabulary at least once. A further 5 were excluded from the analysis of Oscar's Spots to guard against ceiling effects as they had scored more than 90% on the pretest.
* p <.05. ** p <.01. *** p < .0001.

It appears that reading to children had a large effect on children's acquisition of vocabulary knowledge when either condition is compared to the control words. Simply reading to children without providing explanations resulted in significant gains in vocabulary for both books. The effect sizes for these gains were in the medium range that Cohen (1992) described as "an effect likely to be visible to the naked eye of a careful observer" (p. 156). In addition, providing brief explanations of words to the children during the reading session had a much larger effect than reading without explanations. When children had words explained to them, their acquisition gains were more than the gains when words were read but not explained. The effect sizes for explanations were in excess of the effects that Hattie (1993) describes as "large, blatantly obvious and grossly perceptible, like the difference in height between a five-year-old and a teenager" (p. 2).

Additional effect sizes were calculated on the data in Table 6.1. There was an effect size of 0.92 on the difference in gain scores between the explanations and no explanations conditions for both books combined and an effect size of 0.62 on the difference in gains between the no explanations condition and the control words. More than twice as many words were learned in the explanations condition than in the no explanations condition ($d = 0.83$, $p < .0001$). The effects were greater for *Beryl's Box* ($d = 1.15$, $p < .01$) than for *Oscar's Spots* ($d = 0.59$, $p < .05$).

Maintenance Results

The experimental design provided an assessment of whether gains in vocabulary were maintained and whether this could be directly attributed to one or both of the experimental treatments or whether they occurred incidentally. The increase in knowledge of vocabulary from posttest to follow-up test was negligible for both target and control words. Differences and effect sizes were calculated and found to consistently show that children neither acquired new learning, nor forgot what they had learned in the four weeks between the immediate posttest and the follow-up test. Since neither the target words nor the control words had any scheduled exposure over this time, this identical gain suggests that there were no variables confounding the assessment of maintenance. It may be concluded that vocabulary learned through listening to stories being read is maintained. Having explanations does not appear to improve maintenance.

Additional Analyses

Several additional analyses were conducted according to pre-existing vocabulary knowledge, children's attendance, parts of speech of the words presented for learning, pictorial occurrences, and the number of text occurrences using the acquisition data. The same analyses were also conducted on the maintenance data but are not reported because no sizeable differences and effects were detected. This was to be expected because there were virtually no gains or losses shown in the analysis by condition for the maintenance phase data. However, the analyses of the maintenance data confirmed that potential differential effects according to pre-existing vocabulary knowledge, attendance, parts of speech, and pictorial and text occurrences were not masked in the analyses by condition.

Children's pre-existing vocabulary knowledge was assessed using the PPVT-III and an assessment of their reading accuracy using sections of prose selected from the texts. For the purposes of data analysis, children's results for both the PPVT-III and the informal prose reading tests were assigned to upper or lower quartile groups or to a middle group (the second and third quartiles combined). These groups were then termed high, middle, and low. Table 6.2 reports the mean vocabulary raw scores for these groups and their mean gains and their standard deviations (in parentheses) from pretest to posttest. It also reports effect sizes (Cohen's *d*) and tests of significance.

**Table 6.2. Mean Vocabulary Raw Scores and Gains
According to Pre-existing Vocabulary Knowledge**

	Pretest	Posttest	Gain	*d*
PPVT-III Score				
High	5.06 (2.07)	8.06 (1.63)	3.00 (2.43)***	1.61
Middle	5.07 (1.72)	6.46 (2.13)	1.39 (1.86)***	0.72
Low	4.45 (1.60)	6.27 (2.07)	1.82 (1.79)***	0.98
Reading accuracy score				
High	6.06 (1.70)	7.78 (1.96)	1.72 (2.02)**	0.94
Middle	4.72 (1.61)	6.62 (1.98)	1.89 (2.26)***	1.05
Low	4.33 (1.80)	6.14 (2.29)	1.81 (1.60)***	0.88

** $p < .01$; *** $p < .0001$.

When analyzed according to the pre-existing vocabulary knowledge as assessed using the PPVT-III and reading accuracy, all groups' gains were large and statistically significant and there was no difference between the high, middle, and low groups when the gains were analyzed according to reading accuracy. However, when the groups were formed on the basis of the PPVT-III scores, the mean gain was larger for the high group than for the low group ($d = 0.56$, *ns*) and the middle group ($d = 0.79$, $p < .05$).

An analysis according to children's attendance was undertaken to assess the amount of exposure needed to acquire new vocabulary. Irrespective of pre-existing vocabulary scores or experimental condition, children who attended all of the sessions made four times the gains of those who missed one session. Those children who attended all sessions made significant improvements ($p < 0.001$, $d = 0.38$), while children who did not attend all sessions made little gain.

Gains according to parts of speech were analyzed. The greatest gains were made with nouns ($p < .05$) and there were smaller but statistically insignificant gains with verbs and smaller gains still with adjectives.

Two of Elley's (1989) word-related factors, the number of pictorial occurrences of each word in the text and the number of text occurrences of each word, were also analyzed. The only significant relationship was between the number of pictorial occurrences and the gains on target vocabulary from *Beryl's Box* ($p < .05$).

DISCUSSION

Singaporean preschool children learned new vocabulary when they listened to stories. Three readings in successive days resulted in these children making substantial and statistically significant gains. This is an important result considering that these children's language learning is complicated by their bilingual and multilingual environments. These gains required very little effort: a teacher simply read to the children in groups. This is in contrast to Brett et al. (1996) who found that reading without explanations did not result in older children (ages 9 to 11) increasing their vocabulary. However, Brett et al. only exposed the children in their study to a single reading whereas the children in the current study had three readings, as did those in Elley's (1989) study, which also reported that readings without explanations resulted in vocabulary acquisition.

Hearing brief explanations of words during a book reading more than doubled the children's acquisition of target vocabulary. Providing explanations is easily included when reading to children but it seems to have a large effect. This result is similar to those found by Ard and Beverly (2004), Justice et al. (2005), and Elley (1989), who all found that brief explanations of vocabulary during shared reading improves children's vocabulary acquisition. In contrast, Sénéchal and Cornell (1993) did not find that children acquired new vocabulary when they were read to, but their study only provided a single reading.

The gains in vocabulary were maintained for four weeks. This occurred independently of whether the vocabulary was learned with or without explanations. This result confirms that of Elley (1989) whose follow-up at three months showed negligible (2% to 3%) loss of learning but Brett et al. (1996) found better maintenance of words that had been acquired under an explanations condition than a no explanations condition. Ard and Beverly (2004) and Justice et al. (2005) did not assess maintenance in their studies. However, the studies that did assess maintenance provide sufficient evidence to conclude that repeated readings result in words acquired in this fashion being maintained, especially if explanations are provided.

Although there was no evidence in this study that repetitions within the text had any effect on acquisition, Elley found moderate correlations between frequency in text and acquisition. It may be that the nature of his texts, which were selected for older children, had some effect. However, repetition from repeated readings which are spread across days does seem to be beneficial, as the current study and other studies with repeated readings do appear to have had better acquisition and maintenance than those with a single exposure. This conclusion is supported by the attendance data as those children who attended every session (and therefore had more exposures to the words) made substantially greater gains than children who missed one session.

The optimal amount of exposure to new words remains unclear. There are indications that different amounts of exposure are necessary for different children. Precisely how the children might be different is unknown. One possibility is that children's age might be a factor, although there is no clear direction on this when all of the studies mentioned in this report are considered. Since the gains were different for the two books in the current study, it seems likely that there are book-related factors, although what these are is not clear. Nouns were more likely to be learned in Elley's (1989) study and this was also the case in the current study.

Excessive exposure might result in boredom. Leung and Pikulski (1990) reported that children with high pre-existing literacy seemed bored by the third reading of the same text. The notion that the ideal amount of exposure depends at least partially on the ability of the child is supported by Morrow (1984) who reported that repeated readings of texts were especially beneficial for low ability children. It seems possible that children of lower ability may be able to learn as much vocabulary from texts as children with higher ability, given more time and greater exposure. This was not the case in the current study where the children in the top quartile for vocabulary knowledge (as assessed on the PPVT-III) made greater gains than other children.

This result supports the Matthew Effect (Berninger, 1999) in that those children whose vocabulary was already superior made the greatest gains. This only seemed to be the case for children in the top quartile group, with children in the lower quartile making similar gains to the middle half of the children. There were no differences in mean gain scores when the groups were analyzed according to reading accuracy, although this is not surprising as the

PPVT-III is a direct measure of vocabulary knowledge while reading accuracy might involve many factors. There are many possible explanations for the Matthew Effect in this study. Children with higher pre-existing vocabulary knowledge and higher reading ability may have found it easier to understand the context and thus found it easier to derive word meanings from it. These children may also have been more familiar with reading and listening to stories and better able to attend. Another possibility is that general ability or particular aspects of intelligence such as memory are important variables (Robins & Ehri, 1994).

Certain features of the study should be considered when evaluating the findings and their generality. Elley (1989) found no effects in the control groups in his study and this led to a decision in the current study to instead use a design in which all of the participants were exposed to the independent variables, through a counterbalanced design in which each participant was exposed to each book and each condition, including a small number of control words which were not part of the books. In addition, each book was used for each of the independent variables. This counterbalanced design created quasi-control groups and may be claimed to satisfy the purpose for which control groups are usually employed. In fact, it removes many of the potential confounds that may exist in between-groups studies, or when different materials are assigned to different conditions. There were clearly book effects in the results and, had one book been assigned to one condition and the other book to the other condition, the book effects would have masked the effects of the independent variables.

History and practice effects may weaken the results of studies that are conducted over several weeks. However, as no order effects were found it is unlikely that there are any effects due to history or practice. This was also the case in Justice et al.'s (2005) study which extended over 10 weeks with a different book being read each week but in which the books were read in a different sequence to different groups. In the current study, maturation is unlikely to have had any effect because of the shortness of the study and because there were no changes in children's knowledge of the control words over the course of the study.

The study demonstrates that reading to children is an effective and easily implemented way to increase their vocabulary. There are larger effects if teachers also provide explanations. Although the study was conducted with bilingual and multilingual preschool children, the similarity of the results of this study and the results of similar studies, including other studies with bilingual learners (e.g., Elley & Mangubhai, 1983), along with the size of the effects, should allow some confidence in claiming generality to other populations.

Nonetheless, while the effects of reading to children are clear, much is yet to be discovered. More research is needed on issues such as the optimum number of readings, differential effects for age, and how those factors vary according to parts of speech. Another area worthy of study is the Matthew Effect and the degree to which prior knowledge is a salient variable, along with an attempt to identify how prior knowledge functions to produce more learning. Research has yet to reveal why some texts are associated with higher rates of vocabulary learning than others. A better understanding of what types of texts improve learning would aid preschool teachers to select texts and maximize the effects of reading to children as a strategy for teaching vocabulary.

REFERENCES

Ard, L., M, & Beverly, B. L. (2004). Preschool word learning during joint book reading: Effect of adult questions and comments. *Communication Disorders Quarterly, 26*(1), 17–28.

Beck, I. L., McKeown, M. G., & Kucan, L. (2003). Taking delight in words: Using oral language to build young children's vocabularies. *American Educator, 27*(1), 36–39, 41, 45–46.

Berninger, V. W. (1999). Overcoming the Matthew effect: Aiming reading and writing instruction (and research on instruction) at levels of language in an active, social, reflective environment. *Issues in Education, 5*(1), 45–53.

Brett, A., Rothlein, L., & Hurley, M. (1996). Vocabulary acquisition from listening to stories and explanations of target words. *The Elementary School Journal, 96*(4), 415–422.

Butler, D., & Clay, M. (1979). *Reading begins at home: Preparing children for reading before they go to school.* Auckland, New Zealand: Heinemann.

Cheng, V., & Tay, D. (1996). *Resource atlas for social studies* (10th ed.). Singapore: Federal Publications.

Cohen, J. (1992). Quantitative methods in psychology: A power primer. *Psychological Bulletin, 112*(1), 152–159.

Dann, P. (1993). *Beryl's box.* London: HarperCollins Publishers.

Dunn, L. M., & Dunn, L. M. (1997). *Peabody Picture Vocabulary Test* (3rd ed.). Circle Pines, MN: American Guidance Service.

Elley, W. B. (1989). Vocabulary acquisition from listening to stories. *Reading Research Quarterly, 24*(2), 174–187.

Elley, W. B., & Mangubhai, F. (1983). The impact of reading on second language learning. *Reading Research Quarterly, 19*, 53–67.

Hart, B., & Risley, T. R. (2003). The early catastrophe: The 30 million word gap by age 3. *American Educator, 27*(1), 4–9.

Hattie, J. (1993). Measuring the effects of schooling. *SET: Research Information for Teachers, 2*(4).

Jenkins, J. R., Stein, M., & Wysocki, K. (1984). Learning vocabulary through reading. *American Educational Research Journal, 21*(4), 767–787.

Justice, L. M., Meier, J., & Walpole, S. (2005). Learning new words from storybooks: An efficacy study with at-risk kindergartners. *Language, Speech and Hearing Services in Schools, 36*(1), 17–33.

Leung, C. B., & Pikulski, J. J. (1990). Incidental learning of word meanings by kindergarten and first-grade children through repeated read aloud events. In J. Zutell & S. McCormick (Eds.), *National Reading Conference: Literacy theory and research: Analyses from multiple paradigms* (pp. 231–241). Chicago, IL: National Reading Conference.

Morrow, L. M. (1984). Young children's responses to one-to-one story readings in school settings. *Reading Research Quarterly, 23*, 89–106.

Nagy, W., & Scott, J. (2000). Vocabulary processes. In M. Kamil, P. Mosenthal, P. D. Pearson, & R. Barr (Eds.), *Handbook of Reading Research*, Volume III (pp. 269–284). Mahwah, NJ: Erlbaum.)

Robertson, J. (1993). *Oscar's spots.* London: Penguin Books.

Robins, C., & Ehri, L. C. (1994). Reading storybooks to kindergarteners helps them learn new vocabulary words. *Journal of Educational Psychology, 86*, 54–64.

Rose, E. M. (2001). *Singaporean student teachers' use of English and other languages.* Unpublished master's in education thesis, University of Sheffield, Sheffield, UK.

Sénéchal, M., & Cornell, E. H. (1993). Vocabulary acquisition through shared reading experiences. *Reading Research Quarterly, 28*(4), 360–374.

Sénéchal, M., Thomas, E. M., & Monker, J. A. (1995). Individual differences in 4-year-old children's acquisition of vocabulary during storybook reading. *Journal of Educational Psychology, 87*, 218–229.

AUTHOR NOTE

Sandra Kunalan resides in Singapore. She has an MA (Applied Psychology) and is presently raising her five children, including triplets. Dennis Rose was previously an Associate Professor in Special Education at Nanyang Technological University, Singapore and is now a member of the Faculty of Education, University of Auckland, New Zealand.

The study reported in this chapter is based on the first author's MA thesis, which the second author supervised.

The authors gratefully acknowledge the assistance of Dr Gavin Brown, Faculty of Education, the University of Auckland, for his assistance with the calculation of effect size.

Correspondence concerning this chapter should be addressed by email to: d.rose@auckland.ac.nz

In: Challenging Thinking about Teaching and Learning
Editors: C. M. Rubie-Davies and C. Rawlinson

ISBN: 978-1-60456-744-1
© 2008 Nova Science Publishers, Inc.

Chapter 7

SOME CORRELATES OF ACADEMIC PERFORMANCE IN NEW ZEALAND SCHOOLS: THE ASTTLE DATABASE

John Hattie

ABSTRACT

The Assessment Tools for Teaching and Learning Project (asTTle) collected data on the academic performance of more than 90,000 New Zealand students in six subjects—three English-medium and three Maori-medium (reading/panui, writing/tuhituhi, and mathematics/pangarau). At the same time, student responses to a number of valid measures or questionnaires were obtained, providing a secondary data set of asTTle data. For example, students' opinions and evaluations about curriculum, assessment, the asTTle tests, and school subjects were provided by subsamples of students. Additionally, other students provided data on the number of books at home and the degree of parental involvement in their schooling. This chapter outlines factor analyses and examines the correlations of those data to student performance on an asTTle test. Results showed that 24 of these questionnaires had correlations equal to or greater than .20 with academic performance. Most especially powerful (i.e., $r > .30$) were two scales in mathematics (study strategies and working in co-operative groups); four scales in reading (reading importance; teacher interacts and challenges students; confidence in reading from achievement testing; and efficacy in school work); and one scale in writing (confidence in writing from achievement testing). As an example of the kind of analyses possible within the asTTle data set, the effect of sex and year on student attitudes towards parental involvement is explored—females and younger students report much more parental involvement than males and those in secondary school. Further detailed re-analysis of this data is possible and has been started in some areas. The data are available to researchers for such re-analysis.

INTRODUCTION

The major purpose of this chapter is to illustrate the power of analyzing secondary data, reveal how certain characteristics of student attitudes and background variables relate to academic achievement, and provide suggestions as to how best to raise student academic performance. The study is based on a set of secondary data, available to researchers, comprising a range of affective and demographic variables collected in conjunction with standardized academic achievement assessments of reading, writing, and mathematics, and their Maori-medium counterparts of panui, tuhituhi, and pangarau, in New Zealand primary and secondary schools. The research tool that led to the development of these data is the Assessment Tools for Teaching and Learning (known as asTTle). An overview of asTTle is given below, followed by an explanation of the instruments used to obtain the affective and demographic data set. The chapter then focuses on the current study as one example of the type of analysis that can be conducted using the asTTle affective and demographic secondary data set.

THE ASSESSMENT TOOL
FOR TEACHING AND LEARNING

The asTTle software provides teachers with a mechanism for creating a 40-minute test for each subject (reading, writing, and mathematics in English, and panui, pangarau, and tuhituhi in Maori; see Figure 7.1). asTTle contains norms for students in Years 4–12 (Grades 3 to 11 in the United States) and the current Version 4 includes approximately 4,100 items. asTTle is a software application that is available free to all primary and secondary schools in New Zealand and runs on PC and MAC computers, laptops, desktops, and stand-alone and networked platforms. e-asTTle is an internet version that offers many more features for teachers (such as on-screen and computer adaptive testing, some automatic open-ended scoring assistance, 6000-plus extra items, and so on). asTTle allows teachers to obtain graphical reports of student achievement relative to norms, standards, and objectives, and graphical reports of strengths or weaknesses at both individual and group levels in each subject assessed. Further, asTTle provides links to an indexed web catalogue of teaching resources intended to assist with the "What do we do next?" feedback question (see Hattie, Brown, & Keegan, 2003 and www.asttle.org.nz for further details).

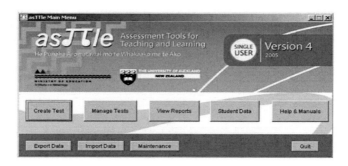

Figure 7.1. Main menu asTTle version 4.

TEST CREATION

When teachers create a test, asTTle gives them control and choice over not only the content, but also over the difficulty of the material within the test. Thus, teachers design a test according to their own understanding of the teaching and learning agenda or needs of their own students. These choices are based on detailed curriculum maps of the six subjects derived from the national curriculum statements (details of the curriculum maps are available as technical reports at www.asttle.org.nz). Teachers are required to focus the test on the content that they believe is essential to progress in the learning area being assessed, since in a single test not all content can be assessed. Teachers choose the proportion of the test desired for each content domain by using the adjustable sliders (Figure 7.2).

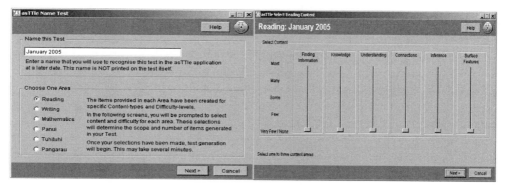

Figure 7.2. Subject selection and content selection menus.

The teacher then chooses the difficulty of the test (Figure 7.3). In New Zealand, teachers expect students to range across multiple levels of achievement within any one class and are encouraged to cater for three levels of achievement when assessing student learning. Teachers are expected to adjust the difficulty mix to fit well with the students being assessed. asTTle permits rich customization in that tests of the same content but of differing difficulty levels can be created and compared, permitting students to receive tests of appropriate difficulty while maintaining common information to teachers about learning.

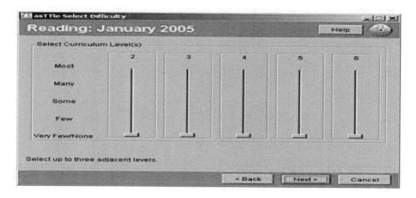

Figure 7.3. Difficulty selection menu.

When teachers adjust the sliders to match their beliefs about the achievement in their class, they are producing an ideal test characteristic curve in two dimensions—content and difficulty. A test characteristic curve defines the range and shape of the difficulties of the items desired in a test. At this point, the asTTle software uses a powerful linear programming heuristic to locate the best set of items that maximize the fit of the created test to this target test characteristic curve, while simultaneously meeting other constraints. These other constraints include: the length of test, the mixture of items by cognitive processing demand, the format of the items in the test, the content or readability of reading passages, minimization of previously used items, maximization of underused items, and order of items in the test. The solution time for e-asTTle is 20–60 seconds. The linear programming heuristic used in asTTle to create the tests is powerful and very efficient and simulations have shown that the fit of item difficulties in the tests are close to engineering industry standards (Johnston et al., 2003).

The life cycle for the development of items is indicated in Figure 7.4. All items have a "signature" that consists of about 20 attributes which were used to guide the development of test items and tasks. Many panels of teacher reviewers and writers were used to critique the item signature for each item and, where possible, improve the item to fit the signature. The item signature attributes included: curriculum difficulty or level, curriculum strand, curriculum objective, curriculum process, and cognitive demand according to the SOLO taxonomy (which can be used to classify whether an item measures surface or deep understanding). The characteristics of the supporting reading passages or stimulus materials were evaluated to ascertain their purpose and appropriateness. Once reviewed, all items were trialled with students, scored, and statistically analyzed. All items were first calibrated using a three-parameter (dichotomous or polytomous) item response model, and items with high guessing parameters and low discriminating values were revised or removed. Teacher judges were used to set standards in terms of curriculum levels for the item difficulties.

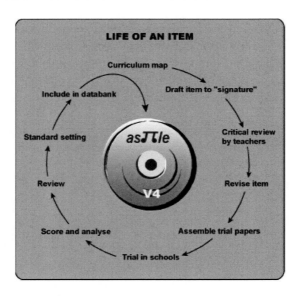

Figure 7.4. Item development cycle.

REPORTS

Having administered the paper-and-pencil test, teachers are offered opportunities to obtain feedback relating to the three feedback questions: "Where are we going?", "Where are we now?", and "What do we do next?" (Hattie & Timperley, 2007). The reports are (a) calibrated to normative performance of populations and subpopulations of interest to teachers and administrators (Console Report), (b) calibrated to curriculum achievement objectives or learning intentions for both individuals and groups (Learning Pathways Report), and (c) calibrated to curriculum standards based on teacher panel-judged cut-scores (Curriculum Levels Report). In this way, teachers can test their interpretations of student learning needs by comparison to criteria, standards, and norms and in so doing identify strengths, gaps, and learning priorities and establish the degree of severity for each. Furthermore, the reports attempt visual, non-numeric communication of performance to better inform teachers' interpretation and resulting decisions on the actions they will take.

An indexed catalogue of teaching resources, calibrated to the curriculum content and difficulties used in creating asTTle tests, has been made available to teachers on the internet through the "What Next" Profile Report. This website allows teachers to answer the third feedback question "What do we do next?" In this way, asTTle fulfils its designed objective of providing teachers with a resource that has the power to improve the quality of their teaching and students' learning.

THE USE AND EVALUATION OF asTTle

The evaluations of the asTTle application have focused on the validity, accuracy, added value, training, and utility standards identified as important in the use of educational technology (Hattie, Brown, Ward, Irving, & Keegan, 2006). As a result of these evaluations, it is argued that users can have confidence that asTTle has demonstrated validity with the curriculum and classroom practice, that the reporting systems add value to teachers' work, and that accuracy of understanding is enhanced with professional development.

asTTle is voluntary and free to New Zealand schools—and this voluntary feature has been critical in its acceptance and use (about 80% of the 2,700 schools are using it in some form and about 30–40% are using it intensively). In the norming sample, for example, more than 90,000 students from more than 700 schools participated, involving more than a thousand teachers. In a recent request for volunteer schools to be part of a pilot study for the next internet version, within a couple of weeks there were requests from more than 400 schools for inclusion, and there were many more who, after the deadline, indicated a desire to be involved.

The evaluations of the items by teachers and students were very positive in terms of appropriateness of content, levels of difficulty, and degree of interest and engagement. Various studies have investigated teachers' understanding of the asTTle reports, the effects of professional development (both in person and via online tutorials), monitoring of the inquiries to the Ministry of Education's Information and Communications Technology (ICT) Help Desk, evaluation of the asTTle website (www.asTTle.org.nz), the manual and support materials, attitudes towards ICT, and experiences related to asTTle and asTTle professional development.

MONOGRAPHS ON THE STATUS OF NEW ZEALAND ACHIEVEMENT

Given that the norming sample was carefully chosen to be nationally representative, it was possible to make some overall conclusions about the status of achievement in each of the six curriculum areas. These results have been published in a series of 10 monographs that were sent to all schools in New Zealand at the end of 2006. These monographs are available from http://www.educationcounts.edcentre.govt.nz/research/soik.html.

The major conclusions from these reports were that the data from the asTTle norming were consistent in many ways with data from many other sources. Generally, although students achieve more each year, rates of progress are not constant across subjects or school years. Although New Zealand students perform well relative to other countries in reading and mathematics, boys, low socioeconomic students, and non-majority ethnicity students consistently score below national means. Writing is generally not well done. The relationship of self-confidence and liking of subjects was shown *not* to be strongly related to achievement.

SECONDARY DATA SET INSTRUMENTS

During the collection of the asTTle norming data, teachers requested that we provide more tasks; these would be used to occupy the time and interest of students who finished early, and also give whole classes extra activities to fill out a class period if testing did not take all the time allotted. This provided an opportunity for the asTTle team to develop questionnaires that would provide a rich source of secondary data for researchers to analyze. Accordingly, requests for suitable questionnaires were made throughout the School of Education at the University of Auckland, were vetted by the asTTle team, and a variety of questionnaires were placed randomly at the back of various asTTle norming tests. Since only a short period of time was expected for this activity, research questionnaires were limited to 10 to 20 items. That meant that some research questionnaires had to be divided among various asTTle tests. Given these constraints, there are varying sample sizes for the various questionnaires and sometimes within a questionnaire. There are 11 questionnaires: attitudes towards assessment, conceptions about assessment, attitudes towards schools and achievement domains, parental involvement in schooling, attitude towards reading and school work, importance of reading and writing, attitude towards mathematics, attitude to and experience of writing, student evaluation of the asTTle tests, attitude to school subjects, and measures of home resources.

For each questionnaire, a maximum-likelihood factor analysis with an oblique rotation was used to identify the best set of factors (the details of each questionnaire, listing the items, and factor loadings are available on request). Each instrument is discussed in turn below.

Attitudes towards Assessment

The items in this questionnaire were derived from Meece and Miller (2001), who studied primary students' achievement goals in literacy activities. From the analyses of the asTTle database, there were five clear factors: assessment can help me learn (e.g., I wanted to do better on this assessment than I have done before); minimize the effort in assessment (e.g., I wanted to get out of having to do much work on this assessment); use assessment to gain praise from others (e.g., I wanted the teacher to think I am doing a good job on this assessment); use deep approaches to assessment (e.g., I asked myself questions as I went along to make sure this assessment made sense); and use surface approaches to assessment (e.g., I did my work on this assessment without thinking too hard).

Conceptions about Assessment

Conceptions about assessment have to do with personal opinions as to the purpose or use of assessment. Brown (2004, 2006) has investigated teachers' conceptions of assessment and found that four major purposes existed among New Zealand primary school teachers. These included: assessment improves the quality of teaching and learning; assessment makes schools and teachers accountable; assessment makes students accountable; and assessment is irrelevant. This instrument was modified to assess students' conceptions of assessment. Detailed analyses of the students' conceptions of assessment have been linked to performance on the asTTle tests in mathematics (Brown & Hirschfeld, 2007) and in reading (Brown & Hirschfeld, 2008). Structural equation modelling was used to relate these conceptions to the various achievements. For example, as shown in Figure 7.5, Brown and Hirschfeld found that reading achievement is most related to student's conceptions of assessment in terms of making them accountable, negatively related to making schools accountable and to conceptions that assessment is fun, and not related to whether they ignored assessment or not. Across all subjects, students who use assessment to self-regulate their learning achieve more, while those who avoid responsibility or who ignore assessment achieve less.

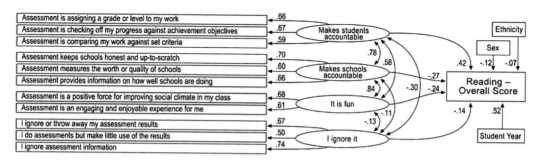

Figure 7.5. Conceptions of assessment and reading achievement.

Attitudes towards Schools and Achievement Domains

There are nine factor scales identified with this instrument: teacher–student relationships (e.g., teachers are interested in students); quality of teaching (e.g., there are high expectations of me in this school); satisfaction and involvement with learning (e.g., I really get involved in my school work); positive peer interactions (e.g., I feel it is easy to get to know other people); enthusiasm for learning (e.g., learning is fun); teachers care about me (e.g., my teacher treats me fairly in class); study strategies (e.g., I finish my homework assignments by deadlines); working in co-operative settings (e.g., I like working in groups), and deep versus surface learning.

Parental Involvement in Schooling

This instrument has been used extensively in the Flaxmere Project, which was an evaluation of home–school relations among five of New Zealand's lowest socioeconomic areas (Clinton, Hattie, & Dixon, 2007). There are four scales: parents discuss school (e.g., I discuss things studied in class with my parents/caregivers); parental encouragement (e.g., my parents/caregivers try to get me to do my best in everything I do); parents talk to my school (e.g., my parents/caregivers attend school meetings); and parents and my future (e.g., my parents/caregivers talk to me about my future career).

Attitude towards Reading and School Work

Many of these items came from Bourke's (1981) *Quality of School Life* inventory. There are three scales: efficacy in school work (e.g., I think my ability is sufficient to cope with school work); self-estimate of achievement (e.g., I get good marks in reading); and academic self-concept (e.g., I feel better about myself when I know I am doing well at school).

Importance of Reading and Writing

Irving (2004) developed an instrument for student evaluation of teaching that identified the characteristics of highly accomplished mathematics teachers. A parallel, but pilot, instrument was devised adapting the characteristics of highly accomplished teaching to the context of the English curriculum. This instrument was attached to asTTle reading tests. There are four scales: efficacy in reading (e.g., I can compare and contrast texts of different styles, purposes, or content); efficacy in writing (e.g., I can write effectively to persuade or influence readers); teacher interacting with and challenging students (e.g., my teacher challenges me to think through and resolve issues); and teacher and family (e.g., the teacher keeps my family informed on a regular basis about my progress in English).

Attitude to Mathematics

There are six scales adapted from Middleton (2002): a positive approach to mathematics (e.g., I do my work in maths because I want to learn as much as possible); mathematics avoidance (e.g., one of my main goals in maths is to avoid looking like I can't do my work); interest in mathematics (e.g., I do my maths work because I am interested in it); teacher challenge (e.g., in maths class, the teacher presses me to do thoughtful work); teacher creates high interest (e.g., my teacher makes learning maths satisfying and stimulating); and teacher and family (e.g., my teacher keeps my family informed on a regular basis about my progress in maths).

Attitude to and Experience of Writing

In assisting asTTle to develop scoring rubrics for student performance in writing (Glasswell, Parr, & Aikman, 2001), seven scoring attributes were identified for six purposes of writing. The items were devised to examine student confidence or ability in doing the various scored aspects of writing and to identify the relative importance of the different purposes in their experience. There are seven factors: structured writing (e.g., I can write a well-formed sentence); surface writing efficacy (e.g., I can write instructions for someone to do something); exposure to surface features of writing (e.g., I have been taught how to punctuate writing); content of writing (e.g., I can select the right content to include in my writing); deep writing efficacy (e.g., I can persuade or argue in writing); exposure to deep features of writing (e.g., I have been taught to take account of the audience or reader); and quality of writing.

Evaluation of the asTTle Tests

As part of asTTle's continuous formative assessment, students were invited to evaluate the test paper they had just completed. Each subject generated slightly different factor structures (details available in Hattie, Brown, Ward, Irving, & Keegan, 2006), but typically involved student enjoyment, confidence to do the questions, liking the test experience, and appropriateness of the logistics of the testing.

Attitude to School Subjects

In each asTTle assessment, students completed a six-item attitude survey (taken with permission from the National Education Monitoring Project studies) and responded using a four-point balanced scale. These items form two inter-correlated scales: liking the subject and a sense of efficacy towards the subject. Confirmatory factor analyses (Otunuku & Brown, 2007) validated this two-factor structure in reading, writing, and mathematics for multiple ethnic groups (i.e., New Zealand European, Maori, Pacific Island, Asian/other, and Tongan students). Otunuku and Brown (2007) found that, for all groups, students liked least and had least confidence in writing, and mean attitude scores were very similar across all groups and ethnicities.

Measures of Home Resources

A home resource question was adapted from the Progress for International Reading Literacy studies (PIRLS) (Mullis, Martin, Gonzalez, & Kennedy, 2003). The PIRLS studies found three major factors for home resources: educational resources in the home; extra resources in the home; and recreational resources in the home. As only one question could be used in subsequent surveys, it was decided to use the number of books in the home for all subsequent surveys—primarily because it is a major variable in the PIRLS survey, was a major marker variable in the "educational resources in the home" factor (Elley, 1992), and had been used in other surveys in New Zealand (see Fletcher & Hattie, 2004). The "Books at Home" question asked students to estimate the number of books at home, prompted by both numbers and illustrated bookshelves; responses ranged from 0–10 books to more than 200 books. A sample of 36,668 students responded to this question.

THE CURRENT STUDY

The current study is one example of the secondary data analysis possible using the affective and demographic data obtained from instruments described above and the achievement scores derived from the asTTle application. Each of the 1,500 items for each of mathematics and reading were administered using a multiple-matrix sampling design—such that each student received about 40 items appropriate to their age level. All items were then assessed using a three-parameter model and items with high guessing and low discrimination were discarded. Only the final set of items was used in the current study, and the total scores were calibrated using a one-parameter model. Given that each item was calibrated simultaneously, it is therefore possible to make comparisons across the various items, and across students across years.

RESULTS

This section reports preliminary analysis of the scales that were correlated with academic performance in the three English language tests of reading, mathematics, and writing. We begin with descriptive statistics for each scaled score and then examine how those scales correlate with the appropriate achievement test. Then we examine how sex and year moderate the effect of these correlations on achievement.

Descriptive Statistics for Scale Scores

Table 7.1 provides the mean, standard deviation, and estimate of reliability (coefficient alpha) for each scale within each instrument. In all cases, the estimates of reliability are sufficiently high to inspire confidence in using these scores. This should provide confidence when using and interpreting total scores on each of these scales.

Table 7.1. Descriptive Statistics for Correlated Scales

Instrument and scales	N	M	SD	alpha
Attitudes towards assessment				
Assessment for learning	399	3.83	2.02	.94
Minimize assessment	399	2.33	1.70	.87
Assess to impress	399	3.09	2.00	.89
Deep approach to assessment	442	2.70	2.04	.87
Surface approach to assessment	442	2.43	1.92	.87
Conceptions about assessment				
Accountability	4564	2.84	1.84	.98
Improvement	2455	2.67	1.82	.97
Irrelevant	5041	2.13	1.47	.94
Validity	430	2.61	1.66	.98
Attitudes towards schools and achievement domains				
Quality of teaching	771	3.85	1.90	.93
Teacher–student relationships	771	3.30	1.78	.90
Satisfaction with learning	325	1.72	1.08	.95
Positive peer interactions	325	1.62	1.04	.93
Enthusiasm for learning	388	2.02	1.04	.91
Teacher cares about me	388	1.53	.90	.89
Study strategies	701	2.91	1.90	.95
Working in co-operative groups	701	3.35	2.20	.91
Deep vs. surface learning	736	1.45	1.25	.95
Parental involvement in schooling				
Parents discuss school	1719	3.71	1.99	.92
Parental encouragement	1719	4.60	2.02	.94
Parents talk to school	1719	3.38	2.06	.78
Parents and future	1719	3.72	2.10	.88
Attitude towards reading and school work				
Efficacy in school work	1668	3.63	1.89	.96
Academic self-esteem	1668	3.65	1.85	.95
Liking reading	1668	3.46	1.90	.89
Importance of reading and writing				
Reading importance	940	2.78	1.71	.98
Writing importance	940	3.07	1.91	.95
Teacher interacts and challenges students	944	3.42	2.02	.97

Table 7.1. (Continued).

Instrument and scales	N	M	SD	alpha
Teacher and family relationships	944	2.16	1.79	.86
Attitude to mathematics				
Math positive approach	399	3.21	1.78	.91
Math avoidance	399	2.16	1.58	.89
Interest in math	704	2.96	1.93	.93
Teacher challenges me	704	3.04	1.77	.91
Interesting and challenging	642	2.68	2.21	.97
Teacher and family relationships	642	1.64	1.87	.85
Quality learning	736	1.45	1.25	.95
Attitude to and experience of writing				
Structure of writing	2858	3.18	1.98	.98
Content of writing	2858	3.29	1.91	.96
Taught surface features	2858	3.37	2.22	.96
Taught deep features	2858	3.26	2.22	.97
Surface writing efficacy	2846	3.25	1.96	.97
Deep writing efficacy	2846	3.19	1.90	.97
Teacher quality of writing	2846	3.11	2.11	.96
Evaluation of asTTle tests				
Reading enjoyable experience	4542	3.74	1.26	.78
Reading logistics of testing	4542	3.76	1.05	.68
Math enjoyable experience	1042	2.74	1.12	.77
Math logistics of testing	1042	3.47	.90	.82
Writing enjoyable experience	1305	3.06	1.93	.92
Writing logistics of testing	1305	2.33	1.73	.80
Attitude to subjects				
Liking reading	26134	1.78	1.88	.96
Reading efficacy	26134	1.88	1.91	.97
Liking writing	22413	1.80	1.23	.88
Writing efficacy	22413	1.75	1.22	.92
Liking math	21933	2.38	1.06	.82
Math efficacy	21933	2.53	1.12	.78

Correlations between Variables

The correlations between attitude to assessment and conceptions of assessment with mathematics achievement (Table 7.2) indicated that four scales had statistically significant correlations with academic performance. Students who conceived of assessment as being about the improvement of learning and for learning, who had a deep transformative approach to assessment, and who agreed assessment was valid were more likely to have higher achievement scores in mathematics. As important, those who conceived testing as part of accountability, as irrelevant, or as a surface approach had no statistically significant relationship with achievement in mathematics. Thus, students who have positive conceptions of assessment as assisting their learning are more likely to be those with higher academic achievement.

Table 7.2. Attitudes and Conceptions of Assessment and Mathematics Achievement

	Mathematics		
Instrument and scales	N	r	p
Attitudes to assessment			
Assessment for learning	399	.18	<.001
Minimize assessment	399	.10	.057
Assess to impress	399	.11	.029
Deep approach to assessment	442	.17	<.001
Surface approach to assessment	442	.06	.199
Conceptions about assessment			
Accountability	276	.05	.410
Improvement	338	.25	<.001
Irrelevant	753	.06	.110
Validity	430	.14	.004

Table 7.3 shows that students had higher achievement in mathematics when they considered that their learning experiences included study strategies, co-operative group work, high quality teaching, excellent teacher–student relationships, where the teacher cared for the student, and where there was an enthusiasm for learning. Increases in mathematics achievement were also associated with parents discussing school with the students, being encouraging, and parents talking to the school.

**Table 7.3. Attitudes to School and Parental Involvement
in Schooling and Mathematics Achievement**

	Mathematics		
Instrument and scales	N	r	p
Attitudes towards schools and achievement domains			
Study strategies	701	.37	<.001
Working in co-operative groups	701	.36	<.001
Quality of teaching	771	.23	<.001
Teacher–student relationships	771	.19	<.001
Teacher cares about me	388	.17	.001
Enthusiasm for learning	388	.12	.018
Deep vs. surface learning	736	.04	.227
Positive peer interactions	325	.00	.961
Satisfaction with learning	325	-.05	.348
Parental involvement in schooling			
Parents discuss school	422	.22	<.001
Parental encouragement	422	.22	<.001
Parents talk to school	422	.20	<.001
Parents and future	422	.15	.001

Attitudes to reading were collected from three different instruments (i.e., attitude towards reading and school work; importance of reading and writing; and NEMP attitude to subjects). Table 7.4 shows that for reading, there were high correlations with all seven different attitudes. Those who had a greater sense that reading was important, whose teachers interacted and challenged them, who had self-efficacy for school work and reading, who liked reading, who had high self-esteem, and who had interactions between the teacher and the family were all associated with increased academic performance.

Table 7.4. Attitudes to Reading and School Work and Reading Achievement

	Reading		
Instrument and scales	N	r	p
Reading importance	940	.42	<.001
Teacher interacts and challenges students	944	.35	<.001
Reading efficacy	26134	.32	<.001
Efficacy in school work	1668	.31	<.001
Liking reading	26134	.29	<.001
Academic self-esteem	1668	.26	<.001
Teacher and family relationships	944	.17	<.001

Attitudes to mathematics were collected from two different instruments (i.e., attitude towards mathematics and NEMP attitude to subjects). Table 7.5 shows that for mathematics, higher academic performance was associated with the perception that the teacher challenged the student, the student had high interest, and the student had a positive approach to mathematics. In contrast, very low or non-significant associations were found for avoiding mathematics, liking of or self-efficacy in mathematics, teacher and family relationships, and use of either deep or surface learning. The lack of positive relations of liking and self-efficacy are contrary to international research findings and worthy of considerable further investigation.

Table 7.5. Attitudes to Mathematics and Mathematics Achievement

	Mathematics		
Instrument and scales	N	r	p
Attitude to mathematics			
Teacher challenges me	704	.29	<.001
Interest in mathematics	704	.24	<.001
Mathematics positive approach	399	.15	.002
Self-efficacy in mathematics	21933	.07	<.001
Liking mathematics	21933	.06	<.001
Deep vs. surface learning	736	.04	.227
Mathematics avoidance	399	-.01	.865
Teacher and family relationships	642	-.02	.536

Attitudes to writing were collected from two different instruments (i.e., attitude to and experience of writing and NEMP attitude to subjects). Table 7.6 shows that for writing, all scales had statistically significant positive relationships with academic performance.

Particularly noteworthy were self-efficacy in writing, liking of writing, efficacy in deep and surface features of writing, and the quality of the writing. It is clear that when teaching writing, there are major dividends in terms of academic performance in building confidence, and in making the students like and enjoy writing.

Table 7.6. Attitudes to and Experience of Writing, and Writing Achievement

	Writing		
Instrument and scales	N	r	p
Attitude to and experience of writing			
Efficacy in writing	21195	.31	<.001
Liking writing	21195	.27	<.001
Deep writing efficacy	2846	.24	<.001
Surface writing efficacy	2846	.23	<.001
Teacher quality of writing	2846	.23	<.001
Content of writing	2858	.22	<.001
Structure of writing	2858	.22	<.001
Taught surface features	2858	.20	<.001
Taught deep features	2858	.19	<.001

An inspection of the writing attitude items with the highest correlations (Table 7.7) permits a deeper analysis of why attitudes are associated with achievement. It is clear that being taught specific writing skills and being able to do those things are powerful predictors of success in writing. It is not merely participating in the activity of writing or having a strong feel-good factor, as might be interpreted from Table 7.6, but rather having been taught specific writing strategies that makes the difference.

Table 7.7. Selected Writing Attitude Items and Correlations with Writing Achievement

Writing attitude items	Correlation
I have been taught to analyse in writing a novel, play, or poem.	.24
I can write a sentence with good grammar.	.24
I can analyse in writing the plot, character, setting, etc. from a text I have read.	.23
I can organize information and write it up in a report.	.23
I have been taught to classify or order information for a written report.	.23
I can recount in writing something I have done or participated in.	.23
I have been taught to write persuasively.	.22
I can present a written argument.	.22
I can punctuate my writing properly.	.22
I can give a written explanation.	.22
I can persuade or argue in writing.	.22
I can write a clear set of instructions.	.22
I can write a recount of events.	.22
I can classify or order information in written form.	.21

The correlations between the students enjoying the testing experience and the achievement scores were all low (Table 7.8). Likewise, student evaluations of the format and logistics of the asTTle test papers had no meaningful relationship to their achievement. Thus there is no evidence that the scores of the students were substantially affected by their enjoyment or otherwise on the tests. Provided testing is relatively enjoyable and the logistics satisfactory, students can perform to their best on the asTTle achievement tests.

Table 7.8. Student Evaluation of asTTle tests and Academic Performance

	Reading			Writing			Mathematics		
Instrument and scales	N	r	p	N	r	p	N	r	p
Testing was an enjoyable experience	1,435	-.06	.026	1305	.11	<.001	1042	-.09	.003
Logistics were satisfactory	1,435	-.01	.774	1305	.02	.404	1042	.00	.895

The correlations between the measure of home resources (books in the home) was .22 with reading ($N = 9,251$, p <.001), .13 with mathematics ($N = 18,633$, $p <.001$), and .19 for writing ($N = 5,910$, $p <.001$).

Moderators of These Correlates of Achievement

To begin to understand how some of these correlates relate to achievement, various moderators or influences of student or school demographic variables (such as sex, year of schooling, and ethnicity) are investigated. There are many other potential moderators in this data set, but only a sample is provided here to demonstrate the potential for further exploration. The asTTle data set contains information about students such as their sex, year, and ethnicity; at the same time, information about school size, type, decile, and location is provided. We provide one example of how the relationship of student-reported parental involvement and academic performance is related to student characteristics.

The example includes 940 girls and 766 boys who had a reading achievement score and who completed the items relating to parental involvement in schooling. These students were in Year 8 ($n = 266$), Year 9 ($n= 854$), Year 10 ($n = 312$), and Year 11 ($n = 274$). The multivariate F-ratio indicated that there were statistically significant differences across the years, and between males and females in terms of the effect of their parental involvement scales and reading achievement, but not an interaction effect (Table 7.9).

**Table 7.9. Multivariate Effect of Sex and Year
on Academic Performance on asTTle tests**

Effects	Lambda	F	Hypothesis df	p
Year	.91	13.90	12, 4485	<.001
Sex	.99	5.36	4, 1695	<.001
Year * Sex	.99	1.05	12, 4485	.395

Parental involvement scale scores decreased for older students across Years 8 to 11, and particularly between Years 8 and 9, which marks the transition from primary to secondary schooling (Figure 7.6). The student-reported involvement of parents also decreased markedly as students moved from primary to secondary school, and continued to decline as the students moved through the secondary school. As important, the degree to which parents encouraged learning was much more critical than whether they discussed schooling, talked with teachers, or were concerned about the students' future. It was parents' encouragement of learning that was the key among these variables.

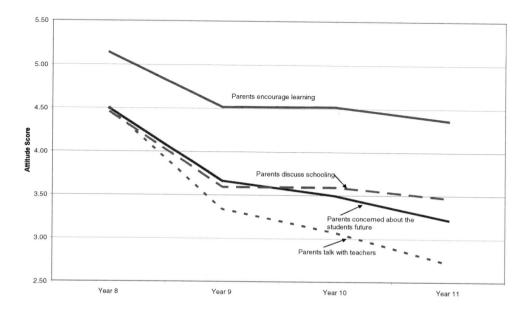

Figure 7.6. Parental involvement attitudes and student school year.

On all four parental involvement scales, females scored higher than males (Figure 7.7). Female students reported a different quality of parental interaction in terms of discussions about school, encouragement to learn, and discussions about the future. The degree to which these self-reports are accurate remains to be confirmed; nevertheless, since some of the parental attitude scales are positively related to academic performance, advice could be given to parents to talk more with their sons about schooling and learning.

When the various correlations of total scores for each group of items with reading, writing, and mathematics are considered, then four factors tend to be consistently among the most important (Table 7.10). They are: challenge, perceived value of the subject, strategies of learning, and the quality of teaching. For reading and writing but not for mathematics, high confidence or efficacy is also important. Less highly correlated but still of some importance are students' conceptions of assessment as assisting in their improvement, and when parents take an interest in and encourage their learning. The logistics of the testing process and the liking or satisfaction of the three subjects are unrelated to the achievement outcomes.

Table 7.10. Correlations between Reading, Mathematics, and Writing and the Various Variables

Reading		Mathematics		Writing	
Reading importance	.42	Study strategies	.37	Writing self-efficacy	.31
Teacher interacts & challenges students	.35	Working in co-operative groups	.36	Like writing	.27
Reading self-efficacy	.32	Math is challenging	.29	Deep writing efficacy	.24
Efficacy in school work	.31	Assessment as improvement	.25	Surface writing efficacy	.23
Like reading	.29	Math is interesting	.24	Teacher quality	.23
Reading enjoyable experience	.27	Quality of teaching	.23	Content of writing	.22
Academic self-esteem	.26	Parents discuss school	.22	Structure of writing	.22
Importance for teacher & family	.17	Parents encouragement	.22	Taught surface features	.20
Assessment as accountability	.16	Parents talk to school	.20	Taught deep features	.19
Assessment as improvement	.14	Teacher-student relationships	.19	Evaluation of writing enjoyable	.11
Parent encourage in schooling	.12	Assessment for learning	.18	Logistic of writing	.02
Assessments is irrelevant	.08	Teacher cares about me	.17		
Parents discuss schooling	.05	Deep approach to assessment	.17		
Parents concerned with future	.04	Parents concerned with future	.15		
Reading logistics of testing	-.01	Positive approach to math	.15		
Writing liking	-.02	Assessment as validity	.14		
Parents talk to school	-.03	Enthusiasm for learning	.12		
		Assessment to impress	.11		
		Minimize assessment	.10		
		Math efficacy	.07		
		Like math	.06		
		Surface approach to assessment	.06		
		Assessment is irrelevant	.06		
		Assessment for accountability	.05		
		Quality of learning	.04		
		Deep vs. surface learning	.04		
		Evaluation of math logistics	.00		
		Positive peer relations	.00		
		Math is a negative experience	-.01		
		Math teacher and family	-.02		
		Satisfied with my learning	-.05		
		Evaluation of math enjoyable	-.09		

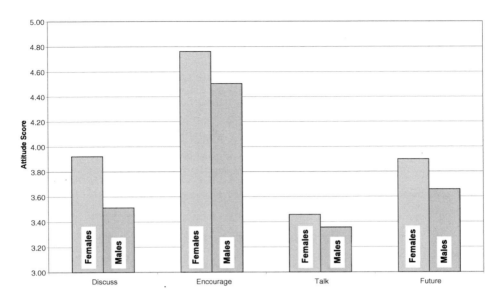

Figure 7.7. Parental involvement attitudes and student sex.

CONCLUSION

The purpose of this chapter is to illustrate the power of secondary data analysis, reveal how certain characteristics of student attitudes and background variables relate to academic achievement, and provide suggestions as to how best to raise student academic performance. The sources for each questionnaire, preliminary statistical analysis, and psychometric properties of the resulting scales from the factor analyses have been provided to illustrate the power of these data for secondary analyses. These achievement data are among the most comprehensive available to researchers in New Zealand, and come from 709 schools and 92,280 Year 4–12 students. The more important scales have been identified and examples given to show that there is sufficient data to examine the attitudes and their relationship to academic performance by student or school demographic characteristics.

The major purposes of these analyses is more to provide pointers to further research rather than informing policy directly. Also, the effect sizes as well as the statistical significance should be taken into consideration when making meaning out of each of the analyses. As noted above, with correlations of the magnitude reported in the tables, an effect size is approximately two times the correlation, and any effect size greater than .20 ($r = .10$) is well worth considering, but an effect size of .40 or greater ($r = .20$) is about or above the typical influence on achievement. Thus, any correlation greater than .20 and statistically significant is well worth pursuing.

The preliminary findings are that liking of and interest in subjects; self-efficacy in subjects; challenging, explicit, and high-quality teaching; student self-regulation of learning and studying especially in response to assessment; and discussions with parents about learning are all positively associated with academic performance. Most of these findings are consistent with the extant research literature, which heretofore had limited New Zealand data to support such claims. However, the data has shown that in certain subjects and for certain populations, self-efficacy does not have a meaningful relationship to academic performance.

It is noted that detailed analyses of the Maori-medium student achievement is a story waiting to be told. In some areas more detailed analyses in Maori medium are being conducted (i.e., conceptions of assessment and attitudes to subjects) which have gone beyond the level of detail presented here. Similarly, school and student effects on the attitude scales and how they affect academic performance need further discussion. Many of the non-significant or zero relationships reported here require theoretically sound explanations as much as the significant ones do. The invitation is offered to readers to access the asTTle data set explore their own models and questions.

REFERENCES

Bourke, S. (1981). *Quality of School Life*. Melbourne, Australia: Australian Council for Educational Research.

Brown, G. T. L. (2001). *Reporting assessment information to teachers: Report of Project asTTle outputs design.* asTTle Tech. Rep No. 15. Auckland, New Zealand: University of Auckland, Project asTTle.

Brown, G. T. L. (2002). *Teachers' Conceptions of Assessment.* Unpublished doctoral dissertation, University of Auckland, Auckland, New Zealand.

Brown, G. T. L. (2004). Teachers' conceptions of assessment: Implications for policy and professional development. *Assessment in Education: Policy, Principles and Practice, 11*(3), 305–322.

Brown, G. T. L. (2006). Teachers' conceptions of assessment: Validation of an abridged instrument. *Psychological Reports, 99*, 166–170.

Brown, G. T. L., & Hirschfeld, G. H. F. (2007). Students' conceptions of assessment and mathematics achievement: Evidence for the power of self-regulation. *Australian Journal of Educational and Developmental Psychology,7*, 63–74.

Brown, G. T. L. & Hirschfeld, G. H. F. (2008). Students' conceptions of assessment: Links to outcomes. *Assessment in Education: Principles, Policy and Practice, 15*(1), 3-17.

Clinton, J., Hattie, J., & Dixon, R. (2007). *Evaluation of the Flaxmere Project: When families learn the language of school* (Commissioned Report to the New Zealand Ministry of Education Research Division No. RMR-832). Auckland, New Zealand: University of Auckland.

Crampton, P., Salmond, C., Kirkpatrick, R., Scarborough, R., & Skelly, C. (2000). *Degrees of deprivation in New Zealand: An atlas of socioeconomic difference.* Auckland, New Zealand: David Bateman.

Elley, W. B. (1992). *How in the world do students read?.* The Hague, Netherlands: International Association for the Evaluation of Educational Achievement (IEA).

Fletcher, R. J., & Hattie, J. A. C. (2004). *Test the nation: The development of an IQ test for New Zealand adults – 2004.* Retrieved 7 February 2008 from http://www.education.auckland.ac.nz/uoa/fms/default/education/staff/Prof.%20John%20Hattie/Documents/John%20Hattie%20Papers/intelligence/Test%20the%20Nation%20(2003).pdf.

Glasswell, K., Parr, J., & Aikman, M. (2001). *Development of the asTTle writing assessment rubrics for scoring extended writing tasks.* (asTTle Tech. Rep. No. 6). Auckland, New Zealand: University of Auckland/Ministry of Education.

Hattie, J. A. C. (2003, October). *Teachers make a difference: What is the research evidence?* Keynote address to the Australian Council for Educational Research Annual Conference on Building Teacher Quality Melbourne, Australia (Reprinted in 'It's official: Teachers make a difference', Educare News, Australia).

Hattie, J. A. (1999, June). *Influences on student learning.* Inaugural professorial address, University of Auckland, New Zealand.

Hattie, J. A. C., Brown, G. T. L., & Keegan, P. J. (2003). A national teacher-managed, curriculum-based assessment system: Assessment Tools for Teaching and Learning (asTTle). *International Journal of Learning, 10,* 771–778.

Hattie, J. A., Brown, G. T. L., Ward, L., Irving, S. E., & Keegan, P. J. (2006). Formative evaluation of an educational assessment technology innovation: Developers' insights into assessment tools for teaching and learning (asTTle). *Journal of Multi-Disciplinary Evaluation. 5.* Retrieved 10 December, 2007 from: http://evaluation.wmich. edu/JMDE/content/JMDE005content/PDFs_JMDE_005/Formative_Evaluation_of_an_E ducational_Assessment_Technology_Innovation_Developers_Insights_into_Assessment_ Tools_for_Teaching_and_Learning_asTTle.pdf.

Hattie, J., & Timperley, H. (2007). The power of feedback. *Review of Educational Research, 77*(1), 81–112.

Irving, S. E. (2004). *The development and validation of a student evaluation instrument to identify highly accomplished mathematics teachers.* Unpublished doctoral dissertation, University of Auckland, New Zealand.

Johnston, R., Brown, G. T. L., Hattie, J. A. C., Sutherland, T., Gregory, D., Hartmann, J., et al. (2003, July). *Evaluation of the asTTle 'greedy' heuristic.* asTTle Advisory Report No. 7. Auckland, New Zealand: University of Auckland, School of Education.

Meece, Judith L; & Miller, Samuel D. (2001, October). A longitudinal analysis of elementary school students' achievement goals in literacy activities. *Contemporary Educational Psychology,* Vol. 26(4), 454-480.

Middleton, M. J., & Midgley, C. (2002). Beyond motivation: Middle school students' perceptions of press for understanding in math. *Contemporary Educational Psychology, Vol. 27*(3), 373-391.

Mullis, I. V. S., Martin, M. O., Gonzalez, E. J., & Kennedy, A. M. (2003). *PIRLS 2001 international report: IEA's study of reading literacy achievement in primary schools.* Chestnut Hill, MA: Boston College.

Otunuku, M., & Brown, G. T. L. (2007). Tongan students' attitudes towards their subjects in New Zealand relative to their academic achievement. *Asia Pacific Education Review, 8*(1), 117-128.

Student achievement findings for cohort 1 schools: February 2004–November 2005 (2006). (Literacy Professional Development Project Report). Wellington, New Zealand: Learning Media. Retrieved December 10, 2007, from: http://www.minedu.govt.nz/web/ downloadable/dl11102_v1/literacy-professional-develoment-project-v2.pdf.

AUTHOR NOTE

John Hattie is a Professor in the Faculty of Education, University of Auckland, New Zealand, and Director of Project asTTle (Assessment Tools for Teaching and Learning). His areas of research include measurement models and their application to educational problems, meta-analysis, and models of teaching and learning. Over the past five years, Professor Hattie has headed a team introducing a model of assessment for teachers in all schools in New Zealand, and thus providing schools with evidence-based information about the teaching and learning. He is editor of the International Journal of Testing, and an associate editor of the British Journal of Educational Psychology.

Correspondence concerning this chapter should be addressed by email to: j.hattie@auckland.ac.nz

In: Challenging Thinking about Teaching and Learning
Editors: C. M. Rubie-Davies and C. Rawlinson

ISBN: 978-1-60456-744-1
© 2008 Nova Science Publishers, Inc.

Chapter 8

ESSENTIAL CONDITIONS FOR EFFECTIVE CRITICAL THINKING IN SCHOOLS

Irene Y. Fung, Michael A. R. Townsend and Judy M. Parr

ABSTRACT

The ability to think critically has been adopted internationally as a core skill in education, and there has been a rapid growth in programmes specifically designed to increase critical thinking and higher order thinking skills in students. Although relatively popular with educators and students, among the criticisms of such programmes is that they have conventionally adopted a narrow *skills-only* approach. A number of educators have argued for a more substantive *skills-plus-dispositions* approach in which both intellectual skills and intellectual character are developed. This latter approach affords the potential for genuine critical thinking that extends beyond restrictive school contexts. In this chapter, we consider that a skills-plus-dispositions approach is sound theoretically, and we propose that there are four essential conditions to an effective skills-plus-dispositions approach to teaching and learning to think critically in daily classroom practice. These conditions include (a) approaching students as thinkers, (b) guiding students to overcome both their intellectual and affective barriers in thinking, (c) promoting participation and contribution in the reasoned discourse of communities of critical inquiry and practice, and (d) engaging critical thinking as an integral element of students' educational experiences.

INTRODUCTION

Educators hold different views on whether developing critical think*ing* or developing critical think*ers* should be the goal of the educational process. Proponents of a *skills-only* approach subscribe to the former educational goal and emphasize developing critical thinking skills and abilities only. In contrast, proponents of a *skills-plus-dispositions* approach focus on the latter goal of developing critical thinkers and emphasize developing both critical thinking skills and dispositions.

Critical thinking cannot operate unless it is underpinned by proficiency in skills and abilities that can assure it is able to happen. A number of critical thinking writers want to distinguish sharply between critical thinking and critical thinkers. They are reluctant to include the non-skills dimension in their conceptions of critical thinking and insist on viewing critical thinking in a strict procedural sense (see, for example, Facione, 1990). To these educators, only abilities and skills are necessary for the distinctive cognitive processes involved in the critical thinking process per se. While critical thinkers are people who have those skills, together with certain valuable dispositions, these dispositions are not, strictly speaking, what is meant by the term critical thinking. These critical thinking educators refer to critical thinking as skills-only, and so refer to the teaching and learning of critical thinking as *skills training*. Such terminology has become part of the popular and official discourse. For example, in the United Kingdom, critical thinking is introduced into the school-leaving examination syllabus as one of a number of core skills (Oxford, Cambridge and RSA Examinations, 2003).

However, many educators are critical of the trend towards a skills-only approach and argue that developing critical thinking dispositions should not be overlooked. They believe that it is the dispositions that determine whether the learner will spontaneously put to use newly acquired effective thinking abilities and skills for problem solving and decision making beyond the instructional context. For example, Baron (1985) argues that the ability factors determine what, in principle, a person can do, whereas the dispositional factors determine what a person does do, within capacity limits. Similarly, Siegel (1988, p. 32) maintains that "a critical thinker is one who is appropriately moved by reasons, one who possesses not only the abilities of rational assessment but a willingness, desire and disposition to follow reason", and argues that failing to develop simultaneously abilities and dispositions will rob critical thinking education of a considerable portion of its depth and significance. Put more graphically, such education will result in "teaching children how to behave at the table while leaving them still disposed to eat like Henry VIII" (Flew, 1982, p. 352). Further, Dewey (1933) saw the interdependence of these two dimensions and argued for their union as a proper conception of critical thinking:

> Knowledge of the methods alone will not suffice; there must be the desire, the will, to employ them. This desire is an affair of personal disposition. But on the other hand the disposition alone will not suffice. There must also be understanding of the forms and techniques that are the channels through which these attitudes operate to the best advantage. (p. 30)

Unfortunately, Dewey's insight seems to have had little effect on the design of many current critical thinking courses and programmes. The current skills-only pedagogy might have been predicated on the assumption that if you possess the abilities and skills for critical thinking, you will automatically put them to use where required. However, it has become clear that this assumption is not warranted, as shown in the results of some recent studies on skills transfer. Empirical findings point to the conclusion that good thinking skills alone may show up well on exercises and tests but, without dispositions to spur the skills into actions, they are likely to remain inactive in real-life situations (Belmont, Butterfield, & Ferretti, 1982; Facione, Giancarlo, Facione, & Gainen, 1995; Facione, Sanchez, & Facione, 1994;

Fisher, 1998; Halpern, 1998; Perkins, Farady, & Bushey, 1991; Perkins, Jay, & Tishman, 1993; Resnick, 1987; Swartz, 1987; Tishman, Jay, & Perkins, 1993).

If students do not also develop the dispositions or have the willingness and commitment to think critically in their academic, personal, or social life, no matter what level of critical thinking skills they possess, it is of *no* practical benefit (Sternberg, 1983). Thus, failing to transfer skills is, in fact, failing to achieve the educational goal that critical thinking education purports to pursue. But, as noted earlier, implementing a skills-plus-dispositions approach is, pragmatically, not easy. This may explain why Dewey's insight noted above has had little effect and why the skills-only pedagogy still continues. This is why it is imperative to identify the necessary conditions that will allow teachers to design and implement programmes that can help students develop simultaneously the required abilities and skills for, and the desirable dispositions towards, critical thinking.

So, what are these conditions? On the basis of the above analysis, we consider that a skills-plus-dispositions pedagogical approach is sound theoretically. In the rest of this chapter, we propose that a skills-plus-dispositions pedagogical approach should be practically possible if four conditions for it are created. We now consider each necessary condition in turn.

CONDITIONS REQUIRED FOR A SKILLS-PLUS-DISPOSITIONS APPROACH

First Condition

The first condition for a skills-plus-dispositions approach is for educators to approach students as thinkers by showing respect for, and upholding, students' right to think, question, challenge, and seek reasons, explanations, and justification (Siegel, 1988), and to acknowledge that students have feelings, desires, values, and beliefs that influence the ways they think and the way they think critically. Students are often seen as mindless or thoughtless by adults, including parents and teachers. Reprimands, for example, are often accompanied by claims that "You didn't think . . ." However, of course, students do think, though their thinking may not be systematic, may be based on faulty or incomplete knowledge, or may be driven by self-interest. Helping students to push their own boundaries of rationality, to overcome and counteract human natural tendencies to err as they think, is the central idea of developing critical thinkers.

Whether or not critical thinking is introduced to students, by the time they enter school they are already able to think and they already have the dispositions to think in a particular way (Bailin, Case, Coombs, & Daniels, 1999). They have their own beliefs, values, goals, interests, and skills that mediate the choice of problem to solve. They are thinking critically in some way, making and criticizing judgements and arguments of various sorts, though their thinking may not be well-reasoned or free from errors, bias, and prejudice.

Using a related argument, Kurfiss (1988) reminds us that teaching for critical thinking does not take place in a vacuum. Students frequently bring with them both a home culture and a peer culture with norms that may be different from those that critical thinking education advocates. Biased thinking is a pervasive and resilient counterforce that does not evaporate when students enter the classroom. Therefore, it would be more helpful to look for ways to teach students to think more effectively rather than assuming that they are not able to think critically.

If the purpose of critical thinking education is to help students to reason in a more *discriminating, self-conscious, self-directed, and self-correcting* way, students should be helped to realize that certain aspects of their thinking practice are valuable and effective and should be retained and further developed, while other aspects of their thinking practice are poor, erroneous, and ethically unacceptable and should be abandoned. Bailin and her associates (1999) suggest that teaching critical thinking is best conceptualized as furthering the initiation of students into complex critical practices that embody value commitments and require the sensitive use of a variety of intellectual resources in making good judgement. This involves not only teaching students the standards, concepts, and principles of critical thinking but also getting them to appreciate the value of changing some of their problematic motives, interests, values, attitudes, commitments, and practices (Bailin et al., 1999; Paul & Elder, 2001).

But, clearly, whether or not critical thinking is introduced into a classroom or school or in everyday situations, the teachers and adults are already communicating certain values, attitudes, expectations, and beliefs to students. "Education" is, in large part, a socialization process, a process that involves the transmission of norms and values, as well as a body of socially approved knowledge and attitudes. The formal or official curriculum contains the sanctioned socially-accepted knowledge, values, norms, and attitudes for students to learn, but there are also the informal rules, beliefs, attitudes, and expectations perpetuated through the actual socialization processes within the classroom or school—what Jackson (1968) and Dreebin (1968) called the *hidden curriculum.* Many writings from the sociocultural perspectives have expressed concern that the values and norms espoused in the formal or official curriculum and taught through lectures, texts, and tests may not be the same as the values and norms that are transmitted by the hidden curriculum taught through the everyday social interactions between adults and students in schools or classrooms (Goodlad & Klein, 1974; Goodman, 1964; Greer, 1972; Illich, 1971). The value of using critical thinking as a tool for self-understanding, self-critique, self-correction, and self-improvement certainly needs to be made explicit to students. However, it is difficult for students to appreciate such value if the teachers and adults in schools—with whom students interact day in and day out—do not appreciate or act in accordance with the value of self-understanding, self-critique, self-correction, and self-improvement.

When students are approached as thinkers, the major concern for educators is not whether students have the ability to think, but how to help students to improve the quality of what and how they think. In this regard, the *Foundation for Critical Thinking* (2001) suggests that if we approach students as thinkers, assign activities which require thinking, model the thinking we expect, and teach students how to assess and improve their own thinking, they will become better thinkers, learners, and persons.

However, if we take seriously the fallible nature of human thinking (Bacon, 1605; Rescher, 1998; Simon, 1982), we should acknowledge that not only students, but also we adults share the natural human tendencies to err as we think. If we care about the quality of our own thinking and practice, we should also commit to developing ourselves into critical thinkers able to evaluate critically our own beliefs, values, and experiences. If teachers are also striving for their ongoing critical thinking development and are committed to self-evaluation of their beliefs, values, and experiences, they should be more able to teach their students by example, rather than just by directives. Through their experiences of both the difficulties and triumphs in changing some of their previously established problematic commitments and practices, teachers will have more insights into how to develop their students into better thinkers. They will be more able to communicate and to reinforce the value of critical thinking in developing better thinkers, learners, and persons.

Second Condition

The second condition for a skills-plus-dispositions approach is for educators to guide students to overcome their intellectual and affective barriers. Critical thinking has often been conceived of as a purely cognitive activity that is above and beyond the realm of feelings, emotions, and desires. This is perhaps because the three aspects of mind—thinking, feeling, and wanting—have been traditionally conceived of and studied as if they function independently of each other. A skills-plus-dispositions approach requires a paradigm shift so that both teachers and students are able to see that critical thinking is operated by a unity of the thinker's mind; that is, the interplay of our thinking, feelings, and wanting (Paul, 1995).

With only a few exceptions, theorists rarely make it explicit that emotions are central to the self-analysis and self-critique of critical thinking processes. But it must be recognized that there are "emotional blocks" to effective thinking (Adams, 1974). Asking critical questions about our previously accepted values, ideas, and behaviours is anxiety-producing: "We may feel fearful of the consequences that might arise from contemplating alternatives to our current ways of thinking and living; resistance, resentment, and confusion are evident at various stages in the critical thinking process" (Brookfield, 1987, p. 7). Paul (1995) points out that "it is very hard to fight against egocentrism, sociocentrism, and ethnocentrism which characterize the mentality of *mine is better*—my ideas, my values, my race, my country" (p. ii). This is because this kind of mentality serves useful and important purposes, and it leads people to feel good about themselves, their group, and their country. But this mentality also fosters an irrational resistance to new or improved ideas. Therefore, Paul argues that if we are to prepare the way for new ideas by rooting out old ones, we need to overcome not only our cognitive/intellectual barriers, but also our psychological/affective barriers. This suggests that to overcome these barriers, two important dimensions of teaching and learning should be incorporated, namely: (a) guiding students to discover how a unity of mind works, and (b) guiding students to evaluate and adjust their personal values.

To overcome the intellectual and affective barriers, the first thing to do is to have a new understanding of how the human mind works. There are major weaknesses to the traditional conception of the mind in which thinking, feeling and wanting are seen as relatively independent. Vygotsky says that such a view makes thought processes appear divorced "from the fullness of life, from the personal needs and interests, the inclinations and impulses, of the thinker" (Vygotsky, 1962, p. 10). It excludes an analysis of human thoughts in terms of the motive forces that direct thought in particular ways. For Vygotsky, motivation in the form of volition was the key to a more useful conception of the human mind:

> Thought itself is engendered by motivation, that is, by our desires and needs, our interests and emotions. Behind every thought there is an affective volitional tendency,

which holds the last answer to "why" in the analysis of thinking. A true and full understanding of another's thought is only possible when we understand its affective-volitional basis. (p. 150)

Vygotsky (1962) argued for the notion of dynamic reciprocity of thought, affect, and volition in meaning making. This fuller conception of the mind enables us to see that "every idea contains a transmuted affective attitude toward the bit of reality to which it refers" (p. 10). It also allows us "to trace the path from a person's needs and impulses to the specific direction taken by his thoughts, and the reverse from his thoughts to his behaviour and activity" (p. 10). These views of Vygotsky have had a profound effect on education. In relation to critical thinking, his understanding shows why it is important to gain command of the full faculties of mind, to self-direct thought, emotions, and desire so they function well altogether. To do this, we need to make our unconscious relationship to our mind *conscious* and *deliberate*. When we are aware that thinking, feeling, and wanting are inter-related, we can deliberately analyze this relationship. In a similar view, Richard Paul argues that we can analyze our thoughts in terms of the motive forces that direct our thoughts into certain decisions and behaviours, or in terms of the influence of our thoughts on our affect and volition; he observes that our feeling and desires do not correct themselves, but they can be corrected through our thinking (Foundation for Critical Thinking, 1997; Paul & Elder, 2001).

Feelings and emotions are closely connected with certain beliefs about their object, and are so responsive to beliefs of certain sorts that they cannot come into being or remain without them. Hence, they can be changed or even removed by changes in those grounding beliefs.

> Anger, for example, requires the belief that I, or something important to me, have or has been harmed by another person's intentional action. If any significant aspect of that complex belief should cease to seem true to me—if I change my view about who has done the harm, or about whether it was intentional, or about whether what happed was in fact a harm—my anger can expect to abate or change its course accordingly. (Nussbaum, 1992, p. 206)

The meaning we create can be grounded in insights, objective reality, a fantasy, or even a dysfunctional interpretation of reality (Paul & Elder, 2001). So, when we are excited by some negative emotions, such as anger, fear, jealousy, helplessness, or hatred, we need deliberately to trace back to the values and beliefs they are based on and evaluate the quality of those values and beliefs. For example, when we feel frustrated in a situation, we can ask ourselves: What is the thinking in my mind that is leading to this feeling of frustration? Is that thinking reasonable? What specifically am I frustrated with? What exactly is the problem here? Is there any possibility that my interpretation of this situation is incomplete or biased? Paul and Elder (2001) suggest that if students of critical thinking regularly keep a journal and reflect on situations that are emotionally significant to them, or that they deeply care about, they will have more opportunities to identify and rectify their egocentric thinking, feelings, and motives.

To overcome both our intellectual and affective barriers in self-analysis, self-critique, and self-correcting processes, it is helpful for us to learn to differentiate between valuational thinking and evaluational thinking. Lipman (1995) who cited Dewey's (1939, p. 5) work on *theory of valuation*, draws a distinction between prizing and appraising, between esteeming and estimating, and between valuing and evaluating. To value something is to appreciate it, to cherish it, to hold it dear, whereas to evaluate is to calculate its worth. Evaluation has to do with deliberate appraisal or assessment on the basis of external criteria and standards. Valuation, on the other hand, can be simply uncritical and biased if it is prizing rather than appraising, and esteeming rather than estimating.

Thinking about what to believe and do is purposeful and intentional. Because the values you see in taking a certain belief or action influence your emotional response to and understanding of that belief or action, purposeful and intentional thinking is, in fact, valuational thinking (Lipman, 1995). In guiding students to critically evaluate and adjust their valuational thinking, Lipman calls for students to learn how to use ethical criteria to distinguish between *what is* and *what ought to be* in their thinking. An example is the ethical criterion of caring about whether what to believe and do is fair and just to oneself and others. In advancing your own values and interests, you need to attend not only to what you take to be important to you, but also to what is important to others. In other words, the ethical criteria for assessing valuational thinking have to do with consideration of the effects on others of advancing your own interests and values. If the effects on others are not ethical, then you need to refrain from advancing your interests and values.

With respect to teaching students evaluational thinking, Lipman (1995) recommends that those students who are able to reflect on who they are should be helped to recognize the sort of persons they could and should want to be. Those students who are able to consider the world as it is should be helped to recognize the sort of world they could and should want to live in. This is a long-term and ongoing undertaking.

Guiding students to evaluate and adjust the personal values that underpin their thinking is essential for building their capacities for taking charge of the meaning, purpose, and quality of their lives—which is the essence of human agency. Students need to reconstruct their habits of thinking, feeling, wanting, and action so as to ameliorate some aspect of their individual and collective experiences. When students see themselves as having self-conscious, self-directed and self-correcting thinking processes, they will experience a range of positive feelings and emotions. As Brookfield (1987) observes:

> We will be able to feel a pleasing sense of self-confidence as we realize that we have the agency to bring about some changes; we will be able to feel joy, release, relief, and exhilaration as we break through to new ways of looking at our personal, academic and political worlds; we will be able to experience a sense of liberation as we abandon assumptions that have been inhibiting our development; and we will be able to experience excitement as we realize that we have the power to change some aspects of our life. (p. 7)

The core value of learning and practising critical thinking is to develop our capability in dealing with the problems and issues we encounter in our public and private life. Guiding students to discover how a unity of mind works, and how to evaluate the personal values underlying their thinking and reasoning, are important in developing this agency.

Third Condition

The third condition for a skills-plus-dispositions approach is for educators to promote students' participation in and contribution to a reasoned discourse. The teaching and learning of critical thinking has often been conducted in a stand-alone programme where individual students are directly taught the general principles and skills for good thinking. Classroom activities are organized around individual students working independently to solve a range of content- and context-free reasoning tasks. The underlying assumption of this instructional approach is that with the mastery of a set of general principles and skills of good thinking, students will be able to apply them in other contexts where critical thoughts are called for. However, a stand-alone programme is unlikely to be effective in promoting skills transfer. This is mainly because the approach fails to provide students with meaningful experiences through which they can internalize the general principles and skills of good reasoning.

To learn to become critical thinkers, Paul and Elder (2001) suggest, we need to learn to become a *critic* of our own thinking and reasoning and to establish new habits of thought. However, for the inner voice of a critic to be incorporated into our own consciousness, Peters (1967, p. 19) suggests "it is important for us to keep critical company" because the dialogue within, the intrapersonal dialogue, is often constructed from the dialogue without, the interpersonal dialogue.

According to Vygotsky, all the higher human mental functions (including voluntary attention, logical memory, reasoning, and the formation of concepts) of a child are experienced twice. They are experienced first through engaging in dialogue with others at the social interpersonal level, and later, internalized as inner voice or "verbal thought" within oneself at the individual intrapersonal level (Vygotsky, 1978; 1999). In other words, the child's verbal thought is socially mediated, influenced by the culture, knowledge, discourse, values, attitudes, expectations, practices, habits, and other elements in the child's social environment. One implication of Vygotsky's sociocultural learning theory is that, without the actual first-hand experience of interacting and reasoning with critical company at the social interpersonal level, it would be difficult, if not impossible, for students to develop the inner voice of a critic's reasoning. Through participating in a reasoned discourse with others in the process of constructing meaning, making decisions, and solving problems, students may gain the in situ experience of reasoning things out together with others in the process of thinking critically. Students may also be more likely to internalize the values, criteria, standards, knowledge, and skills of critical reasoning.

Several critical thinking theorists who share this view suggest that engaging students in a reasoned dialogue or conversation with others who hold different points of view is important for students to internalize the actual critical thinking process. For example, Burbules (1993) argues that thinking critically in real-world situations requires more than a mastery of general principles and skills of good reasoning. In practical, real-world situations, the person who wants to make a reasoned judgement of beliefs and actions has a practical problem to solve in a specific social context in which the person is related to other persons. In other words, the reasonableness of the judgement of beliefs and actions is subject to the process of reasoned inquiry, seen in the thoughts, conversations, and choices that those involved engage in as they pursue some conclusion that has implications for their own interests and well-being. A person's virtues and capacities of reasonableness surface when the person enters into a dialogue and a communicative relation with other persons. The person then strives to make sense of, and be fair to, alternative points of view; to be careful and prudent in the adoption of important positions and actions, and to be willing to admit and self-correct when he or she has made a mistake.

The thrust of Burbules' (1991, 1993) argument is that in an educational process that aims to develop the virtues and capacities of reasonableness, individual learners need to become members of a community of inquiry that promotes and fosters reasonable practice and conduct for individuals and the group. As members of a community of inquiry enter into reasoned dialogue and communication with one another, they together inquire, disagree, adjudicate, explain, or argue their views in the pursuit of an outcome that reasonable, responsible, fair-minded people are satisfied with. As individual learners participating in the reasoned discourse of a community of inquiry, they have opportunities to encounter new, challenging, and often conflicting ideas; to recognize the perspectives, values, and interests of their own and others; and to learn to judge in practice both the applicability and the limits of the general principles and skills they acquire. Gradually, individual learners will be able to see that the process of giving critical feedback to, or receiving it from, others is a necessary condition for the development of their own reasoning powers.

Many educational writings emphasize the social origins of higher mental functioning and recognize the importance of initiating novices into communities of practice (Brown & Campione, 1994; Bruner, 1986; Cole, 1990; Lave & Wenger, 1991; Rogoff, Matusov, & White, 1996; Scribner, 1985) and critical inquiry (Gregory, 2002; Lipman, 1998). They generally see the role of community as essentially shaping the standards by which the quality of people's thinking and their claims to knowledge are ultimately judged. Rorty (1982, p. 166), for example, argues that we must "accept our inheritance from, and our conversation with, our fellow-humans as our only source of guidance". Similarly, Hostetler (1991) maintains that "community is necessary in that standards of judgement and critical judgements themselves are community products ultimately" (p. 10).

Lipman (1991) gives considerable attention to critical thinking in the social context of dialogue and conversation that leads to understanding and good judgement. He recommends that teachers convert classrooms at all grade levels into *communities of inquiry* through conversation governed by norms of critical thought, reasonableness, and mutual respect. Instead of having a course in critical thinking and a course in science, mathematics, biology, or philosophy, students will benefit more if they take a course in scientific reasoning, mathematical reasoning, biological reasoning, or philosophical reasoning, where reasoning skills and the course content are integrated with one another from the very start (Lipman, 1989). Since each intellectual discipline is represented by a set of assumptions, concepts, values, standards, and practices that constitute a way of viewing reality for the members of the community who share them, thinking and content are interdependent and to know a discipline is to know the discourse, logic, rationality, and reasoning processes associated with that specific discipline (McPeck, 1981).

If we take these views seriously, we should focus on encouraging students' participation and contribution in the reasoned discourse inherent in every school curriculum area. For example, in teaching and learning science, students are encouraged to participate in and contribute to the reasoned discourse inherent in the community of scientific inquiry. Therefore, the pedagogical focus is to encourage students' participation in and contribution to the reasoned discourse of these communities of critical practice and critical inquiry. With this pedagogical focus, students should be able to see the value of critical thinking as the *engine* of every critical practice and critical inquiry.

Participation in a reasoned discourse within a community of inquiry will assist students to recognize that knowledge in each discipline is constructed through a particular mode of critical reasoning and inquiry, and that members of the community of critical practice are expected to *act* according to the features of critical judgement that come out of this reasoned discourse. Specifically, participation will help students better recognize the interconnection of the concepts, principles, criteria, procedures, and purposes they are dealing with. It will also help them to see that these are part of the critical inquiry inherent in the tradition of critical practices rather than being isolated, arbitrary, and inexplicable, as many students seem to view them. Further, students should also learn how to articulate and clarify their problems at hand; how to seek, accept, question, or reject ideas from others who have different points of view. They should learn how to do this on the basis of externally agreed criteria and standards; how to solicit help from, and give credit to, others; how to explain their own needs; and how to discern what others need.

However, it should be noted that teachers need to make explicit "the principle of fallibilism" as they encourage students' participation and contribution in the reasoned discourse within communities of inquiry. The principle of fallibilism states that we never take our knowledge, beliefs, and values as *absolute*. Fallibilism, according to the Routledge Encyclopedia of Philosophy (Rescher, 1998), is a philosophical stance towards knowledge and truth. Its central idea is that we can never attain the final and definitive knowledge and truth in matters regarding the world's ways, but have to make do with what is merely probable or plausible. Therefore, we should see all our claims of knowledge of the world, including our best state-of-the-art scientific theories, as provisional and subject to change. It would be contradictory for teachers to hold steadfastly to their own cherished yet possibly problematic beliefs, or to teach in ways that suggest they know all the answers, yet demand that their students think critically.

The essence of fallibilism is that we need to be aware of, and to counteract, three levels of fallibility. One level concerns the fallibility of human inquiries in every discipline and domain, another the fallibility of those who practice them, and the third level the fallibility of students aspiring to competence within those disciplines and domains. To understand a field of knowledge, as Paul and Elder (2001) suggest, "we must understand it realistically" (p. 296). To contribute to it productively, "we must view it as an imperfect construction". To think critically about received knowledge, beliefs, and values does not mean to devalue inherited knowledge, beliefs, and values, or to be sceptical. Rather, it involves enriching them as both individual and collective attainments.

Being aware of the principle of fallibilism helps to guard against blind transmission or indoctrination of community values, knowledge, and beliefs. This is the foundational rationale for building students' capacities and encouraging them to think critically and make their own judgements of whether to accept or reject claims of beliefs, values, and actions. When both teachers and students genuinely share the principle of fallibilism, in Passmore's (1967) words, "they must be alert to the possibility that the established norms themselves ought to be rejected, that the rules ought to be changed, the criteria used in judging performances modified. Or perhaps even that the mode of performance ought not to take place at all" (p. 420). This is what Passmore meant by *a critical spirit*. When the principle of

Swartz, A. M. (1987). Critical thinking attitudes and the transfer question. In M. Heiman & J. Slomianko (Eds.), *Thinking skills instruction: Concepts and techniques* (pp. 58–68). Washington, DC: National Education Association.

Tishman, S., Jay, E., & Perkins, D. N. (1993). Teaching thinking dispositions: From transmission to enculturation. *Theory Into Practice, 32*(3), 147–153.

Vygotsky, L. S. (1962). *Thought and language.* New York: Wiley.

Vygotsky, L. S. (1978). *Mind in society: The development of higher psychological processes.* (M. Cole, V. John-Steiner, S. Scribner, & E. Souberman, Eds.) Cambridge, MA: Harvard University Press.

Vygotsky, L. S. (1999). *Thought and language.* [Translation revised and edited by Alex Kozulin] Cambridge, MA: MIT Press.

AUTHOR NOTE

Irene Fung is a Senior Research Associate at the Open University of Hong Kong, Michael Townsend is Professor of Educational Psychology in the School of Education, Massey University at Auckland, New Zealand, and Judy Parr is Associate Professor in the Faculty of Education, University of Auckland, New Zealand.

This chapter is based on a PhD thesis submitted by the first author to the University of Auckland.

Correspondence concerning this chapter should be addressed by email to: ifung@ouhk.edu.hk

PART 2. RECOGNIZING DIVERSITY

In: Challenging Thinking about Teaching and Learning   ISBN: 978-1-60456-744-1
Editors: C. M. Rubie-Davies and C. Rawlinson   © 2008 Nova Science Publishers, Inc.

Chapter 9

THE ROLE OF EDUCATION IN ETHNIC IDENTITY DEVELOPMENT: THE HYBRID MAORI/PAKEHA EXPERIENCE

Melinda Webber

ABSTRACT

What does it mean to be a person of mixed Maori/Pakeha descent in contemporary New Zealand? In what ways are identities that reflect a dual heritage constructed, or not, through participation in school and university? The complexities involved in articulating an ethnic identity as a person of both Maori (indigenous New Zealander) and Pakeha (European) descent are discussed in this chapter. Issues relating to establishing a sense of belonging that ties a hybrid Maori/Pakeha person to both ethnic groups are examined. It is not only important that Maori, as an indigenous people, articulate and explore their own experiences and realities, but also significant that Maori/Pakeha, as members of both groups, have an opportunity to explore and control their own definitions beyond the constraints set by the dominant groups.

INTRODUCTION

Awareness of ethnic identity and ethnic difference often begin in early childhood (Morland & Hwang, 1981). It is known from social psychological research (Rogoff, 2003) that the development of ethnic identity is context dependent, especially in the early years. Children who attend ethnically diverse schools or reside in ethnically diverse communities are much more likely to become aware of ethnic identity at an earlier age than children in more homogeneous settings (Cross, 1991; Phinney, 1991; Tatum, 1992). Interacting with children from other racial and ethnic backgrounds, in a society that has historically treated ethnic identity as a means of distinguishing groups and individuals, often forces young people to develop ethnic identities early. However, before adolescence they are unlikely to understand the political and social significance associated with their ethnic affiliations. For young children, being a person with a different skin colour may be no more significant than being thin or heavy, tall or short.

In adolescence, the awareness of ethnic identity and its implications for individual identity become more salient. According to Erikson (1968), as children enter adolescence they become extremely conscious of their peers and seek out acceptance from their reference ethnic group. They become increasingly aware of themselves as social beings, and their perception of self tends to be highly dependent on acceptance and affirmation by others. For some adolescents, identification with and attachment to peer groups takes on so much importance that it can override other attachments to family, parents, and teachers (Noguera & Wing, 2006).

It is not uncommon in multicultural settings for pre-adolescent children to interact and form friendships easily across ethnic boundaries—if their parents or other adults allow them to do so (Troyna & Carrington, 1990). However, as young people enter adolescence, such transgressions of ethnic boundaries can become more problematic. As they become increasingly aware of the significance associated with group differences, they generally become more concerned with how their peers will react to their participation in particular cultural groups and they may begin to self-segregate. As they participate in educational institutions, young people also become more aware of the politics associated with ethnic identity, becoming more cognisant of ethnic hierarchies and prejudice, even if they cannot articulate what it means.

Cognisance of ethnicity is not something with which people are born, but is something that is mapped on to them from the first moments of life (with the listing of race on the birth certificate). Ethnic identity does not automatically follow from these early external racial assignments. An ethnic identity instead takes shape over time, through multiple interactions, including familial socialization, participation in ethnic-specific domains, and exposure to the media, school, and other ethnic groups. Schools, in particular, play an important role in both challenging and reproducing conceptions of ethnicity (Apple, 1995; Giroux, 1983).

SCHOOLS AS RACE-MAKING INSTITUTIONS

In schools, ethnicity cannot tell teachers about their students' innate proclivities to learn, to work hard, or to succeed. It cannot provide information about whether their parents care about schooling or believe in hard work. Nor can it provide an insight into the "cultural needs" of ethnic minority students. To say that a child's ethnicity can tell us these things insinuates that children from specific ethnic backgrounds are homogenous. So why does participation in education play such a significant role in ethnic identity development?

Racialization is the formation of understandings about race (Lewis, 2003). Racialization processes are exacerbated in the school context. These processes include how students are ethnically categorized; how boundaries between their ethnic groups are formed, negotiated, and interpreted; and how the processes of racialization and boundary forming affect children's interactions and opportunities. In this way, schools can be considered racially coded spaces (Lewis, 2003) and are significant in the production and reproduction of race, ethnic identities, and ethnic inequality. One's ethnic ascription has the power to shape life chances.

Schools are contexts where we "make each other racial" (Olsen, 1997). Not only are schools central places for forming ethnic identities, but they are key places where we rank, sort, order, and differently equip our children along ethnic lines, even if we hope for schooling to be the great societal equaliser. The way we talk, interact, and act in school both reflects and helps shape our understandings about ethnic hierarchy. This hierarchy in schools is exacerbated through the distribution of funding, through the differentiated expectations that teachers hold regarding the abilities of different ethnic groups, and through an "institutional choreography" (Fine, 1997) of everyday actions incessantly funneling opportunities to some students and not others.

For educators, it is important to understand the process through which young people come to see themselves as belonging to particular ethnic groups, because it has tremendous bearing on the so-called "achievement gap". In the New Zealand context, it has long been documented that school success is valued in Maori (indigenous) communities (Beaglehole & Beaglehole, 1946; Bishop & Glynn, 1999; Ihimaera, 1998). However, many Maori students continue to fare poorly in New Zealand classrooms, especially when compared to their non-Maori counterparts (Bishop, 2003).

There are different opinions about how and why a correlation between ethnicity and achievement exists (Bevan-Brown, 2003; Bishop, 2003; Bishop, Berryman, & Richardson, 2001; Bishop & Glynn, 1999; Fordham, 1996; Macfarlane, 2004; Ogbu, 1978, 2003). Research has revealed that mainstream teachers have lower expectations of Maori children, have failed to effectively identify or reflect on how their practice affects the educational experiences of Maori students, and have had limited support to address these specific issues (Alton-Lee, 2003; Rubie-Davies, Hattie, & Hamilton, 2006). To boost academic performance, many researchers have called for methods of teaching and instruction that build on culture-based values and corresponding behaviours. More particularly, some believe that academic outcomes among Maori students can improve when classroom instructional activities are changed to reflect the behaviours and orientations considered salient in out-of-school contexts (Alton-Lee, 2003; Bevan-Brown, 2003; Bishop & Glynn, 1999).

John Ogbu (Ogbu, 1978; 2003) and Signithia Fordham (1996) are international scholars who suggest other reasons for the underachievement of minority students. Both have argued that minority students from all socioeconomic backgrounds develop "oppositional identities" that lead them to view schooling as a form of forced assimilation to white cultural values. They subsequently come to equate academic success with "acting white". For minority students, such perceptions lead to the devaluation of academic pursuits and the adoption of self-defeating behaviours that inhibit possibilities for academic success.

Other international researchers in this area, Noguera and Wing (2006), challenge Ogbu and Fordham's "acting white" thesis. While carrying out research among high school students in Northern California, they discovered that while some high-achieving minority students are ostracized by their peers, others learn how to succeed in both worlds by adopting multiple identities. These individuals' challenge racial stereotypes and seek to redefine their ethnic identities by showing that it is possible to do well in school and be proud of who they are.

Claude Steele's work on the effects of racial stereotypes on academic performance can also help to provide a compelling explanation for the identity–achievement paradox (Steele, 1997). Through his research on student attitudes toward testing, Steele found that students are highly susceptible to prevailing stereotypes related to intellectual ability. According to Steele, when "stereotype threats" are operative, they lower the confidence of vulnerable students and negatively affect their performance on standardized tests. He also notes that the debilitating effects of stereotypes can extend beyond particular episodes of testing and can have an effect on a student's overall academic performance.

As much of the research illustrates, deeply embedded stereotypes that connect ethnic identity to academic ability have a significant effect on children's academic performance. Children, but especially children from ethnic minorities, become aware of these stereotypes as they grow up in the school context. Beyond these stereotypes, the sorting practices that go on in schools also send important messages to students about the meaning of ethnic categories. For example, in many New Zealand schools, students in the remedial classes are disproportionately Maori (Bevan-Brown, 2003; Macfarlane, 2004) and students often draw conclusions about the relationship between ethnic identity and academic ability based on these patterns. Nasir and Saxe's (2003) research has similarly shown that "too often, minority students believe that they must choose between a positive ethnic identity and a strong academic identity" (p. 13) in order to "succeed" in school.

THE HYBRID EXPERIENCE IN EDUCATION

Ethnic identification can be been considered a key factor in any individual's development. While many models of ethnic/racial identity development (Cross, 1978; Phinney, 1989) address the ethnic identity issues faced by all minority people, few have been able to adequately address the unique issues facing people of mixed descent (Herring, 1995; Poston, 1990). In response to the lack of a model of hybrid identity development, Poston (1990) presented the biracial development model. This model suggests that hybrid individuals develop through five stages: personal identity, choice of group categorization, enmeshment/denial, appreciation, and integration. Participation in the education system is considered a key site where this development is likely to occur, and in particular the "choice of group characterization" stage.

Stage one, personal identity, is characterized by one's identity being relatively inconsistent and dependent on self-esteem developed within the family. This is a critical developmental period for a child. Family members are instrumental in helping a hybrid child feel a sense of belonging and acceptance. The second stage, choice of group characterization, usually occurs at school and may be a time of crisis for a child. During this stage, the child is placed in a situation where he or she is compelled to select an ethnic identity, and thus must choose between parents. The third stage, enmeshment/denial, is characterized by confusion and guilt as a result of choosing an identity that may not be all-inclusive of one's dual ethnic heritage. This stage is characteristic of adolescence when group belonging becomes a central theme for all youth (Newman & Newman, 1999; Poston, 1990). The enmeshment/denial stage is even more difficult for biracial youth because they are struggling with dual-race membership. The fourth stage, appreciation, is a period during which the individual still identifies with one ethnic group but begins to broaden his or her understanding of multiple heritages. This is a time of exploration, resulting from the desire to know one's complete racial heritage. The final stage, integration, is characterized by the individual's ability to recognize and appreciate all of the ethnicities he or she possesses. At this point, the biracial individual feels complete and sees himself or herself as a contributing member of society.

Poston (1990) speculated that with the proper support, biracial individuals could develop a healthy ethnic identity and achieve a sense of wholeness in their lives. However, ethnic identity development is a complex process for some youth, especially as they enter adolescence. These adolescents may encounter conflicting values as they begin to ask "Who am I?" and "Where do I belong?" (Newman & Newman, 1999). These youth may experience guilt and confusion about developing an identity that may not embody all aspects of their heritage (Herring, 1992). They may also be confronted with a lack of social acceptance due to prejudicial and stereotypical attitudes (Newman & Newman, 1999). As a result, some hybrid youth can exhibit a variety of problems that have led researchers to label them "at risk" (Kerwin, Ponterotto, Jackson, & Harris, 1993). These at-risk behaviours include (a) poor academic achievement, (b) off-task behaviour, (c) poor social skills, (d) negative attitudes toward adults, (e) chip-on-the shoulder personas, (f) social isolation, and (g) aggressive behaviours toward peers (McRoy & Freeman, 1986). These behaviours may place the hybrid youth at risk of academic failure.

In contrast, children of mixed descent who are appropriately socialized and knowledgeable usually benefit from their dual heritage. Their families have an opportunity to provide them with a cultural education that is broader than that of mono-ethnic children, giving them both a larger knowledge base and a more informed sense of the world. They can have an enhanced sense of self and identity, and greater inter-group tolerance, language facility, appreciation of minority group cultures, and ties to single-heritage groups than do mono-ethnic people (Thornton, 1996). In addition, they often are able to identify multiple aspects of a situation (or both sides of a conflict) where other people see only one (Kerwin et al., 1993).

At the core of positive learning should be the student's sense of belonging. Belonging is about opening doors for students so that they can see themselves in the various communities within which they live and learn. Children need more flexible, situational, and fluid conceptions of ethnic identity taught in classrooms. From early on, children (particularly those of mixed descent) need to be cognizant of the concept of "third space" (Bhabha, 1994) with regard to self-identification. Bhabha's notion of third space is appropriate here because it opens up a conceptual space that exceeds the insider–outsider, "them and us" representations that currently exist. Dual ethnicity does not mean that individuals have to trace the two original moments from which they, the third, emerged. Rather, in this "third space", their uniqueness as hybrid individuals is dynamic and self-determined. Bhabha's concept of a "third space" is liberating because it introduces a new way of thinking about the hybrid experience. Discourse centred on a "third space", with regard to developing ethnic identities, could release hybrid individuals from a sense of un-belonging, dislocation, and alienation, and instead gives them a sense of partial participation and location within their cultures of origin. It could also provide a platform upon which the hybrid peoples can more comfortably straddle two different, and in the New Zealand context often opposing, cultures.

A NEW ZEALAND EXAMPLE—HYBRID MAORI/PAKEHA

What is to become of the hybrid Maori/Pakeha person who does not fit into one of New Zealand society's designated ethnic categories? This is the dilemma faced by people who are both a part of, and between, two distinct races. Despite the increase of mixed race populations in New Zealand (Kukutai, 2003), institutions collecting demographic information still fail to recognize their status as a separate racial category and continue to challenge them to choose one race. The subsequent labelling uses ambiguous terminology and thus the individual is forced to select "other" to denote the complexity of their heritage. This inability to "fit" into society's racial categorizations results in difficulty determining dual Maori/Pakeha status, roles, and positions relative to both racial groups (Brown, 1990). As Williams (1999) suggests, the social and psychological implications resulting from the lack of affirmation and validation for dual descent can make defining oneself racially especially difficult. Because of society's history of categorization, people of mixed race have been neglected, thus leaving them in a state of marginality because they are so often forced to choose only one racial identity when there is a need to recognize all aspects of their heritage (Rockquemore & Brunsma, 2002; Spickard & Burroughs, 1999; Tizard & Phoenix, 1993, 2002). With this in mind, we need to better acknowledge the existence of multiple realities of the human experience by giving voice to the stories and life experiences of people of mixed race.

A small qualitative study was conducted in 2004 investigating the key influences on identity development for hybrid Maori/Pakeha in New Zealand (Webber, 2007). Issues related to establishing a sense of belonging within both ethnic groups were examined based on the life narratives of six people of dual Maori/Pakeha descent. The study explored the overlap—genetic, cultural, and social—between the two ethnic groups and provided new insights into diversity within the Maori ethnic group: the challenges, issues, and benefits associated with being of mixed Maori/Pakeha descent in New Zealand.

The study revealed that the factors that had the most significant effect on the participants' ethnic identity development were their experiences with "exclusion" and "inclusion" within Maori and non-Maori contexts. A sentiment particularly pertinent in describing the participants' experiences was expressed by Johnston in Kitzenger (1989) when she stated, "Identity is what you say you are according to what they say you can be" (p. 82). This study was as much about how hybrid Maori/Pakeha constructed their own identities as it was about how their identities were shaped by the societal contexts in which they lived.

All the participants had experiences of exclusion and inclusion at one time or another while growing up and felt this was a potent force in their ethnic identity formation. Both exclusion and inclusion are experiences that are centred in power relations and often this meant that the participants felt ignored, trivialized, silenced, rendered invisible, and made "other", or, conversely, included with a true sense of belonging. These experiences often occurred within the participants' immediate communities and families, but were also imposed upon them by other people in their social contexts; for example in school and work contexts.

Experiences of exclusion and inclusion had a significant effect on the ethnic identity formation of all the participants. Being defined and redefined by others, both Maori and non-Maori, were important influences on their sense of belonging as ethnically Maori. Each participant highlighted in their stories the uncomfortable position of feeling powerless in the face of defining mechanisms that sought to "name" and "other" them. Despite factors beyond their control, such as stereotyping and external demands for authenticity (most significantly proficiency in Maori language and "typical" Maori phenotype), all of the participants identified as Maori. Their key for self-inclusion was whakapapa (ancestry) which they believe gave them a right to claim Maori identity. None of the participants talked in any detail about their Pakeha ancestry. All acknowledged it, but this acknowledgement was, overwhelmingly, the most significant reference to it. All of the participants preferred, as adults, to self-identify as indigenous Maori (Webber, 2007).

The critical identity development shift for the participants was coming to understand (as adults, mostly while at university) their right to define and conceptualize their own identity, thus constructing an ethnic identity that defined the whole, rather than parts of themselves. They learnt, as adults, to negotiate for themselves an identity that was situational, fluid, and comfortable. As Hall (1996) points out, like all things historical, ethnic identities constantly undergo transformation. Far from being eternally fixed, they are subject to a continuous "play" of history, culture, and power and at any one time are simply in a process of "positioning". Thus, the participants' experiences with conceptualizing and reconceptualizing, constructing and reconstructing, and articulating and rearticulating their hybrid identities give rise to a constant state of negotiation. Feelings of "in-between-ness" (Meredith, 2004), dislocation (Bhabha, 1994), and "edge-walking" (Krebs, 1999) were merely another stage, factor, or influence on their identity development; not an end point.

Although this study was small and had limitations, the findings help us to re-conceptualize how we view Maori, Pakeha, and hybrid Maori/Pakeha identities in New Zealand. As a starting point, it seems clear that the stereotypes regarding ethnic group membership need to be expanded to incorporate the individuality of those who have adapted positive identities to reflect their ethnic identities, experiences, characteristics, and social-cultural contexts. In being given further opportunities to construct and articulate their dual ethnicity, hybrid Maori/Pakeha may satisfy their own need for continuity, self-esteem, and distinctiveness. Hence, this study argued that attaining a positive dual Maori/Pakeha ethnic identity is an achievement which is poorly understood, under-recognized, and undervalued in New Zealand society. We need to discourage hybrid Maori/Pakeha seeing themselves as disaffiliated and inauthentic, and instead place more emphasis on encouraging them to construct and articulate unique ethnic identities that are vibrant, unique, and fluid.

CONCLUSION

For many years to come, ethnic identity will undoubtedly continue to be a significant source of demarcation within the population. For many people, it will continue to shape where they live, play, go to school, and socialize. People cannot simply wish away the existence of ethnic identity and the associated racism, but they can take steps to lessen the ways in which the categories trap and confine them.

Awareness of the key factors that affect ethnic identity development can caution educators to question their assumptions, to remember their cultural specificity, and to take care in thinking they know too much. The challenge for educators is to be particularly diligent about having high expectations for those students for whom education is one of the few channels to success. All students need access to educational experiences that affirm their cultural and ethnic identities. All students also need access to critical multicultural educational experiences that are honest and confront their assumptions about other ethnic groups. Not enough time is spent in schools helping students to construct positive ethnic identities. Not enough attention is paid to ethnicity as a social category that has a substantial impact on people's lives.

The challenge for educational institutions is to help students to develop more secure ethnic identities that are encompassing of all aspects of their heritage. Bhaba's (1994) notion of "third space" is helpful here because it suggests room for fluidity and change. A "third space" can open up a new category of cultural location where hybrid peoples can constantly negotiate and renegotiate their ethnic identity in relation to their unique historical circumstances.

REFERENCES

Alton-Lee, A. (2003). *Quality teaching for diverse students in schooling: Best evidence synthesis*. Wellington, New Zealand: Ministry of Education.

Apple, M. W. (1995). *Education and power* (2nd ed.). New York: Routledge.

Beaglehole, E., & Beaglehole, P. (1946). *Some modern Maoris*. Wellington, New Zealand: New Zealand Council for Educational Research.

Bevan-Brown, J. (2003). *The cultural self-review: Providing culturally effective, inclusive, education for Maori learners*. Wellington, New Zealand: New Zealand Council for Educational Research.

Bhabha, H. K. (1994). *The location of culture*. London: Routledge.

Bishop, R. (2003). *Te kotahitanga: The experiences of Year 9 and 10 Maori students in mainstream classrooms*. Wellington, New Zealand: Ministry of Education Research Division.

Bishop, R., Berryman, M., & Richardson, C. (2001). *Te toi huarewa: Effective teaching and learning strategies, and effective teaching materials for improving the reading and writing in te reo Maori of students aged five to nine in Maori-medium education: Final report to the Ministry of Education*. Wellington, New Zealand: Ministry of Education Research Division.

Bishop, R., & Glynn, T. (1999). *Culture counts: Changing power relations in education*. Palmerston North, New Zealand: Dunmore Press.

Brown, P. (1990). Biracial identity and social marginality. *Child and Adolescent Social Work, 7*(4), 319–337.

Cross, W. (1978). The Thomas and Cross "Models of psychological nigrescence: A literature review. *Journal of Black Psychology, 5*, 13–31.

Cross, W. (1991). *Shades of black: Diversity in African American identity*. Philadelphia: Temple University Press.

Erikson, E. H. (1968). *Identity, youth, and crisis* (1st. ed.). New York, W. W. Norton.

Fine, M. (1997). Witnessing whiteness. In M. Fine, L. Weis, L. C. Powell, & L. M. Wong (Eds.), *Off-white: Readings on race, power, and society* (pp. 57–65). New York: Routledge.

Fordham, S. (1996). *Blacked out: Dilemmas of race, identity, and success at Capital High*. Chicago: University of Chicago Press.

Giroux, H. (1983). *Critical theory and educational practice*. Waurn Ponds, Victoria, Australia: Deakin University (distributed by Deakin University Press).

Hall, S. (1996). Cultural identity and diaspora. In P. Mongia (Ed.), *Contemporary postcolonial theory* (pp. 110–121). London: Arnold.

Herring, R. (1992). Biracial children: An increasing concern for elementary and middle school counsellors. *Elementary School Guidance and Counselling, 27*(2), 123–130.

Herring, R. (1995). Developing biracial ethnic identity: A review of the increasing dilemma. *Journal of Multicultural Counselling and Development, 23*, 29–38.

Ihimaera, W. T. (1998). *Growing up Maori*. Auckland, New Zealand: Tandem Press.

Kerwin, C., Ponterotto, J. G., Jackson, B. L., & Harris, A. (1993). Racial identity in biracial children: A qualitative investigation. *Journal of Counselling Psychology, 40*(2), 221–231.

Kitzenger, C. (1989). Liberal humanism as an ideology of social control: The regulation of lesbian identities. In J. Shotter & K. J. Bergen (Eds.), *Texts of identity* (pp. 82–98). London: Sage Publications.

Krebs, P. M. (1999). *Gender, race, and the writing of empire public discourse and the Boer War*. Cambridge; New York: Cambridge University Press.

Kukutai, T. (2003). *The dynamics of ethnicity reporting: Maori in New Zealand: A discussion paper prepared for Te Puni Kokiri*. Wellington, New Zealand: Te Puni Kokiri.

Lewis, A. E. (2003). *Race in the schoolyard: Negotiating the color line in classrooms and communities*. New Brunswick, NJ: Rutgers University Press.

Macfarlane, A. H. (2004). *Kia hiwa ra: Listen to culture: Maori students' plea to educators*. Wellington, New Zealand: New Zealand Council for Educational Research.

McRoy, R., & Freeman, E. (1986). Identity issues among mixed race children. *Social Work in Education* (8), 164–174.

Meredith, P. (2004). *A half-caste on the half-caste in the cultural politics of New Zealand*. Unpublished doctoral thesis, University of Waikato, New Zealand.

Morland, J., & Hwang, C. (1981). Racial/ethnic identity of preschool children. *Journal of Cross-Cultural Psychology, 12*(4), 409–424.

Nasir, N., & Saxe, G. (2003). Ethnic and academic identities: A cultural practice perspective on emerging tensions and their management in the lives of minority students. *Educational Researcher, 32*(5), 14–18.

Newman, P., & Newman, B. (1999). What does it take to have a positive impact on minority students' college retention? *Adolescence, 34*(135), 483–492.

Noguera, P., & Wing, J. Y. (2006). *Unfinished business: Closing the racial achievement gap in our schools* (1st ed.). San Francisco: Jossey-Bass (Wiley imprint).

Ogbu, J. U. (1978). *Minority education and caste: The American system in cross-cultural perspective*. New York: Academic Press.

Ogbu, J. U. (2003). *Black American students in an affluent suburb: A study of academic disengagement*. Mahwah, NJ: Erlbaum.

Olsen, L. (1997). *Made in America: Immigrant students in our public schools*. New York: New Press.

Phinney, J. (1989). Stages of ethnic identity in minority group adolescents. *Journal of Early Adolescence, 9*, 34–49.

Phinney, J. (1991). Ethnic identity in adolescents and adults: Review of research. *Psychological Bulletin, 108*(3), 499–514.

Poston, W. (1990). The biracial identity development model: A needed addition. *Journal of Counselling and Development, 69*(2), 152–155.

Rockquemore, K., & Brunsma, D. L. (2002). *Beyond black: Biracial identity in America*. Thousand Oaks, CA: Sage Publications.

Rogoff, B. (2003). *The cultural nature of human development.* Oxford, UK: Oxford University Press.

Rubie-Davies, C., Hattie, J., & Hamilton, R. (2006). Expecting the best for students: Teacher expectations and academic outcomes. *British Journal of Educational Psychology, 76*(3), 429–444.

Spickard, P. R., & Burroughs, W. J. (1999). *We are a people: narrative and multiplicity in constructing ethnic identity.* Philadelphia: Temple University Press.

Steele, C. (1997, June). A threat in the air: How stereotypes shape the intellectual identities and performance of women and African Americans. *American Psychologist, 52,* 613–629.

Tatum, B. (1992). Talking about ethnic identity, learning about racism: The application of racial identity development theory in the classroom. *Harvard Educational Review, 62*(1), 1–24.

Thornton, M. C. (1996). Hidden agendas, identity theories, and multiracial people. In M. P. P. Root (Ed.), *The multicultural experience: Racial borders as the new frontier* (pp. 101–120). Thousand Oaks, CA: Sage.

Tizard, B., & Phoenix, A. (1993). *Black, white, or mixed race? Race and racism in the lives of young people of mixed parentage.* London: Routledge.

Tizard, B., & Phoenix, A. (2002). *Black, white or mixed race? Race and racism in the lives of young people of mixed parentage* (Rev. ed.). London: Routledge.

Troyna, B., & Carrington, B. (1990). *Education, racism and reform.* London: Routledge.

Webber, M. (2007). *Explorations of identity for people of mixed Maori/Pakeha descent.* Unpublished master's thesis, University of Auckland, New Zealand.

Williams, C. B. (1999). Claiming a biracial identity: Resisting social constructions of race and culture. *Journal of counselling and development, 77*(1), 32–35.

AUTHOR NOTE

Melinda Webber is a Lecturer in the Faculty of Education, University of Auckland, New Zealand. She is a Maori/Pakeha New Zealander of Te Arawa and Ngapuhi tribal descent.

Correspondence concerning this chapter should be addressed by email to: m.webber@auckland.ac.nz

In: Challenging Thinking about Teaching and Learning   ISBN: 978-1-60456-744-1
Editors: C. M. Rubie-Davies and C. Rawlinson   © 2008 Nova Science Publishers, Inc.

Chapter 10

KEY COMPETENCIES, GIFTED CHILDREN AND UNDERACHIEVEMENT—WHAT IS THE CONNECTION?

Gay Gallagher

ABSTRACT

Inclusion of key competencies in *The New Zealand Curriculum* (Ministry of Education, 2007) stimulated debate on what these competencies would mean for teachers and students. While some people cautioned against too rapid development towards the implementation of the key competencies into the new national curriculum without adequate consideration of what this would mean in practice, others welcomed the opportunity as a basis for reconsidering curriculum in schools. For underachieving gifted students, the competencies may well hold the key for unlocking their potential, and by assessing students' needs against the key competencies teachers may gain better insight into how to address those needs. However, there are inherent tensions between the competencies that may also contribute to underachievement. These tensions may create opportunities for possible misunderstanding in the assessment of gifted children and add to the complexity for teachers in assessing the needs of their gifted children. This chapter explores examples of such tensions. It illustrates how gifted children manage tensions between key competencies, and the difficulties and potential for misunderstanding that this can raise for teachers in their assessment of their gifted children.

INTRODUCTION

International debate on the key competencies and the "things that everyone should know and be able to do in order to lead a successful life in a well functioning society" (Baker & Mackay, 2006, p. 1) has been vigorous following the 2001 Organisation for Economic Co-operation and Development DeSeCo report (OECD, 2005). In New Zealand, the decision to include key competencies in the curriculum (Ministry of Education, 2007) continues to raise discussion on both the inclusion of a competency framework and the implications for assessment of such competencies. While Reid (2006) advises a gradual and systematic introduction and experimentation with ideas in practice, others are urging consideration of how teachers may assess such competencies as "if they are not assessed, we'll just ignore them" (Hipkins, 2006, p. 31).

In *The New Zealand Curriculum Framework* (1993), each of the curriculum documents was underpinned by *essential skills*. They were organized into eight skills areas: communication skills, numeracy skills, information skills, problem-solving skills, self-management and competitive skills, social and co-operative skills, physical skills, and work and study skills. Key competencies, however, are seen as more complex than just skills. "Capable people draw on and combine all the resources available to them: knowledge, skills, attitudes and values" (Ministry of Education, 2006, p. 11). Key competencies are seen as developing over time, and over contexts that are constantly becoming more complex. The new curriculum (Ministry of Education, 2007) recognizes five key competencies: managing self; relating to others; participating and contributing; thinking; and using language, symbols, and texts.

For underachieving gifted children, consideration and assessment of the key competencies may well be the key to unlocking their potential. Careful analysis of what is happening for these children, and their motivation and reactions, may throw light on their needs far more effectively than assessment of academic content would do. Many writers in gifted education highlight the reason for underachievement as being within the areas of self-management, and, for this reason, recommend supporting the child to be in control of his or her learning (Delisle & Galbraith, 2002; Sisk, 2001).

However, this may be more complex than simply assessing specific competencies. For many gifted children, the complexity is not within the individual competencies, but rather in managing the tensions between the competencies.

MANAGING THE TENSIONS—THREE EXAMPLES

In this chapter, three studies will be used to illustrate the difficulty gifted children may face. The first draws on a study of the personal experience of one gifted boy (Gallagher, 2004). The other two describe the experiences of two gifted children reported in a research project which investigated their transition to school from their early childhood contexts (Gallagher, 2005).

The first example describes the case of a gifted eight-year-old:

> Johan laboriously, but deliberately slowly, works on his Viking presentation due to be completed by midday. He is supposed to present the findings of his inquiry based study to his class after lunch, but it doesn't seem likely that it will be ready in time. When questioned about what is happening, his response explains it all. They [the other children] will not be interested in his study, and they are unlikely to understand. His perception could well be correct. They had been studying swords, longboats, and jewellery. His investigation was on Valhalla, and the beliefs that underpinned the burial practices for a chieftain whereby slaves, wives and the steed were buried along with prized possessions. What had possessed the Viking community to do that?! Johan was not prepared to expose his level of abstract thinking in the public presentation arena of his age peers. (Gallagher, 2004)

This gifted student was making choices, managing himself, making decisions about participation and contributing—all important parts of the key competencies (Ministry of Education, 2006). He was very aware of the effect of his study and ideas on the class, and how they might relate to him because of the complexity of his study. In making his choices, however, he may be viewed as underachieving and underfunctioning (Montgomery, 2002). He could be viewed as being belligerent, and deliberately sabotaging his time allocation. Delisle and Galbraith (2002) would classify Johan as a "selective consumer" (p. 167), in control of what is happening for him. He knows that he has found the answers to the questions he set himself at the outset of his study and is happy to discuss these with an audience that is interested at his level. He is prepared to take the alternative consequences of teacher disapproval and disappointment for non-completion of the presentation task and even peer rebuff.

For this student, the tension is between managing himself, at which he is very skilled, and being asked to relate to the children in the class at a level which he knows will create a further lack of connection on an intellectual level. He is acutely aware of his relationship with others and how his ability and interests distance him from the others. A teacher understanding this complexity may well organize a more appropriate audience with whom Johan can share his study, thus reducing the tension and allowing for his potential to be realized.

Johan's experience illustrates the tension between the two competencies of managing self and relating to others. If teachers were assessing the specific competencies, they would have very clear evidence of behaviours which showed whether Johan was managing himself competently, or relating to others effectively. However, this case study also highlights some of the difficulties as teachers attempt to "tiptoe around the issue of assessment" (Chamberlain, 2006, p. 52). So much will depend on the context, the interpretation of the teacher and his or her knowledge of what the gifted child is doing. This in turn is contingent on the child "disclosing" to the teacher what is happening. It would be very easy for the teacher in a busy classroom to misinterpret what is happening.

The second study illustrates a child's ability to manage himself but effectively avoid disclosure of his ability to the teachers:

> Six year old Tooty completes his maths worksheet, although it was well mismatched to his advanced mathematical ability, and "acts like it was normal" so he doesn't stand out from his peers. He is compliant and conforms. Tooty continues to make choices, as he has done since kindergarten years. Even at kindergarten, his teacher hadn't known of his advanced mathematical skills and computer proficiency. He had chosen not to demonstrate them to her—he didn't like her. She focused on his sporadic attendance patterns over which he had no control. (Gallagher, 2005)

As with Johan, Tooty's behaviour could be interpreted as underfunctioning, underachieving, and very much "selected consumerism" as he chose to dumb down in the presence of his peers. Such behaviour is not uncommon with many gifted students. They may exercise a strong locus of control, even if at times it manifests itself in conforming or rebelling behaviours (Heacox, 1991). However, Tooty's dilemma is also with the tension of the two areas of competency—managing himself and relating to others. Once again any assessment of the key competencies here could highlight his incompetence or recognize the conflict and choices he is making. Once again this is very dependent on the teacher and how the teacher interprets the behaviours, and on the teacher having a sound knowledge of the individual and having an understanding of the needs of gifted learners.

In the third example, Doughnut, the oldest and most advanced in the early childhood centre, is ready for the transition to school:

> She seeks out the company of the teachers in preference to interaction with the younger children. She is highly articulate and enjoys her discussions with the adults. However the teacher interprets this as dependence at a time when independence is expected, and dismisses the child to socialize with the other children. Doughnut chooses to seek solitude, but is reported as being aloof and isolated from her peers. Doughnut is frustrated with the lack of stimulation. At home she throws an enormous tantrum which leaves her mother wondering why. (Gallagher, 2005)

In making choices for herself, Doughnut was thwarted by teacher expectation and lack of opportunity. The teacher's interpretation shows Doughnut as lacking in areas of relating to others and in independence, even though her choices were strong indicators of competency in managing herself. Such an interpretation may illustrate the teacher's limited understanding of the child's need for new and stimulating learning or the need for like-minded peer interaction. Once again, this case study highlights the importance of teachers not only understanding the constructs of each of the key competencies in relation to gifted children but also the tension that is inherent for them in managing the competencies.

CONCLUSION

The concern is that, if these key competencies are to be assessed, any assessment would need to take into consideration the context and need sound knowledge of the individual child and their motivations for making their choices. If the context for the learning places restrictions on the children, then any assessment may not capture the actual level of competency of the child.

In Johan's case, with an inappropriate audience who could not appreciate the complexity and abstractness of his ideas, his chances of success were reduced. For Tooty, the teacher's lack of knowledge and understanding of his behaviours meant the teacher had little insight into the tensions Tooty experienced in making choices and managing the competencies. For Doughnut, teacher interpretation of her behaviours meant that any assessment had not considered the difficulties she was facing in an environment which lacked the stimulation she so desperately needed. As with Tooty, her choices were limited, and therefore her opportunities for displaying her competency were also restricted. The limitations on these children contributed to their perceived underachievement, and assessment of the individual key competencies may not necessarily identify the contributing factors.

Sensitive teachers, knowledgeable about the needs and selected actions of the children, might identify the complexity for the children in making their choices. By careful assessment that considers the context and the influences on gifted children's choices, teachers may be able to identify the complexities the children face in managing the key competencies. This could lead to support for the children in handling the tensions, and help to address areas of underachievement.

REFERENCES

Baker, R., & Mackay, T. (2006). Introduction. In *Key competencies: Repackaging the old or creating the new? Conference proceedings, 2006* (pp. 1–3). Wellington, New Zealand: NZCER Press.

Chamberlain, M. (2006). Address to conference. In *Key competencies: Repackaging the old or creating the new? Conference proceedings, 2006* (p. 52). Wellington, New Zealand: NZCER Press.

Delisle, J., & Galbraith, J. (2002). *When gifted kids don't have all the answers: How to meet their social and emotional needs.* Minneapolis, MN: Free Spirit.

Gallagher, G. (2004). *Differentiated programme for a gifted student.* Unpublished manuscript, Flinders University of South Australia, Adelaide, Australia.

Gallagher, G. (2005). *"They didn't stretch my brain". Challenged by chance: Factors influencing transition to school for gifted children.* Unpublished master's thesis, Flinders University of South Australia, Adelaide, Australia.

Heacox, D. (1991). *Up from underachievement.* Melbourne, Australia: Hawker Brownlow.

Hipkins, R. (2006). Key competencies: Challenges for implementation in a national curriculum. In *Key competencies: Repackaging the old or creating the new? Conference proceedings, 2006* (pp 35–49). Wellington, New Zealand: NZCER Press.

Ministry of Education. (1993). *The New Zealand Curriculum Framework: Te Anga Marautanga o Aotearoa.* Wellington, New Zealand: Learning Media.

Ministry of Education. (2006). *The New Zealand Curriculum: Draft for consultation.* Wellington, New Zealand: Learning Media.

Ministry of Education. (2007). *The New Zealand Curriculum for English medium teaching in years 1–13.* Wellington, New Zealand: Learning Media.

Montgomery. D. (2001). Introduction to Part 1. In D. Montgomery. (Ed.), *Able underachievers* (pp. 1–7). London: Whurr Publishers.

Organisation for Economic Co-operation and Development (OECD). (2005). *The definition and selection of key competencies. Executive Summary.* Retrieved 10 Nov, 2006 from http://www.oecd.org/dataoecd/47/61/35070367.pdf.

Reid, A. (2006). Key competencies: a new way forward or more of the same? *Curriculum Matters 2: 2006.* Wellington, New Zealand: NZCER.

Sisk, D. (2001).Overcoming underachievement of gifted and talented students. In D. Montgomery (Ed.), *Able underachievers* (pp. 127–149). London: Whurr Publishers.

AUTHOR NOTE

Gay Gallagher has had extensive teaching experience at primary school level, and for the last seven years has been a Lecturer in Teacher Education, in assessment and gifted education, in the Faculty of Education, University of Auckland, New Zealand. Her interest in gifted education resulted in her completing an MEd (Gifted Education) through Flinders University in South Australia in 2005.

Correspondence concerning this chapter should be addressed by email to: g.gallagher@auckland.ac.nz

In: Challenging Thinking about Teaching and Learning   ISBN: 978-1-60456-744-1
Editors: C. M. Rubie-Davies and C. Rawlinson   © 2008 Nova Science Publishers, Inc.

Chapter 11

INKING THE PEN: A REVIEW OF SIGNIFICANT INFLUENCES ON YOUNG GIFTED AND TALENTED WRITERS

Lynda Garrett

ABSTRACT

Maximizing individual potential as a gifted writer is recognized as a lifelong developmental process. How this process is individually experienced by young writers as they develop expertise during their primary and secondary school years, and into adulthood, would seem an important focus for researchers in the field. This chapter reviews the literature sourced to date, detailing those endogenous and exogenous influences regarded as of significance to young gifted and talented writers. Concern is expressed at the equivocal, tentative nature of much of the reported research evidence. A greater focus on prospective research is called for whereby young gifted and talented writers are given the opportunity to "voice" their personal beliefs in relation to their development as writers as they are developing expertise. Individual accounts of significant endogenous and exogenous influences on their development as writers at different stages in their development could add greater richness and authenticity to understandings of the talent development process.

INTRODUCTION

This chapter presents some of the significant early endogenous and exogenous influences on gifted writers' developing expertise as identified in the research literature, and includes suggestions on areas that would be fruitful for further research. Current research tends to focus on adult eminence in writing. References to the early influences on the talent development process of such writers involve their recalling personal childhood and adolescent experiences. In some instances, the relevance of such historical reporting in informing present understandings and practice could be questioned. It could be argued that some contemporary influences on young gifted writers and their writing might be quite different from those regarded as previously of significance, while other influences may have gained more, or less, significance. Social contexts for learning and development have changed significantly over time. It is therefore not unreasonable to expect that there might be a shift in both the nature and the extent of significant influences on young gifted writers and their writing.

There is little international research focused specifically on young gifted writers and their personal perspectives of significant influences on their early writing development. Individual writer "voices" are largely missing from research findings. Coleman and Cross (2000, p. 208) stated that they considered "the personal experience of being gifted and talented, especially through childhood, as a relatively unexplored area because the actual experience of the persons from the perspectives of those persons has been missing". A greater emphasis is needed on researching young gifted writers' personal experiences of the significant influences on their writing as they are developing expertise in primary and secondary school settings. Such evidence could then be used to enhance the self-understanding of other young gifted writers, as well as potentially increasing teacher and parent awareness of and responsiveness to the specific needs of this group of young people as they are developing writer expertise.

ENDOGENOUS INFLUENCES

Research findings presented a number of intrapersonal or endogenous influences regarded as being particularly significant to young gifted writers in their early writing experiences. Such influences included evidence of extensive early reading behaviours, including positive responses to being read to from an early age, and a love of and facility with words and language in general. Individual personality attributes, such as high levels of emotional intensity and sensitivity, vivid imaginations, dreams, and the ability to fantasize, as well as a preference for their own company, were also highlighted as significant and positive influences on early writing outputs. It would also seem that young gifted writers maintained a strong sense of personal writer self-efficacy.

Piirto (1999) claimed that children with creative writing talent were precocious and remarkable readers. A study of 160 contemporary American writers suggested that evidence of extensive early reading behaviours was a strong predicator of an early and intense interest in writing for both personal satisfaction and publication. It was further asserted that this intense early interest in reading usually continued into adolescence (Piirto, 1998). It would be interesting to see the extent to which this interest in reading does continue into adolescence, and the degree to which a facility for reading influences writing. There is surely potential for other media such as television, video, the internet, and listening to music to compete for the adolescent's interest and attention, and possibly influence their writing. Interestingly, other researchers cited the lack of an extensive research base and the variation among children as reasons for caution in placing such high significance on the influence of reading on writing ability. (Jackson, 2003; Olszewski-Kubilius & Whalen, 2000).

Adult writers' memories of their youth included a common reference to parents frequently reading to them (Piirto, 1999). This love of being read to was also associated with a particularly keen interest in words and awareness of language generally. Sousa (2006) elucidated further by describing students' "special interest in language features, such as rhyme, accent and intonation in spoken language, and the use of grammar in written texts" (p. 114). It would be reasonable to assume that different children would take an interest in such language features at different stages in their development, and to different degrees. Some variation might also be explained by varied degrees of interest and confidence in different genre; for example, expressive forms of writing such as poetry (Bloland, 2006).

Writing to satisfy emotional needs, rather than to achieve recognition and acclaim, emerged as a common theme in the lives of both adolescent and adult writers (Csiksentmihalyi, 1996; Piirto, 1999; Potter, McCormick, & Busching, 2001). Such needs included the drive to communicate personal thoughts and feelings to a wider audience. Their writing gave them a public "voice" without them having to articulate their thoughts and feelings "in person". Pattison (2003) provided a rare personal student perspective on the significance of publishing one's writing in a public forum: "It's all those words that can't mean anything until you have heard that someone else has heard them. It [the poem] hasn't really existed otherwise" (p. 27). Writers were also motivated to write as a means to gain greater self-understanding and awareness, facilitating a clear sense of self identity (Piirto, 1998). Their writing in this instance had a cathartic purpose, serving as a vital aid to positive personal development.

Potter et al. (2001) reported that an adolescent student "saw his writing as more than a text with a rafted message. He saw it as a presentation of self" (p. 49). Writing has the potential to become a public representation of private and often intensely personal aspects of an individual. Adolescents may experience a particular tension when writing for a public forum or school assessment. They could choose to suppress certain personal thoughts, feelings, or opinions to avoid the risk of exposure or critique. High personal efficacy beliefs could mitigate against this possibility.

Ward (1996) made reference to young gifted writers as loners. It was inferred that producing work of a consistently high standard demanded a solitary writing environment. Piirto (1998) also claimed that writers as children preferred their own company and actively sought solitude. Csiksentmihalyi (1996, p. 66) asserted that "Only those teens who can tolerate being alone are able to master the symbolic content of a domain". Olszewski-Kubilius and Whalen (2000) suggested that young gifted writers exhibited particular sensitivity to stressful home situations, withdrawing into a book or daydreaming. Such perspectives correlated with other explanations relating to gifted children generally which highlighted extraordinary sensitivity and tendencies towards emotional withdrawal into a fantasy world of their own creation (Delisle & Galbraith, 2002).

High levels of emotional intensity and sensitivity, vivid imaginations, and dreams were also highlighted as characteristic of young gifted writers, and as significant motivational forces for writing (Piirto, 1998). However, there is significant danger in generalizing across all gifted writers of all ages. Is it possible that adolescent gifted writers are more likely to seek solitude when writing than younger children? Are younger children more imaginative in their writing than adolescent writers? Do dreams feature more vividly in the lives and writing of young children rather than adolescents? These and other questions indicate potential areas for research into young gifted writers in their primary and secondary school years.

Young gifted writers, particularly adolescents, may have a clear sense of self-concept in relation to their writing ability. Bloland (2006) reported their tendency to write prolifically for their own purposes, including writing in diaries, journals and electronic media and writing song lyrics. Potter et al. (2001) concurred that while almost all of the adolescent writers in their study placed considerable significance on teacher assessments of their writing, as indicators of "school success and as important representations of themselves . . . most of them also retained a sense of themselves as writers that was independent of school definitions" (p. 48).

Writer self-efficacy appeared as a common characteristic of gifted adult writers as well and was regarded as being associated with volition, or the will to write (Piirto, 2002). The strong need to write could link with personal satisfaction gained from successful writing episodes. Such satisfaction could be applicable across all age groups and influenced by a genuine joy or passion for writing. As Jensen (2002) states, "the best writing springs from passion, love, hate, fear, hope" (p. 33). Passion could be heightened for certain individuals depending on their preferred style of writing. A young writer may love to write descriptive, imaginative narrative whereas an adolescent writer may present a passionate transactional argument.

EXOGENOUS INFLUENCES

Research reports highlighted a number of "outside" or environmental influences as being of significance to the development of young writers and their writing. Such influences included family, friends, schools, and teachers, while particular physical locations, artworks, and music could also evoke strong emotional responses in individual writers.

The family can affect the talent development process for young writers in different ways. Van Tassel-Baska (1996) noted that family members could be a source of emotional support and positive encouragement for young writers, acting as valuable mentors in developing their writing abilities. Gifted writers could also use writing as an outlet for traumatic childhood incidents such as the death or serious illness of a parent, or dealing with other unpleasant family experiences such as alcoholism in a parent (Piirto, 1992).

Another important environmental support structure for a writer's development is a group of friends willing to provide positive encouragement and constructive feedback. Piirto (1998) regarded such support as particularly valuable where the friends are writers in their own right. This reference clearly relates to adult gifted writers, with mention made of friends' support in getting writing published. It is feasible to assume that such a relationship could also benefit younger writers in terms of developing expertise in supportive peer relationships.

There is some degree of contradiction within the literature regarding the influence of school and teachers. A common theme emerging from eminent writers' lives was the positive role played by both male and female teachers in nurturing their writing talents (Piirto, 1999). However Piirto (1998) also reported that many young talented writers loathed school and the curricula offered within the classroom setting. This could be particularly significant in relation to the process of adolescent writers realizing their talent, especially in influencing individual motivation to continue writing.

Potter et al. (2001) report that students' "writing motivation was heavily influenced by the extent to which they perceived they were encouraged to write authentic personal texts whose messages were respected by caring teachers" (p. 45). A distinction was made by student writers between "real" writing and writing done as part of school programme requirements (Ward, 1996). Real writing involved author choice and flexibility in terms of writing genre, style, topic, and time allowed for writing. Such writing was usually completed at home. Writing within the school programme setting often involved little or no choice in relation to genre, style, topic, and time allowed. It was regarded as more of a means to an end; a way of meeting curriculum requirements and satisfying the teacher.

Other environmental factors also play a significant role in developing natural aptitudes. Mention is made of the significance of "place" in the writing of gifted female writers, who often chose familiar physical locations from their childhood as settings for their stories (Van Tassel-Baska, 1996). Piirto (2002) reported the powerful influence on writer motivation of natural and unfamiliar settings, including different travel locations as well as artworks and music.

CONCLUSION

Sternberg (2000) refers to giftedness as a continual process of developing expertise throughout an individual's lifespan, while Gagne (2000) highlights the particular importance of the process of talent development throughout childhood and adolescence. Individuals' writing development is likely to be affected by some similar intrapersonal and environmental influences, but possibly to varying degrees and at different points in time. It is also feasible to expect that different individuals could be significantly affected by different influences. Who better to portray the individual variations in experience, than young writers themselves, as they are developing their writing abilities? Research focused on accurate, sympathetic reporting of young writers' "voices", captured as they are developing personally and as writers, has the potential to enhance the understanding, skills, attitudes, and responsiveness of those most intimately involved with our young gifted writer population.

REFERENCES

Bloland, D. G. (2006).*Ready, willing and able: Teaching English to gifted, talented and exceptionally conscientious adolescents*. Portsmouth, UK: Heinemann.

Bloom, B. J. (1985). *Developing talent in young people*. New York: Ballantine.

Coleman, C., & Cross, T. L. (2000). Social–emotional development and the personal experience of giftedness. In K. A. Heller, F. J. Monks, & R. F. Subotnik (Eds.), *International handbook of giftedness and talent* (2nd ed., pp. 203–212). New York: Pergamon.

Csikszentmihalyi, M. (1996). *Creativity: Flow and the psychology of discovery and invention.* New York: HarperCollins.

Davis, G. A., & Rimm, S. B. (2004). *Education of the gifted and talented* (5th ed.). Boston: Pearson Inc.

Delisle, J., & Galbraith, J. (2002). When gifted kids don't have all the answers: How to meet their social and emotional needs. Minneapolis, MN: Free Spirit.

Gagne, F. (2000). Understanding the complex choreography of talent development through DMGT-based analysis. In K. A. Heller, F. J. Monks, & R. F. Subotnik (Eds.),

International handbook of giftedness and talent (2nd ed., pp. 67–79). New York: Pergamon.

Jackson, N.E. (2003) Young gifted children. In N. Colangelo & G. A. Davis, *Handbook of gifted education* (3rd ed., pp.470–482). Boston: Pearson.

Jensen, D. (2002, March/April). Passion, fire, hope 101: Everything I need to know I learned in creative writing class. In *The Utne Reader,* pp. 33–36. Minneapolis: Lens.

Moltzen, R. (2004). Characteristics of gifted children. In D. McAlpine & R. Moltzen (Eds.). *Gifted and talented: New Zealand perspectives* (2nd ed., pp 67–92). Palmerston North, New Zealand: Kanuka Grove.

Olszewski-Kubilius, P. & Whalen, S. P. (2000). The education and development of verbally talented students. In K. A. Heller, F. J. Monks, & R. F. Subotnik (Eds.), *International handbook of giftedness and talent* (2nd ed., pp. 397–411). New York: Pergamon.

Pattison, C. (2003, July 23). Dunedin pupil's creativity flows onto the page. *Otago Daily Times*, p. 27.

Piirto, J. (1998). *Understanding those who create* (2nd ed.). Scottsdale, Arizona: Gifted Psychology Press.

Piirto, J. (1999). *Talented children and adults: Their development and education* (2nd ed.). Upper Saddle River, NJ: Prentice-Hall.

Piirto, J. (2002). *My teeming brain: Understanding creative writers.* Cresskill, NJ: Hampton Press.

Potter, E. F., McCormick, C. B., & Busching, B. A. (2001, October/November). Academic and life goals: Insights from adolescent writers. *The High School Journal,* 45–55.

Sousa, D. A. (2006). *How the gifted brain learns.* Melbourne, Australia: Hawker Brownlow.

Sternberg, R. J. (2000). Giftedness as developing expertise. In K. A. Heller, F. J. Monks, & R. F. Subotnik (Eds.), *International handbook of giftedness and talent* (2nd ed., pp.55–65). New York: Pergamon.

Ward, R. (1996). Writing. In D. McAlpine & R. Moltzen (Eds.). *Gifted and talented: New Zealand perspectives* (pp. 273–280). Palmerston North, New Zealand: Dunmore Press.

AUTHOR NOTE

Lynda Garrett is a Senior Lecturer in primary teacher education programmes in the Faculty of Education, University of Auckland, New Zealand. Her special interests are in gifted education, inclusive education, and the effective differentiation of the content, process, product and learning environment within teaching and learning contexts, to ensure that individual learning needs are met.

Correspondence concerning this chapter should be addressed by email to: l.garrett@auckland.ac.nz

In: Challenging Thinking about Teaching and Learning
Editors: C. M. Rubie-Davies and C. Rawlinson

ISBN: 978-1-60456-744-1
© 2008 Nova Science Publishers, Inc.

Chapter 12

EDUCATIONAL DIFFICULTIES OF OLDER YOUTH IN THE UNITED STATES CHILD WELFARE SYSTEM

Susan P. Farruggia

ABSTRACT

It is widely recognized that youth in foster care are at risk for educational difficulties. However, the specific pathways to these difficulties remain unclear. Using a random sample of older United States youth in the child welfare system in Los Angeles County, California ($N = 188$), the current study examined various indicators of academic success and difficulties, as well as examining a hypothesized model incorporating potential risk factors for those difficulties. On the one hand, the youth in the sample had high rates of education problems (e.g., 35% had been suspended from school, 30% had experienced grade retention). On the other hand, 48% aspired to attend tertiary education or beyond. A cumulative, individual risk index was calculated by standardizing and summing risk factors for poor adjustment. This risk index was associated with a greater discrepancy between educational expectations and aspirations, as well as school instability. School instability was associated with school suspensions, grade retention, and being off-track for graduating from high school and, in turn, school-related problem behaviour. The study highlights the need to address care-related risk in order to help combat school-related risk for these vulnerable youth.

INTRODUCTION

In September 2003, more than 500,000 United States children were in foster care (Administration for Children and Families, 2004). Of those, 67,600 (or 13%) were 16 to 18 years old. Within Los Angeles County, California, as of June 2002, 36,285 youth were in substitute care, 8,268 of whom were aged 15 years and older. Generally speaking, older foster youth are less likely than younger foster youth to return home to their families of origin (Wertheimer, 2002). Typically at age 18, foster care youth leave the custody of child protective services and become responsible for themselves.

The transition to independence creates many difficult challenges, mainly because foster care youth often do not have the personal, social, and institutional resources needed to be successful. An abundance of research—albeit of varying quality—suggests that foster care youth who emancipate out of the system are at risk for poorer outcomes compared with their contemporaries who were not in foster care. For instance, researchers have found that young adults who were formerly in foster care are more likely to drop out of university (Pecora, et al., 2006), be depressed (Cook-Fong, 2000), be incarcerated or in trouble with the law (Benedict, Zuravin, Somerfield, & Brandt, 1996; Courtney, Pilavin, Grogan-Kaylor, & Nesmith, 2001; Festinger, 1983) and experience homelessness (Benedict et al, 1996), and are less likely to be employed (Blome, 1994). Further, 40% of emancipated youth rely upon public assistance to survive (Orangewood Children's Foundation, 2001).

EDUCATIONAL OUTCOMES OF FOSTER CARE YOUTH

Researchers have begun to examine educational outcomes for youth in the child welfare system; an important topic, given the difficulties that many emancipated youth experience during adulthood. Generally speaking, foster care youth have at least twice the academic problems compared with their peers not in care (Evans, 2001). More specifically, former foster youth also have lower levels of educational attainment than their peers. In Reilly's (2003) study of emancipated youth in Nevada, 50% of the sample left the child welfare system without completing high school. Similarly, Courtney et al. (2001) concluded that only 55% of their emancipated sample had completed high school at the 12- to 18-month follow-up and only 9% had entered tertiary education. McMillen and Tucker (1999) report even lower rates of high school completion upon leaving care, with only 33% having graduated from high school or earned their General Education Diploma (a high school equivalency examination).

Youth in the child welfare system also seem to have high levels of educational problems. For instance, Sawyer and Dubowitz (1994) found among their sample of 372 children and adolescents living in kinship care that 45% of the children and 63% of the adolescents had experienced at least one grade retention. (As schools in the United States do not universally use social promotion, some youth will not be promoted to the next grade if they fail to meet specified achievement standards). This sample had lower mathematics and reading scores, as well as lower cognitive and language skills, compared with their age mates not in care.

Further, youth in the child welfare system tend to have high levels of school-related problem behaviour. One such example is school suspensions. McMillen, Auslander, Elze, White, and Thompson (2003), in their study of 262 older youth in the child welfare system, found that 73% had been suspended at least once, with 16% having been expelled from school.

Despite all of these difficulties, youth in the child welfare system tend to have high academic aspirations. In McMillen et al.'s (2003) sample, which had high rates of suspensions and expulsions, 70% of the youth wanted to attend university. Courtney et al. (2001) found that participants in their study had relatively high educational aspirations before their emancipation from foster care; however, many had decreased their aspirations at the 12- to 18-month follow-up after leaving care. Although Courtney and colleagues do nor provide an explanation, it is possible that the young adults found the responsibility associated with their "freedom" to be more difficult than thought before their emancipation. Further, among a sample of current foster youth, high academic aspiration was associated with school performance, as measured by reading abilities (Shin, 2003), similar to findings among community youth (e.g., Schutz, 1997).

RISK FACTORS FOR EDUCATIONAL DIFFICULTIES

Researchers have begun to examine a broad range of risk for maladjustment among at-risk youth. Frequently, resiliency models are used as a theoretical framework for examining adjustment (Luthar & Zigler, 1991) with the inclusion of risk indices becoming more prominent. Two patterns of findings have emerged from this body of work. First, risk tends to cluster in individuals (e.g., Gutman, Sameroff, & Eccles, 2002). Second, and related, the effects of risk are cumulative, with an increase in risk leading, often exponentially, to an increase in poor adjustment (Rutter, 1979). An example of these processes is the Gutman et al. study of academic achievement of young adolescent African American students in the United States. They found a decrease in grades and achievement scores and an increase in absenteeism as risk increased.

Researchers have also examined risk factors for educational difficulties among youth in care. An association between child maltreatment and educational difficulties has become evident. Maltreated youth are more likely to drop out of or be expelled from school (Egeland, 1997; Erickson & Egeland, 2002). Further, children who are maltreated miss more school and perform lower on mathematics and reading achievement tests (Erickson & Egeland). In addition, maltreated youth tend to have high levels of behaviour problems at school (Browne & Finkelhor, 1986; Egeland).

Mental health problems among foster youth also appear to put them at risk for education difficulties. Social-emotional problems at the time of discharge from care are associated with lower educational achievement among adults who had previously been in care (Festinger, 1983). Further, in a study that surveyed caseworkers, one third of the randomly selected youth had a mental disorder (Leathers & Testa, 2006). Caseworkers felt that the youths' mental health problems, along with developmental disabilities and other special needs, put the youth at risk for requiring living assistance as adults.

Placement instability while in care has been found to be a risk factor for lowered educational attainment. For instance, Pecora et al. (2006) found that fewer placement changes was associated with increased likelihood of graduating from high school.

In a line of research on community youth, young people who experienced stressful life events were at risk for poor psychological functioning, including educational problems. For instance, greater numbers of stressful life events were associated with more serious school adjustment problems, fewer education competencies, and lower grades in school (Dubow, & Tisak, 1989; Sterling, Weissberg, Lotyczewski, & Boike, 1985).

THE CURRENT STUDY

The current study examines risk factors for educational difficulties among older youth in the child welfare system. Specifically, it examines how the risk factors associated with being in the child welfare system predict educational outcomes. It is hypothesized that the foster care youth will have high levels of educational difficulties, as indicated by school-related problem behaviour, suspensions, grade retention, being off-track for high school graduation, and a discrepancy between educational expectations and aspirations. In addition, it is hypothesized that foster youth's risk, composed of placement instability, total allegations of maltreatment, number of psychiatric hospitalizations, number of mental disorders, and stressful life events, will be associated with education difficulties. In order to examine the second hypothesis, the care-related risk factors will be combined so as to examine the cumulative effects of risk.

METHOD

Participants

Participants were 188 Los Angeles County youth who were in the protective custody of Los Angeles County Department of Children and Family Services (DCFS). Participants were 84 males and 104 females (45% and 55%, respectively) who resided in non-kin foster homes (59%), group homes (19%), kin foster homes (15%), and other types of placements (7%, e.g., juvenile justice facilities, independent living programmes). The ethnicity of the youth was similar to the ethnic composition of youth in the Los Angeles County child welfare system (40% African American, 36% Latino, 11% white, and 13% other, usually biracial). The foster care youth were at least 17 years old ($M = 17.8$ years, $SD = .78$) and had been in care for at least one year. At the time of administration of the questionnaire and interview, 93% were in school.

Procedures

Adolescents were selected to participate using random sampling from a list of all potential participants provided by DCFS. An individual, in-person interview at a quiet location such as a bookstore or coffee shop was scheduled with each participant. If the participant was in a secure facility, the interview took place there. Before the start of the survey and the administration of the interview, the participant, having been informed that the interviewer was a mandated reporter (that is, legally obligated to report allegations of child maltreatment), signed his or her consent. The Juvenile Court of Los Angeles County, the participants' legal guardian, approved petitions for access to the participants' information, thus providing guardian consent. Also, a Certificate of Confidentiality was secured from National Institute of Health, United States Department of Health and Human Services.

In addition, the research team obtained background information from DCFS case records, such as reason for initial placement, total number of placements, history of abuse, behavioural problems, and psychiatric referrals. Participants were compensated $35 for their involvement in the study.

Measures

Measures for this study are divided into two types: risk factors and educational variables.

Risk Factors

Risk factors included placement instability, total allegations of maltreatment, number of mental disorders, number of psychiatric hospitalizations, and stressful life events. *Placement instability* was calculated by dividing number of placements while in care by length of time in care; thus, the larger the number, the greater the risk. Placement types included shelters, temporary placements, and hospitals as well as the more traditional placements of foster homes, group homes, and independent living programmes which the participants had experienced since first removal from home. Length of time in care reflected the number of months that a participant had spent in an out-of-home placement. Number of placements and time in care were coded from DCFS case files.

Total allegations of maltreatment assessed the number of times physical, emotional, and sexual abuse and neglect allegedly occurred before the child was removed from the parents' home, as well as any alleged instances of abuse or neglect since placement in the foster care system. A total score was calculated for all abuse and neglect that was alleged. Total allegations of maltreatment were coded from DCFS case files.

Number of mental disorders was measured by adding the number of current (within the past two years) Axis I diagnoses. Axis I diagnoses reflect a clinical diagnosis of a mental disorder. The most common diagnoses were learning disorders, mood disorders, and adjustment disorders. If a participant had an Axis II diagnosis (e.g., mental retardation), it was not included. Number of mental disorders was coded from DCFS case files.

Number of psychiatric hospitalizations was the total number of psychiatric hospitalizations that a participant had ever experienced, including any hospitalizations that occurred before the participant was formally taken into care. Number of psychiatric hospitalizations was coded from DCFS case files.

Stressful life events were measured in the survey by a checklist of 22 events. Participants indicated if the particular event had ever happened to them. This checklist was similar to checklists used in other studies to assess exposure to potentially stressful life events in the lives of adolescents (e.g., Compas, 1987). A sample item from this checklist was "suffered a serious illness".

Educational Variables

Educational variables included educational discrepancy, number of high schools, school-related problem behaviour, off-track for high school graduation, grade retentions, and suspensions.

Educational discrepancy, calculated by subtracting educational expectations from educational aspirations, reflected the gap between what the participants aspire to do (educational aspirations) and what they think they will actually obtain (educational expectations). Educational aspirations of the participants were assessed by the question on the survey: "What is the highest level of education that you ideally would like to complete if it were up to you?" Educational expectations were measured by the question on the survey: "Realistically, what is the highest level of education you think you will finish?" The participants responded on a five-point scale to both questions: 0 = *less than high school*, 1 = *high school*, 2 = *two-year college or vocational school*, 3 = *four-year college*, and 4 = *graduate school (PhD, M.D., law degree etc.)*. (As a reminder, in the United States, colleges and universities are both tertiary institutions).

Number of high schools was coded from the participants' DCFS case files. It reflected the total number of high schools that they had attended over the four years of secondary schooling in the United States. A greater number of high schools reflects increased instability in the educational environment.

School-related problem behaviour was a two-item subscale from a 22-item misconduct scale (Greenberger, Chen, Beam, Whang, & Dong, 2000). Respondents indicated on the survey how often on a 4-point scale (1 = *Never*, 2 = *Once or twice*, 3 = *3–4 times*, and 4 = *More often*) they "cheated on tests or quizzes", and "ditched an entire day of school" (i.e., missed school without permission).

Off-track for high school graduation assessed whether or not the participants were making typical progress towards high school graduation. Participants were considered to be on-track if they had already graduated high school or would be graduating at the end of the year as might be expected. They were considered off-track if they had dropped out of school, or were one or more years behind in school. Off-track was coded as "1" and on-track was coded as "0". Off-track for high school graduation was assessed via the survey questions "Are you currently in school?", "Have you graduated from high school?", and "If not, will you graduate this year?"

Grade retention was coded from DCFS case files. It reflected whether or not (1 = *yes*, 0 = *no*) the participant had ever been held back a grade in school.

Suspensions were coded from DCFS case files. "Suspensions" was the total number of times a participant had been suspended from school, regardless of the reason.

RESULTS

Data Screening

All variables were screened for outliers (three standard deviations or more above or below the mean) and patterns of missing data. One variable—number of psychiatric hospitalizations—had outliers. Number of psychiatric hospitalizations was recoded to change all values over seven to seven (seven represented the whole number greater than the mean plus three standard deviations). No patterns of missing data emerged for study variables.

Preliminary Analysis

A risk index was created for individual risk factors using the statistical software programme SPSS. This approach was selected, as previously mentioned research (e.g.,

Gutman, Sameroff, & Eccles, 2002) suggested that risk tends to cluster in individuals and, therefore, risk should be combined to examine cumulative effects. Creation of the individual risk index involved standardizing the risk variables (placement instability, total allegations of maltreatment, number of psychiatric hospitalizations, number of mental disorders, and stressful life events) and calculating the sum of the standardized scores. Case file data were complete for all variables in this study for all participants; therefore, calculating a sum of the standardized scores was possible for all participants.

Descriptive Statistics of Key Variables

Individual Risk Factors

Descriptive statistics for all risk factors are shown in Table 12.1. The foster youth had an average of 6.45 placements while in care. In addition, only 10% of the participants had one placement while in care, whereas 19% had 10 or more placements. For time in care, the participants spent, on average, 116 months in care (just under 10 years), with 26% spending 15 years or more in care. In 2003, 50% of all United States youth in care had been in care for less than a year; only 9% of youth had been in care for more than five years (Administration for Children and Families, 2004).

With respect to number of psychiatric hospitalizations, the sample mean was .60, with more than 20% of the sample having had at least one psychiatric hospitalization. Further, more than 5% of the sample had five or more psychiatric hospitalizations. For number of mental disorders, the mean was 1.08; 61% of the participants had at least one mental disorder, with 29% having two or more disorders. With regard to numbers of child maltreatment allegations, the mean was 4.69 allegations. Only 1% of the sample had no allegations of maltreatment. Further, 10% of the participants had 10 or more allegations. For stressful life events, the mean was .36, meaning that approximately one third of the events had happened at some point in the average youth's life. The most frequent stressful life events were: broke up with a boyfriend/girlfriend (68%), had failing grades (58%), and loved one had a serious injury or accident (55%). Some of the most serious events were less common, but still frequent: sibling died (12%), mother died (16%), father died (17%), friend died (45%), witnessed a family member being seriously injured or killed (25%), and parent in trouble with the law (42%).

Educational Expectations, Aspirations, and Problems

Descriptive statistics for all educational variables are shown in Table 12.1.

Educational aspirations and expectations were examined first. The mean for educational aspirations was 2.59, which was above the midpoint, between vocational degree and four-year university; 58% of the sample aspired to attend a four-year university or beyond. The mean for educational expectations was 2.42, falling below the midpoint, between vocational degree and four-year university; 48% of the sample expected to attend a four-year university or beyond. In order to examine the difference between what the participants aspired to and what they thought they would actually achieve, a discrepancy score was calculated (educational aspirations minus educations expectations). As the mean discrepancy between aspirations and expectations was .18, a statistical analysis was required to determine if this difference was statistically significant, as this number was fairly modest. A paired samples t-test was conducted between educational aspirations and educational expectations which was statistically significant, t (186) = 2.33, p < .05. Foster care youth expected to achieve significantly less academically than they desired to. Regarding this analysis, it is important to note that 10% of the sample had higher expectations than aspirations. Young people in the United States are not allowed to leave school before the age of 18 years without permission from their legal guardian; it is the policy of DCFS that all youth remain in school until completion of high school at a minimum. Therefore, this discrepancy is artificially low, if one is interested in only those who would like to achieve more but feel that they cannot.

Table 12.1. Descriptive Statistics of Key Study Variables

Variable	M (SD)	Percentage
Risk factors		
Placement instability		
Number of placements	6.45 (5.60)	
Time in care (months)	116.16 (67.01)	
Psychiatric hospitalizations	.60 (1.46)	
Number of Axis I diagnoses	1.08 (1.13)	
Allegations of maltreatment	4.69 (3.98)	
Stressful life events	0.36 (0.24)	
Educational factors		
Educational discrepancy	.18 (1.03)	
Educational aspirations	2.59 (1.15)	
Educational expectations	2.42 (0.99)	
Number of high schools	2.51 (1.69)	
Problem behaviour at school	1.62 (.75)	
Number of suspensions	.89 (1.76)	
Grade retention		30%
Off-track for high school completion		35%

Next, number of high schools attended, school-related problem behaviour, grade retention, and number of school suspensions were examined. The average number of high schools attended by these youth was 2.5. Approximately one third (35%) of the sample attended only one high school, reflecting stability in their secondary education. However, 22% of the participants attended four or more high schools, which meant, on average, changing schools every year (as high school is typically four years). Many of the foster care youth experienced a great deal of instability in their secondary school experience.

Regarding school-related problem behaviours, two problems were included: cheated on an exam and ditched an entire day of school. The mean for the combined school-related problem behaviour was 1.62 with 1 = *never* and 2 = *once or twice*. At the item level, 44% had cheated at least once in the past six months, with 5% having cheated more than 5 times. On a related note, 63% had never ditched an entire day of school, while 10% had ditched five or more times in the six months. Similarly, for school suspensions, the mean was .89. Looking at frequencies, 65% had never been suspended from school, which means that 35% had been suspended at some point during high school; 10% of the sample had been suspended three or more times. Most of the participants had engaged in few, if any, school-related problem behaviours.

The final two, somewhat related educational variables were grade retention and being off-track for high school completion. About one third (30%) of the sample had been held back one or more times. Consistent with this, 35% of the sample had not graduated from high school and were not on-track to do so.

Associations among Individual Risk and Educational Variables

A model examining the associations among the study variables was developed. Using the framework of risk and resiliency, it was predicted that foster care-related risk factors (indicated by the risk index) would be associated with a discrepancy between educational aspirations and expectations and the number of high schools. Increased risk experienced by the youth would lead to a decrease in their expectations as their future prospects diminished and an increase in the numbers of schools they attended because of placement instability and the inability of the schools to manage behavioural and mental health problems. Further, it was predicted that educational discrepancy would be associated with more behavioural problems in school and school suspensions because of frustration by the youth. Likewise, it was predicted that number of high schools would be positively associated with grade retention, school suspensions, and being off-track for graduation which, in turn, would be associated with school-related problem behaviours.

Using AMOS 6.0 (Arbuckle, 2005), a model testing these associations among study variables was examined using maximum likelihood estimation.

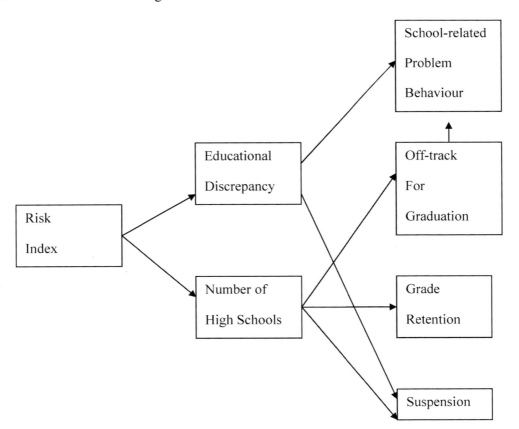

Figure 12.1. Hypothesized relations among risk and educational variables.

Figure 12.1 displays the hypothesized relations among the variables. Although the model had an adequate fit, χ^2 (12) = 16.48, p >.05, CFI = .93; RMSEA = .05, an examination of the various regression weights revealed that two pathways were not statistically significant: between educational discrepancy and school-related problem behaviour, and between educational discrepancy and school suspensions. A new model was tested with these pathways removed. This modified model fitted the data well, χ^2 (14) = 18.75, p >.05; CFI = .93; RMSEA = .04; in addition, all pathways were statistically significant. This final model, including standardized regression weights, is shown in Figure 12.2.

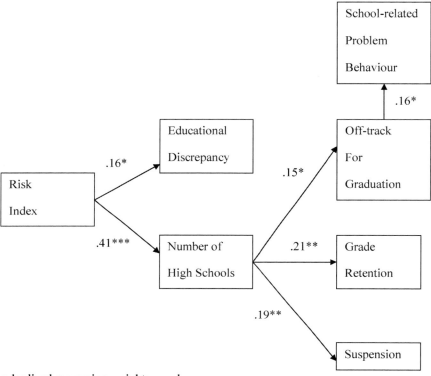

Note. Standardized regression weights are shown.
*p<.05, **p<.01, ***p<.001.

Figure 12.2. Modified associations among risk and educational variables.

Increased cumulative, individual risk, comprising care-related variables, was associated with a greater discrepancy between educational expectations and aspirations and with school instability, which was, in turn, associated with school suspensions, grade retention, and being off-track for graduating from high school, and, in turn, with school-related problem behaviour.

DISCUSSION

Using a random sample of ethnically diverse youth, this study presented risk factors for educational problems among older youth in the child welfare system in the United States. The results suggest that many youth experience high levels of risk, even higher than in other samples of foster youth. For instance, one third of the youth in the Leathers and Testa (2006) sample had a clinical diagnosis, whereas 61% of this sample had at least one diagnosis. This is an important contrast as the participants in both studies were of similar age and foster care status (just prior to emancipation) and randomly selected. Further, both studies used case file data to code this variable.

When examining school-related issues, an inconsistent picture emerges. On the one hand, the participants in this sample had high levels of educational problems, as seen by the high number with school suspensions, grade retentions, and school-related problem behaviour, and one third being off-track for high school graduation. On the other hand, with 65% being on-track for graduation, this sample appeared to be doing better in terms of high school graduation when compared to previous studies which had between 33% and 55% of their samples completing high school after leaving care (Courtney et al., 2001; McMillen & Tucker, 1999; Reilly, 2003). However, although the rates for this study's sample were higher, it is still worrisome that more than one third of the youth were off-track. Emancipating youth will likely have less of a safety net in terms of family support as compared to their peers, so in many ways, it is more crucial for them to have a high school diploma.

The youth in this study, as in previous studies (Courtney et al., 2001), had relatively high levels of academic aspirations. This study further explored this issue by examining the discrepancy between educational aspirations and expectations, finding a significant discrepancy. This discrepancy has important policy implications as the Education and Training Voucher Program of the United States Department of Health and Human Services provides financial support to young adults who have spent time in care to attend post-secondary education (Orphan Foundation of American, 2006). In the state of California, where this study took place, emancipated young adults can receive US$5,000 annually to help pay for educational expenses. Despite this programme and a desire to attend tertiary education, many youth do not expect to achieve their educational aspirations. While the discrepancy is somewhat low, it does include the 10% of the sample who would prefer less education than they expect to receive, which decreases the mean. On a related note, it is important to point out that 10% of the sample was earning more education despite themselves, so to speak. Being in care is likely to be preventing them from leaving school early.

To start to examine potential explanations for the educational difficulties that youth in the child welfare system experience, a model was developed incorporating both individual risk and educational variables. This study, unlike many previous studies, combined risk factors to examine cumulative risk. The final model demonstrated the cumulative effects of risk associated with being in the foster care system on youths' education. One pathway from individual risk was associated with a discrepancy between educational aspirations and education expectations—the greater the risk, the greater the discrepancy. Interestingly, this was a direct association without any educationally-related mediating factors. This discrepancy in beliefs about higher education can serve as an explanation for the lowered educational attainment found in other studies, such as Courtney et al. (2001). If the youth do not expect to achieve at a higher level, despite the fact that they aspire to do so, then they might disengage from school. Future research should examine if this discrepancy does, in fact, lead to lowered educational attainment.

In addition, there was a strong association between risk and high school instability, which was, in turn associated with a greater number of suspensions, grade retentions, a lack of appropriate progress towards high school graduation, and ultimately more school-related problem behaviour. School instability appeared to be the mechanism by which youth in the foster care system end up with greater levels of educational problems. This link demonstrated the importance of trying to maintain youth in their schools and minimizing the effects of being in care that can be addressed, such as placement instability. Future research needs to use longitudinal data to examine causality among these variables as this current study is limited in making such claims because the data is cross-sectional.

In Festinger's (1983) study of emancipated adults, 25% were dissatisfied with the quality and amount of education that they had received while in care. Consequently, more than half felt that an important task of care providers is to prepare foster youth for higher education after leaving care. It appears that, more than 20 years later, these issues remain; foster care youth continue to be educationally under-prepared. Both professionals in the child welfare system and young adults who have emancipated from care have felt that employment difficulties experienced by recently emancipated adults were often a result of poor educational and vocational services while in care (Freundlich & Avery, 2006). As a primary goal of emancipating youth is to be self-sufficient, it seems clear that their educational needs have to be better addressed.

Although this study was conducted in the United States, it has potentially broader implications. Studies on youth from other countries, such as Australia (Delfabbro, Barber, & Cooper, 2002) and France (Dumaret, Coppel-Batsch, & Couraud, 1997) also demonstrate that emancipating youth from those countries are at elevated risk for problems during adulthood. As education becomes more and more important for the successful inclusion in society for young people around the world, it is critical for all youth in care to have their educational needs met.

REFERENCES

Administration for Children and Families. (2004). *AFCARS Report.* Washington D.C.: United States Department of Health and Human Services. Retrieved on October 1, 2005 from www.acf.hhs.gov/programs/cb.

Arbuckle, J. L. (2005). *Amos 6.0 User's Guide.* Spring House, PA: Amos Development Corporation.

Benedict, M. I., Zuravin, S., Somerfield, M., & Brandt, D. (1996). The reported health and functioning of children maltreated while in family foster care. *Child Abuse and Neglect, 20,* 561–571.

Blome, W. W. (1994). What happens to foster youth: educational experiences of a random sample of foster care youth and a matched group of non-foster care youth. *Child and Adolescent Social Work Journal, 14,* 41–53.

Browne, A., & Finkelhor, D. (1986). Impact of child sexual abuse: A review of the research. *Psychological Bulletin, 99,* 66–77.

Compas, B. E. (1987). Coping with stress during childhood and adolescence. *Psychological Bulletin, 101,* 393–403.

Cook-Fong, S. K. (2000). The adult well-being of individuals reared in family foster care placements. *Child and Youth Care Forum, 29*, 7–25.

Courtney, M. E., Piliavin, I., Grogan-Kaylor, A., & Nesmith, A. (2001). Foster youth transitions to adulthood: A longitudinal view of youth leaving care. *Child Welfare Journal, 80*, 685–717.

Delfabbro, P. H., Barber, J. G., & Cooper, L. (2002). Children entering out-of-home care in South Australia: Baseline analyses for a 3-year longitudinal study. *Children and Youth Services Review, 24*, 7–32.

Dubow, E. F., & Tisak, J. (1989).The relation between stressful life events and adjustment in elementary school children: The role of social support and social problem-solving skills. *Child Development, 60*, 1412–1423.

Dumaret, A. E., Coppel-Batsch, M., & Couraud, S. (1997). Adult outcome of children reared for long-term periods in foster families. *Child Abuse and Neglect, 21*, 911–927.

Egeland, B. (1997). Mediators of the effects of child maltreatment on developmental adaptation in adolescence. In D. Cicchetti & S. L. Toth (Eds.), *Developmental perspective on trauma: Theory, research, and intervention* (pp. 403–434). Rochester, NY: University of Rochester Press.

Erickson, M., & Egeland, B. (1997). Child neglect. In J. Myers, L. Berliner, J. Briere, C. Hendrix, C. Jenny, & T. Reid (Eds.), *The APSAC handbook on child maltreatment* (2nd ed.) (pp. 3–29). Thousand Oaks, CA: Sage.

Evans, L. D. (2001). Interactional models of learning disabilities: Evidence from students entering foster care. *Psychology in Schools, 38*, 381–390.

Festinger, T. (1983). *No one ever asked us: A postscript to foster care.* New York: Columbia University Press.

Freundlich, M., & Avery, R. (2006). Transitioning from congregate care: Preparation and outcomes. *Journal of Child and Family Studies, 15*, 507–518.

Greenberger, E., Chen, C., Beam, M., Whang, S. M., & Dong, Q. (2000). The perceived social contexts of adolescents' misconduct: A comparative study of youths in three cultures. *Journal of Research on Adolescence, 10*, 365–388.

Gutman, L. M., Sameroff, A. J., & Eccles, J. S. (2002). The academic achievement of African-American students during early adolescence: An examination of multiple risk, promotive, and protective factors. *American Journal of Community Psychology, 30*, 367–400.

Leathers, S. J., & Testa, M. F. (2006). Foster youth emancipating from care: Caseworkers' reports on needs and services. *Child Welfare Journal, 85*, 463–498.

Luthar, S. S., & Zigler, E. (1991). Vulnerability and competence: A review of research on resilience in childhood. *American Journal of Orthopsychiatry, 61*, 6–22.

McMillen, J., & Tucker, J. (1999). The status of older adolescents at exit from out-of-home care. *Child Welfare Journal, 78*, 339–362.

McMillen, C., Auslander, W., Elze, D., White, T., & Thompson, R. (2003). Educational experiences and aspirations of older youth in Foster Care. *Child Welfare Journal, 82*, 475–495.

Orangewood Children's Foundation. (2001). *Fact Sheet.*

Orphan Foundation of American (2006). *State Voucher Program.* Retrieved on December 1, 2006 from www.statevoucher.org.

Pecora, P. J., Williams, J., Kessler, R. C., Hiripi, E., O'Brien, K., & Emerson, J. (2006). Assessing the educational achievements of adults who were formerly placed in family foster care. *Child and Family Social Work, 11,* 220–231.

Reilly, T. (2003). Transition from care: Status and outcomes of youth who age out of foster care. *Child Welfare Journal, 82,* 727–746.

Rutter, M. (1979). Psychosocial resilience and protective mechanisms. *American Journal of Orthopsychiatry, 57,* 316–331.

Sawyer, R. J., & Dubowitz, H. (1994). School performance of children in kinship care. *Child Abuse and Neglect, 18,* 587–597.

Schutz, P. A. L. (1997). Educational goals, strategies use and the academic performance of high school students. *The High School Journal, 80,* 193–201.

Shin, S. H. (2003). Building evidence to promote educational competence of youth in foster care. *Child Welfare Journal, 82,* 615–632.

Sterling, S., Weissberg, R. P., Lotyczewski, B. S., & Boike, M. (1985). Recent stressful life events and young children's school adjustment. *American Journal of Community Psychology, 13,* 87–98.

Wertheimer, R. (2002). Youth who "age out" of foster care: Troubled lives, troubling perspectives. *Child Trends Research Brief.* Washington, DC: Child Trends.

AUTHOR NOTE

Susan P. Farruggia is a Lecturer in the Faculty of Education, University of Auckland, New Zealand.

This study was supported with grants from the Transdisciplinary Tobacco Use Research Center at the University of California, Irvine; the Murray Research Center at Radcliffe Institute for Advanced Study, Harvard University; the Society for the Psychological Study of Social Issues; and the School of Social Ecology and Department of Psychology and Social Behavior at the University of California, Irvine.

The author wishes to acknowledge Drs Ellen Greenberger and Chuansheng Chen for their invaluable advice on this project, Gary Germo for his assistance with project management, and Mariam Azadian, Department of Children and Family Services, for her aid in navigating the child welfare and juvenile court systems.

Correspondence concerning the chapter should be addressed by email to: s.farruggia@auckland.ac.nz

In: Challenging Thinking about Teaching and Learning   ISBN: 978-1-60456-744-1
Editors: C. M. Rubie-Davies and C. Rawlinson   © 2008 Nova Science Publishers, Inc.

Chapter 13

COMPARISON OF FATHERS', MOTHERS', AND TEACHERS' REPORTS OF BEHAVIOUR PROBLEMS IN 4-YEAR-OLD BOYS

Louise J. Keown

ABSTRACT

This study examined the correspondence between paternal, maternal, and teacher ratings of child behaviour in a community sample of 4-year-old boys. Fathers, mothers, and teachers independently completed the Strengths and Difficulties Questionnaire (SDQ) on 475 boys identified from extensive screening of Auckland, New Zealand, preschools. Comparisons were also made between SDQ scores and interviewer ratings of hyperactivity and conduct problems based on the Parental Account of Children's Symptoms (PACS), for 62 boys. Both fathers and mothers rated their boys as experiencing significantly more hyperactive–inattentive and conduct problems but fewer peer difficulties than did their children's teachers. Fathers also reported significantly more hyperactive–inattentive problems for their sons than mothers did. Moderately strong relationships were found between PACS scores and SDQ hyperactivity and conduct problems scores on father, mother, and teacher questionnaires. Study findings also suggest that to identify children whose behavioural symptoms fall into the abnormal range, information should be obtained from fathers as well as mothers and teachers.

INTRODUCTION

While the important role of fathers in the development of their children's psychopathology is becoming increasingly apparent, fathers have been relatively neglected as informants in research on children's behaviour problems. In particular, few studies have compared reports by fathers, mothers, and teachers of behavioural difficulties in preschool children. Available findings are based mainly on small clinical samples, which have reported mixed results about relationships between fathers', mothers', and teachers' perceptions of child behaviour.

Therefore, a primary aim of the current study was to examine the correspondence between parent and teacher ratings of child behaviour in a large community sample of 4-year-old boys, using the Strengths and Difficulties Questionnaire (SDQ) (Goodman, 1997). These ratings were collected during the screening stage of a two-part study of fathering and mothering of preschool boys with hyperactivity (Keown, unpublished study). A unique aspect of the current study was that all boys were recruited from the same type of preschool with similar hours of attendance and programmes (including some structured time). This overcame a limitation in other preschool studies where useful teacher data on behaviours such as hyperactivity was difficult to obtain, either because some young children did not attend preschool or the variety of preschool settings and programmes made meaningful comparisons difficult. Furthermore, the current study provided the opportunity to examine narrow bands of behavioural difficulties (emotional symptoms, conduct problems, hyperactivity, peer difficulties) in a specific age group of preschool boys using the same instrument across raters.

The study also extends previous research by providing data on some psychometric properties of the SDQ (Goodman, 1997) in a New Zealand sample of 4-year-old boys. More specifically, the validity of the questionnaire as a screening measure for identifying preschool hyperactivity and conduct problems was examined by comparing questionnaire scores with a standardized semi-structured interview measure of child behaviour. There is limited data on the use of the SDQ to screen for behavioural difficulties in samples of preschool children and from countries outside of Europe.

METHOD

The sample consisted of 475 4-year-old boys who were predominantly New Zealand European. Other ethnic origins represented included Maori, Pacific Island, Asian, and non-New Zealand European. Approximately 66% of parents had a post-secondary school qualification. Mean family income was moderately high (equivalent to New Zealand$50,000–$70,000 a year). Participants were identified from extensive screening of Auckland preschools, located in a range of socioeconomic areas. Interview data were also collected from a subsample of these participants, consisting of 25 boys with pervasive hyperactivity and 37 comparison boys, identified on the basis of both mother *and* teacher ratings for hyperactivity on the SDQ.

MEASURES

The study involved the independent completion of the SDQ by each child's father, mother, and preschool teacher. Questionnaire forms were sent to families of all 4-year-old boys attending preschools who had agreed to take part in the study. Teachers were asked to complete questionnaires on boys whose parents had given their permission. The questionnaire consists of five subscales: Conduct Problems, Hyperactivity–inattention, Emotional Symptoms, Peer Problems, and Prosocial Behaviour. The first four subscales are also summed to generate a Total Difficulties score.

Interviewer ratings of hyperactivity and conduct problems were made using the Parental Account of Children's Symptoms (PACS) (Taylor, Schachar, Thorley, & Wieselberg, 1986), a standardized semi-structured interview measure of child behaviour at home. Interviews were conducted with the child's primary caregiver (usually the child's mother).

RESULTS

Mean scores for the SDQ subscales and the Total Difficulties scale were comparable to findings from studies in similar countries that include parent (Hawes & Dadds, 2004) or teacher (Goodman, 2001) SDQ ratings for boys in the 4 to 10-year age range. Both fathers and mothers rated their boys as experiencing significantly more hyperactive–inattentive and conduct problems but fewer peer difficulties than did their children's teachers. Fathers also reported significantly more hyperactive–inattentive problems for their sons than mothers did ($p < .05$).

The correspondence between parent and teacher ratings of child behaviour was examined by computing Pearson product–moment correlations between fathers', mothers', and teachers' scores on the Total Difficulties scale and the Emotional Symptoms, Conduct Problems, Hyperactivity–inattention, and Peer Problems subscales. All correlations were significant at the level of $p < .01$. Agreement was high between fathers and mothers (for total difficulties, $r = .65$; for emotional symptoms, $r = .59$; for conduct problems, $r = .64$; for hyperactivity–inattention, $r = .65$; for peer problems, $r = .54$). In contrast, agreement was low to moderate between parents and teachers. For both parents, the highest level of agreement with teachers was for hyperactivity–inattention (fathers, $r = .30$; mothers, $r = .33$), followed by conduct problems (fathers, $r = .26$; mothers, $r = .25$), then emotional symptoms (fathers, $r = .17$; mothers, $r = .16$). There was higher agreement between mothers and teachers than between fathers and teachers for total difficulties scores (mothers $r = .29$; fathers, $r = .22$) and peer problems (mothers, $r = .36$; fathers, $r = .23$).

Correspondence was also examined by calculating the percentage of boys whose scores fell into the abnormal band (according to SDQ guidelines) based on assessments by two separate raters. In general, more scores were classified in the abnormal band according to fathers' *and* mothers' ratings (ranging from 3.1% for emotional symptoms to 6.8% for hyperactivity symptoms) than for parent *and* teacher ratings (ranging from 0.5% for father/teacher emotional symptom ratings to 4.1% for mother/teacher peer problem ratings). While there were similar levels of agreement between father/teacher and mother/teacher pairs on the percentage of hyperactivity and conduct problem scores falling in the abnormal band, results indicate that it was not unnecessary duplication to get the information from both parents. For example, hyperactivity scores for a total of 18 boys were in the abnormal range according to ratings by either father/teacher pairs or mother/teacher pairs. However, for 11 of these boys, abnormal scores were based on ratings by one parent rather than both parents. For example, 5 were identified by father/teacher pairs only, 6 by mother/teacher pairs only, and 7 by all three raters.

Data from a subsample of boys ($n = 62$) show that interviewer ratings of hyperactivity based on the PACS were significantly correlated with SDQ hyperactivity scores as rated by fathers ($r = .61$, $p < .0001$), mothers ($r = .67$, $p < .0001$) and teachers ($r = .48$, $p < .001$).

Similarly, PACS conduct problems scores were significantly correlated with SDQ conduct problem scores as rated by fathers ($r = .40$, $p < .01$), mothers ($r = .55$, $p < .0001$), and teachers ($r = .42$, $p < .001$).

DISCUSSION

This study contributes new data on fathers as a source of information about behaviour problems in preschool boys and highlights the unique input and perspective of the father in assessing his child's behavioural and emotional well-being. In particular, the finding that fathers reported higher rates of hyperactive–inattentive problems for sons than mothers suggests the possibility of a lower tolerance by fathers of these behaviours in their sons. However, the finding that father/teacher ratings only (rather than mothers' ratings) detected some boys whose hyperactivity scores were in the abnormal range suggests that researchers and professionals should obtain information from fathers as well as mothers and teachers when seeking to identify children with behavioural difficulties for research purposes, and for possible early interventions. Further research might usefully examine possible reasons for disagreements between fathers' and mothers' ratings of child behaviour.

In a finding that is consistent with other studies comparing cross-informant judgements (Achenbach, McConaughy, & Howell, 1987), agreement about child behaviour problems was higher between raters in the same setting (mothers and fathers) than between raters in different settings (parents and teachers). It is likely that the finding of lower agreement across settings reflects different context demands placed on children and different expectations of children's behaviour, and that relationship patterns may differ across contexts.

The associations found between the SDQ and interviewer ratings of hyperactivity and conduct problems are consistent with those obtained by Keown and Woodward (2002) using a similar screening measure—the Preschool Behavior Questionnaire (Behar, 1977). The current results provide support for the validity of the SDQ as a screening measure for preschool hyperactivity and conduct problems.

CONCLUSION

In conclusion, the results of this study demonstrate how data obtained from fathers on behaviour problems in preschool boys can extend information gained from mothers' and teachers' reports. More generally, the findings support the call made by others of a need to increase the inclusion of fathers in research related to children's well-being (Greif & Greif, 2004).

REFERENCES

Achenbach, T. M., McConaughy, S. H., & Howell, C.T. (1987). Child/adolescent behavioral and emotional problems: Implications of cross-informant correlations for situational specificity. *Psychological Bulletin, 101,* 213–232.

Behar, L. B. (1977). The Preschool Behavior Questionnaire. *Journal of Abnormal Child Psychology, 5*, 265–275.

Goodman, R. (1997). The Strengths and Difficulties Questionnaire: A research note. *Journal of Child Psychology and Psychiatry, 35*, 581–566.

Goodman, R. (2001). Psychometric properties of the Strengths and Difficulties Questionnaire. *Journal of the American Academy of Child and Adolescent Psychiatry, 40*, 1337–1345.

Greif, J. L., & Greif, G. L. (2004). Including fathers in school psychology literature: A review of four school psychology journals. *Psychology in the Schools, 41*, 575–580.

Hawes, D. J., & Dadds, M. R. (2004). Australian data and psychometric properties of the Strengths and Difficulties Questionnaire. *Australian and New Zealand Journal of Psychiatry, 38*, 644–651.

Keown, L. J., & Woodward, L. J. (2002). Early parent–child relations and family functioning of preschool boys with pervasive hyperactivity. *Journal of Abnormal Child Psychology, 30*, 541–553.

Taylor, E., Schachar, R., Thorley, G., & Wieselberg, M. (1986). Conduct disorder and hyperactivity-I. Separation of hyperactivity and antisocial conduct in British child psychiatry patients. *British Journal of Psychiatry, 149*, 760–767.

AUTHOR NOTE

Louise Keown is a Senior Lecturer in the Faculty of Education, University of Auckland, New Zealand.

This research was funded by the University of Auckland, The Oakley Mental Health Foundation, and the Auckland Medical Research Foundation.

Correspondence concerning this chapter should be addressed by email to: l.keown@auckland.ac.nz

In: Challenging Thinking about Teaching and Learning ISBN: 978-1-60456-744-1
Editors: C. M. Rubie-Davies and C. Rawlinson © 2008 Nova Science Publishers, Inc.

Chapter 14

QUALITY INDICATORS FOR ALTERNATIVE EDUCATION PROGRAMMES

Avril J. Thesing and Patricia M. O'Brien

ABSTRACT

Alternative education programmes operate outside the mainstream secondary school system in New Zealand as a provision for students with behavioural problems and repeat expulsions. This chapter discusses the findings of a national study of alternative education commissioned by the New Zealand Ministry of Education. The study sought to identify what those who provided alternative education programmes considered to be the indicators of quality, effective programmes. Views on what constituted an effective programme were obtained from three focus groups. These views were then verified and rated by means of a telephone survey by a fourth group of people involved in alternative education provision. Commensurate with the international literature, results suggested that effectiveness in programmes is linked to the combined effort of students, families, and multidisciplinary staff. Criteria for quality programmes in both the focus groups and the survey included a focus on the individual student and having an empathetic environment. There was a strong belief that while alternative education programmes should be accountable and afford the very highest level of professionalism, they cannot be standardized as this would run counter to meeting the criterion of an individual student focus.

INTRODUCTION

Alternative education programmes operate outside the mainstream system in New Zealand secondary schools, under an alternative education policy in which the Ministry of Education provides funding for students aged 13½ to 15 years who have become alienated from the mainstream system (Ministry of Education, 2000). The criteria used for student selection are: being out of school for two terms or more; having had multiple exclusions; having a history of dropping out of mainstream schooling after being reintegrated; or having dropped out of the Correspondence School after enrolment as an at-risk student.

Under the alternative education policy, the Ministry of Education has delegated the management of alternative education programmes to secondary schools. The policy has sought to complement existing truancy provisions by funding a finite number of student places to secondary schools. Each secondary school administers a consortium of providers in its area; these providers are associated with interested community groups and have the appropriate facilities to respond to these students' needs by operating the daily programmes. The policy has resulted in the development of programmes with diverse curricula that are either conducted within the grounds of individual schools or in community locations situated away from the school (Millbank, 2000).

Alternative education programmes are not new. According to Friedrich (1997), they have been documented from the inception of public education in response to the failure of the public system to meet the needs of all students, something that is an ongoing worldwide concern. In New Zealand, in the absence of a separate specialized curriculum, the content of programmes is based on the same New Zealand curriculum that is mandatory in mainstream schools (McCall, 2003). This identifies alternative programmes as having similar goals to those of the mainstream. Civikly (1997) argued that it is not feasible to find an alternative to the mainstream curriculum in which failed students can achieve because the mainstream curriculum represents a comprehensive, traditional body of knowledge. The pedagogies involved have developed to their present status through a considerable history of research and reform and this accumulation is the heritage of all children. However, it is recognized that students are attending alternative programmes because they have many social issues that need addressing before they are able to reconnect with learning (Vaughn, Bos, & Shay Shumm, 2007). As a consequence, during this process of addressing social issues, the major emphasis is upon regaining confidence in basic subjects, particularly literacy and numeracy in applied situations. At the same time, students participate in a range of sport, recreational, cultural, and work-based activities. In addition to the educational focus of alternative programmes, students' other needs are taken care of through a multidisciplinary approach that has health, social, cultural, and judicial components. Consequently programmes are responsive to individual requirements and gradually build on consolidating an individual's strengths.

While students have the advantages of different types of support from many contributing agencies, their daily classes are conducted by two groups of educators—mainstream-trained teachers and untrained educators. The teachers provide trained support for the different programmes operating within their consortium area (with a predominant focus on English and mathematics). The untrained educators staff the daily classes, reinforcing good patterns of attendance, providing social and learning support to students, and liaising with students' families. Usually, the untrained educators do this on the basis of having had a similar background to the students, and through attending short courses made available through a variety of providers. These short courses deal with topics as such as conflict resolution, drug dependency, and adolescent and cultural issues (O'Brien, Thesing, & Herbert, 2001).

Rationale for Alternative Education Programmes

Education has been traditionally viewed by society as a way for young people to gain self-sufficiency and acquire the knowledge and skills needed to ensure a successful transition into adulthood (Oakland, 1992). However, for some youth, achieving these conventions is a particular challenge and this has been instrumental in the development of alternative programmes. According to Rendall and Stuart (2005), such students have long been the target of intervention programmes. This is in part because of the negative outcomes they and their families may otherwise face, but also because once youth has set off on a pathway of disaffection, their behaviour is hard to change. As a consequence, it may become lifelong, precipitating a raft of social ills such as early teenage pregnancy outside stable relationships, sexually transmitted diseases, substance abuse, crime, and unemployment. This affects society as a whole, particularly financially, through the costs of intervention and reparation (Charlton, Panting, & Willis, 2004). Also, when students are not reaching the achievement norms and social expectations of their peers in school, this frequently results in alienation from the school system (Friedrich, 1998). In setting up effective alternative education programmes for these at-risk students, educators have expectations that the students will eventually be able to access the same opportunities in life as their peers in mainstream education.

There is overwhelming evidence that the reason many excluded students are in alternative education programmes is because of disengagement from their mainstream studies through repetitive truancy (Civikly, 1997; Denny, Clark, & Watson, 2004; Freidrich, 1998; Millbank, 2000). Consequently, the students have irretrievable gaps in their learning. The cumulative effect of this upon their self-esteem engenders avoidance behaviour, and truancy is further exacerbated. This is as pervasive in New Zealand as elsewhere internationally (Freidrich, 1998; Charlton, Panting, & Willis, 2004), with 7% of young people having truanted more than 30 times by age 16 (Denny et al., 2004). Irrespective of their potential to achieve, the students' education has been stalled and barriers to learning have been erected; these barriers must be eliminated before any hoped for success in reconnecting them to education in more meaningful ways (Glasser, 1992).

The ideal outcome of a period of intensive individual support in alternative programmes, as perceived by the Ministry of Education, would be for these students to re-enter the mainstream (Ministry of Education, 2000), and one survey (Mitchell, 2003) found 37% of students were successfully re-integrated. However, Mitchell also recognized that this was never an option for some students with significant barriers to learning. For those students, positive outcomes could be developing regular attendance patterns and making progress within a limited range of achievement in literacy and numeracy, while remaining within alternative programmes (Mitchell, 2003).

Effective Alternative Programmes of Education

The literature emphasizes the importance of alternative education programmes being quality interventions—otherwise they have the potential to exacerbate matters for students who have already failed in a mainstream environment. This is particularly critical for students who may be programme participants for the remainder of their school career (Gregg, 1998; Levin, 1989; Mitchell, 2003; Quinn, Rutherford, & Osher, 1999). In seeking to establish appropriate characteristics for alternative programmes, while bearing in mind that the term "quality" as a construct is open to interpretation (Gronlund & Linn, 1985), there are universal understandings, as defined by empirical research, that can be applied. Crawford, Bodine, and Hoglund (1993) interpreted the evaluation of quality as related specifically to the learning context and always carrying with it the maxims of "doing the best" and "being the best" possible.

Alternative programmes are, by virtue of their diverse nature, difficult to assess, yet it is the very quality of individualization that defines excellence in a programme (National Centre for Vocational Education Research, 1999). It would be counterproductive to standardize programmes, and the multiplicity of provision indicates that there is no single best solution (Vaughn et al., 2007). Instead it would appear that quality in alternative programmes, rather than being able to be encapsulated in a standardized model, exists in finding ways to map and co-ordinate diverse approaches that are responsive to the individual needs of students (something that is easier to do where classes are so much more intimate and informal than exist in the mainstream). At the same time, in effective programmes, students and their families require continual monitoring and support by multidisciplinary networks of expertise. However, as in any educational initiative, the policies, programmes, and practices should be continually subjected to close ongoing scrutiny across the whole range stakeholders in order to ascertain that these infrastructures are still working effectively for individual students (Civikly, 1997).

While the diversity of alternative education programmes makes identification of quality indicators complex, the literature demonstrates a high degree of consensus (Bradley, 1992; Glasser, 1992; Friedrich, 1997). Key aspects are:

- individuality of programmes to address the needs of the particular students
- a redefining of learning that re-engages student motivation
- social support for students' problems
- a curriculum that closely follows that of the mainstream, but is authentic
- teachers with special attributes (e.g., ability to work with students with special learning needs or who have social problems)
- the support of a multidisciplinary team
- family involvement.

A feature of these markers of quality is that, with greater or lesser emphasis, they may be seen to closely mirror those in mainstream education (Gladden, 2002; Riordan, 2006). Therefore, it may be conjectured that, as the latter represents a failed environment for these students, reiterating it and expecting them to achieve is an insurmountable challenge. However, there is a strong emphasis throughout the literature that argues positive change may well be achieved through an *alternative delivery* (as opposed to an alternative curriculum) (Civikly, 1997; Glasser, 1992; McCall, 2003). Taking this standpoint, Civikly argued the major hallmark of quality in alternative programmes is the translation of learning outcomes required for all students from conventional mainstream curricula to the more informal, individualized alternative programmes, in creative ways that improve the match between the programme and the student. As a consequence, the student will still be exposed to the same crucial aspects of learning and be challenged and extended, even though he or she is engaged in a more authentic "real world" approach to learning than available through the traditional mode of learning.

Civikly emphasized the importance of not abandoning learning outcomes simply because previous conventional programmes did not meet student needs. This is because the reasons students are operating in alternative programmes will vary widely. Therefore, it should not be immediately assumed that a student's presence indicates an inability to meet the academic requirements of conventional school programmes. However, success in an alternative education programme initially may well be measured by such indicators as improved attendance and social assurance. Civikly cautioned, though, that these should not remain the ultimate goals. Students should eventually move on to academic and work-skills achievement to the same levels as their mainstream counterparts. At the same time, it is acknowledged in the literature that finding ways to impart the same mainstream body of knowledge in different more meaningful and stimulating ways is a considerable challenge (Civikly, 1997; Glasser, 1992; Riordan, 2006; Vaughn, 2004). Nevertheless, there was a general consensus that, however complex the task of curriculum innovation to meet the needs of failed students, there were basic components that promoted success (Civikly, 1997; Clark, Smith, & Pomare, 1996; Donmoyer & Kos, 1993, Quinn et al., 1999).

Effective alternative provision is primarily the responsibility of teachers (DuBeau, Emenheiser, & Stortz, 2003) pedagogically, in the way they set up the environment, and how they relate to the students and their families and access support (Gladden, 2002; Riordan, 2006). Initially, this means teachers must recognize and attempt to address their students' complex personal problems. Then, teachers need to reverse the results of students' negative learning experiences and nurture a sense of self-efficacy (that is, an embedded sense of self-worth and confidence in one's own ability) in the students so that they are able to re-apply themselves (McCall, 2003; Mitchell, 2003). In order to achieve these aims, teachers need to focus their approach on more innovative, flexible ways that engage individual students in real-life situations (Vaughn, 2004). As a consequence, students who are demotivated by knowledge when it is presented within mainstream, compartmentalized subjects will be more inclined to review its usefulness when it is related to the context of their personal lives (Glasser, 1992).

According to Mitchell (2003), the alternative pedagogies that teachers set up need to explore provision of more student friendly, small group home-like venues, where students have greater personal control over their learning on the basis of relaxed discussion and more individualized support. Also, the support of families is important for helping students to reconsider their educational goals, and this, in turn, requires supportive and effective home–school liaison. Community-based multi-disciplinary teams share the responsibility with teachers for establishing and maintaining partnerships with families. The composition of such teams ranges from untrained educators who provide support in the classroom, to members of social, cultural, judicial, and health agencies and local business people.

While innovative approaches may seem to be well within the range of professionally trained teachers, McCall (2003) draws attention to the challenge that presents. Firstly, there are more than average demands on teachers' personal resources, and it requires a particular quality of person to make alternative education their career. Also, a key factor in supporting students entails teachers being able to forge warm, empathetic, individual relationships with difficult students. According to McCall and to others (Vaughn et al., 2007), the quality of these social connections between students and teachers is a significant factor in the provision of the all-important focused individual attention that must accompany alternative education systems. At the same time, as mainstream-trained educators, teachers have to overcome their expectations of operating within that particular pedagogical paradigm. Consequently they must modify and adapt their attitudes and skills when they teach in alternative classrooms (Riordan, 2006). Riordan argues that while this needs to be supported by professional development, the absence of an alternative curriculum and lack of a research base for alternative education training are inhibiting. Likewise, teachers in alternative programmes must generally manage with fewer resources and lesser financial rewards for their efforts than their mainstream counterparts (McCall, 2003).

Because of the difficulties encountered in providing alternative programmes and the increased use of such programmes (Glasser, 1992; Lovey, 1989), the Ministry of Education commissioned research on the indicators of quality in alternative education. It was to this end that the current study contributed. The parameters were set by the Ministry of Education and focused on establishing a database of quality indicators of alternative education programmes. The study included a review of the international literature and a nationwide survey of people who were perceived as local experts because of their daily involvement with New Zealand alternative education programmes.

THE STUDY

The major question posed by the study was "What are quality indicators of effective alternative education programmes?" The study was conducted in two stages. The first stage involved three focus group interviews that provided information about perceived quality indicators. The focus groups were convened in separate areas of New Zealand selected by the Ministry of Education: a North Island city, a provincial town, and a South Island city. The second stage involved a telephone survey of a different group of people that sought their views on the indicators of quality identified by the focus groups.

Participants in both the focus groups and the telephone survey comprised a cross-section of the personnel involved in the various consortia that provided alternative education programmes attached to Ministry of Education-designated schools in the selected areas. They included school principals or programme co-ordinators, teachers, untrained educators, and social work, health, police, marae and local business representatives. Focus group participants were invited by way of a letter to the principal or programme co-ordinator to attend a focus group in their area. The telephone survey respondents were selected by the principals or programme co-ordinators who managed the consortia that were the original contacts for the project. Each consortium's management group suggested two providers from within its particular area. These providers were perceived by the management groups to be operating quality programmes and to willing to participate in the study. In all, 20 people made themselves available for the telephone survey.

Once agreement had been reached with the consortia representatives as to the time and place for the focus groups, and consent was formalized, three focus groups were convened. They each comprised between 10 and 20 individuals and lasted from one to two hours. The discussion in each group regarding the indicators of programme quality was taped. The discussion was developed through researcher prompts that were the result of insights generated from the initial review of literature. After the focus group discussions, the tapes were transcribed and analyzed to identify the most popular indicators of quality as perceived by the focus group participants. These were then developed into a schedule that formed the basis of the telephone survey.

Once the telephone survey participants were recruited, copies of the survey were mailed to them to help them with their responses when the researcher called them. In the survey, respondents were asked to review the quality indicator statements that had been identified from the focus group data. They were then required to verify and rate the importance of these according to their perceptions, as practitioners, of the meaning of quality in alternative education programmes. For this, respondents were required to use a five-point Likert scale: "very important", "important", "neutral", "little importance", and "not important". Respondents were told the indicator statements reflected quality in alternative education programmes as perceived by a sample of providers and they had the opportunity to signify their agreement or not, as well as rate importance. As well, the telephone survey respondents were invited, in an open-ended question, to comment generally upon their own experiences in alternative programmes. Telephone surveys took between 15 and 50 minutes to complete. Subsequently, the individual telephone responses were entered on to a spreadsheet and the means, standard deviations, and frequencies were calculated for each of the indicator sets.

RESULTS

Data from the three focus groups strongly reflected the international literature and local findings that individuality, diversity, and flexibility are key features of quality in alternative education programmes. At the same time, as also identified in the literature, while the *delivery* was alternative, the range of programme characteristics were those generally associated with constituting quality in any mainstream educational programme. Quality indicators, as perceived by those in the focus groups, were categorized into five specific areas of importance—environment, curricula, students, students' families, and programme providers (see Table 14.1).

The indicators that were perceived as signifying quality by the focus groups were then presented as statements to the telephone survey participants to rate according to their beliefs as practitioners. The results show the survey participants endorsed the same indicators of effectiveness for alternative programmes as those in the focus groups. These focused on the need for individualized support for students and their families to consolidate a commitment to the programme. They likewise acknowledged the significance of the multidisciplinary team in providing support for students and their families, and of having both teachers and untrained educators involved in their learning. They also believed traditional teacher training was inadequate for developing alternative education programmes. Teachers identified many gaps in their learning that, although not necessarily pertinent to mainstream education, were essential to providers of alternative programmes; they suggested additional specialized training was needed in the areas of developing more effective, less conventional deliveries; behaviour management; working with students who all have multiple problems; and co-ordinating expertise within multidisciplinary teams.

Although the telephone survey participants were given the opportunity to rate the indicators of effectiveness on a five-point scale, they assessed all the indicators as either "very important" or "important". There were no responses recorded in the "neutral", "of little importance" or "not important" categories. The open-ended question produced further insights into the indicator material already presented rather than providing new categories. In

Table 14.1, the second column shows all the indicators that defined quality within the five categories according to the focus group participants. As these were then presented to the telephone survey participants to rate, the bolded indicator statements represent those deemed "very important" on the five point Likert scale and the un-bolded statements were those deemed "important".

Table 14.1. Indicators of Quality in Alternative Education Programmes as Identified by Study Participants

Five categories of importance	Indicators that define quality within the five categories*
Environment	**Intimate, "unlike school", welcoming** **Student "owned"** **Clear boundaries set/adhered to** **Safety management procedures** Authentic settings: shops, businesses, maraes, farms
Curricula	**Individual student focus, small groups** **Address immediate hierarchy of needs** **Slow-paced activities** **Student choice within the programme** **Regular diagnostic assessment** **Equitable resources with mainstream** **Good transition to/from mainstream** Literacy and numeric focus Authentic learning, no packaged subjects Challenging, changing activities
Students	**Secure commitment/attendance** **Good self-esteem/social development** **Achievements/success valued**
Students' families	**Strong partners in programmes** **Involved in students' learning** **Reinforce programme at home** Use as opportunities for own education
Programme providers	**Empathetic with students** **Maintain strong links to team support** **Maintain strong links to families** **Trained beyond mainstream capacities** Ensure students have daily life essentials Team of teachers and educators Sensitive to individual adolescent needs Use authentic contexts for learning Gender mix of staff

* The indicators of quality are those identified by focus group participants and then presented to telephone survey respondents to rate on a five-point Likert scale. Items in bold represent indicators deemed by survey respondents as "very important" and those not in bold were deemed "important" Survey respondents did not use any of the other three options on the scale, which were "neutral", "little importance" and "not important".

DISCUSSION

This study provides an insight into what those involved in providing alternative education programmes see as indicators of quality programmes. As a group, the participants were all involved in providing alternative education in some way. They included the principals or co-ordinators of the schools managing the alternative programmes, teachers and educators in alternative classrooms, members of the multidisciplinary teams who provided support, and local business people who offered authentic learning experiences within the community.

In commissioning the study, the Ministry of Education sought to establish a database of quality indicators from a review of local and international literature, as well as from the practice-based insights of those involved in providing alternative programmes. The views expressed by the participants in the focus groups and telephone survey are similar to those identified in the research-based literature, which suggests that some confidence can be placed in the summary of perceived quality indicators set out in Table 14.1. At the same time, as also noted in the literature, it must be acknowledged that these indicators of quality are those associated with all effective educational programmes, rather than being confined to those that are alternative. There is the same emphasis in both upon addressing individual students' emotional, social, and educational needs, on diagnostic assessment of progress, and on developing partnerships with families and the provision of wider support in order to engender success (Civikly 1997; Friedrich, 1997; Riordan, 2006; Schulman, 1987). It should be noted, however, that while much is known about effective educational practices, these practices are not necessarily easily implemented in mainstream settings, let alone alternative ones (Gladden, 2002; Riordan, 2006). At the same time, the key to operating effective alternative programmes is focusing on the way in which the programmes can provide better access to some of the important components of success that are difficult to provide in the mainstream. In other words, developing an alternative delivery, as recommended by Civikly (1997), is the favoured approach. Knowing how to accomplish this means identifying how alternative programmes are different from those in the mainstream, in order to realize their potential for providing better support for disaffected students.

The major theme that underpins the quality indicators established in the study (Table 14.1) is the importance of an individual student focus. While this is also a goal in mainstream programmes, it is more difficult to achieve in mainstream education. Not only is there a much higher ratio of students to teachers, but the teachers are likely to be more remote from individual students because they teach subjects rather than being associated with one class. In this regard, the small-group intimacy of alternative classrooms has particular significance in delivering individual support for students who have special problems to negotiate (Glasser, 1992). The more informal approaches that are possible in small groups are better able to promote changed attitudes to learning by focusing on resolving students' present issues and helping them regain ownership of their studies. An important aspect of this is the potential for closer relationships between students and staff that engenders better insights into their problems as adolescents, thereby improving chances of resolution. In turn, the enhanced interest this generates in the students' particular problems has potential to forge closer bonds between the programme providers and families. When families are involved with the programme, many of the issues of attendance and basic needs of food and shelter of the students are addressed. This leads to a greater investment in the programme by both student and family that cannot help but be beneficial to the student's progress, something that was also found by Riordan (2006). This in turn can be instrumental in increasing the viability of the more intense professional support available through the multidisciplinary teams associated with the individual alternative programme. Riordan argues that the inclusion of families and community is the only way to bring about change and improved learning outcomes for students.

CONCLUSION

Quality indicators of alternative education are not difficult to identify, particularly as they so closely resemble mainstream objectives. The problem resides in implementing them effectively. It is evident that alternative programmes have the potential to provide for disaffected students by giving them authentic, "real life" learning that is able to focus more on the range of particular needs of the individual student than is possible in mainstream settings. The advantage of this is that families can also be engaged in the commitment, as well as enjoying the sustained support of multidisciplinary services. However, currently delivery is hampered by the paucity of qualified staff who want to make the difficult arena of alternative programmes their profession. As well, there is the need for those who are trained and who already work in alternative education to have access to appropriate staff development that will permit them to cope with the special challenges that alternative education represents. Nevertheless, any development of an alternative curriculum, either for students or for purposes of staff training, must take into account the need for an individual approach that focuses attention on mode of delivery and excludes standardization of practices. Further research needs to explore how this can be achieved in a way that does not run counter to the criteria laid down by quality indicators.

REFERENCES

Bradley, G. (1992). Increasing student retention. *Youth Studies Australia, 11*(2), 37–42.

Charlton, T., Panting, C., & Willis, H. (2004). Targeting exclusion, disaffection and truancy in secondary schools: An evaluation of an alternative curriculum for older pupils. *Emotional and Behavioral Difficulties, 9*(4), 261–275.

Civikly, J.M. (1997). *Instructor communication habits.* London : Jossey-Bass.

Clark, E., Smith, L., & Pomare, M. (1996). *Alternative education provision: A discussion paper.* Paper commissioned by Te Puni Kokiri. Wellington, New Zealand: Te Puni Kokiri.

Crawford, D. K., Bodine, R. J., & Hoglund, R. G. (1993). *The school for quality learning*: Champaign, IL: Research Press.

Denny, S., Clark, T., & Watson, P. (2004). The health of alternative education students compared to secondary school students: A New Zealand study. *The New Zealand Medical Journal, 117*(1205), 1–12.

Donmoyer, R., & Kos, R. (1993). *At risk students.* New York: State University of New York Press.

DuBeau, T., Emenheiser, D.E., & Stortz, B.A. (2003). Pathways of hope for students left behind: The saga of two students. *Reclaiming Children and Youth, 12*(2), 71–75.

Friedrich, K.R. (1997). *Alternative education for at risk youth. An analytical review of evaluation findings.* Unpublished doctoral dissertation. Texas University, College Station, Houston, TX.

Gladden, R.M. (2002). Reducing school violence: strengthening student programs and addressing the role of school organizations. In W. G. Secada (Ed.), *Review of research in education* (pp.263–99). Washington, DC: American Educational Research Association.

Glasser, W. (1992). *The quality school: Managing students without coercion.* New York: Harper Perennial.

Gregg, S. (1998, November-December). Creating effective alternatives for disruptive students. *The Clearing House,* 107–113.

Gronlund, N. E., & Linn, R.L. (1985). *Measurement and evaluation in teaching.* New York: MacMillan.

Levin P. (1989). Accelerant school: A new strategy for at risk students. *Bloomington Consortium on Education Policy Studies, Bulletin 6.* School of Education: Indiana University, IN.

Lovey, J. (1989). *Teaching troublesome adolescents.* London: David Fulton.

McCall, H.J. (2003). When successful alternative students disengage from regular schools. *Reclaiming Children and Youth, 12*(2), 113–117.

Millbank, G. (2000). *Students at risk, truancy, alternative education.* Wellington, New Zealand: Ministry of Education.

Ministry of Education. (2000). *Process evaluation of school-based alternative education.* Auckland, New Zealand: Ministry of Education.

Mitchell, K. (2003). Finding alternatives. *Tukutuku Korero, 82*(12), 4–6.

National Centre for Vocational Education Research (NCVER). (1999). *Early school Leavers.* Adelaide, Australia: Gillingham.

Oakland, T. (1992). School dropouts: Characteristics and prevention. *Applied and Preventative Psychology, 1,* 201–208.

O'Brien, P., Thesing, A., & Herbert, P. (2001). *Alternative Education: Literature review and report on key informants' experiences.* Report prepared for the Ministry of Education, Wellington, New Zealand: Auckland College of Education, Faculty of Postgraduate Studies and Research.

Quinn, M. M., Rutherford, R. B., & Osher, D. M. (1999). *Special education in alternative education programmes.* ERIC Digest E585. Reston, VA: ERIC Clearinghouse on disabilities and gifted education.

Rendall, S., & Stuart, M. (2005). *Excluded from school: Systemic practice for mental health and education professionals.* London, UK: Routledge.

Riordan, G. (2006). Reducing student suspension rates and engaging students in learning: Principal and teacher approaches that work. *Improving Schools, 9*(3), 239–250.

Schulman, L.S. (1987). Knowledge and teaching: Foundations of the new reform. *Harvard Educational Review, 57*(1), 1–21.

Vaughn, K. (2004). *Beyond the age of aquarius: Reframing alternative education.* Wellington, New Zealand: New Zealand Council for Educational Research.

Vaughn, S., Bos, C. S., & Shay Shumm, J. (2007). *Teaching students who are exceptional, diverse and at risk.* New York: Pearson.

AUTHOR NOTE

Avril J. Thesing is a Lecturer and Researcher in the Faculty of Education, University of Auckland, New Zealand. Avril has taught in several different sectors of education and has research interests in the early years of human development, prematurity and parent support, and special education and community integration for people with intellectual disability.

Patricia M. O'Brien is Director of the National Institute for the Study of Learning Difficulties, Trinity College, University of Dublin, Ireland. Patricia's research interests and publications are in the areas of: inclusive education, advocacy and community participation, and the interface between intellectual disability and the criminal justice system.

Correspondence concerning this chapter should be addressed by email to: a.thesing@auckland.ac.nz or obrienp3@tcd.ie

In: Challenging Thinking about Teaching and Learning   ISBN: 978-1-60456-744-1
Editors: C. M. Rubie-Davies and C. Rawlinson   © 2008 Nova Science Publishers, Inc.

Chapter 15

Turning Up the Volume: Young Adults Reflect on Their Secondary School Experience

Deborah Espiner and Diane Guild

ABSTRACT

The "voice" of students with disabilities typically goes unheard. Valuable insights to strengthen academic and social learning are missed when students are not consulted with or listened to. This chapter describes the use of graphic facilitation to capture the voice of a group of four young adults with special educational needs. Participation in a conference presentation enabled them to share personal ideas about their secondary school experiences with a group of special educators. The special educators who observed the process found that it was an effective way to hear and capture the student voice. It provided them with valuable insights and information for the ongoing development of the meaningful and supportive educational programmes in secondary schools. Listening to the voice of young people and involving them in the design of the educational experience will turn up the volume to ensure that the voice fashions the educational journey.

INTRODUCTION

This chapter focuses on a group of four young adults with special educational needs who volunteered to participate in a conference presentation in which they were asked to reflect on and share their thoughts about their secondary school experiences. The presentation was observed by a group of special educators.

There were three purposes to this presentation. The first was to provide a forum in which the young adults could share their ideas and feelings about their time at secondary school. This would include ways in which the secondary school experience could have been improved for them. The second purpose was to enable the observers to better understand the perspectives of the young adults, through the use of graphic facilitation to increase the observers' engagement with the ideas expressed by the young adults. The third purpose was to demonstrate a process that helped to elicit these ideas and feelings and enabled the observers to really hear what the young adults were saying.

LITERATURE REVIEW

New Zealand is striving to be a more inclusive society. This is the central purpose of the New Zealand Disability Strategy (Minister for Disability Issues, 2001), which provides a framework for increasing the awareness of and responding to the needs of disabled people. To develop a more inclusive society, the New Zealand Disability Strategy advocates recognition of disabled people as "experts on their own experience" (p. 14), which means ensuring that "disabled people are asked what they think" (Ministry of Health, 2001, p. 4). Inclusion will be achieved by eliminating barriers that disabled people may experience when participating in and contributing to society.

Since the 1989 New Zealand Education Act, there has been a focus on increasing the presence and participation of students with disabilities in their local schools. Education provision in New Zealand ranges from regular schools to settings that are highly specialized. The degree of inclusion depends on the climate, attitudes, knowledge, skills, and resources of the school community. The ability of the school to "tune into" and hear the student voice will influence students' presence and participation.

An inclusive school meets the needs of all students through equitable funding, policies, processes, and practices (Booth & Ainscow, 2002; Slee, 2001). Students also must take a full and active part in, and be valued members of, the school community (Fraser, 2005; Nakken & Pijl, 2002). A study in the United Kingdom (Department for Education and Skills, 2001) set out to determine how services delivered by government departments affected children and young people and how children and young people could be involved in developing more inclusive practices. The report reinforces the concept that when students take a role in the decision making at school, practices improve and school citizenship is promoted (Department for Education and Skills, 2001). This report advocates making the shift from assuming "we know best, towards putting those whose lives we affect in the driving seat" (p. 3). Objective 5 in the New Zealand Disability Strategy recognizes the "driving seat" by advocating leadership through a specific action to "encourage disabled people to take part in decision-making as service users . . . within all services that disabled people access" (Minister for Disability Issues, 2001, 5.1, p. 19).

Objective 3 in the New Zealand Disability Strategy lists actions that contribute to providing quality education for disabled people. This includes ensuring that all those involved in education and social services understand the learning needs of disabled people by acknowledging and acting on their ideas, thoughts, and feelings. This is also reflected in the National Administration Guidelines (Ministry of Education, 2007), which require schools to be responsive to and accountable for these needs.

Processes and strategies for involving students in decision making must be explored and developed. The voice of young people is often overlooked, not listened to, or not acted upon. The New Zealand Education Review Office (ERO) reported that the promotion of student participation in decision making is an area for further development:

The participation of students with special needs in school decision-making was predominantly limited to input at a classroom level, mainly into individual learning programmes. Schools need to ensure that students with special needs are provided with real opportunities, matched to student abilities, to participate in school decision-making. (ERO, 2003, pp. 13–14)

Creating opportunities for students to have input into decision making will influence what happens to and around them. The "absent voices of students with disabilities is of particular concern, since their right to be consulted and have a say in decisions affecting their lives is enshrined in current rights-based policy" (Bray & Gates, 2000 p. 58). Ways of sharing experiences and engaging with what is being said will lead to more responsive person-focused approaches to service provision. It is well documented that people have different processing and learning styles (Gardner, 1985; Armstrong, 1987). In order to engage students to the fullest extent, it is important to capitalize on the full range of learning styles rather than focusing primarily on the traditional verbal–linguistic ones.

To increase both engagement with content and interaction with participants, visual techniques are being promoted (Caldwell, Dake, Safly, & Ulch, 2000). Horn (1998) states that visual–verbal language enhances the quality of communication and that combining visual and verbal modes is more effective than words alone. Mayer (2001) supports adding visuals to words and the use of visual–verbal "stand-alone" diagrams. Tierney (2003) supports this, claiming that people retain 10% of information they read, 20% of information they hear, and 50% of information they see and hear.

According to Woolsey (1996), visual communication enables people to concentrate on ideas under discussion and build a framework of shared understanding and learning. People can more quickly integrate and act on information that has been recorded visually (Clegg, 2003; Horn, 1998). The use of visual techniques is also an effective way of disseminating large amounts of information and enabling more collaborative and effective dialogue (Horn, 1998).

Visual language is a growing area that illustrates the effectiveness of using graphics, text, and pictures (Horn, 1998). One process that assists the development of dialogue and understanding through visual–verbal channels is graphic facilitation (Sibbett, 1981). As the name suggests, graphic facilitation has two main components—facilitation and graphic recording. Ideally, two facilitators work with a group—a process facilitator who draws out ideas, issues and themes, and a graphic recorder who captures the ideas expressed by the individual or developed by the group. Ideas are recorded on a large chart in full view of everyone participating. The chart provides a canvas on which the visual dialogue develops. This enables specific details to be recorded while at the same time presenting the "big picture".

Kim and Mauborgne (2002) believe that building the process around a picture creates much better results than using the traditional written format. Furthermore, the chart provides a vehicle for thinking together and capturing and linking multiple perspectives. The resulting graphic contains large amounts of information that can be understood at a glance. Horn (1998) discusses the visual mapping of ideas through the creation of information landscapes (p. 95). He states this type of communication format lends itself well "to broad, systems-level overviews of complex situations or ideas" (p. 63). Furthermore, the use of a large chart enables specifics and details to be recorded and linkages between ideas made apparent as they "positively affect" how we communicate "big ideas." (p. 63).

In addition to stimulating new meaning and insight, the graphic also serves as a group memory for reflection and further development. Sibbett refers to graphic facilitation as "public listening". He claims that participants in a meeting immediately see ideas captured and reframed—making it possible for them to clarify their thoughts. Ownership of the dialogue is enhanced through the participants' identification with the graphics as they are recorded.

THE STUDY

The purpose of the conference presentation was threefold: to provide a context in which young adults (the participants) would feel comfortable expressing their ideas; to provide a context where professionals (the observers) could hear and reflect on the young adults' voices; and to demonstrate a process known to engage both speakers and listeners.

Methodology

The method therefore needed to do more than merely engage the participants in a conversation. The investigation was not designed purely to "survey the terrain" (McCracken, 1988, p. 17) or to conduct an overview, but to "mine it" (McCracken, 1988, p. 17)—to obtain a deeper understanding of individual perspectives and the relationships between them. It was hoped that the combined techniques of focused conversation (Clough & Nutbrown, 2003) and graphic facilitation (Sibbett,1981) would be useful tools for capturing the voices, experiences, stories, new expressions, and new learning in a shared dynamic of communication (Clough & Nutbrown, 2002) that provided both big picture and detail.

Elements of the focus group approach (Merton & Kendall, 1946) also supported the investigation in the way that it enabled a structured dialogue to develop around a chosen topic. It allowed participants "to prompt as well as to 'bounce' ideas off one another" (Waldegrave, 2003, p. 251) and produced "considerable and often complex information in a comparatively short space of time" (Alice, 2003, p. 64). The process encouraged participants to express ideas, values, and beliefs in their own language, highlighting their view of the world (Kitzinger, 1994). Morgan and Krueger (1993) write of the importance of this technique especially when there are power differences between participants and professionals.

The method reflected elements of a focused conversation in the way it elicited the voices of a smaller group of people, exploring how their collective experiences fitted together. The technique of the focused conversation has similar advantages to those of the focus group. Both techniques capitalize on synergism, snowballing, stimulation, security, and spontaneity (Hess, 1968). The key difference between the two techniques is that a focus group typically involves answering a set of questions whereas the focused conversation often raises, rather than answers, questions (Clough & Nutbrown, 2002). As the purpose of the presentation was to capture the voice of the young adults (who had recently left school), it was important that space and freedom be provided to enable the conversation to be directed by them.

Participants

To achieve the intended purpose of the presentation, it was important that the participants were young adults with disabilities who had left school in the last two to three years and who were previously unknown to the researchers. The time frame was relevant to the investigation in that it provided the balance of a distance from the schooling experience while maintaining a recent perspective. A group of four young adults with special educational needs participated to share personal ideas about their secondary school experiences with a group of special educators.

Procedure

In selecting participants, the researchers enlisted the assistance of a person who facilitates regular support meetings of young people with disabilities and their caregivers. The opportunity to participate in this conference presentation and research was discussed at one of the regular fortnightly meetings. Four young adults, two women and two men between the ages of 18 and 23 years, volunteered to participate. All had left school within the past two to three years.

On receiving names and contact details of the participants, the researchers contacted them and their parents. The presentation, the research project, and the practical details were discussed. Information sheets and consent forms were then mailed out to participants and their parents.

Before the presentation, there was an opportunity for the participants to reacquaint with one another and to meet the facilitators. There was also an opportunity to review the process and clarify uncertainties. It was considered vital that every effort be made to put the participants at ease. In a similar way, immediately after the presentation the young adults met with the facilitators for a debriefing on the experience.

For the presentation, participants sat in a semicircle side-on to the observers. This limited eye contact between participants and observers, provided maximum eye contact between participants and facilitators, and enabled everyone to view the evolving graphic.

At the outset of the session, the facilitators explained to the observers the structure of the presentation and the procedure that would be followed. An evaluation form was distributed to observers, who were invited to complete it at the conclusion of the presentation. The evaluation form required observers to reflect, rank, and comment on the process used to elicit participants' voices. The form consisted of four questions that required respondents to provide a ranking on a five-point scale and invited them to make additional comments if they wished.

The facilitators introduced themselves and then invited each participant to introduce him or herself. Three key questions and a number of prompts were used to guide the discussion. Each participant in turn contributed responses relating to what they considered was good about secondary school, what was helpful, and what would have made secondary school better.

A template had been pre-drawn providing the three key words (good, helpful, and better) to provide structure for the participants and to reinforce the direction of the discussion. This template was referred to as a "schoolscape" to convey the idea of developing a "landscape" of participants' ideas (see Figure 15.1).

Figure 15.1. Template of the Schoolscape.

The feelings and ideas of each participant were recorded in a different colour to enable observers to identify and track individual participants' contributions and to assist with analysis of content after the presentation.

Introductions were recorded in the school building in the centre of the graphic. This provided the focal point for all further dialogue. The graphic developed as each segment was introduced and each participant responded. Responses to the questions relating to what participants felt was "good" about secondary school and what they found "helpful" were recorded on the land of the schoolscape. This grounded the discussion and provided a foundation for the next segment, which focused on what would have made school better. These responses were recorded in the sky to represent new ways of doing things, dreams and the winds of change.

RESULTS

The following discussion is divided into three parts. The first part unpacks the schoolscape (illustrated in full in Figure 15.2) which highlights the voices of the young people—the participants. This covers the introduction to the participants (Figure 15.3), the discussion on what was good about school (Figure 15.4), the discussion of what was most helpful for the young people while they were at school (Figure 15.5), and discussion of what could have been better (Figure 15.6). The second part presents the findings collated from the evaluation forms that observers completed at the conclusion of the presentation. The third part presents comments made by the young people in the debriefing session that followed the presentation.

Figure 15.2. The Completed Schoolscape.

The Voices of the Participants

Introductions

The participants were invited to introduce themselves. They were asked to indicate the time lapse since they left secondary school and to talk about their interests, as recorded below (see also Figure 15.3):

Phillip was 21 when he left school two years ago. His ambition is to become a DJ in a night club. This ambition he attributes to his passion for music and self-confidence he feels he gained through participating in speech competitions at school. Phillip is currently training in wrestling and weight lifting.

Taylor is 18—he left school two years ago. Taylor is very interested and informed about trains. He knows the distinguishing features and functions of a variety of trains. He works at Glenbrook Vintage Railway three days a week. Taylor has his Learner's (driving) Licence and is currently working towards his Restricted Licence. He also has an interest in music having auditioned for and competed in New Zealand Idol.

Bronwyn left school three years ago—she is now 22. She is attending a technical institute, has a part-time job at Burger King and is training to be a Youthline phone counsellor. In addition to her interest in counselling, Bronwyn has an ambition to be a spokesperson and advocate for people with disabilities. She is aware of a range of disabilities and is very informed about her own specific disability. Bronwyn is concerned about the implications of having a disability in today's society.

Laura is now 23, having left school two years ago. Laura's interests are in the field of nurturing. She is currently working in a day care centre two days a week. With family support, Laura is developing a boutique business raising plants from seedlings. She is currently restoring glasshouses to plant in readiness for the Christmas market. Laura also enjoys working and being with animals.

Figure 15.3. Introductions.

Each of the four participants was well connected to the community through work and interest pursuits. They had a number of interests and were very clear about their ambitions for ongoing personal development. This provided a basis and an impetus to discuss and reflect on their secondary schooling. It is interesting that although some of these participants had been supported by a special unit, they had all attended a regular secondary school. This may be a contributing factor for their post-school success, as regular school involvement enhances transition into adulthood and promotes wider community involvement and develops career skills (Sax, Noyes, & Fisher, 2001; Carubba, 1998; DiGiacomo, 2002, as cited in MacArthur, Kelly, and Higgins, 2005). Making the transition to adult life and connecting with the wider community is often seen as the "litmus test" of the quality of the school experience (MacArthur, Kelly, & Higgins, 2005, p. 57).

What Was Good about School?

There were five or six common factors identified by each of the participants as being the key to their enjoyment of secondary school (see Figure 15.4). They were all related to the importance of belonging—the sense of community that the participants experienced through social contacts and being linked to the wider school. All the participants had enjoyed opportunities to participate in a range of school-wide activities. These included social events, school camps, speech competitions, and sports events. Having opportunities to discover and develop new skills also featured as important.

The development of relationships appeared to be the most highly valued factor that contributed to participants' enjoyment. They all expressed an appreciation of teachers remembering them and taking an interest in their well-being and academic progress. The importance of relationships in an educational context is well documented in the literature and recognized as being a key factor in the development of social competence and self esteem (Meyer & Bevan-Brown, 2005). Over the past decade, a number of New Zealand research programmes (Alton-Lee, 2003; Hill & Hawke, 2001; Bishop, Berryman, Richardson, & Tiakiwai, 2003; Ministry of Education, 2004) have further demonstrated the importance of relationships in a variety of educational settings.

The following summaries, to be read in conjunction with Figure 15.4, capture the participants' views on what was good about school:

Phillip's secondary schooling was supported through his placement in a unit for students with learning disabilities. This gave him the support he needed in order to participate in school speech competitions. Phillip particularly enjoyed the opportunities to develop friendships in this setting. He appreciated when people noticed, "cared and remembered" him.

Laura enjoyed academic subjects. She mentioned spelling and maths as being particularly enjoyable. Secondary schooling provided her with opportunities to participate in a range of sporting activities. Laura especially enjoyed playing tennis and cricket.

Bronwyn enjoyed being part of the school community. She enjoyed "walking around the school [and being among] happy people". Bronwyn commented that even when she was not directly involved with a group she still felt she belonged. Bronwyn enjoyed interacting with teachers and the interest they showed in her. Science was Bronwyn's favourite subject, particularly the work she did on volcanoes.

Taylor enjoyed his fourth form year the best. He felt that by this time he had learned to find his way around the school and how to interact in the secondary setting. His fourth form recollections included going to school camp and participating in sports. Taylor enjoyed the socials and felt they had provided great opportunities for his musical expression. He appreciated the time teachers took to get to know him and his interests. He felt that they were patient and created opportunities for him to experience a range of activities and develop his strengths.

What Was Most Helpful While at School?

The second question, "What was most helpful while at school?", explored what had been helpful in assisting the participants at secondary school (see Figure 15.5). It was explained to participants that, at the time, they may not have enjoyed or appreciated these aspects but on reflection they realized these had been helpful in their ongoing development. The following summarizes the participants' views.

Bronwyn found the counselling services at school helpful. She also found the kindness of teachers and classmates helpful especially when she felt unwell or had lost some of her gear.

Figure 15.4. What Was Good about School?

Taylor remembered it had been helpful to have support with developing study skills. Being in the unit provided him with support to complete work he was studying in mainstream classes. He found the opportunities to develop practical skills like cooking particularly helpful.

Phillip talked about the importance and value of teachers keeping a "big picture—seeing me as a whole person" when designing learning activities and opportunities.

Laura recalled how helpful it had been when teachers were kind and keen to help her to learn. She remembered in particular her work with teacher aides. Laura found it helpful having the support of teacher aides who asked her questions and worked through problems with her rather than just telling her what to do.

The common theme in the responses was the support the participants had experienced. This support was evident in a variety of forms; for example, counselling, learning how to study, completing work, and developing practical skills.

Figure 15.5. What Was Most Helpful While at School?

Phillip's appreciation of teachers' recognition of the importance of the "whole" person and their taking into account students' interests and strengths demonstrates the value of having education programmes tailored to specific needs and aspirations. The group agreed with this. They also agreed with Laura when she talked about how helpful it had been when teacher aides worked with her to brainstorm and problem solve rather than just giving her the answers. This they found to be a more exciting and meaningful way of learning. The role of the teacher aide is pivotal in the education of students with special educational needs. It is an important and challenging role and New Zealand research recognizes the complex and skilled role teacher aides are expected to undertake in regular classrooms, often without adequate support or training (MacArthur, Kelly, & Higgins, 2005).

What Could Have Been Better?

The common themes identified through the third question, "What could have been better?", present a challenge for teachers and professionals who support students with special needs in secondary schools. The participants' views are given below:

Bronwyn wished people had shown a greater understanding of her disability and the implications this had on her learning. She said it would have helped to have "teachers understanding my learning needs and developing programmes that would help me learn in the mainstream". Bronwyn also commented that "regular communication [by the school] with my parents" would have made secondary school better.

Phillip commented that the only thing that might have enhanced his secondary school experience was "more support at school in times when I was feeling sad".

Taylor wanted "more independence" at secondary school. His suggestions included students "having more say in the rules" and not having to wear a uniform. Considerable discussion and whole group agreement followed Taylor's suggestion that, when they started in the third form, it would have been helpful to "have an older student for a buddy. Someone to give me ideas and show me how to be part of the group—how to behave. Someone to be a friend and help me make friends". He suggested this person needed to be "mature" and have a recognized status "like a head prefect or captain of a sports team".

Laura agreed with all these ideas and indicated she had nothing further to add.

Figure 15.6. What Could Have Been Better?

The findings (see Figure 15.6) clearly indicate the importance of teachers getting to know their students, understanding their disabilities, recognizing the implications of these in the learning and social contexts and being able to take them into account when planning programmes. Teachers need to know students well enough to be able to recognize when they are feeling sad and to provide appropriate support. Regular communication with parents would, as Bronwyn recognized, also assist teachers to be more knowledgeable about and understanding of their students (Fraser, 2005).

There is also potential for fostering and further developing peer support systems in secondary schools. In answering previous questions, all the participants identified the importance of the various forms of support they had received. Taylor's concept of having an older "friend" who would be a positive role model and social skills coach from the beginning of secondary school appealed to the group. Developing positive peer cultures in which young people encourage and support each other is a more effective and encompassing approach (Brendtro & Shahbazian, 2004). When Taylor spoke of wanting more independence by having a say in school rules and not wearing a school uniform, he was identifying the fundamental need students have for power, independence, and decision making in the school context. Positive peer cultures provide numerous opportunities to satisfy this need. Features of a positive peer culture include collaborative problem solving, the creation of safe environments, and the development of interpersonal skills through interacting with older peers who are positive role models. The advantage of such an approach would see secondary schools become more like learning organisations embedded in a culture of positive support rather than pockets of support that is dependent on individuals.

Findings from the Observers' Evaluation Forms

Twenty-one of the 33 observers completed an evaluation form. Almost all qualified their rankings with comments in most sections.

The first question asked observers to indicate how helpful observing this process had been in assisting them to identify possible areas for further development in their professional practice. Responses ranged from helpful to extremely helpful (see Table 15.1, Question 1).

Observers' comments indicated that the process had enabled them to identify possible areas for further development in supporting secondary schools to be more responsive to the needs of students. A range of areas was identified where further support and more effective strategies could be developed. Some of these included social relationships, self-determination, levels of support, inclusive programming, and the lived experience of disability. The importance of listening for the "voice" of the young person was also highlighted in comments that indicated recognition of "the need to ask young people what helps, what is needed and what they think about their school programme".

Other comments reflected how the process had increased observers' understanding and ability to empathize with young people. These comments included that "it gave a real insight into how young people feel about school" and that the conversation "was not as focused on curriculum but more on social (aspects) and being involved in decision making". The process demonstrated to observers that "young people can be involved in decision making about their lives and their future".

The second question asked observers how thought provoking they had found the process. All responses provided a ranking between "thought provoking" and "extremely thought provoking" with a marked number at the higher end of the continuum—82% of observers ranked the process as either very or extremely thought provoking (see Table 15.1, Question 2).

Observers' comments in this section highlighted the way the process had engaged them and enabled them to identify with what the participants said and how they felt. They reported that the process "gave some insight into how varying disabilities are dealt with in the secondary environment" and that to "see a different side to the story is good". Other comments stated that observers had "loved it as it made it real" and "that it was good to hear first hand". One observer commented that the process "made me really think" and another that the technique was "very welcome at a conference such as this". Responses to both these questions demonstrate Sibbett's (1981) theory that graphic facilitation increases understanding through visual–verbal channels.

When asked to rate the facilitation of the process, most respondents indicated they found it to be either very good (20%) or excellent (65%) (see Table 15.1, Question 3). Positive feedback was given about the teamwork demonstrated by the two facilitators and about "the balanced approach". Responses included statements such as the process was "very appropriate . . . well thought through . . . extremely special to be here" and "it will be very memorable". This highlighted an important requirement of effective graphic facilitation—the dynamic between the two facilitators as they share the task of developing the process. One, the process facilitator, has the responsibility of building the connection and relationship with and between the participants and encouraging them to share their ideas. The other, the graphic facilitator, concentrates on capturing, organising, and recording the ideas in a meaningful visual language. At the end of each segment, the graphic facilitator checked the accuracy of the graphic by reporting back to the group.

The effectiveness of the process was further affirmed by responses to the fourth question that invited feedback on how helpful it had been for observers to see a discussion recorded in this way. The majority of respondents found it to be a most or very helpful technique (see Table 15.1, Question 4).

Table 15.1. Summary of Results

Questions	Ranking and number (%)				
How helpful was this process for identifying possible areas for further development in professional practice	Not helpful	Somewhat helpful	Helpful	Very helpful	Extremely helpful
	0	0	33	19	48
How thought provoking was this experience?	Not very	A little	Thought provoking	Very	Extremely
	0	0	19	19	62
How did you find the facilitation of the process?	Poor	Fair	Good	Very good	Excellent
	0	0	15	20	65
How helpful was it to see the discussion recorded in this way?	Not helpful	Somewhat helpful	Quite helpful	Most helpful	Very helpful
	0	0	14	28.5	57.5

A number of comments drew attention to the power of the visuals alongside the facilitation process. Observers stated that such a technique "allowed for a great deal of honesty on the part of the participants" and that it was "great to hear the students' views first hand". They specifically mentioned how much they "loved the visual graphic process" and that "it helped [us] to have a visual idea of what was said". One observer said that "as I have a hearing impairment, it reinforced what I was hearing" and another commented on the usefulness of the feedback at the end of each section as this provided both a clarification and a summary. Several respondents focused on the power of the graphic message and the building up of the template.

Overall, observers indicated the process had highlighted "the frailties and difficulties students faced whilst at secondary school" and that it had demonstrated "the keenness, characters, and courage of the young people" who had participated. The participants' "awareness of their disabilities and how articulate they were in conveying their thoughts" also impressed observers. Remarks included reference to the participants "openness and willingness to share ideas", their "insights", and how "confident and communicative they [the participants] were". "The wonderful attitude and passion [the participants have] for their interests and for life in general" also impressed the observers.

It was obvious by these and other comments that observers had learned "about the frustrations and experiences of students with special needs in school settings", about "the sort of support and intervention that can truly benefit students with disabilities" and about "the different levels of support [needed]—as perceived by participants".

Observers' comments portrayed how impressed they were with the way, "despite blocks and difficulties being put in their way", participants had "positive attitudes towards past endeavours and personal growth" and how the young people could reframe "negative experiences and integrate them into positive learning".

The Debriefing

The participants' positive attitudes commented on by the observers was evident at the conclusion of the presentation. The young adults who participated in this experience were elated. While they felt relieved that the presentation was over, they were also excited about how "great it had been". Naturally, they had been a little apprehensive about talking in front of teachers and sharing their feelings about "how school could be made better". At the same time they recognized the importance of what they had shared. They said they felt proud that they had been able "to teach the teachers". The participants commented that they enjoyed doing this together. They felt supported in the group context and the quieter participants found it easier to speak up once others had spoken.

Seeing their ideas expressed in the colourful graphics was affirming as they realized their ideas were being heard. They all asked if they could do this again. Their celebration of the event continued in more informal chatter in the car on the way home.

CONCLUSION

Kim and Mauborgne (2002) challenge facilitators, when they encounter a complex communication problem, to use graphic facilitation. "Listening to subjects with special educational needs throws into a particular relief all the generically difficult issues of researching voice" (Clough & Nutbrown, 2003, p. 71). The process of graphic facilitation is one way of levelling the inevitable imbalance of power between the researcher and the researched—particularly in a special educational context. In the situation described here, the combination of graphic facilitation and focused conversation techniques proved to be very effective in "turning up the volume on the depressed or inaudible voice" (Clough & Nutbrown, 2003, p. 71). This approach supported the young adults to express their ideas and opinions in front of a group of professionals who were vested with the responsibility of designing and implementing educational programmes, supports, and processes for young people with special educational needs. The "engaged" professionals discovered areas for future development in their own professional practice.

The process worked synergistically. It did more than merely engage the young adults in a conversation. It mined the depths of the young adults' perspectives (McCracken, 1988) by creating a context in which the voices of the young adults were heard. The process gave the professionals insights, made it real, made the professionals think, and presented a different perspective. The essence of the participants' voices was captured in a deeper and more meaningful way providing a "whole" as well as the parts—the specifics as well as the big picture.

Giving the lead to the lived experience of disability by listening to the voice of young people and involving them in the design of the educational experience will turn up the volume to ensure that the voice fashions the educational journey.

REFERENCES

Alice, L. (2003). Power, experience and process in feminist research. In C. Davidson, & M. Tolich (Eds.). *Social science research in New Zealand* (2nd ed.).(pp. 61–68). Auckland, New Zealand: Pearson.

Alton-Lee, A. (2003). *Quality teaching for diverse students: Best evidence synthesis.* Wellington, New Zealand: Ministry of Education, Medium Term Strategy Division.

Armstrong, T. (1987). *In their own way.* New York: Tarcher Press.

Bishop, R., Berryman, M., Richardson, C., & Tiakiwai, S. (2003). *Te kotahitanga: The experiences of Year 9 and 10 Maori students in mainstream classrooms.* Hamilton, New Zealand: Maori Education Research Unit (MERU), University of Waikato.

Booth, T., & Ainscow, M. (2002). *The index for inclusion: Developing learning & participation in schools.* Bristol, UK: Centre for Studies on Inclusive Education.

Bray, A., & Gates, S. (2000). Children with disabilities: Equal rights or different rights? In A. Smith, M. Gollop, K. Marshall & K. Nairn (Eds.), *Advocating for children: International Perspectives on Children's Rights,* pp. 32-41. Dunedin, New Zealand: University of Otago Press.

Brendtro, L., & Shahbazian, M. (2004). Troubled Children and Youth: *Turning problems into opportunities.* IL: Research Press.

Caldwell, B., Dake, D., Safly, M., & Ulch, L. (1999–2000). *Brain based visual education.* Iowa State University, IA. Retrieved 11 April, http://www.public.iastate.edu /~design/ ART/NAB/brain4.html.

Clegg, E. (2003). Visual learning: Building knowledge, innovation and collaboration. *Global Learning Resources, 3*(2). Retrieved August 14, 2006 from http://www.glresources.com.

Clough, P. & Nutbrown, C. (2002). *A student's guide to methodology.* London: Sage.

Department of Education and Skills. (2001). *Learning to listen: Core principles for the involvement of children and young people.* Available from www.dfes.gov.uk/ listeningtolearn.

Educational Review Office (ERO). (2003). *Student participation in school decision-making.* Available from http://www.ero.govt.nz/ ero/publishing.nsf/Content/Student%20 Participation% 20in%20School%20Decision-Making.

Fraser, D. (2005). Collaborating with parents/caregivers and whanau. In D. Fraser, R Moltzen, & K. Ryba (Eds.), *Learners with Special Needs in Aotearoa New Zealand* (pp. 128–154). Palmerston North, New Zealand: Thomson Press.

Gardner, H. (1985). *Frames of mind: Theory of multiple intelligences.* New York: Basic Books.

Hess, J. M. (1968). Group interviewing. In R. L. King (Ed.), *New science of planning* (pp. 51–84). Chicago: American Marketing Association.

Hill, J., & Hawke, K. (2001). *Towards making achievement cool: Achievement in multi cultural high schools* (AIMHI). Wellington, New Zealand: Ministry of Education.

Horn, R. E. (1998). *Visual language: Global communication for the 21st century.* Bainbridge Island, New Zealand: MacroVU Press.

Kim, W. C., & Mauborgne, R. (2002, June). Charting your company's future. *Harvard Business Review*, pp. 77–83.

Kitzinger, J. (1994). The methodology of focus groups: The importance of interaction between research participants, *Sociology of Health*, *16*(1),136–142.

MacArthur, J., Kelly, B., & Higgins, N. (2005). Supporting the learning and social experiences of students with disabilities: What does the research say? In D. Fraser, R Moltzen, & K. Ryba (Eds.), *Learners with special needs in Aotearoa New Zealand* (pp. 49–73). Palmerston North, New Zealand: Thomson Press.

Mc Cracken, G. (1998). *The long interview: Qualitative Research Methods 13*. London: Sage.

Mayer, R. E. (2001). *Multimedia learning*. Cambridge, UK: Cambridge University Press.

Merton, R. K., & Kendall, P. L. (1946). The focused interview. *American Journal of Sociology*, 51, 541–557.

Meyer, L., & Bevan-Brown, J. (2005). Collaboration for social inclusion. In D. Fraser, R Moltzen, & K. Ryba (Eds.), *Learners with special needs in Aotearoa New Zealand* (pp. 168–192). Palmerston North, New Zealand: Thomson Press.

Minister for Disability Issues. (2001). *The New Zealand Disability Strategy: Making a world of difference Whakakauni Oranga*. Wellington: Ministry of Health.

Ministry of Education. (2004). *Enhancing effective practice in special education: A pilot study (research report)* Wellington, New Zealand: Author.

Ministry of Education. (2007). *National administration guidelines*. Wellington, New Zealand: Author.

Ministry of Health. (2001). *The New Zealand Disability Strategy: Making a world of difference Whakakauni Oranga. Pictorial Version*. Wellington, New Zealand: Author.

Morgan, D., & Krueger, R. (1993). When to use focus groups and why. In D. Morgan (Ed.), *Successful focus groups: Advancing the state of the art* (pp. 3–20). Newbury Park, CA: Sage.

Nakken, H., & Pijl, S. (2002). Getting along with classmates in regular schools—A review of the effects of integration on the development of social relationships. *International Journal of Inclusive Education*, *6*(1), pp.47–61.

Sibbett, D. (1981). *I see what you mean: An introduction to graphic language recording and facilitation*. San Francisco: Sibbett & Associates.

Slee, R. (2001). Inclusion in practice: Does practice make perfect? *Educational Review*, *53*(2), pp. 41–61.

Tierney, P. (2003). The competitive advantage of rich media. *American Bar Association (ABA) Journal*, 89(6), p. S4.

Waldegrave, C. (2003.).Focus groups. In C. Davidson, & M. Tolich (Eds.). *Social Science Research in New Zealand* (2nd ed.).(pp. 251–262) Auckland, New Zealand: Pearson.

Woolsey, K. (1996). *Vizability*. Boston: PWS Publishing Company.

AUTHOR NOTE

Deborah Espiner is a Principal Lecturer in the Faculty of Education, University of Auckland, New Zealand. She has a strong background in supporting students with disabilities within the education system. Deborah's considerable experience includes designing and teaching programmes for teachers and human service workers and facilitating Ministry of Education research contracts.

Diane Guild is the Manager of Professional Development and Outreach Services for Mt Richmond Special School, Auckland. Diane's experience includes teaching in all sectors and co-ordinating and facilitating Ministry of Education professional development and research contracts. She is committed to inclusion and the development of learning communities in school contexts.

The authors would like to thank the group of young people whose voices were the basis of this project. Without their energy, ideas, co-operation, and trust this chapter would not have been possible.

Correspondence regarding this chapter should be addressed by email to: debbie.espiner@auckland.ac.nz

PART 3. CHALLENGING PEDAGOGY

In: Challenging Thinking about Teaching and Learning   ISBN: 978-1-60456-744-1
Editors: C. M. Rubie-Davies and C. Rawlinson   © 2008 Nova Science Publishers, Inc.

Chapter 16

REFLECTING FROM MULTIPLE PERSPECTIVES IN MULTIPLE WORLDS: DRAMA AS AN APPROACH FOR ENGAGING STUDENT TEACHERS IN CRITICAL REFLECTION

Paul R. Heyward

ABSTRACT

Many teacher education programmes aim to develop student teachers who can reflect critically from multiple perspectives on issues to do with the practice of teaching. Both the literature and my personal experience reveal that reflection from multiple perspectives rarely occurs. Theorists in the field of drama in education provide insights into how drama can be a powerful tool for engaging people in critical reflection. A range of research suggests that drama can provide unique opportunities for participants to consider matters of human concern from a range of viewpoints. This chapter outlines research that questioned whether using drama could assist student teachers in reflecting from multiple perspectives on a specific educational issue. Central to this discussion is the finding that reflection occurred in two distinct intellectual spaces or "worlds". Implications for teacher education programmes and future research are also explored.

INTRODUCTION

The importance of developing student teachers who can reflect critically on both their practice and issues that affect the teaching and learning process is well established in preservice teacher education literature. Smyth (2001) has suggested that reflection must be conceived as a collective activity that encourages teachers to confront the broader political, social, and cultural structures that perpetuate inequality in the education system and society. Smyth argues that forms of reflection that simply focus on the technical aspects of a teacher's practice lack legitimacy as they disconnect teaching from the existing social and economic relations that privilege some groups and silence others. The notion that reflection should assist people in understanding the social and economic conditions of their existence and thus act as a catalyst for radical change is characteristic of many theorists who propose a critical approach to reflection. Pollard and Tann (1987) argue that we need to encourage teachers to view personal experiences within broader structures and trends. Other writers have suggested that teachers need to be encouraged to question the status quo and be open to examining the underlying assumptions about conventional thinking on teaching and learning (Larivee, 2000; Ward & McCotter, 2004).

Much of the literature on critical reflection in teacher education also points to the importance of encouraging student teachers to reflect from multiple perspectives on issues to do with the practice of teaching. Smyth (2001) was concerned that in the discourse surrounding teaching, one perspective dominated the educational arena—the perspective of managerialism. The effect of the domination of the managerial voice was that teachers came to see themselves as subjects rather than agents of change, and knowledge about teaching practices were seen as "natural" or "common sense" rather than tentative, problematic, and open to question. To arrest the hegemonising influence of managerialism, Smyth argued that a multiplicity of voices needed to be considered during the reflective process. If student teachers were exposed to a range of perspectives on educational issues, then they would see that all perspectives, even the powerful ones, were shaped by social forces.

Smyth is not alone in promoting a view of critical reflection that encourages teachers to view issues of practice from multiple perspectives (Braun & Crumpler, 2004; Brindley & Laframboise, 2002; Dixon, Snook, & Williams, 2000; Larivee, 2000; Ward & McCotter, 2003). Larivee argued that if teachers are to recognize that they have filters that limit their range of responses towards issues that emerge in their practice, they need to be encouraged to view issues from new vantage points. In reflecting from multiple perspectives, there is the potential for teachers to become aware of their filters and therefore increase their range of possible responses to difficult issues (Larivee, 2000). Similarly Brindley and Laframboise (2002) suggested that if student teachers are going to move beyond their own previously unexamined world views they need to be encouraged to reflect from multiple perspectives. For Dixon et al. (2000), the development of the thinking professional relies on a teacher education programme that enables student teachers to analyze problems from multiple perspectives in order to move towards satisfactory solutions.

As a lecturer attempting to engage students in critical reflection from multiple perspectives, I had become increasingly frustrated that the critical reflection advocated by theorists such as Smyth was only occurring to a very limited extent in my work with student teachers. It was evident that most student teachers struggled to view educational issues from any perspective but their own.

Several writers in the field of reflection and professional development have provided explanations for why student teachers may have difficulty in reflecting from the perspectives of others. Argyris (1990), an author in the field of organizational management, argues that reflection is often subverted into a reflective loop, because when people reflect on an event or issue, they only consider perspectives of which their prior experience has made them aware. It is therefore understandable that when reflecting, people ignore perspectives that are not in their realm of experience (Argyris, 1990). Similarly Brookfield (1995) argued that reflection often becomes a self-confirming cycle within which accepted assumptions come to shape future actions, which are then used to confirm the validity of the original assumption. In her research into professional development with teachers, Timperley (2003) has explained why teachers might ignore certain information even when their experience has made them aware of its existence. She has argued that a barrier to sustained change in the practice of teachers is that discrepant new information is often filtered through old belief systems.

Argyris' concept of the reflective loop resonated with me. It was clear that most student teachers in my classes were totally unaware of other important perspectives necessary to reflect critically on specific educational issues. The problem I faced was that if student teachers were to confront their assumptions about teaching in an open-minded manner, then they needed to be made aware of, and understand, multiple perspectives on the issues involved. However, if in the reflective process they only considered perspectives of which their own experience made them aware, or perspectives that were concomitant with their existing belief systems, then it was unlikely that they would come to understand the filters they used to validate certain ideas and invalidate others. The reflective loop required a circuit breaker and, from my previous experience, I believed that drama could provide the necessary charge.

Numerous researchers and practitioners have explored how drama can develop the reflective capacity of student teachers in preservice teacher education programmes. Raphael described his regular use of drama to assist his student teachers to reflect on their practice as beginning teachers (Raphael & O'Mara, 2002). Salvio (1994) used playwright Bertolt Brecht's rehearsal methods to encourage her student teachers to reflect on how emotions can affect pedagogic intentions. Whatman (2000) found that the use of drama in secondary teacher education was more successful in developing the necessary reflective and performance skills required for effective teaching than traditional technicist approaches. Whatman concluded that student teachers who were experienced in drama were more capable of taking on the role of the teacher as performer and that their understanding of the acting required in classroom teaching enhanced their capacity to reflect on their practice. Similarly Griggs (2001) argued that the more student teachers know about the performance skills required of actors the more capable they are of reflecting on their practice.

While various researchers have elaborated on the use of drama to encourage students to reflect on their teaching, others have used drama to reflect on sociopolitical issues that affect teachers' work. For example, Kaye and Ragusa (1998) investigated how the participatory theatre of Augusto Boal assisted student teachers to reflect on the social and political context of education in the culturally diverse setting of urban Los Angeles. They found that the use of Boal's methods provided a safe environment in which student teachers could critically reflect on issues to emerge from both course work and their school placement experiences. Similarly, Greenwood (2002) found that the use of participatory process drama helped a group of New Zealand student teachers to reflect on their understandings of the Treaty of Waitangi. Greenwood (2000) conducted her research with a group of student teachers from the small Northland settlement of Panguru and found that drama provided a safe environment within which student teachers could challenge the various perspectives of other participants.

The power of drama to assist learners to understand multiple perspectives on issues and events that affect their lives has also been explored by a number of educators in school and early childhood contexts. Walkinshaw (2004) suggested that when drama is used in the classroom, students are encouraged to move beyond their own feelings about a given situation and reflect on how other people might respond to the same situation. Wilhelm and Edmiston (1998) have advocated for drama's potential for helping middle school learners construct their own personal meanings of the world around them. Wilhelm and Edmiston argued that such personal meaning-making occurs as a result of students' ability to take on and critique multiple perspectives through drama. Similarly Martello (2001) found that when children in early childhood settings are encouraged to take on roles, they are able to try out different perspectives first hand and as a result "resolve points of tensions between perspectives or beliefs" (p. 206). Morris (1998) explored the effect drama can have on learning in social studies. He found that when drama was used as an approach to teach social studies content, students were more likely to empathize with the people about whom they were learning. Similarly Taylor's (1998) research found that drama enabled students to reflect from multiple perspectives on issues affecting the lives of the people studied. Taylor discussed the importance of process drama (where the purpose is to participate in learning rather than to present drama to an audience, and where participants decide the direction of the drama) in challenging participants' perspectives and making them accountable for the position taken within a drama. He contended that good process drama should demand that students are clear about their perspective or viewpoint and make themselves available for interrogation. For Taylor, it is the ability of students to engage in dramatic material from multiple perspectives that ensures critical reflection can occur through drama.

While research clearly demonstrates that drama can assist participants to reflect on matters of human concern from multiple perspectives and assist student teachers in reflecting on issues related to their practice, there has been little research into how drama assists student teachers to reflect from multiple perspectives.

THE CURRENT STUDY

The current study was designed to investigate student teachers' perceptions of the use of drama as a teaching approach in a preservice teacher education context. Two classes of 25 student teachers were involved in exploring a specific educational issue through structured role play as part of their second year professional inquiry paper entitled "The Moral and Political Nature of Education and Teaching". The details and structure of the drama experience are described below. Following their involvement in the role play sessions, all student teachers were asked to participate in the current study, and 29 of the 50 chose to take part. The data collection methods were designed to find out how student teachers perceived drama assisted their ability to critically reflect on a specific educational issue from multiple perspectives.

The specific issue chosen for this research project was based on an article by Angela Gregory that appeared in the New Zealand Herald on July 25, 2003. The article ran under the headline "Higher Expectation Key to Child Literacy" and outlined how the then New Zealand Minister of Education, Trevor Mallard, was highly pleased with the results of a research study into literacy levels of primary students in some low socioeconomic primary schools in South Auckland (Gregory, 2003). The research, entitled Picking up the Pace, was conducted by researchers from the University of Auckland and contributed to the much wider Ministry of Education-funded intervention, Strengthening Education in Mangere and Otara (SEMO) (Ministry of Education, 2003). The SEMO intervention had aimed to significantly raise educational achievement in the South Auckland communities. One of the conclusions drawn by the Picking up the Pace lead researcher, Helen Timperley, was that high teacher expectation was a factor that contributed to the raising of literacy levels of children involved in the study (Ministry of Education, 2003; Timperley, 2003). This particular finding was emphasized in a speech given by the Minister of Education at the launch of the Picking up the Pace report (Mallard, 2003), and that subsequently became the focus of Gregory's (2003) article.

Following the launch of the Picking up the Pace literacy initiative and the associated press coverage, the Quality Public Education Coalition (QPEC), a group set up to lobby for the adequate government funding of public education, responded to what it thought was an unfair portrayal of the professionalism of teachers working in low socioeconomic communities (Minto, 2003). Another group to voice concerns regarding the findings of the Picking up the Pace research, and the subsequent decision by the Minister of Education to invest $10 million dollars in replicating the initiative in other areas, was the Education Policy Group of the Massey University College of Education. This group raised issues about the methodology employed by the University of Auckland researchers (Education Policy Group, College of Education, Massey University, 2003). The response from the Massey group resulted in a strong defence of the research study by the University of Auckland researchers and led to an ensuing claim and counter-claim via the media and academic journals (Timperley, 2003; Nash, 2003).

As the issue regarding the effect of teacher expectations on the achievement of low socioeconomic learners elicited such strong responses, it was suitable for inclusion in the Bachelor of Education (Teaching) Professional Inquiry module "The Moral and Political Nature of Education and Teaching". A key learning outcome for student teachers in this course was to "examine and evaluate political, economic, educational, social and cultural (macro) issues which affect teachers' work" (Auckland College of Education, 2005, p. 6). To assess the ability to meet this learning outcome, student teachers were required to maintain a learning log of educational issues covered in the popular press and within this log they were to provide an analysis of multiple perspectives on selected issues. The learning log contained three articles, two chosen by lecturers, and one self-selected. The 2003 Gregory article was one of the lecturer-directed learning log items in 2004 and 2005.

To help student teachers gain an understanding of multiple perspectives on the "teacher expectation" issue outlined above, it was decided to use drama as a teaching approach. The form of drama used was "structured role play" as it ensured lecturers could direct the drama towards an exploration of specific perspectives. Bolton and Heathcote (1999) have suggested that structured role play allows leaders greater control than more open forms of process drama in which students decide on the direction of the drama. It is important to note that the use of role play in the current study did not take the form of traditional role plays where students simulate a real-life work problem with an audience focusing on how accurately the performance re-enacts the real life experience. Rather, the focus was on the learning that occurred within the context of the role play.

The class was divided into three groups. The first group was the Minister of Education and the teachers involved in the Picking up the Pace research, the second was QPEC, and the third was the Education Policy Group of Massey University. It was explained to the students that they were to be involved in the launch of a major literacy initiative that had emerged from the SEMO project. Students were supplied with role cards and background literature that explained the position of the group of which they were to be members during the structured role play.

METHODOLOGY

Newman, Ridenour, Newman, and De Marco (2003) have argued that a prerequisite for valid research is a systematic exploration of the purpose, or purposes, of the research. To this end, the study drew on Newman et al.'s typology in which they articulate nine potential reasons for conducting research. Three were relevant to the current investigation: understanding complex phenomena; generating new ideas; and personal, social, and/or organisational impact.

The study has been influenced by the evidence and by my belief that drama has the capacity to assist learning and, therefore, should play a prominent role in teacher education programmes. Newman et al. (2003) have explained how personal beliefs provide a lens through which the purpose of research is determined. In my study, the purpose for conducting the inquiry was threefold. First, and most importantly, the aim was to investigate how the phenomenon of drama as a teaching approach was understood by student teachers. Secondly, the study sought information about whether or not drama was a useful approach in assisting student teachers to understand multiple perspectives on a particular issue. Thirdly, it was hoped that the research might add to the body of knowledge or the generation of ideas regarding the use of drama in teacher education contexts.

For Newman et al. (2003), the research purpose must precede both the research question and the methodology if the research is to have any validity. In the current study, the examination of the underlying reasons for conducting the research underpinned both the research question and the methodology. The key question guiding the research design was: "In what ways does approaching an educational issue through drama help student teachers to reflect on the issue from multiple perspectives?"

In order to answer this question and to fulfil the purposes of the study, a mixed-methods research design was used. Greene, Caracelli, and Graham (1989) have defined mixed methods as those that "include at least one quantitative method (designed to collect numbers) and one qualitative method (designed to collect words)" (p. 256). The study used a questionnaire to obtain quantitative data to provide a broad statistical understanding of whether or not student teachers perceived that drama assisted them in reflecting from multiple perspectives on a specific educational issue. This was followed by a qualitative exploration of individual stories, which used information from interviews and responses to open questions that had been included in the questionnaire (Creswell, 2002). Priority was given to the qualitative data as both the amount of data and the emphasis in the data analysis favoured the qualitative data (Creswell, 2002).

The two classes from which participants were drawn were selected on the basis that the student teachers had experienced drama as a teaching approach in class, and I could access them easily. In both these classes, drama was used to explore the specific moral or political issue that affected teachers' work that was the basis for the research. Therefore these students had experiences relevant to the research question. Such a sampling technique has been described as convenience sampling (Creswell, 2002; Neuman, 2000; Sarantakos, 1998) as the sample is convenient to the researcher and available for the study.

Twenty-nine student teachers agreed to participate in the research study and completed the questionnaire. Of these, 11 indicated they would be willing to take part in the semi-structured interviews, of whom 8 were randomly selected to take part in the interviewing process.

The data analysis for both the interviews and the open questions in the questionnaire was based on the grounded theory approaches originally developed by Glaser and Strauss (1967). Initially, open coding was used by reading through data and making brief notes on data of particular interest or relevance to the research question. An ongoing memo was maintained through this open coding stage on which notes were made on possible categories of data. The next stage of the data analysis process was axial coding. Strauss and Corbin (1990) describe axial coding as the reassembly of fractured data through the process of making connections between the categories established at the open coding stage. In the current study, possible connections between the categories established in the open coding stage were identified and recoded as new categories. The final stage of the grounded theory process involved selective coding in which the categories established in the axial coding stage were further refined to generate core ideas and generalizations. Two of the main overarching generalizations to emerge from this grounded theory analysis were that reflection from multiple perspectives occurred during the structured role play within the dramatic world constructed for the role play, and also outside the dramatic world after the structured role play had concluded.

The quantitative data from the questionnaire were analyzed by initially calculating the number of respondents who answered each of the two quantitative questions. The questions asked participants to indicate how helpful they found drama in assisting them to understand multiple perspectives on an educational issue and how the drama experience had helped them in analyzing multiple perspectives in their learning log assignment. In answering these questions participants indicated their answer by circling a point on a five-point Likert scale. For each point, the number of participants who responded to each was tallied up and converted into a percentage.

FINDINGS

In their ratings of the benefits of drama in helping them understand and analyze multiple perspectives, most respondents perceived that drama had assisted their understanding of an educational issue from multiple perspectives, with 93% scoring the effect as four or five on the rating scale (17% very helpful and 76% extremely helpful). The other 6% found it moderately helpful (3%) or not very helpful (3%).

Most respondents perceived that drama had assisted their analysis of an issue from multiple perspectives recorded in their learning log, with 97% scoring the effect as four or five on the rating scale (28% very helpful and 69% extremely helpful). The other 3% found it moderately helpful.

Not only did participants indicate that drama assisted their learning, but the majority of participants were also able to explain how this learning occurred. All eight interview participants were aware of the learning processes that occurred for them during and as a result of the role play. These learning processes led them to understand and recall multiple perspectives relevant to the issue explored. Learning processes involved participants reflecting on the issue from the perspective of the character they played as well as from the perspectives of characters played by their classmates. A number of responses to the open questions in the questionnaire also demonstrated an awareness of how learning occurred through drama. Throughout the following discussion, interviewees are identified by a pseudonym followed by an abbreviation of interview (int). Respondents to the questionnaire are referred to by the abbreviation of questionnaire respondent (QR) followed by the number assigned to their questionnaire (between one and 29).

Many of the participants attributed their learning to the fact that the drama was both hands-on and realistic. Both interview participants and questionnaire respondents described how the physical hands-on nature of drama ensured that learning occurred:

> I think because it's enjoyable and because it's hands on that it is definitely a beneficial approach. (Jane, int.)

This sense of hands-on physical involvement was closely associated with the element of time.

Many participants articulated an awareness of how learning occurred in the present and as a result how they experienced the event and ideas rather than reading and discussing them retrospectively.

> It helped make the perspectives seem more real and made it interesting. I felt that I didn't tune out as I usually do when a lot of paper is shoved at me. (QR 7)

Although participants showed an awareness of how the experiential nature of drama assisted their learning in the moment, the drama also had an effect on their understanding in the longer term. Many participants described how the drama experience helped them analyze multiple perspectives in their learning log after the role play.

> When I was writing my learning log I could visualize back to our drama session who was who and who thought what. I could then compare the similarities and differences between the perspectives. (QR 13)

However Fran felt the drama had a negative effect on her learning log analysis as she focused too much on the characterization of each perspective instead of looking for similarities and differences between them:

> It made me characterize each one a little bit too much and I didn't really link them well enough. I did actually separate them out probably a little bit too much. (Fran, int.)

Some participants believed that the hands-on experiential nature of drama led to deeper, more meaningful learning that resulted in them internalizing their understanding of multiple perspectives.

> For me it was a lot more deeper learning, a lot more meaningful learning than just listening to the lecturer. (Catherine, int.)

While learning may have been deep and meaningful, many participants also discussed how the experiential nature of drama ensured that the learning was fun.

There is a purpose behind it but sometimes it [the drama] just alleviates the pressure and you think this is fun. You come away thinking "Oh I learnt something, I was having fun and learnt something", now that's great. (Brenda, int.)

However, although many commented on the fun nature of drama, Donna and Eric also described how learning occurred as a result of people taking the drama work seriously.

It's [participating in drama] not being stupid, you're not being stupid, it's quite a serious thing. (Donna, int..)
You see we took it on really seriously and so you sort of took on the role seriously. (Eric, int.)

Many of the participants commented on how their participation in the role play demanded they listen attentively to their classmates. Eric was aware of how the experiential nature of drama, although fun, demanded his attention to what his fellow class members were saying.

It's happening in front of you and you're involved in that and you don't want to look silly as well so you want to make sure you know what's happening so you can keep up. (Eric, int.)

Listening to the perspectives of others and hearing the perspective of the character they were playing in the role play was not always a comfortable experience for several of the participants. Brenda's response was typical:

Well the teachers, as we were, we'd been given all these wonderful opportunities, I sort of felt maybe we were being unjustly accused. (Brenda, int.)

Some participants were able to discuss how they reflected from, and on, a range of perspectives while acting in the dramatic world. Heather was surprised at how strongly she could hold a viewpoint within a role with which she disagreed when out of role. When discussing how the drama helped her form her own perspective on the issue she observed:

After reading the material and understanding who you are supposed to be portraying, how quite firm you can be about that perspective. (Heather, int.)

Eric was also interested in how strongly he was able to identify with the character he portrayed even though he personally disagreed with the perspective of this character.

I've been tricked or something into believing what Mallard was saying because I was trying to defend him and I took on his role so I don't know if that subconsciously made me really want to believe what he was saying. (Eric, int.)

Some participants commented on how playing a character within role in the role play allowed them to confront their own beliefs and values.

When you're acting for something that you actually don't agree with, having to defend it [the perspective of her character] made me question some things but again, I felt it reinforced my own viewpoint. (Avril, int.)

Brenda described how when she was playing the role of a teacher who believed that the low expectations of teachers in low socioeconomic areas contributed to children's underachievement, she contemporaneously considered whether she personally agreed with this position. Brenda felt that this deeper questioning of her own beliefs would not have happened had she only read about the perspective she was playing:

> Becoming that role you actually begin to form an opinion yourself rather than just reading it so you can develop it and while you might read it on paper and think oh yeah I agree with that, it is teacher expectations, when you actually come to do it you suddenly think hang on a minute, I don't want to be blamed for something I have no control over. . . . You're actually taking on a role and you're in that role. It's not so much your own opinion. It lets you think about your own opinion but you are not that person [myself]. (Brenda, int.)

Many participants reported on how their participation in the role play affected their personal position of the issue under exploration. While Donna and Avril were aware of how they confronted their own perspectives on the issue while in role, a number of other participants were able to discuss how the drama helped them develop their own perspective on the issue after the role play.

> You reflected on everybody else's multiple perspectives and turned it into your own and what you believed and your position. (Donna, int.)
> Debating the different perspectives . . . influenced my own opinion regarding the issue. (QR 5.)

However the drama had little impact for Fran on the formation of her personal position. When asked how the drama had influenced the development of her own position on the issue she answered.

> Did it influence me? No it just brought it to my attention and made me think about it. (Fran, int.)

A number of participants discussed how, after the drama sessions, they were motivated to inquire into the perspectives explored during the role play. Some participants suggested that their involvement in the drama motivated them to read more closely the supporting material provided in class.

> I guess I took a better look at the articles in finding key statements. What was important in the articles for me to analyse multiple perspectives. (QR 12)

Avril and Brenda indicated that they were motivated to read beyond the readings supplied in class.

> I actually looked up on the websites, got into QPEC to find out anything else they had, got into the Massey University website to find out exactly what they said rather than just an excerpt. . . . I started looking for stuff and actually reading stuff, letters to the editor . . . (Avril, int.)

So I got far more interested in who those people were and why their perspective was what it was . . . it just actually quirked my interest really. (Brenda, int.)

Participants were often aware of the emotional reaction they experienced within the drama, as well as the emotional reactions of their classmates.

It was emotive, the real feeling that I picked up from each of the group's perspectives.... the scientists were a little upset [with Mallard] and then the teachers jumped to Mallard's assistance. (Heather, int.)

DISCUSSION

Reflecting from Inside a Dramatic World

The use of the term dramatic world refers to the experience of participants when they occupy the role of somebody else in a created world. O'Neill (1995) referred to the dramatic world as "an imagined elsewhere with its own characters, locations, and concerns, developing in accordance with its own inner logic" (p. xi). It was clear that the experience of being inside the dramatic world was pivotal to the participants' ability to reflect from multiple perspectives.

Many student teachers indicated that when they were engaged in the dramatic world they were aware of the demands that being in role placed on their attention. They believed that their attention to the task was heightened because they had to listen in order to participate and keep up with what was happening within the dramatic world. Bolton (1992) suggested that when participants believe that something important is going to happen within the dramatic world, they develop a responsibility towards their role. This sense of responsibility was discussed by one student teacher when she explained that the reason she listened so attentively to the perspectives of others was so she could be convincing in her role.

I had to be open to comprehending my role and listen to the others in order to be convincing in my role. (QR 24)

To Bolton (1992), the act of listening in the dramatic world is more demanding than that required in direct experience because of the extra dimension of responsibility participants feel towards keeping the drama alive. Morgan and Saxton (1987) and O'Neill (1995) suggested that active listening in the dramatic world sustains belief in the world and its happenings as it assists participants in establishing congruency in their role, and how to be appropriately responsive to other characters and responsibly cope with the freedoms they hold to change the direction of a drama. The participants in the current study were helped to reflect on the issue from multiple perspectives as a result of attentively searching for clues about both their role and the role of their classmates and teacher. The imperative that propelled this attentiveness was a commitment to keeping the narrative action of the drama moving in a direction that maintained the integrity and plausibility of the dramatic world so something worthwhile could occur.

Many student teachers discussed the unpredictability of being involved in the dramatic world and the unexpected challenges they received within role. These challenges occurred because of participants' feeling that their character's perspective was in opposition to their own personal position, or came as a result of unexpected attacks on their character's perspective from other characters in the role play. In either case, the experience of learning in the dramatic world led some student teachers to feel confused, challenged, and uncertain. Taylor (1998) argued that good drama should challenge participants to defend the perspective of their character, even when it was one with which they might personally disagree, as such internal confusion could enhance the learning process. Bolton and Heathcote (1999) suggested that new insights become available for participants in drama as they have a foot in two worlds: They can watch themselves playing their role in the fictional world while keeping one foot in the real world as spectator and as such constantly compare the ideas being expressed by their character with their own values and beliefs. Boal (1995) described this state of belonging to two worlds simultaneously as metaxis. Many student teachers discussed how they operated in two worlds by reflecting on the issue from the perspective of the character they were playing while simultaneously considering their personal viewpoint.

> When you're acting for something that you actually don't agree with, having to defend it [the perspective of her character] made me question some things but again, I felt it reinforced my own viewpoint. (Avril, int.)

Experience in two worlds simultaneously allowed for reflection from multiple perspectives. An important finding in the current study was how this experience of metaxis resulted in cognitive conflict and cognitive dissonance.

Cognitive conflict refers to the confusion learners go through when their ideas are challenged by others (New, 1998) and cognitive dissonance to a conflict between belief and behaviour (Reber, 1995). Both were present when participants were operating in the dramatic world.

During the structured role play, student teachers were forced to defend the perspective of their character while simultaneously being made aware of views which previously they may not have considered. In experiencing cognitive conflict in role, participants were experiencing learning in two worlds. While they may have been managing a response that was concomitant to their character's perspective, they were also aware of the personal views they held in the real world and how these were similar to, or different from, those of the characters played in the role play.

Some student teachers provided insights into how acting in the dramatic world, while mindful of the real world, was an experience that not only created cognitive conflict but also cognitive dissonance. A number of participants described instances of internal conflict when they discussed how learning within the dramatic world meant they had to act as if they believed in a perspective that was not aligned to the position they held in the real world. Brenda, who played a teacher in the role play, was able to describe how she simultaneously agreed with her character's position while personally questioning how such a perspective would have an effect on her role as a teacher in the real world. Fogarty (1994) has suggested that this type of role taking is a powerful way of promoting metacognition as it reduces ego-centred perceptions of the world and allows participants to actively hypothesize how others might react to situations. For Bolton (1992), the opportunity drama provides for participants to exist in a state of metaxis ensures that reflection through drama is more powerful than reflection in real life. He reasoned that the participant in drama, unlike the participant in real life, must be constantly aware of maintaining the believability of the dramatic world while reflecting on how the words and actions they perform in this world relate to their personal beliefs and values.

Many student teachers were able to describe how their participation in the dramatic world helped them to develop their own perspective on the issue.

> It made me really form my own opinion and take bits and pieces from all of them and think well I like that idea and I believe that's true so I'll take that on board, yeah it helped me form or clarify my own . . . perspective. (Eric, int.)

For Boal (1995), such a finding is consistent with the process of metaxis as he suggested that the dramatic world is essentially a rehearsal space where participants can practise in order to modify their real life. It is the extrapolation back from the fictional to the real that completes the process of metaxis, as was the case in this study where participants could try out the perspective of their character and use this experience to shape their own position.

Reflecting from Outside the Dramatic World

Participants in the current study revealed that reflection on, and from, multiple perspectives was not confined to the dramatic world but continued after the role play had concluded. Many student teachers discussed how their experience within the dramatic world was easily recalled after the conclusion of the role play. They observed how, following the drama, they were better able to understand the supporting literature on the issue, and the perspectives presented. They also discussed how the drama helped their written learning log work as they had a clear understanding of how different perspectives compared and contrasted. Participants reported the ability to relate their reading and writing to an actual event showing that the dramatic experience became a memory that informed new experiences.

> You could sort of flick back to the scene in class and something might have made it more solid or concrete having acted out the different perspectives so coming to write it, I think subconsciously it might have had an effect. (Eric, int.)

These findings are consistent with a range of research projects that have found that drama experiences can assist the recall of educational concepts learnt through drama (Duatepe, 2005; Edmiston, 2003; Fleming, Merryl, & Tymms, 2004; Morris, 1998; O'Neill, 1995).

When participants look back on a drama in which they have been involved, the narrative threads of the experience reveal themselves in a way that could not occur within the dramatic world. Some of the student teachers described how, long after the role play had concluded, they were able to return to the drama in their head and then remember events and conversations as if remembering a film or play.

> You're recalling the situation, the position you were in, that's how it was for me so I was able to instantly go oh this is what, this is where it's from. (Fran, int.)

Bolton has suggested that it is not until the drama is over that participants are able to recall the drama as a narrative (Bolton, 1992; Larivee, 2000).

Most student teachers reported a high level of comprehension of supporting literature provided after the completion of the drama. The structured role play ensured that key perspectives covered in the supporting literature were elaborated on during the drama and it is possible that this is why participants were able to comprehend the literature after the role play had concluded. It is important to note that some participants believed they would not have been able to understand the supporting literature if it had been handed to them without the accompanying role play. This finding is consistent with a range of studies which have found that following the use of drama in a classroom context, students were able to gain greater comprehension of reading material which they previously had difficulty understanding (Booth, 2000; Rose, et al., 2000; Wilhelm and Edmiston, 1998).

A number of student teachers were able to reflect on the perspectives presented in the supporting literature as they read because they could return to the role play in their head and recall the characters who presented specific perspectives. They were then better able to approach the issue from these multiple perspectives when they were writing up their learning log analysis. Wilhelm and Edmiston (1998) suggested that when students return to a text explored through drama they were more capable of analyzing the multiple voices inherent in the text. They argued that the in-depth analysis that can happen after a drama, occurs because students are able to re-enter the dramatic world and independently use the techniques experienced in the drama to move around this world and reflect from the perspectives explored in the drama. It was clear from participants' responses that the structured role play assisted them in comprehending supporting literature.

> You've already got the base for what you needed to really learn and then you can go away and you can go through, look at the readings and sort of pick out what you need. (Donna, int.)

Involvement in the structured role play motivated student teachers to find out more of about the different perspectives explored in the drama. Some participants reported that their curiosity was aroused to the extent that they read beyond the supporting literature and searched for internet sites and articles on the various groups portrayed in the role play. Avril's motivation to read more widely was also a result of her frustration that her classmates did not have a good understanding of their perspectives during the role play and this meant she needed to read more widely after the session.

> I sort of had to look for the stuff myself because some people didn't understand what they were reading. (Avril, int.)

Booth (2000) observed that drama encourages participants not to be satisfied with immediate, simplistic solutions but encourages the peeling away of layers that serve to distort meaning. Similarly Heathcote and Bolton (1995) argued that good role play educates participants to ask relevant questions on issues explored in the drama. For Avril, some of the ideas put forward in the dramatic world did not appear entirely accurate and this led her to seek out the truth about the groups represented in the role play. Her recognition that there was more to be known about the issue than was elicited through the role play contributed to her wide reading on the issue. Avril acknowledged that it was unlikely she would have read as widely if she had not been involved in the role play. This finding is consistent with O'Neill's (1995) observation that encounters in the dramatic world motivate participants to reflect on the world in a different way. In the case of Avril, she was committed to reflect on the issue explored from perspectives beyond the scope of the role play.

CONCLUSION

While the current study is limited by the small number of participants involved, it does provide a rich account of how learning occurred through drama for a specific group of student teachers. Findings suggest that the experience of being involved in a structured role play assisted student teachers to reflect from multiple perspectives during their engagement in the dramatic world and after the role play had concluded. In proposing her framework for critical reflection, Larivee (2000) suggested that teachers needed to challenge themselves to see issues in education from previously unconsidered vantage points. It is only then that they become aware of the filters they used to confirm some responses to situations and dismiss others. The current study found that the thinking promoted within the dramatic world allowed participants to analyse their filters in a way that is difficult to attain in real life. Taylor (1998) has given some insights into how drama can make personal filters visible in his observation of how drama transports participants above and beyond themselves to where they can pay witness to their own values and the values of others. It is the opportunity drama provides through metaxis that allows participants to simultaneously reflect from the perspective of their character while also reflecting on how they have come to hold their own personal perspective. Although the processes that occurred inside the dramatic world certainly assisted most student teachers to reflect on an educational issue from multiple perspectives it is important to point out that the reflective process did not stop the moment they stepped out of role and re-entered the real world.

Drama assisted participants in reflecting on and from multiple perspectives outside of the dramatic world. The structured role play provided participants with a clear visual memory of the various perspectives portrayed which enabled them to re-enter the dramatic world to compare and contrast multiple perspectives when writing their learning log assignment. Many participants believed that the drama contributed to their ability to comprehend the supporting literature they were given at the conclusion of the role play. Some participants attributed their motivation to read beyond the set supporting literature to their involvement in the role play while others believed that had it not been for the drama it was unlikely they would have been motivated to read the set readings. It is important to note that in the case of Avril, her motivation to read more widely was because of her frustration that she was not getting all the information she required from her involvement in the structured role play. Avril felt her classmates had not researched their roles rigorously enough which left her with gaps in her understanding about various perspectives that she addressed through pursuing her own research.

The findings confirm that student teachers perceived that drama assisted them in reflecting on an educational issue from multiple perspectives, and suggest that the use of structured role play assisted them in engaging in a form of critical reflection promoted by

Larivee (2000) and Smyth (2001). The ability of graduates to critically reflect on their practice is an important outcome for many teacher education degrees. Therefore I believe the findings of this study have implications for teacher education providers who aim at developing critically reflective teachers and for curriculum design in higher education.

The student teachers did believe that drama assisted them to better understand the content and concepts integral to the course in which they were studying. Many participants commented that they believed more drama in the classes of their teacher education programme could benefit their learning. Much literature on drama in education has also found that drama has been beneficial in assisting learning in a range of educational and vocational settings (Bolton, 1992; Bolton & Heathcote, 1999; Booth, 2000; O'Neill, 1995; Wilhelm & Edmiston 1998). The findings of the current study provide some evidence as to why learning through drama should continue to occur in a wide range of courses in preservice teacher education.

REFERENCES

Argyris, C. (1990). *Overcoming organizational defenses: Facilitating organizational learning.* Boston: Allyn & Bacon.

Auckland College of Education. (2005). *Module 911.721/731: The moral and political nature of education and teaching: Module booklet.* Auckland: Author.

Boal, A. (1995). *The rainbow of desire: The Boal method of theatre and therapy.* New York: Routledge.

Bolton, G. M. (1992). *New perspectives on classroom drama.* Hemel Hempstead, UK: Simon & Schuster Education.

Bolton, G., & Heathcote, D. (1999). *So you want to use role play? A new approach in how to plan.* Stoke on Trent, UK: Trentham Books.

Booth, D. (2000). Reading stories we construct together. In J. Ackroyd (Ed.), *Literacy alive! Drama projects for literacy learning* (pp. 6–15). Oxon, UK: Hodder & Stoughton.

Braun, J. A., & Crumpler, T. P. (2004). The social memoir: an analysis of developing reflective ability in a pre-service methods course. *Teaching and Teacher Education, 20*(1), 59–75.

Brindley, R., & Laframboise, K. L. (2002). The need to do more: promoting multiple perspectives in preservice teacher education through literature. *Teaching and Teacher Education, 18*(4), 405–420.

Brookfield, S. (1995). *Becoming a critically reflective teacher* (1st ed.). San Francisco: Jossey-Bass.

Creswell, J. W. (2002). *Educational research: Planning, conducting, and evaluating quantitative and qualitative research.* Upper Saddle River, N.J: Merrill.

Dixon, H., Snook, I., & Williams, R. (2000, November). *Conflicting perceptions. Teachers, technicians or professionals?* Paper presented at the Teacher Education Forum of Aotearoa New Zealand, Christchurch, New Zealand.

Duatepe, A. (2005). *The effects of drama based instruction on seventh grade students' geometry achievement, van Hiele geometric thinking levels, attitudes toward mathematics and geometry.* Unpublished doctoral dissertation, Middle East Technical University, Turkey.

Edmiston, B. (2003). What's my position? Role, frame, and positioning when using process drama. *Research in Drama Education, 8*(2), 221–230.

Education Policy Group, College of Education, Massey University. (2003). *Literacy research in South Auckland: A critique.* Retrieved April 3, 2006, from http://www.qpec.org.nz/index.html#x1-63000

Fleming, M., Merrell, C., & Tymms, P. (2004). The impact of drama on pupils' language, mathematics, and attitude in two primary schools. *Research in Drama Education, 9*(2), 177–197.

Fogarty, R. (1994). *Brain compatible classrooms.* Australia: Hawker Brownlow.

Glaser, B. G., & Strauss, A. L. (1967). *The discovery of grounded theory: Strategies for qualitative research.* Chicago: Aldine.

Green, J. C., Carracelli, V. J., & Graham, W. F. (1989). Toward a conceptual framework for mixed-method evaluation designs. *Educational Evaluation and Policy Analysis, 11*(3), 255–274.

Greenwood, J. (2000). *The group the body and the real.* Christchurch, New Zealand: Christchurch College of Education.

Greenwood, J. (2002). Marking the unmarked: Using drama cross-culturally in teacher education in New Zealand. *System Research and Behavioural Science, 19*(1), 323–329.

Gregory, A. (2003, July 25). Higher expectation key to child literacy. *The New Zealand Herald,* p. 10. Section A.

Griggs, T. (2001). Teaching as acting: Considering acting as epistemology and its use in teaching and teacher preparation. *Teacher Education Quarterly, 28*(2), 23–37.

Heathcote, D., & Bolton, G. M. (1995). *Drama for learning: Dorothy Heathcote's mantle of the expert approach to education.* Portmouth, UK: Heinemann.

Kaye, C., & Ragusa, G. (1998). *Boal's mirror: Reflections for teacher education.* Paper presented at the 79th Annual Meeting of the American Research Association, San Diego, California.

Larivee, B. (2000). Transforming teacher practice: Becoming the critically reflective teacher. *Reflective Practice, 1*(3), 293–307.

Mallard, T. (2003). *Family background does not need to restrict learning.* Retrieved August 20, 2004, from http://www.beehive.govt.nz.

Martello, J. (2001). Drama: Ways into critical literacy in the early childhood years. *The Australian Journal of Language and Literacy, 2*(3), 195–207.

Ministry of Education (2003). *Shifting the focus: Achievement for learning: A summary of the sustainability of professional development in literacy – Parts 1 and 2.* Retrieved April 2, 2004, from Ministry of Education website: http://www.minedu.govt.nz.

Minto, J. (2003). *Literacy report welcomed but government interpretation deliberately misleading.* Retrieved August 20, 2003, from http://qpec.org.nz.

Morgan, N., & Saxton, J. (1987). *Teaching drama.* London: Hutchinson Education.

Morris, V. (1998). Teaching social studies through drama: Student meanings. *Journal of Social Studies Research, 25*(1), 3–26.

Nash, R. (2003). One pace forwards two steps backwards. *New Zealand Journal of Educational Studies, 38*(2), 249–254.

Neuman, W.L. (2000). *Social research methods: qualitative and quantitative approaches (4th ed.).* Boston: Allyn & Bacon.

New, R. (1998). Theory and praxis in Reggio Emelia: They know what they are doing and why. In C. G. Edward, L. Gandini, & G. Forman. (Ed.), *The hundred languages of children: The Reggio Emelia approach-Advanced reflections* (pp. 261–284). London: Ablex.

Newman, I., Ridenour, C. S., Newman, C., & De Marco, G. M. P. (2003). A typology of research purposes and its relationship to mixed methods. In A. Tashakkori & C. Teddlie (Eds.), *Handbook of mixed methods in social and behavioural research* (pp. 167–188). Thousand Oaks, California: Sage.

O'Neill, C. (1995). *Drama worlds: A framework for process drama.* Portsmouth, UK: Heinemann.

Pollard, A., & Tann, S. (1987). *Reflective teaching in the primary school: A handbook for the classroom.* London: Cassell.

Raphael, J., & O'Mara, J. (2002). A challenge, a threat and a promise: Drama as professional development for teacher educators. *Melbourne Studies in Education, 43*(2) 24–29.

Reber, R. S. (Ed.). (1995). *Penguin dictionary of psychology.* London: Penguin.

Rose, S., Parks, M., Androes, K., & Mc Mahon, S. D. (2000). Imagery based learning: Improving elementary students' reading comprehension with drama techniques. *Journal of Educational Research, 94*(1), 55–69.

Salvio, P. (1994). What can a body know? Refiguring pedagogic intention into teacher education. *Journal of Teacher Education, 45*(1), 53–61.

Sarantakos, S. (1998). *Social research* (2nd ed.). South Melbourne: Macmillan Education Australia.

Smyth, J. (2001). *Critical politics of teachers' work: An Australian perspective.* New York: Peter Lang.

Strauss, A.L., & Corbin, J.M. (1990). *Basics of qualitative research: Grounded theory procedures and techniques.* Newbury Park, CA: Sage Publications.

Taylor, P. (1998). *Red coats and patriots: Reflective practice in drama and social studies.* Portsmouth, UK: Heinemann.

Timperley, H. (2003). School improvement and teachers' expectations of student achievement. *New Zealand Journal of Educational Studies, 38*(1), 73–88.

Walkinshaw, A. D. (2004). *Integrating drama with primary and junior education: The ongoing debate.* Lewiston, N.Y: Edwin Mellen Press.

Ward, J., & McCotter, S. (2004). Reflection as a visible outcome for pre-service teachers. *Teaching and Teacher Education, 20*(3), 243–257.

Whatman, J. (2000). Learning new roles. In J. O'Toole, & M. Lepp. (Eds.), *Drama for life. Stories of adult learning and empowerment* (pp. 245–254). Brisbane, Australia: Playlab Press.

Wilhelm, J. D., & Edmiston, B. (1998). *Imagining to learn: Inquiry, ethics, and integration through drama.* Portsmouth, NH: Heinemann.

Author Note

Paul Heyward is a Senior Lecturer in the Faculty of Education, University of Auckland, New Zealand. His research has focused on how drama can be used as a teaching approach to assist learning in a range of educational contexts.

This chapter is adapted from a dissertation completed as part of a MEd at the University of Auckland in 2006.

Correspondence concerning this chapter should be addressed by email to: p.heyward@auckland.ac.nz

In: Challenging Thinking about Teaching and Learning   ISBN: 978-1-60456-744-1
Editors: C. M. Rubie-Davies and C. Rawlinson   © 2008 Nova Science Publishers, Inc.

Chapter 17

GIFTED EDUCATION IN TEACHER EDUCATION: IS IT MORE THAN JUST A ONE-OFF LECTURE?

Tracy Riley and Catherine Rawlinson

ABSTRACT

This chapter outlines the results of an investigation of the extent and nature of current provisions of gifted education in preservice and inservice teacher education in New Zealand. The results show that gifted education in preservice teacher education is more than just a one-off lecture; however, questionnaires and document analysis show that at both preservice and inservice levels, the gifted education content is not comprehensive. Suggestions for how teacher education providers can innovatively address gifted and talented education are also presented in this chapter.

INTRODUCTION

As a result of the New Zealand Ministry of Education's Initiatives for Gifted and Talented Learners (2002), and the change to the National Administration Guidelines (giving specific reference to gifted and talented learners), there has been greater demand for gifted education in teacher education. The initiatives arose from recommendations made by a Working Party on Gifted Education, appointed by the Minister of Education in 2001, that:

> the Ministry of Education recommend to all providers of teacher education that their programmes include course content specifically aimed at preparing pre-service teachers to understand and cater for the needs of gifted and talented learners. (Working Party on Gifted Education, 2001, p. 29)

Following this recommendation, the New Zealand Teachers Council, which establishes and maintains standards for teachers' qualifications, advised that programmes leading to teacher registration should include content about teacher responsiveness to students with exceptional abilities. The initiatives also provided increased opportunities for professional development for advisors and teacher educators working in gifted education (i.e., annual professional development meetings, or hui, that were held annually from 2002 to 2005).

In 2004, Riley, Bevan-Brown, Bicknell, Carroll-Lind, and Kearney provided anecdotal evidence regarding the status of gifted education in teacher education. They reported four delivery models:

- integration of gifted content across a variety of papers and programmes
- inclusion of a gifted module or component in a compulsory, inclusive education paper
- optional stand-alone papers, usually in the third year of preservice education
- postgraduate papers and specialized qualifications.

Despite these different options, they concluded that "the bottom line regarding compulsory pre-service teacher education remains that described by the Ministry of Education in 2000: it is seldom addressed" (Riley et al., 2004. p. 154).

In 2005, the Ministry of Education funded the research reported in this chapter: an investigation of the extent and nature of teaching and research in gifted education within the major providers of teacher education. The primary research purpose was to gather both quantitative and qualitative information regarding the delivery of gifted education content within preservice and inservice education. The researchers were seeking the answers to who, what, when, where, how, and why questions, so as to provide future directions in teacher education.

METHODS

Prior to the study, approval was sought and received from the Massey University Human Ethics Committee. Eighteen teacher educators from the six major providers took part in this study. This was a purposive sample of those who had been involved in the professional development meetings. The number of teacher educators from each provider varied from one to four, because of the unique nature of each institution's provisions in gifted and talented education. Similarly, their roles as teacher educators varied, with most participants indicating that gifted and talented education teaching and research was "secondary" to their other responsibilities (e.g., mathematics, special education). Institutional and individual consent was obtained for all participants.

Both qualitative and quantitative data were obtained through:

- questionnaires (exploring gifted education paper and/or programme details such as title, level, delivery mode, and enrolment figures; key topic areas for teaching content and assessment; textbooks and resources; advantages and disadvantages of delivering gifted education in teacher education; future plans; collaboration within and across institutions; Ministry of Education initiatives and support)
- document analysis (e.g., teaching materials/resources such as study guides, sets of readings, and assignment guidelines)
- focus group discussion (for clarification and elaboration of questionnaire responses).

The questionnaire responses were analyzed for frequency of response; the open-ended questions and interviews were analyzed for broad, recurring themes. Initial questionnaire results were shared at the professional development meetings in 2005, and participants were invited to contribute to a focus group discussion. This discussion mainly revolved around professional collaboration and future initiatives.

RESULTS

The focus of this chapter is on preservice and postgraduate education. Other results are reported in Riley and Rawlinson's 2006 paper presented at the Rising Tides National Gifted and Talented Conference, in Wellington, New Zealand.

Preservice Education

All six institutions reported gifted education in primary preservice education; four included content at the early childhood and secondary levels. Gifted and talented education was integrated across curriculum and professional practice papers, and compulsory inclusive education papers included between two and five hours of content (e.g., one or two lecture slots). Characteristics of gifted learners, enrichment/acceleration, and inclusive classroom strategies were the key areas of focus in the inclusive education papers—school and community-based provisions, and policies and procedures were seldom addressed. It was also reported that the majority of institutions offered specialist gifted education papers. These were single semester, optional papers, usually in the final year of teacher preparation.

General feedback from teacher educators about gifted education at the preservice level was that although all students were being exposed to content in this area, "We only touch the tip of the iceberg". As one respondent stated, "What we do is not enough". The teacher educators recognized the importance of the area, but were struggling to adequately provide depth of coverage; while this did vary from individuals across and within institutions, overall the members of this sample were aware of the need for more time, resources, specialist teachers, and collaboration both institutionally and individually.

Postgraduate Education

Three of the six institutions reported integrating gifted education content across a range of postgraduate papers, and four institutions offered specialized papers. Postgraduate student research in gifted education was reported at five institutions. The content of specialist papers included a strong emphasis on the Ministry of Education initiatives, definitions, characteristics, identification, and programming, but little opportunity for hands-on practical learning opportunities. "Depth of study" was reported as the most common advantage of these papers; however, only one institution offered postgraduate qualifications in gifted education (diploma and certificate). The disadvantages of specialized papers were specific to each institution's administrative structures, rather than generalizable.

Summary of Results

In summary, the results demonstrate that at preservice and inservice levels, gifted and talented education is occurring, at varying degrees, at each of the six teacher education providers. Gifted content is integrated within compulsory, inclusive education papers; however, this is limited to between two and five hours. While there are specialized papers on gifted education, these are only available as optional courses. All six providers emphasized that there were opportunities for student research in gifted education. At the postgraduate level, there were specialized papers available; however, there is no master's degree in gifted education offered by any New Zealand teacher education provider. This differs from what is offered overseas (e.g., the United Kingdom and America). There is also a lack of practical, hands-on teaching opportunities for those participating in specialized papers at both preservice and postgraduate levels.

CONCLUSION

Results from this study showed that gifted education in New Zealand preservice teacher education is more than just a one-off lecture, but questionnaires and document analysis illustrated that the content is not comprehensive. The demand for gifted education courses at both preservice and inservice levels will no doubt grow, as the Education Review Office focuses on evaluating the effectiveness of programmes in New Zealand schools, and the need to cater for diversity continues to be a priority.

Several suggestions were made by teacher educators about how to innovatively address gifted and talented education:

- a compulsory preservice paper in gifted education
- greater integration of gifted content across a range of appropriate papers at both preservice and postgraduate levels
- a master's degree in gifted education, giving consideration to collaborative, cross-institutional development and delivery.

A major recommendation from this research is that it is timely for each teacher education institution to carry out an in-house investigation of the extent and nature of teaching and research in gifted education. This should lead to the development of a scope and sequence of content, especially in preservice education, and it could also lead to collaborative, cross-institutional postgraduate programmes.

REFERENCES

Working Party on Gifted Education. *Report to the Minister of Education*. (2001). Wellington, New Zealand: Ministry of Education (2001). Retrieved April 29, 2002 from http://www.executive.govt.nz/minister/mallard/gifted_education/index.html.

Ministry of Education. (2002). *Initiatives in gifted and talented education*. Wellington, New Zealand: Office of the Minister of Education.

Riley, T., Bevan-Brown, J., Bicknell, B., Carroll-Lind, J., & Kearney, A. (2004). *The extent, nature and effectiveness of planned approaches in New Zealand schools for providing for gifted and talented students— Full report.* Wellington, New Zealand: Ministry of Education.

Riley, T., & Rawlinson, C. (2006, August). Teacher education in gifted and talented education in New Zealand. In T. Riley & J. Bevan Brown, *Rising Tides Conference Proceedings* (pp. 111–116). Wellington, New Zealand: National Gifted and Talented Conference 2006.

AUTHOR NOTE

Tracy Riley is a Senior Lecturer in the School of Curriculum and Pedagogy at Massey University, New Zealand. She specializes in gifted and talented education, teaching undergraduate and postgraduate papers and supervising postgraduate student research. She is a member of the Ministry of Education's Sector Advisory Group on Gifted Education and has served in many leadership roles as a researcher and policy advisor. She is co-editor of APEX: The New Zealand Journal of Gifted Education, and on the editorial board of Gifted Child Today magazine. In 2007, she was awarded a National Tertiary Teaching Award for Sustained Excellence.

Catherine Rawlinson is a Senior Lecturer in the Faculty of Education, University of Auckland, New Zealand. She was the representative for the Colleges of Education on the New Zealand Ministerial Working Party on Gifted Education and she has provided leadership for professional development of teachers in gifted education in many schools. Currently she writes and teaches courses for undergraduate and postgraduate students as well as supervising postgraduate research. She is also involved in Ministry of Education contracts associated with gifted education.

The authors would like to acknowledge the Ministry of Education funding for this research.

Correspondence concerning this chapter should be addressed by email to: T.L.Riley@massey.ac.nz or c.rawlinson@auckland.ac.nz

In: Challenging Thinking about Teaching and Learning   ISBN: 978-1-60456-744-1
Editors: C. M. Rubie-Davies and C. Rawlinson   © 2008 Nova Science Publishers, Inc.

Chapter 18

WEB 2.0 IN THE CURRICULUM OF THE FUTURE: EXPLORING THE EDUCATIONAL POTENTIAL OF NEW DEVELOPMENTS IN WEB-BASED DIGITAL TOOLS

John Roder and Tony Hunt

ABSTRACT

The World Wide Web of the internet has been changing rapidly throughout its short existence, but has recently developed in particularly significant ways. The major feature of the second generation Web (Web 2.0) is the way in which users become creators and publishers of online content rather than merely passive readers. This theoretical chapter considers the potential effect that such changes may have on the process of education, focusing specifically on the use of "wikis" (web pages that can be jointly edited by users over the internet), for shared construction of online content by students. This discussion is contextualized by reflection on an initial trial in which wikis were used by one of the authors in a teacher education course. The wider implications of this technology for educators are considered in relationship to current views of the changing nature of education and the role that information and communication technology plays in learning and teaching.

INTRODUCTION

A wide range of authors are claiming that the World Wide Web is changing and that this change has been significant enough to be called "Web 2.0" (Alexander, 2006; Lamb, 2004). A quick search on Google reveals that much is currently being written about the rise of what we now think of as "version 2" of the Web; it has been called the "social Web", with reference to the "social software" which is its defining feature. Shirky defines social software simply as "software that supports group interaction" (2003, cited in Owen, Grant, Sayers, & Facer, 2006, p. 12).

This recent phenomenon fits well with the original vision for democratic agency (that is, participation in and engagement with the world, and the means by which something is accomplished) developed by Tim Berners-Lee, the "father of the Web". Berners-Lee's designs were for a "read/write" Web that would be a space to enact the collective desires for communication and data sharing in a global scientific community (Gillies & Cailliau, 2000). Technological constraints of the early 1990s made this difficult to achieve beyond its specialized roots. Important Web tools that have since appeared as part of this recent cultural and technological revolution include blogs, wikis, social bookmarking, social networking sites, podcasting, and the use of RSS feeds (sometimes known as Really Simple Syndication). These types of software are briefly explained, followed by a discussion of their implications for education.

Alexander (2006) reminds us that internet-based social software is not new, in itself. We have had email, listservers, news groups, and discussion-board messages since the early days of the internet, before the development of the World Wide Web. Tim Berners-Lee began with a vision of the Web as a highly interactive space in which it was easy for users to contribute and edit the content. As the Web became more popular, a few providers made information available to a wider audience. The dominant emphasis over the first decade was on increasing the sophistication of the multimedia experience provided for the web page visitor (Lamb, 2004). The opportunity for most web users to write to the Web was extremely limited; only those with specialist software, coding knowledge, skills, and access to a server could contribute.

The democratizing face of today's Web 2.0 is clearly evident in the phenomenal proliferation of blogs. "Blogging" is now an ubiquitous form of expression on the Web, where "bloggers" create commentary on many aspects of the world today, from the mundane and ultra-personal through to political comment and, in many cases, concerns with the nature of Web 2.0 social practices themselves. They publish their writing in online web logs (or blogs) which can be thought of as a hybrid between a personal web page and a journal. A blogger then engages in a form of online journalism, but is not necessarily someone who has had traditional journalistic training or writing experience. What makes blogs such a significant social phenomenon is that anyone with access to the Web can share their ideas with few of the restrictions of traditional publishing. The number of blogs has gone from near zero in early 2003 to more than 70 million today, and continues to grow at the rate of 120,000 a day. (Sifrey, 2007)

To the army of bloggers, the Web is no longer simply a source of information, or means of private email communication, but an opportunity to express their authorial "voice" to a global audience. The other significant feature of blogs is their ability to reflect collective interests and shared discussions. This is most obvious when features are provided for linking between blogs, or for enabling readers to add their own comments.

Social bookmarking sites enable the sharing online of an individual's bookmarks which link to web-based materials, so that others can access the interests and links of anyone else in that community. In social bookmarking, users "tag" their bookmarks with keywords which they believe are significant for searching by others. This lifts the activity to a level of distributed cognition where it is believed that the knowledge is built and modified across a social group rather than held by individuals (Scardamalia & Bereiter, 1994). These sites are not restricted to simply sharing bookmarks: they could involve the uploading of photos, such as the well known phototagging site Flickr, or involve content focused on particular purposes, such as the people meeting each other in social networking sites (e.g., Myspace, Facebook, or

WAYN). The tagging affords new mindsets about searching, opening up new kinds of community behaviour, and potentially new ways of learning.

Podcasting involves the digital recording of sound and the uploading of these files to the Web. They can be accessed from particular interest sites that are set up to share podcasts, such as online radio stations offering an archive of programmes. Alternatively they could be an integral part of a blog where the authoring is a mix of audio and written texts. As bandwidth has become less of a problem, this has extended to video podcasts.

What has dramatically changed the nature of this online sharing activity is the use of syndication through RSS feeds. Traditionally, Web users have searched for, and retrieved, information but RSS feeds enable them to specify in advance the information that they wish to receive. Any blog or podcast site (and indeed many other web services) can be linked to in this way. When a change occurs on such a site, anyone with a feed is updated with the new information. This is often characterized as the move from "push" broadcasting to "pull" narrowcasting (Owen et al., 2006). It is this syndication technology that allows bloggers, for example, to aggregate what is called microcontent from various other sites (e.g. news sites and the sites of other bloggers). This sense of people being connected through content which is dynamically updating is another feature of Web 2.0's social character.

Wikis allow people to upload their own content to shared web pages which others can easily edit. The word "wiki" is derived from a Hawaiian term "wiki wiki", meaning "quick". Wikipedia is the best known example of this format. It is an online encyclopaedia that is written by its readers and to which any internet user can contribute; the widest source of expertise is available for writing and editing and the work can continually evolve and update itself. The same principle has been applied to writing of many kinds, often within small, closed communities, rather than on the wider internet. The crucial feature of a wiki is that it is designed to allow online collaboration by a number of authors.

The purpose of this chapter is to indicate some of the relationships between these types of applications and changes to our thinking about the purposes of education, our understanding of learning, and the way we enable the match. This will be illustrated by describing the educational use of one of these tools, the wiki, which Alexander (2006) suggests is "the application most thoroughly grounded in social interaction" (p. 36).

The development of Web 2.0, with its emphasis on interaction, democratization of knowledge, connectivity, and personal involvement reflects wider changes in society which characterize the post-industrial information age economy, and these changes pose challenges for educators which will are discussed below.

THE WEB IN TEACHING AND LEARNING

The interactive online tools that characterize Web 2.0 are the latest in a long line of technological innovations that have been applied to educational purposes. The impact of technological innovations on classroom practice has been, in general, negligible (Cuban, 1987; Cuban, 2001) and the educational benefit of information and communication technology (ICT) are elusive in practice (Chandler, 1992; Pea and Sheingold, 1987). Despite predictions of transformative effects from ICT, and undoubted examples of its effective use, this outcome is depressing. Considering more than two decades of research on ICT in education, Nichol and Watson lament that, "Never in the history of education has so much been spent by so many for so long, with so little to show for the blood, sweat and tears expended" (2003, p. 132).

Aviram (2001) proposes some reasons for this lack of effect: schools need time to adapt; teachers, having grown up in an ICT-poor environment, are having difficulties adapting; the technology is still immature; and education is, by nature, conservative. The most convincing reason, in Aviram's view, is that the structure of educational organisations creates a major impediment to ICT-related change.

This view is representative of a widespread belief that the major social and economic changes which are now occurring—such as the "information explosion", globalization, the digital revolution in information and entertainment, and e-commerce—call for a major change in the structure of education systems and institutions. Not only are these changes created, to a large extent, by developments in ICT, but ICT is seen as providing important means for dealing with their effects.

There is evidence that major changes in society have influenced education in the past: It can be argued that our current educational system is intimately connected with the technology of the industrial age. Sociological commentary on education, based on the work of Bowles and Gintis (1976), Bernstein (1971), and Bourdieu (1977), has emphasized the role of educational institutions in social reproduction (Apple, 1990), specifically in facilitating the provision of labour for industry (McKinnon, Nolan, & McFadden, 1992) and maintaining the divisions between the workers and the managerial and ruling elites. Tyack (1974) asserts that the educational reformers who created American urban schools in the nineteenth century were impressed by "the order and efficiency of the new technology and forms of organisation they saw about them. The division of labour in the factory, the punctuality of the railroad, the chain of command and co-ordination in modern business—these aroused a sense of wonder and excitement" (p. 28).

We need to consider whether changes associated with our increasingly networked society will also have an effect on curriculum in schools and tertiary education.

Bernstein (1971) identified two major forms of curriculum, the collection type and the integrated type. In the collection type of curriculum, the learner collects favoured content, dependent on views of what is valued knowledge, to satisfy evaluation criteria, whereas in the integrated curriculum the various components are not independent, but "held in open relation to each other" (p. 204).

McKinnon et al. (1992) argue that the collection type of curriculum has provided the major way in which students have been socialized into industrial society. Associated with this curriculum are traditional pedagogical practices and evaluation methods which reinforced the hierarchical structure underpinning working and social life.

In recent years, however, changes in the modes of production have been dramatic. These have been popularized by Alvin Toffler (1990) who wrote about what he called "de-massification" in highly technological societies whereby the new computer-based technology is leading to the breakdown of large units into smaller ones through the easier access to knowledge which the technology provides. Technological development and knowledge production are both growing at increasing rates, accompanied by growth in service-based industries and changes in the labour market which have resulted in higher levels of unemployment for less skilled workers and an increase in the number who can be classified as working in the information sector (Aoyama & Castells, 2002).

The concept of the knowledge society (Gilbert, 2005) has gained wide currency in the last decade, as illustrated in New Zealand by government-sponsored "Knowledge Wave" conferences, national strategies, and political rhetoric. Gilbert makes the point that traditionally people have tended to think of knowledge as "stuff" that you have, and education the process of collecting that knowledge. She sees the knowledge society as being based on a new view of knowledge as an active process. This represents an increased emphasis on knowing rather than inert knowledge. This view reflects the arguments of Lyotard about knowledge in a post-modern society (Lankshear, 2003). Lankshear draws attention to changed perceptions of epistemology resulting from an increasingly digital society, networked technologies, and neocapitalism. These changes include a favouring of procedural knowledge over propositional knowledge and distributed knowledge over individual knowledge. We are much more concerned with creating new knowledge as an outcome of education than collecting existing knowledge, because we are increasingly seeing economic success, and even survival of the human species, as requiring this capacity.

Such changes are widely seen as demanding a curriculum of Bernstein's "integration" type, in which the boundaries between subjects are more fluid, and views of socially valued knowledge are changing. Knowing a large number of facts about a subject becomes progressively less important when accessible information is growing exponentially, while knowledge of techniques for selecting and evaluating information becomes increasingly important. Understanding underlying principles as a basis for organizing knowledge becomes more valuable than memorization and regurgitation.

Under such a curriculum, the pedagogy is likely to become less didactic and require that students develop more self-regulation and accept greater responsibility and control over their own learning. This occurs best when students are intrinsically motivated by engaging their personal interests, natural inquisitiveness, and concerns for social and environmental issues. We expect, therefore, that the school will take more responsibility for creating learning conditions that encourage these things, and that teaching and learning will become much more of a collaborative exercise. In such pedagogy, learning is seen as a process where individuals play an active role in building their own intellectual structures.

Evaluation within this kind of education "tends to emphasize assessment of the developing ways of knowing rather than the attainment of states of knowledge" (McKinnon et al., 1992, p. 12). Criterion-referenced and achievement-based assessments are more consistent with this approach, compared with the commonly employed standardized tests, external examinations, and norm-referenced testing of traditional education. Whereas the collection-type curriculum favours evaluation which ranks individuals for selection purposes, the alternative, integration-type curriculum aims to provide information to assist in determining the most appropriate kind of programme for the learners through formative assessment.

It is increasingly argued that alternative approaches are required today to equip all students with broader-based skills for this knowledge society. Information handling skills, interpersonal skills, communication skills, listening skills, and the ability to prioritize, negotiate, and innovate will all be of greater importance. The kind of educational programmes that are likely to promote these skills are those identified as developing a decade and a half ago by McKinnon et al. (1992) in which learning becomes more personalized and active, with an emphasis on problem solving rather than memorization, flexible organisation of time, grouping and spaces, and the use of a wide range of media and sources of information.

Despite the lack of convincing evidence of widespread change of this nature, commented on above, a growing body of literature affirms the potential for change in limited ways. In the past decade, technological change has provided tools more useful for learning and made them ubiquitous. The developing power of computer processors and software have enabled computers to become easier to use, capable of a wider range of communicative functions, and more embedded in daily life. The growth of the internet has made them a ubiquitous source of information and entertainment, and encouraged more people to use them for communicating with their family, friends and the world at large. No longer is the act of publication on the Web restricted to those with highly specialized knowledge skills. It is this ability to write the internet, as well as read it, which makes the Web 2.0 developments potentially powerful in education.

In a recent review of teacher learning with digital technologies, Fisher, Higgins and Loveless (2006) conclude that:

> Digital technologies can play a role as tools which afford learners the potential to engage with activities. The use of such tools may extend or enhance their users' abilities, or even allow users to create new ways of dealing with tasks which might also change the very nature of the activity. The technologies can also provide limitations and structure to activities, influencing the nature and boundaries of the activity. (p. 19)

They describe the affordances of such technologies in terms of four groups of purposeful activities: (a) knowledge building, (b) distributed cognition, (c) community and communication, and (d) engagement. These kinds of activity fit well with the directions of change in learning needs identified above.

The term "affordances" used by these authors has become common in writing about e-learning and has its roots in cognitive psychology and the study of human–computer interaction. John and Sutherland (2005) suggest that the concept is concerned with potentiality. They suggest it can be a useful lens through which to view pedagogical implications of a technology and how we as agents act in response to its opportunities or constraining influences. At one level this could be seen in terms of the physical effectiveness of the ICT tools and environments, while at another level, they argue that what the tools and resources "afford" may be more determined by the perceptions of users rather than merely the features of those tools.

The kind of technology which has driven many of the changing needs of society are also providing some of the tools, now beginning to appear in Web 2.0 which can, perhaps, assist in providing educational programmes to satisfy them. This chapter now considers the authors' experience in implementing a course using one of these tools.

WIKI USE IN TEACHER EDUCATION

To investigate the use of wikis for shared knowledge construction in an educational context, a wiki tool was introduced into a teacher education course being taught using a blended, flexible approach. Participants were practising teachers who were working towards a degree qualification, and the course began with an initial four days on campus before moving fully online for the remainder of the semester. Moodle was chosen as the learning management system for a number of reasons, including the blog and wiki tools which were easy to manage. The focus of this course was on ICT, its effect on society, and the critique of its use in educational contexts, and therefore this setting seemed to provide an ideal space to explore the affordances, or perceived potentialities, of Web 2.0. The initial belief of the authors, one of whom was the course lecturer, was that the inclusion of student-created wikis would provide an opportunity to develop better alignment between course objectives, course content, and the teaching approach. Ongoing reflection on the part of the authors supported this, and it is these reflections that are now discussed.

Changing ideas about the nature of knowledge, digital-influenced epistemologies, shared knowledge construction, distributed cognition, and engagement in communities of learning were just some of the concepts that would ideally be encountered throughout the course. The experiences were designed to explore and critique these as concepts, and also provide an authentic experience of a learning environment that would allow participants to develop their own informed values and dispositions. The authors' experiences in other online learning environments suggested that students' depth of insight was more likely to be present when there was meaningful infusion of the educational technology in the design of the course. In this case, it was believed that the co-construction of wikis would stimulate such informed insights; it was believed that the synergies and conditions afforded by this rich engagement with wikis would provide scaffolding experiences to help students appreciate the philosophies, theory, and practice of ICT-infused education.

The work around wikis formed the larger part of the second half of this course. It was set up as the vehicle for learning, with groups publishing the findings of their investigations into different aspects of pedagogy involving e-learning. The wiki product, the critique of significant ideas, and the processes revealed through ongoing planning and review, comprised one assessed task, worth 60% of the final grade. A study of the different approaches to assessment made possible through the use of wikis would be worthy of further study and is only briefly described here.

The significant feature of the assessment was the split of marks between the individual's contribution (50 marks) and the group's (10 marks) for the planning work on the structure of the wiki. The ability to split marks this way in a project with aspects of collaborative authorship is made possible by a wiki's ability to track the history of contributions and the features that reveal comments made behind the scenes as the wiki is built. Group members took responsibility for different aspects of the overall wiki but were still able to leverage off the planning and support of others. Indeed, students' own marks would improve wherever they could elaborate on meaning in their own sections by thoughtful hyperlinking into other areas of the work. This was seen as an important feature of working with wikis. There are tensions here that require careful thought in the design of the teaching; however, this appears to offer a way forward in the quest for alternative assessment techniques which address the "I" and the "we" in group projects, where a single group mark is not seen to be adequate or entirely valid.

The wiki was clearly one of the major tools in the course, but it was also part of a comprehensive online learning environment which also included forums to discuss any and all aspects of the course, along with a glossary tool that each group worked on and other integrated message systems. Apart from the new work with wikis, the course lecturer was already well used to online teaching using a range of communication tools to scaffold community building processes. The lecturer's style of teaching was aimed at being strategic and enabling positive interdependence, in contrast to a lecturer-centric orientation which encourages dependency on the lecturer as the sole teacher in the group, the central hub of all interaction, and the font of all knowledge. Expectations and group strategies were established early in the course to encourage students to share experiences, debate theory, provide opinion, and justify positions. The significance of social, critical, and digital literacies was signalled early on. The lecturer believed that these were key elements of the pedagogy needed for the innovative ways of learning employed in the wiki project.

Initially it seemed that the students found the collaborative aspect of the online assessment task daunting, but given that they already knew each other from the on-campus sessions, they approached the project with considerable faith. This fluctuated as they became more aware of what they were involved in. The lack of familiarity with the software on the part of the lecturer and technical support staff contributed to the technical level of challenge faced by the students. The Moodle environment enabled participants to add comments in forums set up to support the task, as well add comments to each page or contribution in the wiki. Students' commentary at first generally described, in quite positive terms, how the task was highly engaging. In a number of reports, the comments were about the motivating nature of the work and how it could be seen as "taking over" their lives. There appeared to be a sense of pride developing, which was related to how they were establishing their identity. Changes in these messages came when constraints overtook early success. These were both technical and social. Such problems could arise, for example, if a participant were attempting to introduce multimedia images and events without a solid understanding of the principles, and could not get adequate support from others. Another conceptual challenge arose out of the ease with which multiple hyperlinked pages could be created. This started to overwhelm some individual contributors when they had not fully engaged in joint planning.

Towards completion of the course, a forum was created to enable students to look back over the experience. The invitation was made to participants, encouraging them to share their reflections on lessons learnt, their own expectations, their comments on alignment and match with course intentions, and any other matters they felt were significant. As the assessment task drew to a close, most participants reported some satisfaction with what they felt they had learned. Events at times had emotionally stretched people and this was also acknowledged. Feedback was often expressed in terms of their technical and process skills and quite strongly referred to their understanding of course themes, the processes they had been engaged in, and the insights they had made into their own areas of investigation. This was a group of teachers who were aware of the importance of an open and safe learning environment and had experienced how essential this was in very real ways throughout the wiki building process.

The culmination of this commentary provided rich feedback on what could be done differently in future courses, including a lot of thinking around the role of the lecturer, and the role of the students who were, themselves, teachers. Comments ranged from the view that more support was needed ahead of the task, to the more predominant notion that success comes from a wide range of elements, including access, timing, prior experience, group responsiveness, and students' abilities to adjust to new roles. These anecdotal remarks appear to reinforce some of the original perceptions of the authors; namely, that the very nature of the community learning embodied in wiki building seems to invite highly reflective and useful feedback.

DEVELOPING VIEWS OF THE WEB IN EDUCATION

Looking over the course, and at the activity surrounding the wiki in particular, the authors believe that the students' engagement in wiki building had helped them to appreciate a new view of knowledge construction and its place in learning and teaching. Noting that the topics and themes chosen for investigation in the wiki projects were designed to take a critical view of the links between ICT and curriculum, it was possible to discern shifts in thinking as the content of each wiki developed. Students made statements about ICT-influenced pedagogies having the potential for learning to be less predictable and linear, more adaptive, more self-regulatory, and with more potential for increased student responsibility. They perceived that this arose out of participation in community activity. Moreover, the notion of individual knowledge was seriously challenged by the sense that, as group members, they were as strong as their ability to connect to knowledge that had been developed as a result of interdependence and collaboration. This included the way that participants capitalized on the thinking that was distributed across the group. An emerging and quite complex sense of procedural knowledge, multiliteracies, distributed cognition, agency, and engagement stood out as both the content and the curriculum in this rich immersive experience.

In the Web 2.0 world, the focus is on aggregating and connecting microcontent from a range of digital sources. Both Alexander (2006) and McWilliam (2005) talk about challenges to authorship at a level quite different from what has been valued in the past—that of borrowing from other sources and remixing various designs of meaning and multimodal representations to suit new literary purposes. Academics are well used to the challenges of plagiarism. When the boundaries blur, it becomes considerably more challenging, especially for novices who may become seduced by the availability of so much information on the Web. Lankshear (2003) points us toward an epistemological shift in what is valued, suggesting (following Lyotard) that, in future, "truth" as we know it may not be required. Lankshear proposes that in a knowledge society the value is in the exchange of information and fitness for purpose. He argues for a construct that encompasses what he terms "digital epistemologies". In this he suggests that the move from the physical atoms of analogue media, and the realities of a print-constrained existence, to a more virtual "bits and bytes" digital world has changed not only the medium in which information exists, but more significantly how knowledge is produced through the affordances of the web, new digital media, and fundamental shifts in social practice. Knowledge construction competencies may be more aligned with processes of digital connectedness, discernment, and collaboration. With such sites for knowledge construction as Wikipedia, the notion of fully individual knowledge artefacts disappears in favour of paradigmatic shifts where, as Lankshear puts it:

> a particular "assemblage" of knowledge that is brought together—however momentarily—in the product of an individual may more properly be understood as a collective assemblage involving many minds (and machines). (p. 184)

Supporting this position, McWilliam (2005) promotes a view of an eminently emergent and remixable curriculum. She draws on the term "redaction" to capture the act of adapting and repurposing of a mixture of sources and media to create suitable new literary forms. Seely Brown (2002) picks up on the theme, asking how we make judgements in this kind of information and media rich web environments. He sees favour in the description of this "web-smart" redaction as being akin to "bricolage", a term from the work of Levi-Strauss that is used to describe the finding of "concrete" material to build something that is seen as important. The students' developing skills as they built their wikis fit well with Seely Brown's description of what it takes: "Judgment is inherently critical to becoming an effective digital bricoleur" (p. 14).

The wiki building experience created some doubt for the teacher participants about their traditional views of literacy. It enabled them to critique some of their experiences and their current understandings of digital literacies with reference to changing social and cultural practice on the Web. Indeed, a major theme of the course was the educational imperative for new modes of curriculum that might address multiple literacies such as information literacy, critical literacy, media literacy, social literacy, digital literacy, and all forms of multi-modal and multimedia literacies (Kellner, 2004; Lankshear and Knobel, 2003). Understanding the power agendas and discursive relationships between technology, literacy, and learning is made more accessible through engagement in the production of knowledge and how meaning is made in these new digitally integrated media (Lankshear & Snyder, 2000).

The authors believe that learning to see how language works in different contexts that are increasingly less unitary and individualistic, and encompass more "hybridity", is a key element of this multiliteracy imperative (Cope, Kalantzis, & New London Group, 2000). Another form of hybridity relevant to the debate and scope of this course is the mix of integrated and hyperlinked media using oral, written, and visual modes of language and the linguistic skills to read meaning in these usually web-based hypertextual hybrids. Supporting the earlier argument around engagement, Kress (1997) argues that meaning making in the multimedia arena requires creative agency as a key to literacy competency. Students, more than ever, need to be creators of these hybrid texts as a significant aspect of their educative journey towards becoming critical consumers of new media.

McWilliam (2005) takes the sense of a paradigm shift further, arguing that a "pedagogy of unlearning" is needed in order to create a match with the competencies required by a fluid modern society. She argues that traditional notions of curriculum and teaching practices have left students unprepared for a society valuing critical integrative skills. Building on the notion of redaction and bricolage referred to earlier, it is the ability to aggregate and remix content according to rapidly shifting purposes that she points out would be more congruent with the needs of contemporary fluid society. McWilliam grounds this view of teaching through contrasting images of what she names as teachers' "seven deadly habits". Three examples from traditional dogma give an idea of what the wiki builders were asked to critique and respond to around their own "unlearning": teachers should know more than students; teachers lead—students follow; teachers assess—students are assessed. There was little from the wiki-building experience that supported their traditional notion of teaching, literacy, or curriculum. In contrast to traditional "habits", and when reflecting on the question of suitable pedagogical frameworks, the research of Lingard and Mills (2002) resonated with the students' integrative approach to pedagogy encompassing domain knowledge, intellectual challenge, digital literacies, critical literacies, metacognitive strategies, connectedness, and supportedness. These were not only seen in discussion and reading, but were felt by them as student participants through the overall engagement in complex rich tasks and productive action (Lingard & Mills, 2002).

The process of shared knowledge construction with its dimensions of connectedness and supportedness can also be looked at in terms of its alignment with Lave and Wenger's theories concerning communities of practice (1991). They posit that acquiring and developing knowledge is seen as an inherently social activity. Learning is mediated by the social beliefs and practices valued by the group. Learning is seen as a complex of mediated interactions involving the experience and knowledge that they bring to the group, or take from the group. Levels of expertise are both directly and indirectly influenced by the richness of interaction across the group as a whole. A key theme in their theory is the notion of "legitimate peripheral participation" where novices watch from the edges as part of their learning in the group. This is often talked about in cyberspeak as "lurking".

What characterizes an effective community of practice is the quality of interaction between "novices" and "experts" as they share their knowledge. The more members interact with each other, frequently swapping between novice and expert roles depending on what they have to offer, the more they become insiders to the groups' new cultural practices, and the more likely their learning is to be richer.

Contributions in the wiki building process were not restricted to a member's own group. Some course participants stimulated thinking in other groups through comment and questions appearing across the group forums. Ideas and resources were shared. This was certainly not universal, but in more traditional arenas it is unlikely to be valued at all, and hence unlikely to happen. Paradoxically more interdependence of this order fosters greater independence on the part of individuals. As an example, if more than one individual's contributions fell back then it became difficult for the group to establish direction or reflect on the more complex issues as they emerged. Owen et al. (2006) suggest that this is a feature of social software; group action requires individual action and in turn acts as a catalyst to further individual agency. It would be misleading to think this kind of synergy serendipitously took place: co-construction of loose community guidelines, and models of how these might be enacted, was seen as an essential element in the lecturer's role. Talk among the community about the way they were sharing, including lecturer responsiveness, provided further examples and helped to drive shifts in the kind of participation that was valued.

In reading the online talk, it was clear that learning through full engagement and community interaction did not happen for everyone. Those who felt they remained "outsiders" during the events became less likely to make shifts in their insight into curriculum change. Conversely those who worked to become "insiders" during the wiki experience, seemed, even after only a little experience, to indicate that they needed to confront their beliefs about teaching and learning. They reflected on shifts in their own ways of learning. This included some deeper insights into the nature of an integrative curriculum, especially changes in knowledge and knowledge construction.

Table 18.1, derived from the work of Nonaka and Takeuchi (1995), lists the kind of processes conducive to developing shared knowledge construction that are similar to those experienced in this course. Nonaka and Takeuchi are describing a process of creation that has come to be seen as symbolic of what many Japanese companies are using as they respond to the demands of the knowledge society.

Table 18.1. Processes Conducive to Shared Knowledge Construction

The process of creation is seen as taking place within a spiral, in the following stages	
Stage	What the stage involves
Sharing ideas with colleagues in half-formed and loose ways	Sharing current tacit knowledge
Using others to help you clarify and explain your ideas	Moving from tacit to explicit knowledge
Seeing and fitting your ideas into the pattern of ideas generated in the framework around you	Moving from individual to new group concepts; a new explicit knowledge
Working within and developing from that framework	From new explicit to new tacit
This stimulates a new cycle of knowledge creation at both an intra- and inter-organisational level	

Note. Summarized from Owen et al. (2006, p. 34), based on the work of Nonaka and Takeuchi (1995).

An analysis of these processes suggests considerable complexity when compared with traditional tightly controlled processes for developing an individualistic view of knowledge and knowledge transmission. Scardemalia and Bereiter (1994) describe this shared cognitive activity as distributed cognition, the strength and evidence manifesting itself in the actions across the whole group or community. In their work on Knowledge Forum, an educational software environment designed in the early 1990s to help and support knowledge building communities, they argue for an ecological view of learning. In this view the computer-mediated interactions afforded by shared community "knowledge spaces", now common in the Web 2.0 era, were seen to provide the necessary conditions and support for knowledge building.

No longer does clear hierarchical authority, seen perhaps as the traditional teacher's role, work in this kind of community interaction. Nor is the ability to prescribe ahead of time every step in a process of learning likely to suit the complex environments of the post-industrial society. In its place, cultural conditions need nurturing where loosely coupled arrangements allow for authority to shift depending on context and timing. Much of the planning given in this scenario emerges from within the task and overall learning experience. Learning conditions of this order also respect complexity, taking a connectivist, networked, and systemic view of formal and informal educational processes (Downes, 2005; Davis & Sumara, 2006). An essential feature here is the ability of members in a system to evolve self-organizing behaviours, where they learn about learning from the very collaborative networking processes that they are engaged in. The more successful groups of students building their wikis appeared to exhibit this loosely-coupled learning behaviour, reflecting similar kinds of self-regulative cultural practices that have found their existence in the norms and shifts which constitute the "cyberculture" known as Web 2.0.

CONCLUSION

The development of new forms of communication and interaction on the internet, which comprise this phenomenon of Web 2.0, may be seen as indicative of changing patterns in social systems and also as drivers of such change. To disentangle cause and effect is beyond the scope of this chapter, but it is clear that many commentators see these changed communication patterns as providing both challenges and opportunities for educators.

Reflection on the experience of teaching a course in which the students used wikis for the collaborative construction of reports of their shared research into the nature of e-learning have given the authors confidence that this is a technique worthy of deeper investigation. The use of wikis has indicated important features of the learning which can occur in the process of the activity, together with some of the associated problems that need to be dealt with. These experiences indicate that shared knowledge construction mediated by such online tools may be a potent stimulus to learning. The next stage in this research will be to investigate more thoroughly student learning that occurs under these conditions. Educators need to have a deeper understanding of the conditions under which learning occurs in the Web 2.0 environment, including the knowledge and skills required of the teacher and the learners, and the technical requirements which support the process.

The extent to which such methods of learning and teaching prepare students for what appears to be a changing global society are even more difficult to assess. If a fundamentally different curriculum is necessary to meet the changed needs of society that are predicted by many writers, there is a possibility that the kind of interactive tools which comprise Web 2.0 may help to contribute to the demand in such a curriculum for new forms of interaction and collaboration.

REFERENCES

Alexander, B. (2006). A new wave of innovation for teaching and learning [Electronic version]. *Educause Review, 41*(2), 33-44. Retrieved 20 March, 2007, from http://www.educause.edu/apps/er/erm06/erm0621.asp.

Aoyama, T., & Castells, M. (2002). An empirical assessment of the informational society: Employment and occupational structures of G7 countries, 1920–2000. *International Labour Review, 141*, 123–160.

Apple, M. W. (1990). *Ideology and curriculum.* New York: Routledge.

Aviram, A. (2000). From "computers in the classroom" to mindful radical adaptation by education systems to the emerging cyber culture. *Journal of Educational Change, 1*, 221–352.

Bernstein, B. (1971). *Classification and control* (Vol. 1). London: Routledge & Kegan Paul.

Bigum, C. (1993). Curriculum and the mythinformation technologies. In B. Green (Ed.), *Curriculum, technology and textual practice* (pp. 81–105). Geelong, VIC. Australia: Deakin University.

Bourdieu, P. (1977). *Outline of a theory of practice.* Cambridge, Cambridge University Press.

Bowles, S., & Gintis, H. (1976). *Schooling in capitalist America.* London: Routledge & Kegan Paul.

Chandler, D. (1992). The purpose of the computer in the classroom. In J. Beynon & H. Mackay (Eds.), *Technological literacy and the curriculum* (pp. 171–196). London: Falmer Press.

Cope, B., Kalantzis, M., & New London Group. (2000). *Multiliteracies: Literacy learning and the design of social futures*: South Yarra, VIC. Australia: Macmillan.

Cuban, L. (1987). *Teachers and machines: the classroom use of technology since 1920.* New York: College Press.

Cuban, L. (2001). *Oversold and underused: Computers in the classroom*. Cambridge Mass.: Harvard University Press.

Davis, B., & Sumara, D. J. (2006). *Complexity and education: Inquiries into learning, teaching, and research*. Mahwah, NJ: Lawrence Erlbaum Associates.

Downes, S. (2005). *An introduction to connective knowledge*. Retrieved 15 October, 2007, from http://www.downes.ca/files/connective_knowledge.htm.

Fisher, T., Higgins, C., & Loveless, A. (2006). *Teachers learning with digital technologies: A review of research and projects*. Bristo, UKl: FutureLab.

Gilbert, J. (2005). *Catching the knowledge wave? The knowledge society and the future of education*. Wellington, New Zealand: New Zealand Council for Educational Research Press.

Gillies, J., & Cailliau, R. (2000). *How the web was born*. Oxford: Oxford University Press.

Kellner, D. (2004). *Technological transformation, multiple literacies, and the re-visioning of education* [Electronic version], 43. Retrieved 4 May, 2006, from http://www.gseis. ucla.edu/faculty/kellner/essays/technologicaltransformation.pdf.

Kress, G. (1997). *Before writing: Rethinking the paths to literacy*. London: Routledge.

John, P., & Sutherland, R. (2005). Affordance, opportunity and the pedagogical implications of ICT. *Educational Review, 57*(4), 405–413.

Lamb, B. (2004). Wide open spaces: Wikis, ready or not [Electronic version]. *Educause Review*, 39, 36–48. Retrieved 5 January,2007, from http://www.educause.edu/ir/library/pdf/erm0452.pdf.

Lankshear, C. (2003). The challenge of digital epistemologies. *Education, Communication and Information, 3*(2), 167–186.

Lankshear, C., & Knobel, M. (2003). *New literacies: Changing knowledge and classroom learning*. Buckingham, UK: Society for Research into Higher Education and Open University Press.

Lankshear, C., & Snyder, I. (2000). *Teachers and techno-literacy: Managing literacy, technology and learning in schools*. St Leonards, NSW. Australia: Allen & Unwin.

Lave, J., & Wenger, E. (1991). *Situated learning: Legitimate peripheral participation*. Cambridge, UK: Cambridge University Press.

Lingard, B., & Mills, M. (2002, October). *Teachers and school reform: Aligning the message systems*. Paper presented at the New Zealand Council for Educational Research conference "Teachers make a difference: What is the research evidence?", Wellington, New Zealand.

McKinnon, D. H., Nolan, C. J. P., & McFadden, M. (1992). *Changing education: Towards productive and collaborative practice*. Canberra: Australian Federal Government.

McWilliam, E. (2005). Unlearning pedagogy. *Journal of Learning Design, 1*(1), 1–11.

Nichol, J., & Watson, K. (2003). Editorial: Rhetoric and reality – the present and future of ICT in education. *British Journal of Educational Technology, 34*(2), 131–136.

Nonaka, I., & Takeuchi, H. (1995). *The knowledge-creating company: How Japanese companies create the dynamics of innovation*. New York: Oxford University Press.

Owen, M., Grant, L., Sayers, S., & Facer, K. (2006). *Social software and learning* [Electronic version]. Retrieved 3 July, 2007, from http://www.futurelab.org.uk/research/opening_education/social_software_01.htm.

Pea, R., & Sheingold, K. (1987). *Mirrors of mind: Patterns of experience in educational computing*. Norwood, N.J.: Ablex.

Scardamalia, M., & Bereiter, C. (1994). Computer support for knowledge building communities. In T. Koschmann (Ed.), *CSCL: Theory and practice of an emerging paradigm* (pp. 249–268). Mahwah, NJ: Lawrence Erlbaum Associates.

Seely Brown, J. (2002). *Growing up digital* [Electronic version]. *USDLA Journal, 16*. Retrieved 10th April, 2007, from http://www.usdla.org/html/journal/FEB02_Issue/article01.html.

Sifry, D. (2007). *Sifry's alerts: The state of the live web*, 5 April, 2007. Retrieved 13 April, 2007, from http://www.sifry.com/alerts/archives/000493.html.

Toffler, A. (1990). *Powershift : Knowledge, wealth, and violence at the edge of the 21st century*. New York: Bantam Books.

Tyack, E. (1974). *The one best system: A history of American urban education*. Cambridge, Mass: Harvard University Press.

AUTHOR NOTE

John Roder is a Senior Lecturer in the Faculty of Education, University of Auckland, New Zealand. He is currently the Chair of the University of Auckland Information Technology Faculty Forum. His research interests lie in e-learning leadership, online communities of practice, emerging multiliteracies, connectivism, e-portfolios, and web-based personal learning environments (PLEs).

Tony Hunt is a Senior Lecturer specializing in educational technology in the Faculty of Education, University of Auckland, New Zealand. He is currently Acting Head of the Centre for Educational Design and Development in the Faculty. His research interests lie in e-learning for schools and tertiary education, flexible and distance education, information and communications technology in secondary schools and the education of teachers in these areas.

Correspondence concerning this chapter should be addressed by email to: j.roder@auckland.ac.nz and t.hunt@auckland.ac.nz

In: Challenging Thinking about Teaching and Learning   ISBN: 978-1-60456-744-1
Editors: C. M. Rubie-Davies and C. Rawlinson   © 2008 Nova Science Publishers, Inc.

Chapter 19

WHO WERE THEY? WHERE DID THEY GO?
A BRIEF ANALYSIS OF A COHORT OF GRADUATING
TEACHERS OF THE DEAF

Nanette L. Gardner

ABSTRACT

This study was driven by the desire to find out how many of the 1999–2006 cohort of graduates from a one-year programme for training teachers of the deaf moved directly into the field of deaf education on completion of training. The initial question asked was "Where did they go?" The question "Who were they?" became relevant because of the assumption that if students were selected carefully enough they were more likely to move into the specialist field. The results present an encouraging picture, with the greater percentage of the cohort under consideration moving directly into the field.

INTRODUCTION

This brief analysis explores two key questions in relation to a New Zealand qualification for teachers of the deaf, the Diploma in Education of Students with Hearing Impairment. The questions are, firstly, "Who were the teachers who undertook the diploma?" and secondly, "Where did they go on completion of the diploma?"

The diploma has been offered since the early 1970s. A one-year full-time programme, it was initially delivered by teacher training colleges in Christchurch and Auckland until, in 2000, it became a national course based at the Auckland College of Education (now merged with the University of Auckland).

In addition to the one-year diploma, a new initiative was developed in 2002 to offer part-time training over two years off-campus. This targeted teachers working in teacher of the deaf positions who did not have the specialist training and were unable to relocate to Auckland for full-time study. The combination of full-time and part-time options is similar to those at the

University of Manchester in Britain, where a full-time one-year diploma and a two-year part-time diploma are available.

The New Zealand diploma was developed by tertiary education staff in close collaboration with professionals from the deaf education field in order to meet employment needs and professional requirements. Principle 12 of the National Plan for the Education of Deaf and Hearing Impaired Children and Young People in Aotearoa/New Zealand, (DEANZ, 2005) states that "All specialist teachers and specialist educators employed in the education of deaf and hearing impaired children and young people are appropriately qualified" (p. 31), and lists 18 further goals specifically related to training. Kelston Deaf Education Centre in Auckland and van Asch Deaf Education Centre in Christchurch are the two primary employers of teachers of the deaf nationwide.

The delivery of the diploma involves the university as tertiary provider, the deaf education centres as centres of expertise as well as future employers, and a third party, the Ministry of Education, which allocates a fixed number of study awards a year for teachers to study the diploma.

A study award contributes to fees and expenses, and pays a teacher's salary for the year of study release (Ministry of Education, 2007a). Teachers who are not eligible for a study award can also complete the diploma as fee-paying students.

Initially, a study award brought with it a bond to teach in the field upon graduation; however, this requirement ceased in the mid-1980s. This raises the question of whether, without a bond and hence no obligation other than possibly a moral one to enter the specialist field, graduates of the diploma actually move into deaf education employment. The Ministry of Education needs to ensure that allocation of study awards does, in fact, fulfil the need for trained specialist teachers who move into employment in the specialist field.

The two deaf education centres look to the diploma graduates to ensure an ongoing supply of teachers of the deaf to provide a qualified national workforce. In New Zealand, it is not possible to get permanent employment in deaf education in a deaf education centre, resource class, or as a resource teacher of the deaf without specialist training. By comparison, a British report in 2005 notes that while legislation required that teachers of the deaf employed by schools had an additional qualification, in fact a lack of trained specialist teachers meant 44% of resource centres for deaf children did not have fully qualified staff (Wakefield & Mackenzie, 2005, p. 17).

For the current study, the question "Who were they?" was asked because of the implication that if applicants were chosen carefully enough they would be more likely to move into deaf education upon graduation. Factors considered were gender, ethnicity, previous training, whether the graduates were study award recipients or fee-payers, geographical location of home, and age. The second question "Where did they go?" would provide exact figures for this seven-year period on how many moved directly into deaf education positions on completion of the diploma. The latter question also provided information about what happened to those who did not move into deaf education.

To find answers to these questions, the cohort of 99 teachers who completed the diploma between 1999 and 2006 was examined. This cohort provided a sufficient number of graduates to detect trends and suggest answers to the questions under consideration.

DIPLOMA GRADUATES—WHO WERE THEY?

Of the 99 teachers in the cohort who completed the diploma between 1999 and 2006, 79 completed the full-time one-year diploma in Auckland; 20 completed the part-time two-year diploma in various centres; 93 were study award recipients and 6 were fee payers; 11 were male and 88 were female. Of the 99, 9 students were early childhood trained, 75 were primary trained, 13 were secondary trained, and 2 were trained speech-language therapists.

Deaf education is administratively divided into four regions: Auckland/Northland, Waikato/Bay of Plenty, Central, and Southern. When the diploma became Auckland-based in 2000, there were concerns as to whether teachers from southern areas would be prepared to relocate to Auckland for the year. If not, there was a potential negative consequence of a non-specialist trained workforce in more rural and southern areas.

Of the 79 on-campus students, 49 came from Auckland/Northland; 8 were from Waikato/Bay of Plenty; 12 were from Central; 7 were from Southern; and 3 were from overseas. Of the 20 off-campus students, 3 were from Northland; 5 were from Waikato/Bay of Plenty; 8 were from Central; and 4 were from Southern.

Putting both groups of figures together, the regional spread was 52 students from Auckland/Northland, 13 from Waikato/Bay of Plenty, 20 from Central, and 11 from Southern.

With an increasingly diverse student population in New Zealand, ethnicity was also a relevant factor. The category of Deaf is the self-selection by a deaf person whose communication of choice is New Zealand Sign Language and cultural identity is Deaf. Of the total cohort, 75 were European New Zealanders; 7 were Maori; 12 were Deaf; and 5 were "other" (this included Indian, Filipino, and South African).

While not a criteria for entry on to the diploma, age was also considered in the statistics of "Who were they?" Of the total: 19 students were in the 20–30 age band; 35 were in the 30–40 band; 31 were in the 40–50 band; and 14 were in the 50 plus band.

DIPLOMA GRADUATES: WHERE DID THEY GO?

Of the 99 teachers in the cohort, 85 moved into deaf education or "affiliated" positions upon completion of the diploma. A closer look at the 85 reveals that 27 moved into deaf education classrooms either at one of the deaf education centres or in a resource class for deaf children at a mainstream school and 37 moved into itinerant (or resource) teacher of the deaf jobs—positions that are managed by the regional services of the deaf education centres. Eleven teachers took other jobs within deaf education—three moved into day relief positions, two took speech language therapy positions, and six moved into deaf education overseas (four in Australia and two in England).

Ten of the 85 moved into "affiliated" positions—that is, positions not directly within the deaf education services, but where newly acquired expertise in deaf education would be well used. These positions included three who worked for GSE (the special education group within the New Zealand Ministry of Education), two who completed further studies before moving into deaf education, one in the deaf–blind unit at Homai National College for the Blind, and four who returned to their special school positions as resource teachers for deaf students within their special school populations.

Of the 14 teachers who did not move into deaf education or affiliated positions, one left education altogether, two did not enter deaf education directly after graduation because they had babies, and the remaining 11 returned to mainstream positions.

Geographically, where were the deaf education jobs? Did students who trained in Auckland stay in Auckland, or were regional needs being met? Excluding the six who went overseas and the 10 who moved into affiliated positions, consideration of the 69 of the 85 who moved directly into deaf education employment in New Zealand indicates that 34 moved into deaf education employment in Auckland/Northland while 35 moved into deaf education employment in the other three regions: 8 to Waikato/Bay of Plenty, 15 to Central, and 12 to Southern.

DISCUSSION

The gender balance, 11 males from the total of 99 students, compares with gender figures within the wider teaching population of 28.3% males in state and state integrated schools in 2007 (Ministry of Education, 2007b).

The age bands could be considered in various ways. Two-thirds of the teachers came from within the 30–50-year age band. This reflects the mid-career nature of the training, but may be seen as educating an aging workforce. On the other hand, 54 of the 99 were below 40 years of age, compared with 45 being over 40. It could be asked if it is better to train and employ a younger group who then have travel, marriage, and families ahead of them, or an older group who not only have years of experience but may be less likely to have major changes in life circumstances. Longer term figures would be needed to provide a picture of what actually happens and whether age should be a consideration for recruitment. Interestingly, the 2005 Royal National Institute for the Deaf report calls on the British Government to "provide 30 bursaries for the next three years for trainees under the age of 30" (Wakefield & McKenzie, 2005, p. 1). If this age stipulation were applied in New Zealand, only 29 of the 99 students under consideration would have been eligible for Ministry study awards.

While from 1999 to 2004, there were between one and four Deaf students on the diploma each year; this dropped back to one in 2005 and none in 2006, probably as a result of the increasing range of tertiary options available to Deaf people.

The geographical spread for employment within deaf education on graduation indicates half the teachers taking employment in Auckland/Northland and half distributed across the other three regions. This closely reflects where students initially came from: 52 students came from the Auckland/Northland region and 44 from the other regions combined. It also reflects where job vacancies arose within the regions. These figures match population needs and would seem to allay the concern about an untrained rural and southern workforce. With regard to the six teachers who went directly overseas on completion of training, while this is not the preferred outcome, it is pleasing to note that the New Zealand qualification is recognized in Australia and Britain.

Fifteen years ago, most teachers of the deaf did their "apprenticeships" working in classrooms at the deaf education centres or in resource classes for deaf children before moving later in their careers into itinerant positions. With government policy changes, parental preference for mainstream education, improved technology (particularly the advent of cochlear implants), and comprehensive support services, most deaf and hearing impaired children are now in their local schools and more newly trained teachers of the deaf are moving directly into itinerant positions (now renamed as resource teacher of the deaf positions). Course content needs to reflect this change of employment patterns.

The ethnicity of the trainee teacher intake does not match the ethnicity range of the deaf/hearing-impaired student population. Given current recognition of the importance of like role models as well as the need to foster close parent/professional links, this is a concern. The low numbers of Maori teachers and lack of Pacific Island teachers is particularly noticeable and needs to be addressed with future recruitment as well as providing continued encouragement for Deaf teachers of the deaf to move into the field. This mismatch between ethnicity or cultural identity of professionals in teaching and the students they teach is a recognized issue in other western nations where cultural diversity is increasing. Andrews (2003, p. 259) states, in reference to postgraduate training for professionals in deaf education in the United States, that "with ethnic-minority enrolments rising to nearly 45% of all deaf student enrolments a need exists for deaf and multicultural professionals to lead K-12, community college, and university teacher-education programs". Of the applicants for their postgraduate programmes, "only 13% of applicants were from multicultural or deaf backgrounds".

There is also the question of whether the "others" who did not move into either deaf education or affiliated fields are lost to deaf education. I would argue that, with 85% of the deaf and hearing impaired student population in mainstream classrooms, even if study award recipients did not fulfil their obligations to work in deaf education on graduation, they nonetheless become a valuable resource within the wider education community.

This brief study has only considered the situation immediately following graduation, but other valuable data would be revealed from longer term follow up. For example, of the 1999 group of six students, one returned to a mainstream position, three went overseas, and only two moved directly into deaf education in New Zealand. This might initially be seen as a concern, yet in 2006, all six students were back in New Zealand and working in deaf education.

CONCLUSION

So who were they? In a nutshell, the majority of the cohort who completed the diploma between 1999 and 2006 were primary trained women teachers of European New Zealand descent, from the North Island, aged between 30 and 50, and who completed the one-year full-time course in Auckland on study awards. It must be acknowledged that while answering the initial question, this brief analysis reveals nothing about the depth of experience, skills, enthusiasm, and commitment that this group has brought to deaf education and to deaf children and their families.

And where did the cohort go? Overall, figures indicate that the majority of teachers do move into deaf education upon completion of the diploma, a minority move into related fields, and a very small minority "disappear"—although taking additional knowledge and skills with them. It must be emphasized that these figures only consider placement for the year immediately following graduation. Follow-up data would provide a better long-term picture as to how long graduates stay in the field and movement over time. Long-term retention, however, probably has as much to do with employer initiatives, professional development, and further employment opportunities within the field as it does with initial motivation and training.

With the amalgamation of the Auckland College of Education and the University of Auckland, the diploma was restructured and renamed as a specialist pathway within the Graduate Diploma in Special Education. The Ministry of Education study awards and the specialist needs of the field of deaf education remain. It will be important to ensure that the qualification continues to meet the requirements of the study awards and the employment and professional needs of the field by careful selection of candidates for the training and continual reflection on course content as professional roles change to meet new challenges within the field.

REFERENCES

Andrews, J. F. (2003). Benefits of an EdD program in deaf education: A survey. *American Annals of the Deaf*, 148(3), 259–266.

The British Association of Teachers of the Deaf (BATOD). (2006). *Training as a teacher of the deaf.* Retrieved September 2, 2006 from http://www.batod.org.uk.

Deaf Education Aotearoa New Zealand (DEANZ). (2005). *National plan for the education of deaf and hearing impaired children and young people in Aotearoa/New Zealand* (September 2005 revised edition). Retrieved May 25, 2007 from www.deafed.org.nz.

Ministry of Education. (2007a). *Study awards for teachers: HI study awards for teachers of the hearing impaired.* Retrieved May 25,2007 from www.minedu.govt.nz/goto/studyawards.

Ministry of Education. (2007b). *Teaching staff as at April 2007.* Retrieved January 18, 2008 from http://www.educationcounts.govt.nz/statistics/schooling/ts/teaching_staff/teaching_staff_april_2007.

Wakefield, V., & Mackenzie, S. (2005) *At the heart of inclusion: The role of specialist support for deaf pupils.* Royal National Institute for the Deaf (RNID) Report. Retrieved July 20, 2007 from http://www.rnid.org.uk/Content.aspx?id=84923andciid=195817.

AUTHOR NOTE

Nanette Gardner is a Senior Lecturer in Deaf Education in the Faculty of Education, University of Auckland, New Zealand. She has worked in the field of Deaf education for a number of years, initially at Kelston Deaf Education Centre, and then at the New Zealand Cochlear Implant Programme, before being seconded into the above position in 1999.

The material in this chapter was initially presented informally to a Meeting of the DEANZ (Deaf Education Aotearoa New Zealand) Forum in 2006.

Correspondence concerning this chapter should be addressed by email to: n.gardner@auckland.ac.nz

In: Challenging Thinking about Teaching and Learning   ISBN: 978-1-60456-744-1
Editors: C. M. Rubie-Davies and C. Rawlinson   © 2008 Nova Science Publishers, Inc.

Chapter 20

EFFECTIVE MENTORING OF STUDENT TEACHERS: ATTITUDES, CHARACTERISTICS AND PRACTICES OF SUCCESSFUL ASSOCIATE TEACHERS WITHIN A NEW ZEALAND CONTEXT

Lyn McDonald

ABSTRACT

This chapter reports on the findings of a research project which identified and described the attitudes, characteristics, and practices of four associate teachers within a New Zealand context. The purpose of the research was to investigate associate teachers' supervision styles and to identify what makes them successful. Data were collected from associates, visiting lecturers, and student teachers. The findings indicate that to be effective, associate teachers need to motivate student teachers, find out about their learning needs, discuss their perceptions about teaching, and model effective teaching practice. Associate teachers should also provide regular feedback and ensure that their classroom supports student supervision. The findings confirmed the importance of the supervision practices of the associate teacher.

INTRODUCTION

This chapter argues that student teachers are more likely to have successful practicum experiences (the period of time student teachers spend in schools) if associate teachers (classroom teachers who supervise student teachers completing their practicum) demonstrate certain attitudes, characteristics, and practices. This is the finding of my research study into the role of associate teachers in preservice education, based on collective evidence from a number of associate teachers, student teachers, and visiting lecturers (lecturers from teacher education institutions where the student teachers are enrolled). This finding is supported by Mayer and Austin (1999) who stated the practicum is an essential and important part of preservice teacher education and its success is dependent to a large extent on the associate teacher and his or her supervision practices.

My research (McDonald, 2001) indicated that an effective associate teacher needs to motivate student teachers, find out about their learning needs, discuss their perceptions about teaching, and model effective teaching practice. Associate teachers should also provide regular feedback and ensure that their classroom is supportive of student supervision. Student teachers should have the opportunity to engage in critical reflection. The data collected in the study supported the idea that associate teachers' own personal pedagogy should be effective, that they should have up-to-date curriculum and professional knowledge, and should also be clear communicators with the ability to talk and listen to students. The findings confirmed the importance of successful practicum experiences for student teachers in their development as an effective practitioner.

Further findings from the study showed that encouraging and implementing better supervision practices by associate teachers led to higher calibre student teachers and ultimately improved learning and teaching for children in the classroom. In order for the practicum to realize the potential it has as a significant learning experience for future teachers, changes need to be made based on notions of empowerment, collaboration, and reflection. This argument (Dobbins, 1996) aligns with the move over recent years from a teacher-dominated approach of associate teachers in student supervision to a more learner-dominated approach of inquiry and investigation. It has also led to a change from the associate teacher being the problem solver, decision maker, and goal setter to the student teacher and associate teacher working in a collaborative, problem solving way with joint decision making and goal setting.

Much has been written about the role of the associate teacher and it is evident that they have a big responsibility in facilitating the effective learning of the student teacher in the practicum classroom. Mayer and Austin (1999) point out that helping students negotiate their own professional identities within a reflective and goal-directed framework is central to their professional growth. This requires not only a positive personal and professional relationship involving open and frank communication, but also a provision for student teachers to become more active and critical learners rather than passive recipients (Pinder, 1999). This will teach them the subtle and overt ways of acting like a teacher (Ovens, 2003) and with all the knowledge, thinking, and behaviour that is associated with becoming a teacher.

Dobbins (1996) has shown that student teachers' learning in the practicum is a complex business. One of the reasons it is complex is because the experience is different for each student and each associate teacher. Everyone brings different experiences, both personal and professional, to the classroom. Therefore it is a necessary prerequisite for a successful practicum that students have an associate teacher who is communicative, reflective, and supportive, and who has clear beliefs and philosophies in regard to teaching and supervision. Lang (2000) commented in her research that the great majority of the kinds of qualities that associate teachers recognized as contributing to the perfect student teacher fell into what Dobbins described as the personal qualities.

The research of Yost, Sentner, and Forlenza-Bailey (2000) states that teacher educators should strive to provide preservice teachers not only with course work that provides them with a solid foundation for their thinking, but with the opportunities to make essential connections between practical experiences and their base of theoretical knowledge. Ball (2000, p 241) argues that "subject matter and pedagogy have been peculiarly divided in the conceptualization and curriculum of teacher education and learning to teach". This has meant that teachers have often been left to their own devices to link subject matter, knowledge, and pedagogy. Ball further suggests that being able to complete this linking is fundamental to teaching, and associate teachers have to be able to teach all student teachers this core task.

This chapter examines each of the attitudes, characteristics, and practices identified as best supervision practices and the importance of this in the supervision of student teachers. It also examines some of the issues and tensions that preservice teacher education needs to address, in order to ensure the quality and success of practicum experiences for both associate teachers and student teachers.

The research discussed was a case study of four associate teachers in the Auckland area. These teachers worked in preservice education in partnership with the Faculty of Education at the University of Auckland. The teachers were identified as being effective by student teachers and visiting lecturers. Four visiting lecturers participated in the study to look at what they perceived to be effective attitudes, characteristics, and practices of associate teachers. They were invited to participate from feedback received from students and associate teachers. Three groups of six third-year students were asked to volunteer to take part in semi-structured group interviews. Data were collected from associate teachers, student teachers, and visiting lecturers by means of a semi-structured face-to-face audiotaped interview. Their responses were analyzed and grouped into common sets of themes; for example, teachers' content knowledge, role models, personal pedagogy, reflection, feedback, communication, personal professional qualities, and professionalism.

FINDINGS

Issues and Tensions

There were a number of issues and tensions which arose for student teachers and associate teachers during practicum. An important issue related to the lack of training for associate teachers and to the effectiveness or ineffectiveness of supervision practice. Other issues referred to by student teachers were the lack of feedback and guidance by associate teachers, and the feeling of powerlessness that resulted from this for students. The assessment practice of passing or failing a practicum was an issue for some students, as were the constraints of working in someone else's classroom. Some student teachers mentioned concerns about associate teachers who were directive in their supervision practice, and expected the student teachers to be "clones of themselves".

There were also issues and tensions for associate teachers. One associate was concerned about having to hand over her class to a student teacher, and then have the student teacher lose control and management of it. Some student teachers, according to a few associate teachers, displayed an arrogant attitude and the associates felt intimidated by this. One associate teacher indicated that maybe supervising the student teachers required too much time and effort for very little reward, both professionally and financially.

These issues and concerns about lack of feedback and guidance are in keeping with the views of Groundwater-Smith (1993, p. 137) who noted: "The practicum experience is one fraught with difficulties, dilemmas and challenges as the student attempts to negotiate his or her way along a hazardous path of professional policies and practices". In the current study, student teachers and associate teachers indicated that they dealt with and interpreted these difficulties in many ways. Some had success and saw the issues as a challenge while other associate teachers struggled with the issues.

Edwards and Collinson (1995) comment that many associate teachers regard their role as complex and one that requires preparation and training, which in some cases may not occur because of lack of resources and time. There is also the fact that being a good classroom teacher does not always guarantee a teacher will be an effective mentor or associate teacher:

> What our data suggests is that mentoring is not an instinctive activity which can be carried out by good practitioners as another layer of their professional function as class teachers. (Edwards & Collinson, 1995, p. 9)

Mentoring or supervision has a set of skills which have to be learnt and a knowledge base which requires training (Sanders, 2000). It was clearly indicated in the current study, by all groups, that associate teachers need to have this training and preparation, as the following comment indicates:

> It is so important for associate teachers to have the training in the required skills of supervision. They have to be effective practitioners and role models for the students. They can't be narrow in their approach. Also the trainers of these associates need to be effective practitioners with current or recent classroom experience. (Visiting lecturer)

All student teachers in the study expected the associate teachers to have read the practicum brief and been to a briefing meeting beforehand. These meetings are organized and run before practicums by lecturers at the teacher education institution, but it is not compulsory to attend. Teachers, on becoming associates, also have access to training programmes run by these lecturers. Visiting lecturers and student teachers confirmed that these courses or briefings assist in building up the associate teacher's knowledge base, and should be part of their professional development. The courses include the skills of supervision and building of reflective practice. However, many associate teachers never attend any form of professional training, as reflected by the comment from one lecturer who stated:

> I think it has to be given more than just lip service. I think it actually has to be resourced and that means providing staff. (Visiting lecturer)

Because the importance of supervision for student teachers cannot be underestimated, processes that promote the involvement of student teachers in reflection and action are said to have the most successful outcomes (Gibbs, 1996). Price and Sellars (1985, p. 21) indicate that "excellent supervisors use basic principles of clinical supervision in that they are collegial, non-directive and supportive rather than coercive in style and seek to foster professional autonomy in students under their care". The skills of collaboration, reflection, feedback, and support are skills which result in more effective supervision practices by associate teachers of student teachers.

Student teachers in the current study mentioned several issues. They felt that some associate teachers were being neglectful in their approach, through their lack of feedback, and offering little guidance to them.

One associate I had, actually only allowed me to teach what she said I could teach. There was no collaboration and then I had to plan it all myself with no guidance. (Student teacher)

I was often left to fend for myself with no feedback or guidance. I sort of got left to do it and I felt neglected. (Student teacher)

Cameron and Wilson (1993) commented that such neglectful and directive styles are characterized by low student teacher satisfaction, and low communication between student and supervisor. Students in the current study mentioned that, when presented with these styles, they had been afraid to take risks because there was little collegiality and support from the associate teacher.

Associate teachers also referred to issues and tensions. One associate teacher in the study experienced having a student lose control over the class, and leaving the associate to "put it all back together".

A number of times I've had my class turned upside down and then away goes the student. It's taken me usually about a week to get them back on track. (Associate teacher)

For this associate, the stress of dealing with such an incident was too much and had become difficult. Another associate experienced a few student teachers who were arrogant in their attitude. The associate found that, under those circumstances, it was difficult to build up any sort of professional relationship. A third associate commented that she had been intimidated at first by the professional language the student teacher used. Several associates also mentioned the time and effort that had to be put in to be an effective associate, listing feedback, discussions, reflections, and disruption to the classroom as examples. In these instances, the associates' initial enthusiasm, dedication, and sense of mission was replaced with expressions of stress, reluctance to have students, and dissatisfaction with role of being an associate (Sanders, 2000).

Thus, both associate teachers and student teachers experienced a number of issues and tensions. Associate teachers considered that student teachers should be prepared to assume some responsibility for their learning processes within the practicum. Likewise, student teachers considered associate teachers should be prepared to assume responsibility for their role in supervising and guiding student teachers into the professional role of teaching.

Successful Associate Teachers

Because practicum involves an interpersonal and interactional process between student teacher and associate teacher, the teaching and learning that occur are therefore complementary concepts, and the activities of the student teacher and the associate are linked (Cooper, 1999). In the current study, visiting lecturers, associate teachers, and student teachers all indicated that the characteristics, attitudes, and practices of excellent associate teachers included an ability to motivate student teachers and in most cases be motivated by them. This involved the teachers finding out about students' needs and interests, and discussing and critiquing their own perceptions about teaching practice. All three groups in the study mentioned that associate teachers need to be able to give regular feedback to student teachers, be supportive and reflective, and have a passion and enthusiasm for teaching.

According to student teachers, this passion needs to be reflected in clear interpersonal skills of communication, being approachable and a good listener. Four of the student teachers also commented that the way associate teachers teach is clearly reflected in the fun and inventiveness of their learning activities, and the teaching and learning strategies used. It was also noted by all of the visiting lecturers and student teachers that strong pedagogical practice and curriculum knowledge was essential.

Personal Pedagogy

Associate teachers should aim to provide student teachers not only with a solid foundation for their thinking, but with opportunities to connect practical experiences with their theoretical knowledge (Yost, Sentner, & Forlenza-Bailey, 2000). This was evident in the current study. Student teachers indicated that associate teachers with a sound knowledge base were able to explain their pedagogy to them clearly. The following comment illustrates the importance student teachers placed on a knowledge base.

> Associate teachers have to have content knowledge, because you're trying to understand teaching and kids, and if associates don't have the skills or experience to tell you what is happening, it makes a really huge gap. (Student teacher)

McNamara (1994) indicated that the teacher's knowledge of the subject matter and the skills necessary to apply knowledge in the classroom are of central importance for practical pedagogy. This concept was also evident in the current study, as the following comment indicates:

> To be a successful associate you have to have good curriculum knowledge, you have to have a variety of learning styles you use effectively, and can model them for student teacher . . . (Associate teacher)

It is also necessary for the associate teacher to have not only sound subject knowledge but be able to apply this knowledge effectively in the classroom. Shulman (1987) and Reagan (1993) highlight the importance of teachers possessing a sound knowledge base that is clearly visible to student teachers. In the current study, it was generally felt that as student teachers gained experience, they might begin to think differently about subject matter and, in fact, classroom practice may reshape their pedagogical content knowledge. According to Shulman (1987) knowledge and experience are closely intertwined characteristics of good teachers. Teacher education is characterized by concerns with quality and professionalism, and in order to achieve quality education there is a need for high quality teachers who have sound content and subject knowledge. In the current study, associate teachers, student teachers, and visiting lecturers alike confirmed that teachers need to be able to explain their practice while at the same time being critical and reflective.

Role Models

It was clear from comments made by both visiting lecturers and student teachers that the ability of the associate teachers to model teaching practice and behaviour is extremely important.

> I think it's so important for our student teachers to experience excellent teaching and excellent role models because there's a flow on effect. It inspires them, and the idea of having high standards and high expectations of children and achieving excellent outcomes, is essential. A highly proficient practitioner as a role model is vital. (Visiting lecturer)

All three groups indicated that, for a start, the associate teacher needs to want to guide the student teacher professionally. Associate teachers should be talking about their own beliefs, and own thinking processes while at the same time encouraging student teachers to think more deeply about their own practice. Such a process, with the assistance of an associate teacher, helps student teachers understand and negotiate the process of socialization, which is, as Zeichner and Gore (1990) comment, also inherent in becoming a teacher.

Reflection

It was generally recognized by associate teachers and visiting lecturers that it was important for students to develop a critical awareness of their own practice, and that the practicum played a vital role in this process. The associate teachers were aware that they needed to ensure that student teachers have opportunities to develop reflective practice. Klenowski (1998) suggests that the process of reflection will encourage student teachers to be innovative and developmental in their teaching and learning, and that reflection practised within a supportive environment, encourages them to take risks and be able to articulate on their actions. This was also identified by the following comment by a participant in the current study:

> Student teachers need to be taught to engage in practice, reflect on practice and articulate practice, which in turn will better help them understand and improve their practice. (Visiting lecturer)

The importance of reflection is not for the associate teacher to demonstrate and explain how practice should be carried out, but for the student teacher to be given the opportunity for self-analysis and reflection in connection with his or her own teaching. The focus then is on how the associate teacher transfers professional knowledge to the student teacher.

Feedback

All student teachers mentioned the importance of regular, clear, constructive feedback from associate teachers, and the relevancy and necessity of this. This feedback can be through formal, informal, formative, or summative assessment. Feedback can be defined in two ways: as information about the quality of work, or as the effect it has on learning. Feedback is, as Hinett (1998) suggested, not just looking backwards, but also about looking ahead to improve performance and learning. As one participant said:

> Student teachers love feedback both oral and written. We can go home and look at it and reflect on the feedback and when we're planning we can refer back. (Student teacher)

Associate teachers should, then, be able to provide experiences in teaching practice needed by student teachers to progress and develop. It is often the continual communication between associate teacher and student teacher, and the constructive criticism and feedback, that is needed for this to occur.

Relationship between Associate and Student Teachers

The dynamics of the interactions between associate teachers and student teachers is an important issue. Lang (2000), in her research, commented that significant numbers of student teachers preferred associates who allowed them to experiment and take risks; associates who did not expect the student to be a "clone of themselves". By making mistakes and "having a go", students would learn. This was evident also in the current study, where student teachers constantly indicated the importance of being able to "try things out" without worrying about repercussions. This demonstrated confidence and faith in the student:

> Just being a good listener, being approachable and friendly, being well organized and a good manager in your class as well, that's what I think is an effective associate. (Associate teacher)

Personal professional qualities such as enthusiasm, flexibility, being supportive, and approachable, and having a sense of humour rated highly with student teachers as being characteristics of effective associates:

> Having an enthusiastic, lively associate is wonderful- one who truly loves their job with a passion. It stands out in what they say, what they do and is so obvious. (Student teacher)

Associate teachers and student teachers commented on the importance of the relationship between associates, student teachers, and staff in general at a school, with both groups saying it could only enhance the teaching and learning opportunities for all parties. This positive, professional, collaborative relationship between associate and student teacher involves open and frank communication where constructive criticism can be given and received more easily. Blunden (1994) commented that from a student teacher's viewpoint, good supervisors are friendly, approachable, and supportive and have pedagogic knowledge and advice to give.

Mayer and Austin (1999) suggest that an effective associate is not only committed to the teaching profession, but is an articulate upholder of that profession. They go on to suggest the idea that the associate teacher is acting as a "gatekeeper to the profession" and that it is their role to build and maintain teaching as a high status profession. It is about showing a passion and love of teaching and being able to pass this on. This view was also evident in the current study:

> If you didn't love it and didn't like being with kids and having a laugh and things like that you'd just be the worst associate in the world, because you'd just pass on those ill feelings. (Associate teacher)

Associate teachers mediate student teachers' learning by supporting their acquisition of practical and professional skills (Fairbanks, Freedman, & Kahn, 2000), and these skills are so important. They relate to the guidance, mutual learning, and friendship between associate teachers and student teacher.

CONCLUSION

The study discussed in this chapter provides evidence of strong links between associate teachers and student teachers in practicum experiences. The findings highlight the importance of positive practicum experiences and excellence in supervision from associate teachers for student teachers. The quality and success of that practicum is dependent on the role and effectiveness of the supervising teacher (Koerner, 1992). Observation of successful associate teachers who effectively model teaching practice will, as indicated in the study, help lead student teachers to innovation and development in their own teaching practice.

It is clear that there are a number of issues and tensions for both associate teachers and student teachers. As Martinez, Coombes, and Rigano (2001, p. 17) point out, practicum experiences should be where both associate and student teachers engage in a partnership with opportunities for "construction, reconstruction and renewal of the teaching profession".

Ensuring better supervision practices by associate teachers would lead to a higher calibre of student teachers and ultimately improved learning and teaching for children in the classroom. The importance of associate teachers as supervisors has been clearly established, and associate teachers' views on teaching and learning, their curriculum and professional knowledge, and their interpersonal skills are important for student teachers to observe in the development of their own pedagogy and teaching style.

REFERENCES

Ball, D. (2000). Bridging practices—intertwining content and pedagogy in teaching and learning to teach. *Journal of Teacher Education, 51*(3), 241–247.

Blunden, R. (1994). I can teach, but I don't have to teach like Killer Miller. *The Journal of Teaching Practice, 14*(1), 26–47.

Cameron, R., & Wilson, S. (1993). The practicum: Student teacher perceptions of teacher supervision roles. *South Pacific Journal of Teacher Education, 21*(2), 155–168.

Cooper, L. (1999). Pedagogical approaches to student supervision in social work. *Research Monograph: No 3.* Melbourne, Australia: Practical Experiences in Professional Education.

Dobbins, R. (1996). The practicum: A learning journey? *Waikato Journal of Education, 2,* 59–72.

Edwards, A., & Collinson, J. (1995). What do teacher mentors tell student teachers about pupil learning in infant schools? *Teacher and Teaching Theory and Practice, 1*(2), 265–279.

Fairbanks, C., Freedman, D., & Kahn, C. (2000). The role of effective mentors in learning to teach. *Journal of Teacher Education, 51*(2), 102–112.

Gibbs, C. (1996, October). *Enhancing student teaching through interventionist supervisory strategies.* Paper presented at the New Zealand Council for Teacher Education Conference, Palmerston North, New Zealand.

Groundwater-Smith, S. (1993). *Introducing dilemmas into the practicum curriculum.* Paper presented at the Fifth National Practicum Conference, Sydney, Australia.

Hinett, K. (1998, August). *The role of dialogue and self assessment in improving student learning.* Draft paper presented at the British Educational Research Association Annual Conference, Queen's University of Belfast, Northern Ireland.

Klenowski, V. (1998). *Enriching pre-service teacher knowledge of assessment.* Paper presented at the British Educational Research Association Annual Conference. Queen's University of Belfast, Northern Ireland.

Koerner, M. (1992). The co-operating teacher: An ambivalent participant in student teaching. *Journal of Teacher Education, 43*(1), 46–56.

Lang, C. (2000, August). *Perfect student teachers/perfect associate teachers: Do the perceptions match?* Paper presented at the Teacher Education Forum of Aotearoa-New Zealand Conference, Christchurch, New Zealand.

Mayer, D., & Austin, J. (1999, January). *It's just what I do: Personal practical theories of supervision in the practicum.* Paper presented at the Fourth Biennial International Cross-Faculty Practicum Conference of Association of Practical Experiences in Professional Education, Christchurch, New Zealand.

Martinez, K., Hamlin, K., & Rigano, D. (2001). *Redirecting the supervisory gaze.* Paper presented at the Practical Experience in Professional Education Conference, Melbourne, Australia.

McDonald, L. (2001). *Successful associate teachers: Beliefs, attitudes and practices within a New Zealand context.* Project submitted in partial fulfilment of the requirements for the degree of Master of Educational Administration, Massey University, New Zealand.

McNamara, D. (1994). *Classroom pedagogy and primary practice.* Routledge: New York.

Ovens, A. (2003). Learning to teach through the practicum: A situated-learning perspective. In B. Ross & L, Burrows (Eds.), *It takes two feet: Teaching physical education and health in Aotearoa New Zealand* (pp. 76–89). Palmerston North, New Zealand: Dunmore Press.

Pinder, H. (1999). *Breaking new ground: Redefining the practicum two years further on.* Paper presented at the Fourth Biennial International Cross Faculty Practicum Conference, Christchurch, New Zealand.

Price, D., & Sellars, N. (1985*). A synthesis of effective supervisory teacher behaviours in the final year of the primary practicum.* Report to Queensland Board of Teacher Education, Brisbane, Australia.

Reagan, T. (1993). Educating the reflective practitioner: The contribution of philosophy of education. *Journal of Research and Development in Education, 26,* 189–196.

Sanders, M. (2000*). Increasing associate teacher competence and confidence.* Unpublished research completed at Bethlehem Institute of Education, Tauranga, New Zealand.

Shulman, L. S. (1987). Knowledge as teaching: Foundations of the new reform. *Harvard Educational Review, 57,* 1–22.

Yost, D., Sentner, S., & Forlenza- Bailey, A. (2000). An examination of the construct of critical reflection: Implications for Teacher Education programming in the 21st century. *Journal of Teacher Education, 5*(1), 39–48.

Zeichner, K., & Gore, J. (1990). Teacher socialization. In W. R. Houston (Ed.), *Handbook of Research on Teacher Education* (pp. 329–348). New York: Macmillan.

AUTHOR NOTE

Lyn McDonald is a Senior Lecturer in the Faculty of Education, University of Auckland, New Zealand.

Correspondence concerning this chapter should be addressed by email to: l.mcdonald@auckland.ac.nz

In: Challenging Thinking about Teaching and Learning   ISBN: 978-1-60456-744-1
Editors: C. M. Rubie-Davies and C. Rawlinson   © 2008 Nova Science Publishers, Inc.

Chapter 21

THE PRACTICUM'S CONTRIBUTION TO STUDENTS LEARNING TO TEACH

Mavis Haigh, Heather Pinder and Lyn McDonald

ABSTRACT

This chapter reports on early findings of a research project carried out by the practicum team in the Faculty of Education at the University of Auckland. The project explored how the practicum experiences embedded in a teacher education programme contribute to student teachers learning to become teachers. The research questions were: "What do student teachers learn about becoming/being a teacher when on practicum?" and "What factors enable or hinder student teachers learning to be teachers during the practicum?" The initial analysis indicates complex patterns regarding what the student teachers have learnt about teaching and being a teacher, how they have learnt this, and what enabled or hindered this learning.

INTRODUCTION

Within the context of preservice teacher education, the importance of the practicum component for prospective teachers has been well documented (Guyton & McIntyre, 1990; Mayer & Austin, 1999, Oosterheert & Vermunt, 2003; Smith & Lev-Ari, 2005). Not only should teacher educators strive to give student teachers the course work that provides them with solid foundations but they should also provide opportunities for student teachers to make essential connections between practical experiences and their theoretical knowledge (Yost, Sentner, & Forlenza-Bailey, 2000).

However, research studies such as those by Dobbins (1996) and Haigh and Ward (2004) have shown that student teacher learning in the practicum is a complex business. Not only do the various participants bring unique personal and professional perspectives to the classroom, but each practicum experience will differ depending on the context and the personal dispositions of those involved. Furthermore, student teachers are confronted by an increasingly diverse and changing environment in which they are required to accommodate often conflicting and ambiguous demands. So what are the benefits of the practicum experience and what do student teachers learn during their time in schools that progresses their journey to becoming a teacher?

Since the 1990s, the approach to student teachers' learning during practicum has undergone constant change. Like their teaching counterparts, preservice teachers have felt the effect of education policy, with its calls for improved teacher quality and student achievement (Haigh & Tuck, 1999; Scott & Freman-Moir, 2000). During this decade, a technocratic approach, which provides ready-made solutions for teachers to apply in teaching and learning situations, was no longer considered appropriate when preparing student teachers for an increasingly complex environment that they entered as beginning teachers. Neither was a technocratic approach to teaching and learning deemed fitting in a climate that sought improved teacher quality through personal endeavour (Fullan, 2002). During the 1990s, there were moves towards a greater emphasis on professionals' reflective practice and an inquiry approach to teaching and learning (Butler, 1996; Smyth, 1989). Whether the emphasis on reflective practice and an inquiry approach have enhanced the quality of teacher learning, however, continues to be debated (Hagger, Burn, & Mutton, 2006).

Much has been written about student teacher experiences during practicum that describe factors that either contribute to or detract from learning and professional growth (Cameron & Wilson, 1993; Dobbins, 1996; Hayes, 2001). A prevalent concept has been the promotion of student teachers as active rather than passive participants, giving rise to discussion about how this is best achieved (Cochran-Smith & Paris, 1995; Zeichner, 1990). As a result of such discussion, practicum goals have been reconceptualized and technicist requirements have been replaced by professional activity that engenders greater personal growth and self-direction (Martinez, 1998).

The notion that student teachers should be engaged in their own learning through personal inquiry and reflection has become central to concepts of professional growth (Schon, 1987; Tickle, 1994). Reflective practice is viewed as a vehicle whereby student teachers can analyze, appraise, and synthesize their work with a view to improving their practice (Dobbins, 1996; Zeichner, 1990). Quality learning for student teachers during practicum, therefore, means challenging beliefs and practices while also assuming greater responsibility for personal learning and the outcomes of practicum. A key feature of learning to teach in this "participatory view" (Edwards & Protheroe, 2003, p.230) is an ability to make informed decisions about what was happening in the classroom and to develop a wider range of appropriate responses. Instead, what frequently occurs in response to a high stakes assessment situation is student teachers' reluctance to "rock the boat" and hence engage in critical conversations (Wilson, Floden, & Ferrini-Mundy, 2002, p. 195).

While there is a great deal of literature about the benefits and constraints of the practicum, there is less research that examines what student teachers learn during their time in schools. As Wilson et al. (2002) have argued, the earlier practicum literature tended to be small-scale interpretative studies that focused more on student and associate teacher attitudes than on "what prospective teachers actually learn" (p. 197). More recent practicum literature, however, has begun to emerge that throws some light on student teachers' learning during their practicum. Some of these findings have confirmed that the practicum environment extends well beyond the classroom to encompass the broader social, cultural, and political concerns that inevitably affect student teachers' learning as well as their personal well-being.

Edwards and Protheroe's (2003) research, for example, revealed student teachers focused more on the delivery of a planned curriculum than on pupils as learners. When questioned about their growing competency, student teachers most frequently mentioned: growing confidence in interpreting the curriculum for children; greater understanding of what children could do; and using resources to support curriculum delivery. Student teachers, therefore, found themselves shaping their view of classroom pedagogy and their role as a teacher within an accountability-driven environment. As such, the context promoted effective performance rather than risky attempts to interact and support pupils' learning (Edwards & Protheroe, 2003).

In contrast, when Burn, Hagger, Mutton, and Everton (2003) investigated student teachers' thinking, they discovered a high level of concern for pupils' learning and an awareness of the complexity of teaching. Moreover, these concerns occurred even at the early stages of their development.

Another study by Smith and Lev-Ari (2005) investigated what student teachers perceived were the important components of their teacher education programme for acquiring professional knowledge. The content knowledge that student teachers considered contributed most to their professional knowledge arose from the practicum experiences. Aspects such as class management, dealing with unexpected problems, developing a concept of self as an educator, application of practical knowledge, pedagogical knowledge, decision making during teaching, and beliefs in pupil ability were rated highly. Student teachers also regarded course work integral to their practicum learning with respect to both curriculum and pedagogical knowledge (Smith & Lev-Ari, 2005).

Powerful influences on what student teachers think and learn during the practicum are associated with the beliefs and knowledge of the associate teacher (Wilson et al., 2003). Indeed, the role of the associate teacher has dominated a large part of the practicum literature and been viewed as critical in advancing student teacher learning (Burgess & Butcher, 1999; Cameron & Wilson, 1993; Feiman-Nemser, 2001; Hayes, 2001; Mayer & Austin, 1999). Ball (2000) reported that a vital part of how the practicum helped a student teacher to learn to teach related to how an associate teacher facilitated their understanding of the links between subject matter knowledge and pedagogy. Mayer and Austin (1999) emphasized the important role the associate teacher played in helping student teachers negotiate their own professional identities within a reflective and goal-directed framework.

In their research, Fairbanks, Freedman, and Kahn (2000, p. 111) state that learning to teach, like teaching itself, "is neither simple nor explicit". Thus finding some answers to complex questions such as "What do student teachers actually learn during the practicum?", "How does this learning occur?", and "What are the enabling and hindering factors of this learning?" may advance discussions about what learning takes precedence. It may also enable greater insight into the different ways that practicum experiences are interpreted and how student teachers learn to become teachers.

The aim of the current research project was to identify what student teachers learn during the practicum, how they acquire this learning, and how the practicum experience enables or hinders their professional growth as teachers.

RESEARCH DESIGN

The participants in the study were selected from one cohort of second-year primary student teachers on their third assessed practicum of four weeks' duration. Triads of the student teacher, associate teacher, and visiting lecturer were obtained by randomly numbering the cohort and selecting every twentieth student teacher. Site access to the schools was first negotiated, followed by approaches to student teachers, associates, and visiting lecturers.

Six researchers each interviewed two student teachers within three weeks of the completion of the second practicum experience in the second of three years of an undergraduate primary teacher education degree. The interviews were semi-structured in nature with lead questions relating to what the student teachers had learned about becoming teachers during the practicum, how they had learnt this, and what they considered to have enabled and hindered this learning. Once all the data were collected and transcribed, a series of team meetings was held to establish coding protocols and to build consistency across the team when coding the interviews. Consistency of coding was necessary as the data were to be aggregated to establish frequency of references to a particular aspect. Three pairs of researchers were assigned specific aspects of the findings to report on. These were "What did the student teachers learn?", "How did the student teachers learn this?" and "What enabled or hindered this learning?" The authors of this chapter represent one of each of these pairings.

The analysis and interpretation draws on data from only 10 of the 12 student teachers, as one of the researchers was able to interview only one student teacher, and a taping-transcription problem meant that data from one other student teacher could not be included. The coded data was drawn from all of these 10 student teachers' transcripts. Discussion among the team members carrying out the coding indicated that the frequency of the items themed for the purpose of this study as "what", "how", and "enabling and hindering" codes was relatively consistent across all students.

In this chapter, the students are identified through their link with the researcher who interviewed them. For example R1, S1 indicates the first of the two students interviewed by the first listed researcher.

FINDINGS

The findings will first be reported under the three headings of "What did student teachers learn?", "How did student teachers learn?", and "Factors that enabled and hindered student teacher learning". Quotations are identified by the researcher (R) who gathered and coded the data (e.g., R1) and by the student being interviewed (e.g., S4).

What Did Student Teachers Learn?

"What did they learn?" indicators that were coded from the student teachers' interviews can be grouped into four main categories: teacher skills and knowledge, becoming a professional, managing the learning environment, and realities of teaching (see Table 21.1). There was a total of 288 identified "what" codes.

**Table 21.1. Percentage of Indicators Coded as
What Student Teachers Learnt on the Practicum**

Percentage of coded indicators	Indicators (%)
30–44%	*Teacher skills and knowledge* (41) Creating a learning environment Planning, curriculum, assessment knowledge
15–29%	*Becoming a professional* (24) Developing a teacher identity Organizational matters, e.g., time management Enhancement of practice through reflection *Managing the learning environment* (23) Behaviour management Routines
1–14 %	*Realities of teaching (complexity)* (12) Multiple people, interruptions, tasking School structure and systems

Note. N "What" Indicators = 288.

A total of 41% of the statements were identified as "what" indicators related to teacher skills and knowledge, such as how to create a learning environment, how to plan teaching episodes—both long-term and short-term—and how to use curriculum documents. References to assessment practice was a significant feature. The student teachers talked about learning how to do running records and about the differences between formative and summative assessment purposes and practices:

> Just because we've talked about it heaps in Education I was wondering what it was going to be like in the classroom but it was really good just to sit down with my AT [associate teacher] and do formative feedback and also I learnt heaps about how they do their summative assessment as well. (R6, S1)

Twenty-four per cent of the "what" codes related to becoming a professional; and covered aspects such as developing a teacher identity, being prepared, showing initiative, being organized, and enhancing their practice through critical reflection:

> She actually gave a lot of feedback which I took into account for my reflections, a totally different teaching environment, it was a lot more child-centred than I had previously seen. (R5, S2)

The practicum was also seen as a context in which to develop and be comfortable with one's own style of teaching, to develop a personal presence:

> Everybody's got his/her own style and I think it's important for a student to try and find this because if you're thrown into your own classroom and you haven't figured out what it is yet, you're going to be treading water. (R5, S3)

Managing the learning environment, managing group teaching, establishing routines, and developing behavioural management strategies made up 23% of the "what" response codes. Comments such as this were frequent:

They never learn if you yell at them but talking to them in a firm manner, telling them my expectations, and getting to know them, their abilities, their needs, their interests. (R1, S 2)

Time management was also an important part of student teacher learning during the practicum. References included concerns about being prepared on time and establishing routines, systems, and structures:

Be organized. That's the main thing. Be organized and be flexible so if something needed changing at school I'd stay late or be there early to change it to make sure that I was prepared for the day. (R5, S2)

Finally, 12% of the "what" responses were grouped together around notions of developing a better understanding of the realities and complexities of teaching. This grouping included learning about the multiple numbers of people that teachers deal with during the day, the frequent interruptions, and learning about school systems and structures. As one student teacher stated:

Before it was just about how to teach and now it seems to be more not just the actual teaching but all the other things that are involved in being a teacher. Like the meetings and the catering for everyone and the assessment. You're more aware of the environment as well, much more aware of everything. (R1, S1)

How Did Student Teachers Learn?

"How did they learn?" indicators that were coded from the student teacher interviews were grouped into seven main categories: opportunities to practise, learning from the associate teacher, response to practicum requirements, engagement in professional dialogue, feedback, invisible effects, and self-evaluation (see Table 21.2). There were a total of 221 identified "how" codes.

Student teachers indicated most frequently that they learnt from being actively involved ("hands on", "getting stuck in", and being able to "have a go"). Within the category of opportunities to practise, experimentation was referred to most frequently (39%), closely followed by time and involvement (34%), and risk taking (27%). The comments made by the student teachers reflected a taken-for-granted attitude that the practicum was where learning about teaching and being a teacher occurred:

You obviously can't learn in any other way than by just doing it. (R3, S2)
[Practicum provides a] chance to experiment a bit. (R1, S1)
Just being able to go in there and do stuff. (R2, S2)
Hands on stuff. . . . My associate teacher was willing to let me have a go and not stress if I made a mistake. (R6, S2).

When student teachers spoke about their active involvement, they often talked about moving outside their comfort zone, taking risks, and having a go. Indeed, stepping outside their comfort zone (or even being pushed) was seen as important for professional growth:

I definitely went out of my comfort zone. (R1, S1)

Well if you can't step outside your comfort zone and do all those sorts of things well then you are not going to achieve . . . you are never going to push yourself that bit further and doing something new. (R3, S2)

Everyone needs to have a practicum where they are totally out of their comfort zone. (R6, S2)

Table 21.2. Percentage of Indicators Coded as How Student Teachers Learnt on the Practicum

Percentage of coded indicators	Indicators (%)
20–29%	*Opportunities to practice* (28) Experimentation Time (involvement) Risk taking Learning from the associate teacher (24) Direct and deliberate Incidental
10–19%	*Response to practicum requirements* (15) Involvement in school meetings Documentation/documenting requirements Engagement in the assessment process Goal setting Critical reflection Theory/practice/making links *Engagement in professional dialogue* (13) *Feedback* (11) Constructive Frequency Type (oral/written) Feed forward (response/action)
0–9%	*Invisible effects* (7) Dispositions Prior knowledge Preparation Environment *Self-evaluation* (2)

Note. N "How Indicators" = 221.

The second most frequently referred to category was learning from the associate teacher. This category accounted for 24% of the total references and was subcoded under two main aspects—"direct and deliberate" factors such as modelling, and "incidental" factors such as general observation of the associate teacher's practice.

Within this category, 32% of the references were made to incidental factors while 68% referred to a "directed" associate teacher approach. In fact, "direct and deliberate modelling" by the associate teacher provided the highest number of references over all the subcoded elements, comprising 36 references of the 221 in total. Student teachers tended to regard direction and modelling as a positive learning experience. Only 2 of the 10 student teachers made greater references to "incidental" factors than they did to "direct and deliberate" factors.

Student teachers' willingness to learn by imitation and adopt the practices modelled by their associate teacher was apparent in the number of indications made on this point. Comments linked to this factor included:

> She always told me exactly what I needed to do. (R1, S1)
> The associate teacher was very helpful and I accepted and wrote down everything I saw [and heard] because it was very useful for my teaching. (R1, S2)

There appears to be some security in being told what to do when learning within a complex environment that is fraught with tension and ambiguity. In addition, there can be reassurance when, as some student teachers indicated, the associate teacher's style suited them. There were also occasions where student teachers who had affirmed learning from direct modelling also indicated that they had been allowed to try out new ideas and take risks.

Student teachers frequently mentioned that they learnt through observation in a variety of contexts. Types of observation mentioned included observing teacher behaviours, observing programmes, observing the environment itself, and observing children. A regular feature of learning through observation related to learning that resulted from their interactions with children. The use of phrases such as "seeing" and "knowing the children" suggested that, at times, student teachers' learning occurred through some form of "osmosis" and sensitive awareness. The student teachers strongly asserted that a great deal of their learning occurred in this manner, but it was not always clear what specific learning had occurred. References were often vague and student teachers tended to speak in generalities:

> As much as I learned from my associate teacher I learned more from the kids in the way that they worked and I would pick up on things. . . . Being there was my biggest learning thing with those kids. (R3, S2)

Almost all the student teachers interviewed had a high regard for their associate teacher and experienced a positive practicum. Staff, along with the school environment, provided a strong influence on their learning success. Being part of the learning environment enabled student teachers to engage in professional dialogue with others as well as their associate teacher. Such experiences were much valued by the student teachers who made reference to them.

Only 13% of the references were attributed to the category of professional dialogue. Asking questions was often associated with professional dialogue, as student teachers sought to gain understanding, develop new strategies, and make connections with previous leaning. Planning, organisational, and behaviour management concerns were prominent:

> Whenever I could I just made sure I asked questions and reflected on things. (R1, S1)

Again, it was not always clear what learning actually arose from the professional conversations. At times, discussions appeared to be based more on "being told what to do" (R1, S1). The dialogue appeared, in this respect, to be one-way rather than a two-way communication. At other times, discussions were used to share professional knowledge and to reflect upon personal learning. As one student stated:

> I think discussion was really important. . . . We had lots of times where we would sit down and we would just reflect on what happened during the day and what worked and what didn't work and what we would change next time. (R2, S1)
> Another said: "I thought about it in my head and how to resolve it. (R3, S1)

Although a relatively small percentage (15%) of the overall responses were coded as responses to practicum requirements, the combined aspects coded in this category rated third highest of the seven main categories. Documenting and completing requirements, along with attending meetings, were the most frequently mentioned aspects.

It may be that personal disposition also had an important role to play in terms of how student teachers learnt during their time in someone else's class. Dispositional aspects that appeared to affect how student teachers learnt included:

- ability to develop relationships
- ability to establish effective communication (and ask questions)
- personal qualities such as enthusiasm, adaptability
- professionalism (prior preparation).

Comments indicating the possible effect of dispositional factors included:

> There were some issues but I turned them into learning experiences. (R2, S2)
> I can communicate with probably just about any person I actually come into contact with . . . work and study habits . . . actually being motivated. (R5, S2)

Other invisible effects that appear to have influenced how student teachers learnt during the practicum are covered in the section on factors that enabled and hindered student teacher learning.

Factors That Enabled and Hindered Learning

The data displayed in Table 21.3 indicate the significance of the development of professional relationships to the learning that occurs for student teachers when they are on practicum. It is apparent that these relationships have the potential to be both significantly enabling or hindering. Other factors that that were identified in the student teachers' interviews as significantly enabling or hindering their learning to become teachers were the context of the placement (both structurally and culturally), practicum requirements, the student teachers' preconceptions and prior experiences, and the nature of the communication developed between the practicum players. The disposition of the student teachers was also identified as a factor that regulated student teachers' learning.

This section will continue to use the student teacher's voice to describe the six aspects of the practicum that were identified most frequently as either enabling or hindering. These factors are professional relationships, structure of the context, practicum requirements, preconceptions about the practicum, prior experiences, and communication.

Table 21.3. Percentage of Indicators Coded as Enabling and Hindering

Percentage of coded indicators	Enablers (%)	Hinderers (%)
30% plus	Relationships (35)	
20–29%		Structure of context (22) Relationships (20)
10–19%	Disposition (16) Communication (11) Culture of context (10)	Practicum requirements (14) Preconceptions (14) Prior experiences (13)
1–9%	Structure of context (9) Prior knowledge and experience (7) Practicum requirements (5) Personal and pedagogical philosophy (3) Preconceptions (2) Personal circumstances (2)	Communication (8) Disposition (5) Philosophy (2) Culture of context (1) Personal circumstances (1)

Note. N enabling codes = 235; N hindering codes = 79.

Professional Relationships

The main professional relationships that we would expect the student teacher to develop during the practicum are with the associate teacher (and other staff in the school), the visiting lecturer, and the classroom students, and these were all shown to have significant enabling or hindering features (Table 21.4).

Table 21.4. Percentages of Enabling and Hindering Professional Relationships

Types of enabling relationships as % of total enabling relationship indicators ($n= 83$)	Types of hindering relationships as a %of total hindering relationship indicators ($n = 16$)
Associate teachers (46) Other staff in school (27) Children (17) Wider school community (6) Visiting lecturers (2) Other student teachers (2)	Associate teachers (37) Other staff in school (6) Children (13) Wider school community (13) Visiting lecturers (25) Other student teachers (6)

The findings revealed that associate teacher–student teacher relationships may be enabling (46% of all enabling relationship codes, $n = 83$) or hindering (37% of all hindering relationship codes, $n = 16$) of student teacher learning during the practicum. Being able, and encouraged, to establish a strong, warm professional relationship by an associate teacher who was welcoming was seen as enabling the student teachers' learning to be a teacher:

> My associate, I think it was more a personality thing, but we really got on, so like, she could have been like a friend of mine. Admittedly she was older than me but she was so nice and really welcoming. (R2, S1)

Establishing that relationship early with the associate teacher was also important. Student teachers who met with their associates before the practicum began recognized this as a significant factor in building the relationship and thus enabling their learning; for example:

I met her before the practicum. We sat down for about a day and we went through all the planning and how the kids work and everything like that. I felt so much more relaxed when I walked into the classroom the first day. It was really neat. (R4, S1)

Relationships between the associate teacher and the student teacher were not referred to by many of the student teachers in the study as having the potential to hinder their learning to be a teacher. However, one student teacher did indicate that associate teachers who did not spend time with their student teachers, perhaps because of the demands of their other roles in the school, could restrict the student teachers' learning. Even though one associate teacher had indicated to the student teacher that she had not spent much time discussing the student teacher's work because she "thought the [student teacher] could do it", the student teacher was concerned and confused about the lack of time the associate was spending with her:

She didn't spend nearly as much time with me as the [other associate teachers] have with the other students and I always thought that was really bad, but then I suppose it's a good thing, but then at other times you don't know if you're doing OK or not. . . . I didn't know until the final days that I was actually fine and that I was doing exactly what [she] wanted me to do, but going along and just doing and not actually know, you're kind of like—. (R2, S2)

Visiting lecturer–student teacher relationships may enable (2%) or hinder (25%) of student teacher learning during the practicum. Visiting lecturers were not very often referred to by the student teachers in this study as enabling of their learning. However, for one student teacher a visiting lecturer who spent time in her classroom over two days was perceived as having a significant input into her teaching:

The next day I had someone from [the teacher education provider] come and she was there for the next two days . . . and we changed everything [relating to the teaching of mathematics] and the way we taught was different. When I say we, I taught but she was giving me feedback all the time. (R1, S1)

Not knowing the visiting lecturer before the practicum placement may hinder student teacher learning:

Having someone you don't know and you've never met before can, it makes you, it made both of us [student teachers] kind of panic and they had no idea who we were, that can swing both ways, it can be a good thing and it can be a bad thing, but we were constantly scared of what this person is going to think of us. (R2, S2)

School children–student teacher relationships may enable (17%) or hinder (13%) of student teacher learning during the practicum. Feeling that they understood and were able to relate to the children they were teaching facilitated the student teachers' learning to become teachers. This may have been a simple recognition that the student teacher found it easy to relate to children of a particular age:

I find that year level [Year 4] quite easy to relate to. (R2, S2)

However, some student teachers struggled with knowing what kind of relationship to build:

> They [children in class] still know you're a student teacher. So you've got to watch some kids. They just want to be your friend because they still know you're a student teacher. You've just got to make sure that you show them that you are a teacher. (R2, S2)

Establishing professional relationships with the children was enhanced when the associates insisted that the children recognize the student teacher as a teacher:

> The kids were really good at recognizing that yes, I wasn't an official teacher, but they still saw me as a teacher. My associate was really good and said to them, although she's here as a student teacher, she's on the same level as me in teaching. . . . They have a lot of teacher aides coming in an out of the class all the time and she said, "She's not a teacher aide. I don't want you to think that she is a teacher aide, because it's not what she is". (R3, S2)

Establishing professional relationships with the children sometimes presented the student teachers with a challenge and where these relationships were slow to develop, the student teacher's practicum experience was affected negatively. For example, a younger student teacher found that establishing appropriate relationships with children only five or six years younger than her was more difficult than if the children had been younger:

> It's quite difficult because I am straight out of high school . . . sometimes they just see me as an older sister or an older friend and I have to maintain that professional distance. (R4, S1)

Structure of the Context

The structure of the classroom, the set-up of the school, the layout and functioning of the staff room, and access to resources were all perceived to help (9% of all enabling codes, $n = 235$) or hinder (22% of all hindering codes, $n = 79$) the student teachers' learning. For one student teacher, the situation that she found herself in was initially perceived as hindering but she was able to turn the experience into one that supported her learning:

> On two occasions [I've been] in a team teaching situation. I had one teacher who was the DP [deputy principal] and then I had another teacher that came in the afternoon and so there was a difference. . . . They had different things on and so many other things to think about that there were times when I felt a bit lost as to what I should be doing. There was that uncertainty but then I was able to turn it round into a learning thing and just plan for the day and do what I was able to do. (R2, S2)

The structure of the classroom and the layout of the desks were perceived as a block to this student teacher who had hoped to teach using group activities:

> She did have quite a rigid structure in her class and the way the class was set up made it very, very hard to teach groups in that classroom because they were all facing the board and the front of the classroom was little so there wasn't much room to do anything else. . . . I did role plays one day and moving the desks around was such a mission. (R1, S1)

Practicum Requirements

As well as being required to build up a portfolio documenting their placement, the student teachers on this practicum were required to set personal professional goals. These goals became enabling (5%) when they became a driving force for the student teachers' learning:

> My goal was to get more teaching experience and more feedback because I didn't really get any feedback in either of my two last practicums. (R1, S1)

Other practicum requirements such as the keeping of formal observation and planning records were seen by some to cut across time they might put into planning for their teaching, and thus were perceived as hindering (14%) learning:

> There was so much documentation. . . . I could have done more planning if there was less time [on] documentation. There was definitely an expectation that we did a certain amount [of documentation] because if there wasn't enough then it wouldn't be enough evidence that you had passed. (R6, S1)

Preconceptions about the Practicum

Preconceptions of the school and the class they were to teach in did influence the student teachers' learning. The student teachers met their associates before the placement began and formed views regarding the class, and this was perceived as both enabling (2%) and hindering (14%) learning:

> I'd never been with five year olds before, they are a bit young . . . and I thought "Oh, my goodness. (R2, S1)
> The first week I was there I was absolutely petrified. I didn't want an intermediate. (R3, S2)

Prior Experiences

Previous teaching experience (whether on practicum or through previous teaching in another country) strongly influenced the student teachers' learning, particularly with respect to the attitudes that they took into the placement (enabling = 7% and hindering = 13%):

> [My goal came] from previous practicums basically because I had really muddled up last time. (R1, S1)
> It's very interesting to find and to see lots of different ideas, different methods, different teaching approaches and styles [different from those she was used to in previous teaching in another country]. (R1, S2)
> I've also been a teacher's aide for 10 years. (R5, S2)

The culture of past practicum placements also influenced the attitudes that student teachers took into their new learning situation. For example, one student teacher was concerned whether the staff in her new practicum placement would be as unwelcoming as those in her last placement school:

[The atmosphere] at my last one was really cold, I went to the staffroom once and I was there by myself. . . . For the rest of the time I stayed in the classroom. . . . I tried again but it's so hard when you're not welcomed. (R2, S1)

Communication

Developing open lines of communication was frequently mentioned by the student teachers as an enabler (11%) of student teacher learning. This communication might occur at the planning stages:

Within this school they did a lot of sharing ideas of how they're implementing different things into the classroom. They just share ideas, like PD [professional development], it was really good that communication between different teachers. I went to lots of meetings and they all varied with the staff involved and the whole school communicates a lot via email. (R2, S2)

Or it could be feedback after the student teacher had taught:

Written feedback [was helpful to me]. I would have liked more of that. Yeah, even her verbal feedback was food because it was just straightforward and easy to follow. (R1, S1)

Occasionally a communication difficulty hindered (8%) the learning:

Because they [associate principals] are syndicate leaders as well they've always . . . got so much else on [it's hard to find the time for discussion]. When you get a really busy associate it is hard and you don't want to interrupt their time. They don't have that time always to sit down and talk and you don't want to go "Hey, can I have some time here?" (R2, S2)

DISCUSSION

Our findings appear to support what others have already asserted about the importance of the practicum for student teacher learning (Guyton & McIntyre, 1990; Mayer & Austin, 1999, Oosterheert & Vermunt, 2003; Smith & Lev-Ari, 2005). Similar to the findings of Smith and Lev-Ari (2005), our student teachers regarded the practical components of their programme very highly in terms of supporting their growing professional knowledge. The student teachers in our study indicated that they learnt planning and assessment strategies and how to create a learning environment when on the practicum. However, learning about the complexities and realities of teaching did not feature highly in these student teachers' conversations. A possible reason for this could be that the interviews occurred after their fourth practicum. Perhaps they were now more accepting of the challenges of the teaching profession. Nor did they often mention learning about specific curriculum subject areas. Where curriculum was mentioned, it was either in reference to mathematics or to the use of curriculum documents when planning for and assessing learning.

With regards to how the student teachers learnt, they considered they learnt best by being actively involved in practical hands-on experience and by being deliberately directed by their associate teacher while also being allowed to experiment and take risks. Stepping outside their comfort zone, as well as engagement in practicum requirements, also featured regularly with respect to enabling professional growth.

It was pleasing to see the prevalence of student teachers' references to stepping outside their comfort zone. At the same time, while risk taking and experimenting are synonymous with stepping outside a comfort zone, it was surprising to see student teacher preparedness to do this given the desire for emotional security that is so often sought during practicum (Hastings, 2004). Additionally, although assessment of student teacher performance can sometimes be problematic when encouraging student teacher risk taking, such concerns did not feature in our study. Hence further examination of these aspects is worth pursuing.

It was also of interest to see that student teachers referred to associate teacher "direction" nearly as much a risk taking and experimentation as a factor in how they learnt. For many student teachers, "being directed" while being allowed to "experiment" appeared to work in a positive way. The frequency of references to experimentation, when combined with references to risk taking, provided 19% of the "how?" indicators. When compared with "deliberate and directed assistance" (16% overall), an interesting mix arises that is again worthy of closer analysis.

The findings reveal a lack of reference to self-evaluation and this is a concern given the critically reflective underpinnings of their teacher education programme that emphasizes evaluation and reflection (Smyth, 1989). Only three references were directly made to critical reflection in all of the recorded interviews. On the other hand, perhaps the regularity in which student teachers made reference to stepping outside their comfort zone might indicate a preparedness to look at alternatives and confront practices, which, in itself, is a feature of reflection.

Neither did feedback, as one form of professional dialogue, feature highly in our study. Whether this was because of student teachers not receiving feedback or not expecting to receive feedback as a result of past experience is yet to be determined. We did find a small amount of evidence to suggest that professional dialogue was occurring between the student teachers and their associate teachers. As with Edwards and Protheroe (2003), the student teachers' comments about this dialogue did not reveal deep discussions about the understandings embedded in practice. However, unlike the student teachers in Edwards and Protheroe's study, the student teachers in our study appeared to be more focused on their pupils as learners rather than being concerned about personal performance. This supports the findings from Burn, Hagger, and Mutton's (2003) study. What constitutes professional dialogue and what conversations are more productive to personal professional growth require further examination.

With regard to what the data revealed about the enablers and inhibitors to student teacher learning during the practicum, the most frequently mentioned enabler was the development of professional relationships, whether they be between the associate and student teacher, the visiting lecturer and student teacher, or the children and the student teacher. These findings support earlier research reports from Cameron and Wilson (1993), Pinder (1999), and Ovens (2003). Relationships were also the second most frequently mentioned inhibiting factor. The structure of the context—the classroom layout and expectations of behaviour, aspects of the school such as the staff room, and resource availability—also had the potential to enable or hinder the student teachers' learning to be a teacher.

It became very apparent to the researchers that the student teachers' disposition and personal traits such as a passion for teaching, willingness to use their initiative, resilience, adaptability, degree of introversion or extroversion, and risk taking were potentially significant enablers or hindrances. The student teacher's disposition, prior knowledge, and personal or pedagogical philosophies appeared to mediate the practicum experiences in ways that experiences that enabled learning for one student teacher might be a hindrance for another's learning.

A small-scale study such as this has its limitations because of the fact that it reports data from just 10 primary teacher education student teachers. However, a strength of the study is its richness of data. We are making no attempt to generalize these findings and leave it to the reader as to what significance is attached to the findings.

CONCLUSION

Practicum learning remains problematic. In the literature, we are reminded that it is not possible for teacher education programmes to fully prepare student teachers for the reality of full-time teaching (Northfield & Gunstone, as cited in Loughran, Brown, & Doecke, 2001). Nor should preservice programmes be expected to fulfil this expectation when learning about teaching is constructed as more than just socializing a novice teacher into the profession (Loughran et al., 2001). This study has alerted us to aspects of the student teachers' practicum experience that need further investigation. Aspects requiring deeper examination are the factors that are currently relatively invisible, such as the influence of disposition and student teachers' prior knowledge. An apparent lack of focus on curriculum concerns (both pedagogy and subject matter) also requires further consideration. We have identified that professional relationships can both enable or hinder student learning, but this aspect would benefit from further study, particularly in regard to the role of the visiting lecturer and the undoubted emotional nature of the practicum (Hargreaves, 1998). Such studies would best be suited to qualitative approaches. We also plan a large-scale quantitative study framed from these findings.

REFERENCES

Ball, D. (2000). Bridging practices – intertwining content and pedagogy in teaching and learning to teach. *Journal of Teacher Education, 51*(3), 241–247.

Burgess, H., & Butcher, J. (1999). To challenge or not to challenge: The mentor's dilemma. *Mentoring and Tutoring, 6*(3), 31–46.

Burn, K., Hagger, H., Mutton, T., & Everton, T. (2003). The complex development of student teachers' thinking. *Teachers and Teaching: Theory and Practice, 9*(4), 310–331.

Butler, J. (1996). Professional development: Practice as text, reflection as process, and self as locus. *Australian Journal of Education, 40*(3), 265–283.

Cameron, B., & Wilson, S. (1993). The practicum: Student teacher perception of teacher supervision styles. *South Pacific Journal of Teacher Education, 21*(2), 155–167.

Cochran-Smith, M., & Paris, C. (1995). Mentor and mentoring: Did Homer have it right? In J. Smyth (Ed.), *Critical discourses on teacher development* (pp. 181-202). London: Cassell.

Dobbins, R. (1996). The practicum: A learning journey. *Waikato Journal of Education, 2*, 59–71.

Edwards, A., & Protheroe, L. (2003). Learning to see in classrooms: What are student teachers learning about teaching and learning while learning to teach in schools? *British Educational Research Journal, 29*(2), 227-242.

Fairbanks, C., Freedman, D., & Kahn, C. (2000). The role of effective mentors in learning to teach. *Journal of Teacher Education, 51*(2), 102–112.

Feiman-Nemser, S. (2001). Helping novices learn to teach: Lessons from an exemplary support teacher. *Journal of Teacher Education, 52*(1), 17–30.

Fullan, M. (2002). The change leader. *Educational Leadership, 59*(8), 16–23.

Guyton, E., & McIntyre, D. (1990). Student teaching and school experiences. In W.R. Houston (Ed.), *Handbook of research on teacher education.* New York: Macmillan.

Hagger, H., Burn, K., & Mutton, T. (2006, September). *Practice makes perfect? Learning to learn as a teacher.* Paper presented at the British Educational Research Association, Warwick, England.

Haigh, M., & Ward, G. (2004). Problematising practicum relationships: Questioning the "taken for granted". *Australian Journal of Education, 48*(2), 134–148.

Haigh, M., & Tuck, B. (1999, December). *Assessing student teachers' performance in practicum.* Paper presented at the Australian Association of Research in Education, Melbourne, Australia.

Hargreaves, A. (1998). The emotional practice of teaching. *Teaching and Teacher Education, 14*(8), 835–136.

Hastings, W. (2004). Emotions and the practicum: The co-operating teacher's perspective. *Teachers and Teaching: Theory and Practice, 10*(2), 135–147.

Hayes, D. (2001). The impact of mentoring and tutoring student primary teacher's achievements: A case study. *Mentoring and Tutoring, 9*(1), 6–21.

Loughran, J., Brown, J., & Doecke, B. (2001) Continuities and discontinuities: The transition from preservice to first year teaching. *Teachers and Teaching: Theory and Practice, 7*(1), 7–23.

Martinez, K. (1998). Preservice teachers adrift on a sea of knowledges. *Asia-Pacific Journal of Teacher Education, 26*(2), 97–108.

Mayer, D., & Austin, J. (1999). *It's just what I do: Personal practical theories of supervision in the practicum.* Paper presented at the Fourth Biennial International Cross-Faculty Practicum Conference of the Association of Practical Experiences in Professional Education, Christchurch, New Zealand.

Oosterheert, I. E., & Vermunt, J. D. (2003). Regulating knowledge growth in learning to teach: The role of dynamic sources. *Teachers and Teaching: Theory and Practice, 9*(2), 157–173.

Ovens, A. (2003). Learning to teach through the practicum: A situated learning perspective. In B. Ross & L Burrows (Eds.), *It takes two feet: Teaching physical education and health in Aotearoa New Zealand* (pp. 76–89). Palmerston North, New Zealand: Dunmore Press.

Pinder, H. (1999, January). *Breaking new ground: Redefining the practicum two years further on.* Paper presented at the 4th Biennial International Cross-Faculty Practicum Conference of Association of Practical Experiences in Professional Education. Christchurch, New Zealand.

Schon, D. (1987). *Educating the reflective practitioner.* San Francisco: Jossey Bass.

Scott, A., & Freman-Moir, J. (2000). *Tomorrow's teachers: International critical perspectives on teacher education*. Christchurch, New Zealand: Canterbury University Press.

Smith, K., & Lev-Ari, L. (2005). The place of the practicum in pre-service teacher education: The voice of the students. *Asia Pacific Journal of Teacher Education, 33*(3), 289–302.

Smyth, J. (1989). Developing and sustaining critical reflection in teacher education. *Journal of Teacher Education, 40*(2), 2–9.

Tickle, L. (1994). *The induction of new teachers*. New York: Cassell.

Wilson, S., Floden, R., & Ferrini-Mundy, J. (2002). Teachers' preparation research: An insider's view from the outside. *Journal of Teacher Education, 53*(3), 190–204.

Yost, D., Sentner, S., & Forlenza- Bailey, A. (2000). An examination of the construct of critical reflection: Implications for teacher education programming in the 21st century. *Journal of Teacher Education, 5*(1), 39–48.

Zeichner, K. (1990). Changing directions in the practicum: Looking ahead to the 1990s. *Journal of Education for Teaching, 16*(2), 105–131.

AUTHOR NOTE

Mavis Haigh is an Associate-Professor and Associate Dean: Postgraduate, Heather Pinder is a Principal Lecturer and the Primary Practicum Co-ordinator, and Lyn McDonald is a Senior Lecturer in the Faculty of Education, University of Auckland, New Zealand.

The authors wish to acknowledge the data gathering and analysis contribution from the other members of the Practicum Research Team: Helen Hedges, Jenni Jongejan, Rhona Leonard, and Jeanne Sheehan.

They also acknowledge a research grant from the former Auckland College of Education Research Grants Committee that enabled them to carry out this research.

Correspondence concerning this chapter should be addressed by email to: m.haigh@auckland.ac.nz

PART 4. ENHANCING PEDAGOGY

In: Challenging Thinking about Teaching and Learning
Editors: C. M. Rubie-Davies and C. Rawlinson

ISBN: 978-1-60456-744-1
© 2008 Nova Science Publishers, Inc.

Chapter 22

ETHICAL ISSUES IN PRACTITIONER RESEARCH: TEACHING AND LEARNING RESEARCH INITIATIVE LESSONS

Mary Hill

ABSTRACT

School-based practitioner research by teachers in partnership with university researchers can produce improved outcomes for students as well as valuable knowledge about how schools achieve these outcomes. However, significant ethical issues can and do arise during such practitioner research projects. This chapter explores some ethical issues that arose in one such project, describes how these were addressed, and suggests ways of anticipating and managing challenges in practitioner research.

INTRODUCTION

Ethics, in the context of research, are typically discussed in terms of conventional empirical research paradigms. In such contexts, the focus is on interactions with participants to access information to meet the research objectives. In these circumstances, ethics are taken to refer to doing no harm, ensuring confidentiality and/or anonymity, managing risk, not distorting the data, and so on. However, as with practitioner research in other allied fields, practitioner research in education is based upon the assumption that the teachers are both researchers and participants simultaneously. Not only are they researchers of their own practices but they are undertaking the research in order to take significant action to change the very institution they are investigating, usually as the investigation proceeds. While some commentators believe that conventional research ethics are compromised in undertaking practitioner research (e.g., Murray & Lawrence, 2000), this chapter argues that teacher researchers require strong understanding of both conventional research ethics and practitioner research to underpin the iterative ethical decision making that must be made as intertwined research and practice proceed. This understanding is especially important when practitioners carry out research in partnership with academic researchers as a way of implementing policy to improve school effectiveness.

Recently in New Zealand, as elsewhere (e.g., the Teaching and Learning Research Programme in the United Kingdom), government officials have realized that

> despite the fact that research about pedagogy is a potentially invaluable record of the work of teachers, there is stronger ownership of that knowledge by researchers than teachers and teachers are rarely named as co-authors in research reports about their work. (Alton-Lee, 2006, p. 4)

One initiative of the Ministry of Education in New Zealand to address this low involvement of teachers in both research and the use of valuable research findings about effective practice has been the Teaching and Learning Research Initiative (TLRI). Launched in 2003, the TLRI is funded NZ$2,000,000 per year to support projects involving teachers and researchers that build knowledge about teaching and learning, enhance the potential of research findings to inform practice, and use this knowledge to improve outcomes for learners (Teaching and Learning Research Initiative, 2007a). TLRI projects, therefore, typically (though not exclusively) combine practitioner and academic researchers within one- or two-year projects focused on investigating changed teaching practices both for the benefit of the school, early childhood centre, or tertiary institution, and to increase research knowledge, influence policy, and build research capability nationally. These intentions are explicated in the TLRI principles as the practice, strategic, and research values respectively. Specifically, the TLRI aims to

> build knowledge through partnership research about teaching and learning, use this knowledge to create improved outcomes for learners and create partnerships between practitioners and researchers to maximize the value and usefulness of research. (Teaching and Learning Research Initiative, 2007b, p. 1)

This chapter draws on one TLRI-funded project—the Great Expectations project (Hill et al., 2006)—to exemplify the ethical issues that can arise from partnership practitioner research. Carried out by teachers from six schools and two university researchers over 2004 and 2005, this project sought to meet the TLRI aims by investigating how practices within each of the six schools might lead to increased student performance. Within the Great Expectations project, all of these schools were focused upon improvement and held high expectations for their students. The schools covered a range of deciles (socioeconomic levels) and locations, and drew students from communities with diverse ethnic and cultural groups. While it is the case that the principals of each of these schools initiated contact with the university researchers to make the proposal that led to the Great Expectations project, their primary focus always remained on how the results could improve teaching within their particular schools through cycles of action research. The university researchers, however, while supportive of improved learning outcomes in the partnership schools, also had specific research interests in advancing school improvement through teacher inquiry, distributed leadership, and coaching. Both had experienced, directed, and written about action research previously (e.g., Hill, 2000; Robertson, 2000).

This chapter begins with a brief review of literature related to action research and ethics. In particular, this section highlights the kinds of ethical issues that can arise when the government sponsors action research for school improvement and also insists that this work be carried out in partnership with academic researchers for the purposes of increasing school improvement knowledge and building research capability. The chapter then narrows in focus to explain the particular TLRI project in which the ethical issues explored in the rest of the chapter arose and how data about these issues were collected. The ethical issues are listed and then described prior to discussion and conclusion about the need to build the ethical decision making of practitioner researchers on the base of conventional research ethics in order that they can manage such tensions, dilemmas, and challenges when they do arise in action research.

PRACTITIONER INQUIRY AND ETHICAL ISSUES

Sagor defines action research as

> [a] disciplined process of inquiry conducted by and for those taking the action. The primary reason for engaging in action research is to assist the actor in improving or refining his or her actions. (2005, p.1)

However, action research describes a broad category of practices ranging from an emphasis on personal reflection to claims that action research can lead to greater social justice for disempowered groups (Cardno, 2003). Carr and Kemmis (1986) provided a useful three-level distinction between technical, practical, and emancipatory kinds of action research. Technical action research is oriented towards functional improvement measured in terms of its success in changing particular outcomes of practices; practical action research has similar technical aspirations for change but also aims to inform the practitioners so that they can make wise and prudent decisions. Carr and Kemmis (1986) explain that a third kind of action research, termed emancipatory or critical, aims not only at improving outcomes and improving the self-understandings of practitioners, but is also intended to assist practitioners to critique their own social or educational work and work settings. This kind of action research aims at changing the cultural, social, and historical processes of everyday life to intervene in not only the practice but also the setting (or, as it could be described, the work, the worker, and the workplace).

Debate exists about the extent to which practitioner action research can both serve to change practice at the local level in policy-driven directions and be emancipatory, as described above by Kemmis. Some go as far as to argue that current versions of action research claim to be emancipatory but are actually tools to support policy directives or encourage compliance with government programmes (Carr & Kemmis, 2005). Brown and Jones warn that this situation, where the government sponsors teacher research for dual purposes such as in the TLRI, is problematic and can lead to issues that threaten the conduct of the research, among them ethical issues. They state that

> [emancipatory action research] draws on an uneasy alliance of two alternative research perspectives: (a) the insider perspective of teachers focusing on their own actions; and (b) research motivated by attempts to influence policy across broader sections of the teaching force. It may work in my classroom . . . but it is a different matter

making it stick as national policy. Further, research agendas are not easily harmonized with conflicting assumptions and motivations held by different agencies, not least those assumptions built into the infrastructure within which education practices take place. (2001, p. 4)

Tensions can also arise between the insiders (teacher researchers) and their academic research partners (outsiders), particularly when research purposes, methods, and outputs are viewed differently from each perspective. The very nature of what research evidence is considered to be is also sometimes disputed. Teachers acting as researchers in their own schools may consider changes in individual student behaviour and performance to be valid research evidence in contrast with the wider notions of research evidence that government agencies such as the Ministry of Education may hold as aspirations for system-wide change. These tensions are well known and written about in the literature (e.g., Coghlan & Brannick, 2005; Lee and van den Berg, 2003). Murray and Lawrence (2000) list six main ways these tensions can play out, the sixth of these regarding ethical issues. They state that practitioner research is not amenable to be carried out under conventional research ethics:

> Conventional ethics governing access to the research venue, confidentiality of information and the privacy of research subjects may all be compromised by the privileged role/status position of the practitioner and the presumption of the autonomy that accompanies this position. Indeed the interpersonal conditions in classrooms and of tutor work may be a primary source for the bias and contamination of data. (Murray & Lawrence, 2000, pp. 18–19)

While the very nature of emancipatory action research carried out by teachers may not fit neatly within conventional research ethics, it is critical that teacher researchers understand and employ ethical decision making. Robinson and Lai (2006) spend time in their text, Practitioner Research for Educators, guiding practitioners about ethical decision making in their research endeavours. In particular, Robinson and Lai indicate that free and informed consent and the prevention of harm are paramount factors in ethical decision making. They provide five principles to guide ethical decision making in practitioner research. These can be summarized as:

- There are no rules to follow—only awareness of ethical principles and wise application to your particular context.
- Ethical decision making is a kind of problem solving.
- Where you can, involve others in making ethical decisions that affect them.
- Use conversations and test your own and others' assumptions about the effect of research on others; for example, do not assume that everyone wants to be anonymous.
- Work on increasing the benefit to participants as well as minimizing harm.
- The more potential benefits that teachers see in a research project, the more risks they may be prepared to take. (Principles adapted from Robinson & Lai, 2006, p. 71.)

Sensible as these principles are, putting them into practice can still be very challenging especially when both insiders and outsiders are engaged in research partnerships to simultaneously improve practice within schools and across education systems more generally.

ETHICAL ISSUES IN PRACTICE:
TENSIONS, COMPLICATIONS AND DILEMMAS

In the Great Expectations project used as an example throughout this chapter, the aim was to conduct emancipatory action research to change the teaching, the teachers, and the school structures to facilitate improved outcomes for the diverse students within each of these school sites. But because of the principles of the TLRI, the schools/university partnership was also charged with a wider mission of investigating how this emancipatory research could build knowledge about school improvement and increase research capability. Building teacher researcher ethical understanding within emancipatory action research as an aspect of building research capability, therefore, was one of the aims of the wider project.

The teacher researchers and university researchers worked together to write the funding proposal and establish a conceptual framework for the project. Each school then selected a group of teacher researchers who took responsibility for writing that school's research questions and deciding what data needed to be collected and how it would be collected within the constraints of the project's conceptual framework. In order to progress the project and investigate the extent to which the teacher researchers were able to research their own schools' practices and improved outcomes, five full project meetings were held. At these meetings, data were collected about the individual school outcomes as well as on how the teachers experienced their role as researchers (Robertson & Hill, 2005).

In order to gather data about how the teacher researchers experienced their role as researchers, and explore the issues arising for them, each project meeting was audio-recorded in full, the university researchers kept field notes, and all those attending the meetings undertook reflective writing about their experiences as researchers in the project. Although the meeting tapes were not transcribed in full, parts were transcribed to investigate areas of interest. The teacher researchers also filled in a survey about their participation as teacher researchers in the project and data concerning teachers as researchers were collected as field notes by the university researchers during visits to schools and meetings. One area of interest that emerged from analysis of the data was the ethical tensions, complications, and dilemmas that continued to arise throughout the project.

From the outset of the project, conventional research ethics guided practice. Therefore, an application for ethical approval was submitted to the institutional ethics committee at the partner university. All six school projects were covered within the application which, in line with convention, emphasized that participation was voluntary, sought informed consent from all parties, and assured participants that their identities would remain confidential to the researchers. The application also explained how teacher researchers would be on the look out for situations that might have the potential to cause harm (such as work intensification, publication of student achievement details, and the like) and would address these immediately should they arise. The application stated that the Privacy Act would be adhered to throughout the project and that no conflicts of interest had (at that point) been identified but that should any arise they would be acknowledged, dealt with and declared in the appropriate manner. The application acknowledged that every effort would be made to work in a manner sensitive to cultural diversity and individual differences. Finally the application mentioned that several of the teacher researchers were also postgraduate students and would gain ethical approval for their personal studies (which in some cases overlapped with the TLRI project). The university institutional committee approved the application and the project began.

Even before the first meeting was held, however, ethical issues arose (see Table 22.1). These questions arose specifically because this was emancipatory action research in partnership with academic researchers who were interested in how the findings from the individual school projects might inform governmental objectives expressed as the TLRI principles. Had these projects been either site-specific action research projects designed to improve outcomes at each of the schools or an interpretive investigation carried out by the researchers on varying school practices, these issues might not have arisen. The nature of the partnership between the teacher researchers and the university researchers and the nature of emancipatory action research, it appears, simultaneously increased research capability and exacerbated the ethical dilemmas.

The New Zealand Association for Educational Research (NZARE, 2007) sets out ethical guidelines under "General Principles" and then provides three sets of more specific principles: principles relating to research participants; principles relating to research personnel; and principles relating to research reports. The aspects described as guidelines under each of these headings can be thought of as conventional ethical guidelines in educational research. These include avoiding harm and adverse effects, confidentiality, informed consent, acknowledgement, and assent from children. The Great Expectations project ethics application considered and followed these conventional guidelines, but even then issues arose that challenged the approved procedures (see Table 22.1). Each of these ethical issues is exemplified and discussed below.

Table 22.1. Ethical Issues Debated by the Great Expectations Project Team

Ethical issue	Questions debated
Confidentiality/ anonymity	Will teachers and students (and others) data be reported anonymously or will there be a chance they could be identified? If so, how should they be informed about this? Will it be written up? Published? If so, by whom? Whose name should go on the report? Why? If teacher researcher names go on the published papers, how is confidentiality to be maintained for the rest of the teachers? Will participants be photographed, videoed, taped? If so, is this for the research project or is it part of professional development? Or for teaching and learning purposes? What about presenting at conferences, can I show photos of the school? Teachers? Students? Samples of students work?
Informed consent	Is this "research" or "teaching"? Whose informed consent is necessary? Advisable? How should this be carried out?
Power and control	Who makes the decisions and holds the power in the partnership?
Conflicts of interest	Is there a conflict of interest? If so, how do we solve it? Can the participants withdraw their information? If so, when and how? Will the students' marks/grades be affected? If so, is this a harm or a benefit? Could staff promotions be affected by this project? If so, is this a harm or a benefit? How might this need to be managed?
Cultural issues	Are there cultural/translation issues involved? Who in the school will read the report before it is published? Is compensation or koha (gift) offered?

Confidentiality/Anonymity

One of the first ethical issues faced brought the conventional principle of participant confidentiality into conflict with the right of the researcher to be acknowledged for his or her work. Because in emancipatory action research the participants are also the researchers, it is often difficult to know how to proceed when details of such projects are made public. Early on in the project, the national TLRI co-ordination team asked for a summary of the intended project, including the names of schools and researchers, to put on the website. After consultation, the Great Expectations research team declined this request. Although aligned with the aims of emancipatory research, where all partners in the research should be acknowledged for their work, had this information been published it would have compromised the explicit promise to the participants to keep their identities confidential. The desire of the national TLRI co-ordination team to celebrate teacher research and express true partnership through publicizing teacher researchers (as well academic researchers' names) directly challenges conventional research ethics.

Confidentiality also arose as an issue when the first round of papers and presentations were being prepared for publication. To ensure that they maintained the confidentiality of their co-teachers, students, and their families, the teacher researchers decided that only the university researchers' names should be used as authors. The university researchers repeatedly raised this as an issue with the teacher researchers. The university researchers, having the emancipatory nature of the research in mind, were not happy that the teacher researchers would not be recognized as the authors and investigators in their own projects. The teacher researchers, on the other hand, did not feel able to relinquish the promise of confidentiality that they had made to their colleagues in their schools, nor were they ready to renegotiate with their school colleagues about confidentiality. Therefore, through discussion and informed decision making (Robinson & Lai, 2006), the research team (all of the teacher researchers and university researchers together) decided not to include the teacher researchers names at that point.

During the second year of the study, however, the university researchers still felt conflicted about the fact that the teacher researchers (and their school colleagues) who were the prime investigators were not able to be recognized as such. Within the schools, changes to teaching and the way the schools operated were becoming very evident as a result of the projects. The teachers were audio- and videotaping classroom and school action as evidence of improved student outcomes and the teacher researchers began to express a desire to present their findings along with some of the recorded data at practitioner and research conferences. After much discussion among the research team, the decision was made that the teacher researchers would renegotiate confidentiality within their school communities so that they could publish and present their work publicly. While this example of an ethical challenge may appear uncomplicated, in practice it was complex and took time and negotiation to work through.

Conventional ethical guidelines hold that the teachers and students, as participants, should have the right to have their identities kept confidential but because the teacher researchers were both researchers and participants, tensions arose over this aspect. Early in the project, especially during the first year when trust was being established, pseudonyms were negotiated and used in publications and when communicating information to the TLRI co-ordination team. But over the second year of the project, because of the increasing desire to share authorship, the nature of the project in each school, and the desire for equality in the partnership arrangements, all of the teachers involved in the project in each of the schools negotiated to reveal the names of their school and teacher researcher identities. This was time consuming as it needed to be formalized with the principal and board of trustees, with all the teachers, and with any students and their parents whose identities might be revealed. However, the effort to make these changes as the project proceeded was extremely worthwhile because they had the effect of equalizing the power relationships within the project, and thus led to more emancipatory outcomes (Robinson & Lai, 2006).

As Murray and Lawrence (2000) point out, practitioner research methodologies, and the confidentiality issues that surround them, are rather more complex than within methodologies that correspond to conventional research ethics. Because of the public dimension of practitioner research and the commitment to emancipatory outcomes, confidentiality and publicity have to be negotiated throughout the project, not just decided by researchers before the project begins. Robinson and Lai (2006) suggest that in practitioner research, ethical decision making becomes a problem solving process rather than an agreed set of practices approved by a committee in advance.

Additionally, the Great Expectations teacher researchers regarded the situation as no different from those they faced in teaching (Patterson, Santa, Short, & Smith, 1993). They believed that it was their ethical duty to do the best they could for every student and teacher within the constraints of their work. Because they were confident that their research indicated positive changes within their schools, they approached their fellow teachers, students, principals, and boards of trustees to gain permission to present at the conferences, author reports, and show approved video clips. Thus they renegotiated the informed consent gained at the outset of the project in order to enact the emancipatory intentions of their collaborative research efforts (Carr & Kemmis, 1986).

Informed Consent

As the issue of confidentiality above attests, gaining informed consent for emancipatory action research may need to be an iterative process. In conventional research designs, informed consent is most often gained only once from each participant because the research design in conventional projects is worked through in advance and presented to each participant for consent before he or she takes part. As exemplified above, although initial informed consent was gained from participants in the Great Expectations project, throughout the project there were occasions on which informed consent needed to be renegotiated and newly gained.

A major reason this iterative process of gaining different or changed informed consent was necessary was that as each school research team communicated the findings of each cycle of research back to the participants within the school, the process of institutional change necessitated yet a new cycle of research to investigate the changed practices. Because the researchers within the school were also the principal and teachers, and because they were increasingly taking on all the roles of researcher, more and more they wanted to claim the process and findings of research as their own. Claiming work in the field of research requires publication and presentation. Therefore, emancipatory research, which involves collaborative institutional action, also leads to the need to gain consent to make the findings public. Thus, as Carr and Kemmis explain, emancipatory practitioner research is an empowering process for participants; "It engages them in the struggle for more rational, just, democratic and fulfilling forms of education" (1986, p. 205). This brings with it, however, the responsibility to constantly inform and gain the voluntary consent of all participants regarding their participation as the project proceeds.

What was sometimes not at all clear, however, was the extent to which the teachers and the students in the Great Expectations project were research participants in comparison with the extent to which they were just involved in regular teaching and work. The ethics application indicated that the students would be involved only in their regular work and that no extra personal data would be gathered about them. This was the case, but in some schools, where the teachers saw very large potential benefits in building learning communities and assisting each other to improve their practice, they started to use video footage and achievement data to gather evidence about their practice. In cases where this happened, the opinion of the teacher researchers was that the video footage and the student learning meetings to examine the achievement data and plan interventions as a result were teaching work rather than practitioner inquiry. From a university research vantage point, however, such activities could have been viewed as research and thus they should be subject to informed consent.

As with the confidentiality issues above, an iterative approach to these issues was employed as they arose. In most cases, the teacher researchers took the lead in decision making and problem solving about such issues. As Robinson and Lai (2006) suggest, by working to increase the benefit to participants, as well as minimizing the harm, the teachers were motivated to build in student learning meetings and video observations of each other in order to improve their practice for the benefit of their students—and they deemed it to be teaching rather than research. At other times, activities were deemed to be research by these same teacher researchers. For example, when they needed to know how successful their fellow teachers thought holding student learning meetings had been as a strategy, informed consent was gained from all the teachers who agreed to participate in responding to a questionnaire.

Power and Control

Issues of power and control were also aspects that the project team needed to keep in mind and discuss as the project proceeded. As Lankshear and Knobel (2004) warn, researchers (whether teacher researchers or their university counterparts) often find themselves on the "strong" side of uneven power relations that develop during research projects. As they suggest, the research may be backed by the authority of the school, or by a university or government agencies, making it difficult for potential participants to decline the invitation to participate or withdraw when they feel uncomfortable. Because the lead teacher researchers in the TLRI were either the principal or a deputy principal in each of the schools, the potential for teachers to feel pressured to participate was high. One way the research team addressed this was that, initially, only a volunteer sample of teachers from each school was included. In one school, only one teacher volunteered in the first year. In the rest, up to half the school participated. In the second year other teachers were invited to join in as they felt comfortable to do so. However, the extent to which the teacher researchers felt under pressure to take part was never completely clear.

Conflicts of Interest

These tensions around the potential for participants to feel pressured to take part might well have originated as potential conflicts of interest. Thus special care needed to be paid to ensuring the dignity and integrity of the participants was kept intact throughout the project in order to reduce this possibility. One important way that the research team used to avoid such conflicts was to establish and maintain reciprocal relationships within the school-based projects. Such reciprocity is established, usually, through the exchange of favours and commitments that build a sense of mutual identification (Glazer, 1982, cited in Glesne & Peshkin, 1992, p. 122). Lather (1991) and Robertson (2000) also argue the critical importance of reciprocity. Throughout the Great Expectations project, each teacher researcher worked hard on this aspect. For example, in one school the teacher researchers took on the assessment data input and analysis role to relieve the pressure of workload on classroom teachers; in another, the teacher researcher/principal released teachers from their teaching at times so that they could undertake aspects of the research project such as group meetings to analyze student achievement data. In a third, the principal used substantial resources to free up the entire research team every Wednesday to gather data and implement changed practices throughout the school.

An interesting outcome of this reciprocal action was that the number of teacher researchers increased in all but one of the six schools during the duration of the project. In each of these schools, new teacher researchers joined the research team, assisted with gathering and analyzing data, presented at seminars and conferences, and attended the research team meetings at the university. The data gathered from these teachers at the research team meetings and through field observations indicated that they had developed trust in the research project and were motivated to join the research team because they were benefiting from their participation.

Throughout the Great Expectations project, other conflicts of interest did arise for both the teacher researchers and the university researchers. These could be as simple as the time commitments demanded by the project affecting time for teaching, knowing which "hat" one was wearing when, or making decisions about what to include in a presentation or publication when privy to information as both a researcher and a teacher. In conventional research, where the researcher is an outsider, although conflicts of interest can arise, it is often not as difficult to sort out what to prioritize and how to proceed. Teacher researchers, however, are insiders and are teachers first and then researchers.

While Halasa (1998) argues that teacher researchers can think of themselves as doubly bound to ethical behaviour both as teachers and researchers and lists ways in which these responsibilities can be achieved in practice, the teacher researchers did confront situations where ethical decision making was needed to think their way through tensions between their role as teacher and researcher. Using an ethical decision-making process as described by Robinson and Lai (2006, p. 71) assisted in working through these dilemmas, but at times it was necessary for the teachers to step aside from the researcher role in order to avoid a serious conflict of interest. For example, during a research meeting at one school, the teacher researcher/principal was advised that a child had failed to arrive at school that morning. Without another thought, both the teacher researcher/principal and the university researcher set out into the community to locate the missing pupil. While this was an obvious decision about how to proceed, there were other times when it was less obvious that a conflict of interest existed.

Cultural Issues

A final set of issues confronting the project exemplified in this chapter arose in relation to the cultural differences within and between schools. Conventional research ethics indicate that where there is the potential for the research to affect particular cultural groups, special care should be taken to consult with the appropriate communities of interest to ensure that the effects are not detrimental. In the Great Expectations project, all of the schools identified particular cultural groups within their school communities that might be affected by the research they were undertaking. However, these effects were usually positive. For example, one school was sited in a very low decile area and all of the children within the school came from Pacific Island families. The project in this school was to use particular teaching strategies on a school-wide basis to increase reading comprehension levels to the national average by the time their students reached high school age. To monitor progress towards this goal, the teacher researchers at this school used one particular measure repeatedly throughout the project. Although the school achieved their aim by the end of the two years of the project, at times they struggled to use the measurement tool effectively. Ethical issues, not anticipated at the beginning of the project, arose regarding the extent to which publicizing their difficulties might occur.

The university researchers, as mentioned earlier, were looking across the projects to identify issues that might be common across the school projects in order to improve research capability and inform government policy about school improvement and teacher inquiry. The problems that the teachers in this school experienced were related in part to the knowledge of the teacher researchers about the measurement tool and in part to how to use assessment for research purposes. Added to this were the cultural differences and ways of relating between the university researcher and the teacher researchers. Although at first it was not ethical to highlight the difficulties experienced by these teacher researchers, following work between the university researcher to assist the teacher researchers to understand and use the tool, and renegotiation of informed consent within the school to present the results publicly, it became possible to sensitively reveal these results. These issues were subtle and relate to social justice issues arising from emancipatory research. As Reason and Bradbury put it, action research practitioners "need to make choices which have implications for the quality and validity of their work" at the same time as they are working to "liberate the human body, mind and spirit in the search for a better, freer world" (2006, p. 2).

CONCLUSION

As demonstrated through the examples above, emancipatory action research in schools carried out in partnership with university researchers can and should be based firmly upon conventional research ethics principles and guidelines. However, it is not enough to consider ethical issues at the beginning of such projects and then implement a set of practices spelt out in advance. As the examples above indicate, as the cycles of action research proceed, constant ethical decision making is required and the agreements negotiated at the beginning of a project may need to be changed and renegotiated. This calls for teacher researchers (and their university partners) to have relatively strong understandings about both conventional educational research ethics and knowledge and understanding of ethical decision making in practice. While teachers do come to the research field with a set of professional ethics, building knowledge and understanding of ethical decision making for research, particularly in emancipatory action research, requires support.

When teachers are working as researchers in partnership with researchers from an institution with an ethics committee such as a university, those committees along with the researchers are strong allies in support of ethical considerations and usually provide advice and guidance before and during the life of the project. Rather than seeing institutional ethics committees as foes to battle with in order to be able to get on with a project, the best advice is to see them as advisors who can assist teacher researchers to sort through ethical dilemmas and provide guidance when the way forward may not be clear.

Institutional ethics committees have an educative role to play in building such ethical knowledge and understanding among practitioner researchers. Many teacher researchers are also postgraduate students undertaking action research projects, such as the ones in the Great Expectations project, for qualification purposes. Institutional research ethics committees do not always include experienced action researchers among their members and therefore can exacerbate the tensions action researchers experience by requiring hard and fast adherence to pre-specified requirements throughout the life of a project. Having more flexible processes that encourage researchers to vary the conditions of their ethical approval and change the nature of these through shared ethical decision making could assist practitioner researchers to meet and solve such tensions and issues when they arise.

As well as having a strong understanding of conventional research ethics and knowing and following the appropriate ethical guidelines for research, the evidence from the Great Expectations project indicated that it is important for teacher researchers to have a strong grasp of practitioner research theory and practice. It is acknowledged that, of course, teacher researchers are teachers first and foremost. Therefore, professional ethics will be to the fore in decision making. But teacher researchers also need to make decisions in situations that they will not meet regularly, if at all, in a teaching context. The examples of using video footage for public presentations and publishing research findings described above are just two of these types of situations teacher researchers might encounter. Making use of authoritative texts, such as Robinson and Lai's (2006) book Practitioner Research for Educators and undertaking postgraduate study and research fieldwork under the supervision of experienced academics are two ways in which this knowledge and understanding can be gained. Working in research partnerships that include a scholarly approach to learning about how to make ethical decisions when they arise is another (Robertson & Hill, 2007).

Finally, there are policy lessons to be learnt from the issues that have been discussed in this chapter. Increasing research capability, improving teaching practice, and reducing educational disparities are all worthwhile aims for schooling. However, combining all of these aims within every practitioner project can be problematic. In particular, as exemplified in this chapter, combining site-based emancipatory action research projects with cross-site investigations aimed at influencing policy at both local and national levels brings with it attendant tensions, complications, and dilemmas for both the teacher researchers and university partners. These issues need to be highlighted and resources allocated to ensure that sufficient researcher education is available to build research capability in dealing with ethical, as well as other, issues when they arise in practice.

REFERENCES

Alton-Lee, A. (2006). *Iterative best evidence synthesis: Strengthening research, policy and practice links to improve outcomes.* Paper presented to the 4th Policy Conference: Policy Evolution, OECD, The Hague, Netherlands. Retrieved 12 August 2007 from http://search.minedu.govt.nz/search?q=research+policyandbtnG=SEARCHandentqr=0an dsort=date%3AD%3AL%3Ad1andoutput=xml_no_dtdandbtnG.y=10andclient=default_f rontendandbtnG.x=13andud=1andoe=UTF-8andie=UTF-8andproxystylesheet=default_frontendandsite=default_collection.

Brown, T., & Jones, L. (2001). *Action research and postmodernism: Congruence and critique.* Buckingham, UK: Open University Press.

Cardno, C. (2003). *Action research: A developmental approach.* Wellington: New Zealand Council for Educational Research.

Carr, W., & Kemmis, S. (1986). *Becoming critical: Education, knowledge and action research.* Geelong, Victoria, Australia: Deakin University Press.

Carr, W., & Kemmis, S. (2005). Staying critical. *Educational action research, 13*(3), 347–358.

Coghlan, D., & Brannick, T. (2005). *Doing action research in your own organization.* (2nd ed.). London: Sage.

Glesne, C., & Peshkin, A. (1992). *Becoming qualitative researchers: An introduction* (2nd ed.). White Plains, NY: Longman.

Halasa, K. (1998). *Annotated bibliography: Ethics in educational research.* Retrieved 19 August 2007 from www.aare.edu.au/ethics/aareethc.htm.

Hill, M. (2000). *Remapping the assessment landscape: Primary teachers reconstructing the assessment landscape in self-managing primary schools.* Unpublished doctoral thesis, University of Waikato, Hamilton, New Zealand.

Hill, M., Robertson, J., Allan, R., Bakker, T., Connelly, D., Grimes, M., et al. (2006). *Great expectations: Enhancing learning and strengthening teaching in primary schools with diverse populations through action research.* Teaching and Learning Research Initiative. Retrieved 19 August 2007 from http://www.tlri.org.nz/publications/.

Kemmis, S. (2006). Exploring the relevance of critical theory for action research: Emancipatory action research in the footsteps of Jurgen Habermas. In P. Reason & H. Bradbury (Eds.), *Handbook of action research* (pp. 94–105). London: Sage.

Lankshear, C., & Knobel, M. (2004). *A handbook for teacher research: From design to implementation.* Maidenhead, Berkshire, UK: Open University Press.

Lather, P. (1991). *Getting smart: Feminist research and pedagogy with/in the postmodern.* New York: Routledge.

Lee, S., & van den Berg, O. (2003). Ethical obligations in teacher research. In A. Clarke & G. Erickson (Eds.), *Teacher inquiry: Living the research in everyday practice* (pp. 93–102). London: Routledge Falmer.

Murray, L., & Lawrence, B. (2000). *Practitioner-based enquiry.* London: Falmer Press.

New Zealand Association for Educational Research (NZARE). (2007). *Ethical Guidelines.* Retrieved 19 August from www.nzare.org.nz/about.html.

Patterson, L., Santa, C., Short, K., & Smith, K. (1993). *Teachers are researchers: Reflection and action.* Newark, Delaware: International Reading Association.

Reason, P., & Bradbury, H. (2006). Introduction: Inquiry and participation in search of a world worthy of human aspiration. In P. Reason & H. Bradbury (Eds.), *Handbook of action research* (pp. 1–14). London: Sage.

Robertson, J. M. (2000). The three R's of action research methodology: Reciprocity, reflexivity and reflection on reality. *Educational action research, 8*(2), 307–326.

Robertson, J.M., & Hill, M. F. (2005, July). *Practitioner research: How valid is the experience?* Paper presented at the biennial conference of the Association for Qualitative Research Conference, La Trobe University, Melbourne, Australia.

Robertson, J., & Hill, M.F. (2007). Developing the platform with postgraduate researchers. In J. van Swet, P. Ponte, & B. Smit (Eds.), *Postgraduate programme as platform: A research-led approach* (pp. 197–215). Rotterdam, Netherlands: Sense Publishers.

Robinson, V., & Lai M. (2006). *Practitioner research for educators: A guide to improving classrooms and schools.* Thousand Oaks, CA: Corwin Press.

Sagor, R. (2005). *The action research guidebook.* Thousand Oaks, CA: Corwin Press.

Teaching and Learning Research Initiative (2007a). *About the TLRI.* Retrieved 12 August 2007 from http://www.tlri.org.nz/about.html.

Teaching and Learning Research Initiative (2007b). *Partnership, 7,* 1–4, June.

Teaching and Learning Research Programme. (2007). Retrieved 19 August 2007 from http://www.tlrp.org/index.html.

Author Note

Mary Hill is Associate Dean Research in the Faculty of Education, University of Auckland, New Zealand. Her research and teaching interests are in assessment for learning, and practitioner and teacher education research. Before working as an academic she was deputy principal of a large primary school. She has extensive experience in leading and mentoring practitioner research projects, is deputy chair of the University of Auckland's Human Participants Ethics Committee and Deputy Chair of the New Zealand Council for Educational Research.

Correspondence concerning this chapter should be addressed by email to: mf.hill@auckland.ac.nz

In: Challenging Thinking about Teaching and Learning
Editors: C. M. Rubie-Davies and C. Rawlinson

ISBN: 978-1-60456-744-1
© 2008 Nova Science Publishers, Inc.

Chapter 23

ASSESSMENT LITERACY TRAINING AND TEACHERS' CONCEPTIONS OF ASSESSMENT

Gavin T. L. Brown

ABSTRACT

The low status of teachers' assessment literacy is well-established and there are many calls for increased training as a means of redressing this deficiency. It is often not noted that teachers' already have conceptions of what assessment is and these beliefs need to be addressed as part of teacher change endeavours. This chapter reports a study of 525 New Zealand primary school teachers and relates their conceptions of assessment to their levels of assessment literacy training. A well-fitting model of teachers' conceptions of assessment had four inter-correlated conceptions—"assessment makes students accountable"; "assessment makes schools and teachers accountable"; "assessment is irrelevant"; and "assessment improves teaching and learning". The amount of assessment literacy training teachers reported was broken into five categories: none; some preservice hours; inservice workshops or seminars; completed undergraduate paper; and completed postgraduate paper. No statistically significant differences in conceptions of assessment mean scores were found across the five categories of assessment literacy training. While it is possible that the amount and kinds of training are irrelevant to conceptions, a number of alternative explanations for this null result are present in the literature, including lack of attention to teachers' belief systems, overly short period of training, and poor quality of the training.

INTRODUCTION

Assessment literacy is "the ability to design, select, interpret, and use assessment results appropriately for educational decisions" (Quilter, 1998, p. 4). This kind of literacy is a natural consequence of how both validity and the role of assessment have come to be understood. Validity is "an integrated evaluative judgement of the degree to which empirical evidence and theoretical rationales support the *adequacy* and *appropriateness* of *inferences* and *actions* based on test scores or other modes of assessment" (Messick, 1989, p. 13). Validity, thus, is a judgement that the decisions made as a consequence of the assessment were appropriate, defensible, sound, trustworthy, and legitimate.

Assessment reform movements in the last quarter of a century have shifted from an over-reliance on standardized tests provided by external agencies to an increasing involvement of the teacher's formative judgements about the qualities of learning in light of curriculum intentions and sociocultural theories of learning (Gipps, 1994; Shepard, 2001, 2006; Willis, 1994). As Kane (2006) has made clear, teachers are expected to make a series of qualitative interpretations about observed student performances, rather than just interpretations of test scores. These interpretations occur as teachers interact with students in the classroom and are not simply recorded for later interpretation. Thus, an assessment-literate teacher is one who creates, chooses, administers, interprets, responds to, records, and reports assessment information in such a way that those decisions can be shown to be adequate and appropriate.

There has been much research indicating that the vast majority of teachers, principals, and administrators have limited understanding of the more technical qualities of assessment information (e.g., reliability, validity of inferences, and statistical terminology), whether it be derived from their own assessments of a student, from external standardized test marks, or from their own in-class performance assessments (Black & Wiliam, 1998; Cizek, 1995; Hambleton & Slater, 1997; Impara, Divine, Bruce, Liverman, & Gay, 1991; McMillan, Myran, & Workman, 2002; Mertler, 1999; Plake, Impara, & Fager, 1993; Quilter, 1998; Schafer, 1993; Stiggins, 1998, 1995). For example, Gipps, Brown, McCallum, and McAlister (1995, p. 2) argued that primary school teachers' understandings "of issues in assessment was very limited; while there was widespread use of standardized tests of reading and mathematics, there was little understanding of how the scores were derived, or what they meant, and no understanding of issues such as reliability and validity".

It was widely accepted that New Zealand primary teachers had faulty assumptions and beliefs around the normal curve distribution 1 to 5 grades they used to record student achievement throughout the 1980s (Ministry of Education, 1990). Among New Zealand secondary school teachers it was argued that, notwithstanding the inappropriate over-emphasis on assessment for certification, teachers needed greater expertise in assessment to assure the community that there was national consistency of standards (Ministry of Education, 1990). Later research reported that many experienced teachers had had little training in assessment philosophy or practices despite having responsibility for implementing assessment changes in their schools (Bourke, Poskitt, & McAlpine, 1996). In contrast, by the time the research reported in this chapter was conducted, many research reports suggested that teachers were attempting to make formative use of assessment. For example, many primary schools were using many standardized achievement and diagnostic assessment tools and most teachers surveyed reported that they frequently or always altered the way they taught their students as a result of the information (Croft, Strafford, & Mapa, 2000). Hill (1999) found through in-depth discussions with 32 primary teachers three major patterns of assessment practice (i.e., unit assessment, head note assessment, and integrated systematic assessment). Regardless of dominant style, most teachers assessed their students for diagnostic and improvement purposes (i.e., to identify their strengths and weaknesses in progress towards curriculum objectives and to evaluate the quality of teaching programmes) (Hill, 2000).

However, the dual emphasis in the national assessment policy (Ministry of Education, 1994) on improvement and monitoring purposes have made themselves felt in teachers' understanding and use of assessment. Hill (1999) reported that the teachers she interviewed experienced significant tensions between the competing uses of administrative accountability and formative improvement. Likewise, detailed interviews with 40 associate teachers (i.e., those who mentor student teachers in field practice) reported that a majority of those teachers conflated the formative and the summative practices despite having a reasonably robust understanding of formative assessment (Dixon & Williams, 2002). Aitken (2000) reported the same conflation of purposes among 20 secondary school teachers of English and argued that the administrative purpose was overwhelming teachers' ability to offer formative assessment. Timperley (2003) reported in her survey of teachers' use of running record assessments of reading performance in the first two years of school that the administrative, accountability uses of the data superseded the use of the data to inform or improve teaching programmes. A detailed study of six teachers' feedback practices in mathematics found that less than one fifth of the oral feedback provided to students was oriented towards describing achievement, and the bulk was oriented towards the effort and attitudes of the learners (Knight, 2003). These small-scale studies make it difficult to paint a clear picture of the state of assessment literacy among New Zealand primary teachers. However, it is likely that there is less assessment literacy present in the population of teachers than is expected or required by the country's assessment policy.

A wide range of causes for teachers' poor assessment literacy has been identified. These include educators' fear of assessment and evaluation (Stiggins, 1995); lack of time to assess well (Stiggins, 1995); false or inappropriate public perceptions about the state of current assessment practices (Stiggins, 1995); insufficient appropriate training of teachers in the sound use of a wide range of assessment practices (Arter, 2001; Hambrick-Dixon, 1999; O'Sullivan & Johnson, 1993; Schafer, 1993; Stiggins, 1995, 1998); unsatisfactory "assessment literate" leadership on the part of administrators and principals (Cizek, 1995; Popham, 2000; Schafer, 1993; Stiggins, 1995, 1998); lack of compulsory credentialing in assessment literacy (National Research Council, 2001; Stiggins, 1995, 1998; Worthen, 1993); the reluctance of teachers to believe that they need professional development in this realm (Hargreaves & Fullan, 1998; Worthen, 1993); staff developers with low levels of expertise (Dixon & Williams, 2003); and overwhelming policy pressure to focus on summative and accountability uses (Hill, 1999; Timperley, 2003).

In response to these causes for low levels of assessment literacy, many American educational professional associations and state and local authorities have adopted standards of professional competence for teachers that include assessment literacy (Cizek, 1995; Stiggins, 1995). In their 2001 report, the United States National Research Council's Committee on the Foundations of Assessment put forward recommendations for the improvement of assessment in American schools including the preservice and continuing professional development of teachers in understanding how student learning can be assessed (National Research Council, 2001). Similarly, the Commission on Instructionally Supportive Assessment, convened by five school leadership organisations in 2001, listed among its requirements the expectation that states ensure educators receive professional development that is focused on how to optimize children's learning based on the results of instructionally supportive assessment (Baker, Berliner, Yeakey, Pellegrino, Popham, Quenemoen, et al., 2001). In New Zealand, a working party of assessment experts claimed that "existing programmes in teacher training are deficient in terms of time allocated and the nature of courses offered" in assessment and that there was a serious lack of expertise in assessment within the teacher education community (Ministry of Education, 1990, p. 62). Further, the working party reported that there were serious deficiencies in the provision of inservice professional development and they recommended that "all teachers be provided with one week of inservice training in assessment within the next five years, and that such training be funded by the Ministry of Education" (Ministry of Education, 1990, p. 64). It should be noted that even a week's training would be considered inadequate by experts in teacher change; long-term, collaborative, and inquiry-oriented programmes of professional development are most likely to achieve the type of change envisioned by assessment literacy (Bell & Cowie, 2001; Richardson & Placier, 2001).

However, these recommendations about requiring teachers to become assessment literate and be given professional development in assessment may not be able to resolve teachers' misunderstanding or misuse of assessment. The development of assessment literacy demands a shift from norm-referenced scoring and the assumption that only students are responsible for learning outcomes. This means that the teacher's belief systems about the nature and purpose of assessment have to be involved in any effective professional development around assessment (Hargreaves & Fullan, 1998). More generally, it is assumed that teachers' reasoning for their practices, which are their means of solving educational problems, is resistant to modification partly because research-based training often misses the issues relevant to teachers and because new interventions are not understood as needing to compete for belief (Robinson, 1998; Robinson & Walker, 1999). In other words, the advocates of increased teacher assessment literacy are trying to solve an educational problem (e.g., lack of formative feedback to students after an assessment event as a symptom of poor assessment literacy) without taking into account the pre-existing reasons and beliefs teachers have for their current practices. Indeed, the National Research Council (2001) listed student beliefs, but not those of teachers, among the many advances in the sciences of thinking and learning that have an effect on assessment use.

This chapter provides an overview of the assessment policies, practices, and professional development contexts that were current in New Zealand when the research was conducted. Then, it briefly reviews the conceptions of assessment that teachers have, before reporting the results of a survey which analyzed New Zealand primary teachers' conceptions of assessment in light of the amount of assessment literacy training or professional development they had experienced. In the discussion of the results, implications for assessment literacy training and professional development are suggested.

NEW ZEALAND CONTEXTS

The New Zealand education assessment policy (Ministry of Education, 1994) expects that school-based assessment will improve students' learning and the quality of learning programmes and be used to report progress and provide summative information. Although aspects of national testing are hinted at within the policy (e.g., transition point assessment), to date, despite efforts to introduce such systems (Government of New Zealand, 1988), New Zealand has no national, compulsory, externally-mandated assessments in primary schools. Thus, the interpretive and decision-making practices and beliefs teachers and schools have about assessment are what really matter. The policy makes clear that teachers are expected to be able to operate standards-based, achievement-based, competency-based, and norm-referenced assessments, as well as evaluate teaching and learning programmes. Classroom-based assessments are meant to be indexed to curriculum achievement objectives and levels; indeed, teachers are expected by National Administration Guidelines to monitor and report student learning against the curriculum objectives and levels.

The policy expects teachers to use a range of assessment methods including: informal assessment, observation, student self-assessment, student peer-assessment, conferencing, portfolios, benchmark exemplars, and tests. Teachers are expected to use moderation procedures to ensure consistency across classes, ensure that assessments are valid, reliable, manageable, fair, and unbiased, and meet the learning needs of disabled and specially-able students. The evidence collected of student learning is meant to be recorded and reported to students, parents, school governors, and other appropriate government agencies. Clearly, New Zealand teachers are expected to have a high level of assessment literacy, consistent with the formal definitions of validity.

These expectations and legal requirements clearly depend upon teachers having a high level of understanding and involvement in assessment practices (Gipps, 1994). In the context of American high-stakes testing, Firestone, Mayrowetz, and Fairman (1998, p. 98) advised, "steps must also be taken to increase their capacity to teach in new ways . . . teachers will need to understand short-term issues such as what it takes to score well on those tests. They may also need the deeper pedagogical content knowledge to help students learn the basic subjects at a more profound level". As a result, teachers require profound knowledge of the content being taught, of the various ways to teach that material, of the various ways to assess that material, and robust theories about how learning of that content occurs.

Currently in New Zealand, completion of at least one course or paper on assessment is normally required of undergraduate teacher preparation programmes; these courses are usually in the range of 36 to 50 hours long. Once employed, responsibility for further professional development of teachers is devolved to New Zealand schools which can access Ministry of Education-funded assessment tools and professional development resources.

The Ministerial Working Party on Assessment for Better Learning (Ministry of Education, 1990, p. 64) recommended that assessment "training programmes should be interactive, rather than involve direct instruction, with course facilitators using the experience and data provided by the teachers themselves". Consequently, the major government-funded professional development resource between 1995 and 2001 was the Assessment for Better Learning (ABeL) project which involved about 400 schools a year each for a two-year programme (Education Gazette, 2002). The programme was explicitly intended to increase teachers' assessment literacy and knowledge and application of formative or improvement-oriented assessment practices (Ministry of Education, 2001). A formal evaluation found that the programme was associated with substantial, beneficial effects in most participating schools (Peddie, 2000). Such results included better school-wide assessments, changes in teacher thinking, greater understanding of assessment, and improved reporting.

Another source of professional development in assessment was teacher involvement in various assessment research projects which made use of teacher informants and teacher assessors, such as the National Education Monitoring Project (NEMP), the Assessment Resource Banks (ARBs), the Assessment Tools for Teaching and Learning Project (asTTle), or the National Exemplar Project (Crooks, 2002). However, Gilmore (2000) reported that about half of the 152 teachers surveyed who had acted as teacher assessors for NEMP between 1995 and 1997 claimed to have gained broader knowledge of or insights into assessment, while only one sixth reported increased use of a wider range of assessment tasks in their classrooms. Dixon and Williams (2003, p. 37) suggested that the focus of the short school-based professional development sessions on benchmark exemplars from the National Exemplar Project had been more to do with "what to assess, and the measurement of learning, rather than where they sensed it should be, on the formative utilisation of information".

More powerful and effective professional development was reported as a consequence of a series of formative assessment development workshops embedded in a two-year assessment research project in one curriculum area (Bell & Cowie, 2001). Although the research took place after the data collection reported in this chapter, the findings of the evaluation of the professional development associated with the release of the Assessment Tools for Teaching and Learning (asTTle) software in 2003 are pertinent. The teachers who were given professional development preferred "practice-oriented training sessions, disliked lectures or reading manual . . . agreed that several short sessions of training with time in between to practice was optimal, and moderately agreed that professional development was more beneficial if there had been time to try things out before hand" (Hattie, Brown, Ward, Irving, & Keegan, 2006, pp. 30–31). Further, those who had not received professional development related to asTTle made use of and benefited from the self-teaching resources that had been supplied with the system (e.g., context sensitive help, a free-phone helpline for IT issues, the online manual, and so on).

Thus, it is possible to conclude that the need for assessment literacy is as great in New Zealand as it is anywhere, that there are some promising signs of assessment literate teachers being effective, and that there is a large supply of relatively brief assessment professional development opportunities available to teachers. However, the track record of those professional development activities in terms of raising assessment literacy is inconclusive. It would also appear that only in the best of the professional development activities is attention paid to teachers' conceptions of assessment.

CONCEPTIONS OF ASSESSMENT

Teachers' conceptions are "more general mental structure[s], encompassing beliefs, meanings, concepts, propositions, rules, mental images, preferences, and the like" (Thompson, 1992, p. 130) which have arisen largely from the person's experience of the phenomenon, and, in the case of teachers, most likely from their experience of education as students (Pajares, 1992). Thus, conceptions act as a framework through which a teacher views, interprets, and interacts, with the teaching environment (Marton, 1981). Conceptions are not uniform and simple (van den Berg, 2002), nor are they necessarily logically consistent (Cheung & Wong, 2002; Kahn, 2000; Rex & Nelson, 2004). Conceptions of various educational processes such as teaching, learning, assessment, and curriculum have been shown to be interconnected (Brown, 2006a; Dahlin, Watkins, & Ekholm, 2001) and strongly impact on educational practices and outcomes (Pajares, 1992; Clark & Peterson, 1986; Thompson, 1992; Calderhead, 1996).

Consistent with the theories of reasoned or planned behaviour (Ajzen & Madden, 1986; Fishbein & Ajzen, 1975), research into teachers' conceptions of assessment has focused on the purposes or intentions that assessment has (Brown, 2004, 2006b; Stamp, 1987) rather than on the types of assessment used (e.g., Dixon, 1999; Gipps, et al., 1995; Hill, 2000; McMillan, Myran, & Workman, 2002; Quilter, 1998). Three major purposes for assessment exist (Heaton, 1975; Torrance and Pryor, 1998; Warren & Nisbet, 1999; Webb, 1992): that is, assessment improves teaching and learning, assessment makes students accountable for learning, and assessment makes schools and teachers accountable. Further, a rejection of valid educational purposes can be seen in teachers treating assessment as fundamentally irrelevant to the life and work of teachers and students (Brown, 2004; Bulterman-Bos, Verloop, Terwel, & Wardekker, 2003; Garcia, 1987; Philippou & Christou, 1997; Rex & Nelson, 2004; Saltzgaver, 1983; Stamp, 1987; Warren & Nisbet, 1999). Brown (2002) developed a self-report instrument capable of identifying teachers' levels of agreement towards four inter-correlated, major conceptions of assessment (i.e., assessment improves teaching and learning; assessment makes schools and teachers accountable, assessment makes students accountable, and assessment is irrelevant).

It has been shown that greater assessment literacy is correlated with more positive attitudes toward classroom assessment (Quilter, 1998; Quilter & Chester, 1998), but training in assessment may have very little effect on changing teacher trainees' assessment conceptions (Stamp, 1987). Thus, increases in assessment literacy may be pointless if teachers' underlying purposes or conceptions of assessment remain purely administrative (e.g., assessment makes students accountable; assessment makes schools and teachers accountable) or negative (i.e., assessment is irrelevant). For example, a teacher who conceives of assessment as fundamentally irrelevant may actually be quite expert in interpreting assessment results, but is persuaded that assessment of learning is inappropriate in his or her context. This is not to say that such a teacher is actually wrong—it may well be that an assessment with significant negative consequences is irrelevant to the teacher's work in the classroom. If increased levels of training in assessment are associated with greater commitment to improvement purposes then it could be argued that assessment literacy training is contributing towards an assessment for learning paradigm. On the other hand, if assessment literacy training is associated with greater levels of accountability of schools and teachers, then the training contributes to teachers exercising greater responsibility for student outcomes. Thus, it is useful to understand how teachers' conceptions of assessment are affected by the level of assessment literacy training they have had.

LINKING CONCEPTIONS TO ASSESSMENT LITERACY TRAINING

The research reported in this chapter of New Zealand primary school teachers' conceptions of assessment took place within a policy and practice context of self-managed, low-stakes assessment for the purpose of improving the quality of teaching and learning. Simultaneously, schools are expected to report student performance against the objectives of various curriculum statements to parent communities, while central agencies seek to obtain evidence and surety that students and schools are meeting expected standards and outcomes.

The study reported here involved a survey which was administered in 2001 to New Zealand primary school teachers of Years 5 to 7 (students nominally aged 10 to 12). The survey included conceptions of assessment items and asked participants to indicate the kinds of assessment training they had experienced. Thus, the relationship of conceptions of assessment to training could be explored.

A total of 525 teachers answered the conceptions of assessment questionnaire. The teachers in the study were for the most part New Zealand European (83%), female (76%), highly experienced with 10 or more years teaching (63%), employed as teachers rather than managers or senior teachers (54%), employed in contributing or full primary schools (89%), and well trained with three or more years training (55%). Three key demographic characteristics of the teachers in this study reasonably reflect those of the New Zealand teaching population who were 87% New Zealand European ethnicity, 71% female, and 50% long service in 1998 (Sturrock, 1999). Thus, data in this study were from a relatively homogenous population of full and contributing primary school teachers and which reflected accurately significant demographic characteristics of the New Zealand teaching population.

Teachers were asked to indicate, on a non-exclusive basis, what kind of assessment training they had participated in. The options were arranged hierarchically from none, through some hours as part of preservice training, half- to one-day workshops or seminars, to completion of formal courses in assessment at the undergraduate or postgraduate levels. The participants were asked to select all categories of assessment literacy training that applied to them (Table 23.1).

Table 23.1. CoA-III Participant Assessment Literacy Training

Amount and type of training	Total N (% of participants)[a]
None	76 (14)
Some hours in preservice training	183 (35)
Half- to one-day workshop or seminar	220 (42)
Completed undergraduate paper	114 (22)
Completed postgraduate paper	29 (6)
Other	111 (21)
Total[b]	733

[a] Percentage calculated against total of 525 participants. [b]Total exceeds 525 as participants were instructed to select all that apply.

About one in seven teachers noted that they had had no training in assessment, while a third had received some hours on assessment as part of their preservice teacher training. Nearly half had attended a half- to full-day workshop or seminar on assessment at some time in their service as teachers. This is somewhat greater than the 34% of teachers who reported participating in assessment professional development in the period March 1997–March 1998 (Sturrock, 1999). Perhaps this result reflects the growing supply of assessment-related professional development opportunities provided in the half-decade before the survey. However, just over one in five had completed an undergraduate paper or course on assessment, while only one in 20 had finished a postgraduate paper or course. This value is not significantly different from the 26% of teachers in Years 0 to 5 who, in a survey of use of diagnostic assessment tools in literacy and numeracy, reported participating in tertiary courses including some assessment component since pre-service training (Croft, Strafford, & Mapa,

2000). However, this result is well below those expected by the 1990 ministerial working party on assessment (Ministry of Education, 1990).

In addition, teachers supplied alternative other types of assessment training that they had participated in. Of the one in five who had received training in assessment through other means, four categories accounted for just over three-quarters of all alternative methods (n = 86). These included participation in Ministry of Education-funded assessment improvement contracts such as Assessment for Better Learning (n = 33), school-based inservice courses (n = 29), attendance at short courses (n = 11), and components of courses (n = 13). Because of the wide diversity of low frequency response categories offered by teachers these data were not used in the analysis. Nevertheless, these results show that the plethora of government-funded professional development activities was clearly reaching out to all schools and teachers.

Thus, it is considered that this sample of teachers also accurately represented New Zealand teachers' levels of assessment literacy training. Generally, very few primary school teachers had received any extensive formal course work in assessment, while relatively brief inservice workshops and preservice lectures accounted for the bulk of assessment literacy training. This overall lack of systematic assessment literacy training is consistent with international trends (Black & Wiliam, 1998; Plake & Impara, 1997; Stiggins, 2001).

The data used here to report teachers' conceptions of assessment are taken from a confirmatory factor analysis (CFA) of teachers' responses to the 50-item Conceptions of Assessment Inventory (Brown, 2004). CFA determines the estimates of all parameters simultaneously that most nearly reproduce the matrix of observed relationships in a data matrix (Klem, 2000). Specification of a model includes identifying observed variables that load on to latent first-order factors and the relationship of the first-order factors to second- or higher order latent factors or other first-order factors. In CFA, relationships between variables and latent factors that are not theoretically expected are set to zero, while the expected relationships are free to load on their appropriate factors (Byrne, 2001). A general advantage of CFA is that it does not ignore, unlike regression or general linear model approaches, the error variance parameters and thus leads to more accurate estimation of relationships (Byrne, 2001; Thompson, 2000). The quality of fit for the specified model to the underlying data matrix is statistically tested with a number of effective measures (i.e., indices which are least affected by sample size or model complexity). For example, the Tucker-Lewis Index (TLI) (a goodness of fit index) should be greater than .90, while the Root Mean Square Error of Approximation (RMSEA) (a badness of fit index) should be simultaneously below .08 (Hoyle, 1995).

Briefly, the Conceptions of Assessment inventory consisted of nine first-order factors, four of which loaded on to the conception "assessment improves teaching and learning", three of which loaded on to the conception that "assessment is irrelevant", and the remaining two factors represented the conceptions "assessment makes students accountable" and "assessment makes schools and teachers accountable". Thus, the measurement model consisted of the nine factors structured into four inter-correlated conceptions of assessment and had good psychometric fit characteristics (χ^2 = 3217.68; p = .000; df = 1162; RMSEA = .058; TLI = .97). Mean scores for the four conceptions showed that these teachers moderately agreed with the improvement and student accountability conceptions, while rejecting the school accountability and irrelevance conceptions.

Fortunately for assessment professional developers, the conceptions of assessment exhibited by some of the teachers in this survey appeared to be positively aligned with assessment literacy (Table 23.2). Between a third and a fifth of teachers strongly agreed with the assessment for improvement conception and less than 2% agreed strongly that assessment was irrelevant. However, small minorities (around 10%) strongly disagreed with the notion that assessment could improve student learning, was valid, or described student performance. Addressing these conceptions within the context of assessment professional development seems a necessary precursor to effective teacher change.

Table 23.2. Percentage of Teachers by Agreement Level for CoA-III Scales

Conception of assessment	Disagree (%)	Low agree (%)	Strongly agree (%)
Assessment improves teaching	2.9	59.6	37.5
Assessment is inaccurate	14.3	59.2	26.5
Assessment improves student learning	11.8	65.5	22.7
Assessment describes learning	10.7	72.0	17.3
Assessment makes students accountable	24.4	65.1	10.5
Assessment is valid	30.1	62.9	7.0
Assessment makes schools and teachers accountable	53.3	43.8	2.9
Assessment is bad	62.5	35.8	1.7
Assessment is ignored	79.2	20.0	0.8

The conceptions of improvement and school accountability were moderately and positively correlated ($r = .58$); in other words, as they agreed with the conception that "assessment improves teaching and learning", they tended to agree with "assessment makes schools accountable". This association suggested that primary school teachers in this survey had accepted or fully engaged with the two primary objectives of the national assessment policy (i.e., assessment leads to improvement of student learning and assessment is used to improve school programmes and demonstrate school effectiveness). The positive association of these two conceptions is consistent with Hill's (1999, 2000) results. It would appear that within the context of self-managing schools and relatively low-stakes assessment policies, teachers are not afraid to use assessment as a means of professional accountability.

Multivariate analysis of variance (MANOVA) determines whether mean scores for multiple variables differ by category to which each case belongs by analyzing the ratio (F) of within group and between group variances for all variables of interest simultaneously. This means that while observed mean scores may be different across variables and categories, the probability of the differences occurring by chance (given the number of cases, variables, and categories) can be determined. When the probability (p) for a certain F ratio is greater than .05, it is accepted that the variation in mean scores are most likely because of chance or error rather than systematic differences by category. Remembering that the other category represented a wide range of participant-supplied training experiences, the MANOVA analysis used just the five pre-set categories of assessment literacy training and the nine assessment factors. No statistically significant differences in mean scores for the nine assessment factors for each amount of assessment literacy training were found; that is, the probability for the observed F statistic was greater than .05 (Table 23.3). Thus, the amount of assessment literacy training this group of teachers reported participating in made no statistically significant difference to their conceptions of assessment.

**Table 23.3. Multivariate Results CoA-III Subscales
by Assessment Literacy Training**

Effect	n^a	Hypothesis df	Wilks' λ	F	p
No training	76	9	.98	1.38	.20
Some preservice hours	183	9	.99	.48	.89
Workshop or seminar	220	9	.98	1.18	.31
Completed undergraduate paper	114	9	.97	1.57	.12
Completed postgraduate paper	28	9	.99	.48	.89

[a] Sum is greater than 525 since multiple responses were permitted.

DISCUSSION

The premise of assessment literacy training is to ensure that teachers can interpret assessments for appropriate educational decision making. This study has shown that increased levels of assessment literacy training were not associated with a greater commitment to improvement purposes, nor were they associated with reduced commitment to accountability or irrelevance conceptions of assessment. Teachers with no or little training of any sort in assessment had mean scores for each conception that were statistically indistinguishable from those with quite substantial assessment development experiences. The teachers were equally committed to using assessment to improve teaching and learning and to demonstrate student accountability.

We cannot conclude whether this pattern of conceptions of assessment existed before the assessment literacy training, whether the training was consistent with the teacher's pre-existing conceptions, whether the training successfully created the current pattern of conceptions, or whether the training was irrelevant to the pre-existing conceptions. However, based on reports of assessment professional development in New Zealand reviewed earlier, it is possible that the professional development experienced by these teachers did not explicitly focus on teachers' beliefs or conceptions underlying the nature and purpose of assessment or intend to modify those conceptions. It is more likely that the training focused on a specific skill, knowledge, or ability designed to address a small aspect of the process of making interpretive decisions about the quality of student learning (Shepard, 2001). It seems even more likely that the inservice experience of teachers within their school-based policies, practices, and contexts had substantially more effect on shaping their conceptions of assessment than any training or development they experienced (Richardson & Placier, 2001). In other words, socialization in the school's professional community might have had more effect than all the assessment literacy training offered.

Alternately, it may be that the professional development opportunities, whether inservice or preservice, simply were not very good quality. The data available in this study indicated no more than 6% of teachers had participated in the explicit assessment literacy improvement programme ABeL, a proportion far too small to use in detecting meaningful differences. However, the reviewed literature suggested that the quality and effect of assessment professional development was erratic. We must also consider that it is likely teachers would assimilate new assessment philosophies and practices into their pre-existing conceptions, unless explicit and sustained attention is paid to modifying the organizational context in which individuals are being asked to change their thinking (Richardson & Placier, 2001). For example, Kahn (2000) pointed out that high school language arts teachers appeared to assimilate new assessment practices (e.g., portfolios, co-operative learning, and lifelong learning,) into long-standing transmission, teacher-oriented, accountability-type assessment and learning frameworks. The challenge of assessment literacy professional development then is to successfully transform teacher thinking and practices.

It is also possible, though the intervention research has yet to be done, that teachers' conceptions of assessment cannot be changed. Conceptions may be so deeply ingrained from years of experience of assessment in their own schooling (Pajares, 1992), that it may not be possible to change their conceptions. The record on individual teacher change is not promising, but organizational context change research (e.g., widespread change of policy and process within a school or nation) has suggested belief changes are possible with a combination of approaches (Richardson & Placier, 2001). While it has been shown that certain conceptions of assessment are associated with greater educational outcomes for secondary school students (Brown & Hirschfeld, 2007; 2008), it has not yet been shown that any conceptions of assessment held by teachers are associated with greater educational outcomes for students. It may be that it is not necessary to change teachers' conceptions of assessment into any pattern; however, this possibility would fly in the face of much other research which suggests teachers' thinking is powerfully linked to practices and outcomes.

Nevertheless, since teachers' beliefs and thinking filter, define, and interpret how they practice and implement assessment, it is important that assessment literacy developers pay attention to teacher's pre-existing conceptions of assessment. It would appear that too much of the current debate about assessment literacy focuses too much on the declarative knowledge and not enough on teachers' conceptions or belief systems (Cizek, 1995; Popham, 2000; Schafer, 1993; Stiggins, 1995, 1998). Professional developers need to keep in mind that, at least in their own minds, teachers already understand what assessment is—they "know" that assessment is about improving teaching, or certifying student learning, or motivating students, or fulfilling administrative requirements, and so on. More assessment training is likely be understood and interpreted in the light of those conceptions, and information not consistent with enhancing the teachers' current or dominant conception of assessment is likely to be rejected or assimilated. The use of the Conceptions of Assessment inventory in its abridged form (Brown, 2006b) could be a useful component in any assessment professional development exercise.

CONCLUSION

The evidence from this representative sample of New Zealand primary school teachers suggested that the assessment literacy training they had experienced did not affect their conceptions of the purposes of assessment. If assessment literacy training is to be effective, it should probably deal with teachers' conceptions as much as it deals with declarative or procedural knowledge requirements. It may also be that all assessment professional development processes have to be restructured so that they are capable of creating substantial and permanent change.

REFERENCES

Aitken, R. (2000). Teacher perceptions of the use and value of formative assessment in secondary English programmes. *set: Research Information for Teachers*, (3), 15–20.

Ajzen, I., & Madden, T. J. (1986). Predictions of goal-direct behavior: Attitudes, intentions, and perceived behavioural control. *Journal of Experimental Social Psychology*, 22, 453–474.

Arter, J. A. (2001, April). *Washington assessment professional development program evaluation results*. Paper presented at the Annual Meeting of the National Council on Measurement in Education (NCME), Seattle, WA.

Baker, E. L., Berliner, D. C., Yeakey, C. C., Pellegrino, J. W., Popham, W. J., Quenemoen, R. F. et al. (2001). *Building testing to support instruction and accountability: A guide for policymakers*. Retrieved February 20, 2004, from http://www.aasa.org

Bell, B., & Cowie, B. (2001). Teacher development for formative assessment. *Waikato Journal of Education*, 7, 37–49.

Black, P., & Wiliam, D. (1998). Assessment and classroom learning. *Educational Assessment: Principles, Policy and Practice*, 5(1), 7–74.

Bourke, R., Poskitt, J., & McAlpine, D. (1996, June). *Assessment for Better Learning: Realities and Rhetoric*. Paper presented at the New Zealand Council for Teacher Education Conference: Teacher Education to Standards. Dunedin, New Zealand.

Brown, G. T. L. (2002). *Teachers' conceptions of assessment*. Unpublished doctoral dissertation, University of Auckland, Auckland, New Zealand.

Brown, G. T. L. (2004). Teachers' conceptions of assessment: Implications for policy and professional development. *Assessment in Education: Principles Policy and Practice*, 11(3), 305–322.

Brown, G. T. L. (2006a). Teachers' instructional conceptions: How learning, teaching, curriculum, assessment, and self-efficacy interconnect. In A. P. Presscott (Ed.), *The concept of self in education, family and sport* (pp. 1–48). New York: Nova Science Publishers.

Brown, G. T. L. (2006b). Teachers' conceptions of assessment: Validation of an abridged instrument. *Psychological Reports*, 99, 166–170.

Brown, G. T. L., & Hirschfield, G. H. F. (2007). Students' conceptions of assessment and mathematics achievement: Evidence for the power of self-regulation. *Australian Journal of Educational and Developmental Psychology*, 7, 63–74.

Brown, G. T. L., & Hirschfield, G. H. F. (2008). Students' conceptions of assessment: Links to outcomes. *Assessment in Education: Principles, Policy and Practice*, 15(1), 3-17.

Bulterman-Bos, J., Verloop, N., Terwel, J., & Wardekker, W. (2003). Reconciling the pedagogical goal and the measurement goal of evaluation: The perspectives of teachers in the context of national standards. *Teachers College Record*, 105(3), 344–374.

Byrne, B. M. (2001). *Structural Equation Modeling with AMOS: Basic Concepts, Applications, and Programming*. Mahwah, NJ: LEA.

Calderhead, J. (1996). Teachers: Beliefs and knowledge. In D. C. Berliner & R. C. Calfee (Eds.), *Handbook of educational psychology* (pp. 709–725). New York: Simon & Schuster Macmillan.

Cheung, D., & Wong, H.W. (2002). Measuring teacher beliefs about alternative curriculum designs. *The Curriculum Journal, 13*(2), 225–248.

Cizek, G. J. (1995). The big picture in assessment and who ought to have it. *Phi Delta Kappan, 77*(3), 246–249.

Clark, C., & Peterson, P. (1986). Teachers' thought processes. In M. Wittrock (Ed.), *Handbook of research on teaching.* (3rd ed., pp. 255–296). New York: MacMillan.

Croft, A. C., Strafford, E., & Mapa, L. (2000). *Stocktake/evaluation of existing diagnostic tools in literacy and numeracy in English.* Wellington, New Zealand: New Zealand Council for Educational Research.

Crooks, T. J. (2002). Educational assessment in New Zealand schools. *Assessment in Education: Principles Policy and Practice, 9*(2), 237–253.

Dahlin, B., Watkins, D. A., & Ekholm, M. (2001). The role of assessment in student learning: The views of Hong Kong and Swedish lecturers. In D. A. Watkins & J. B. Biggs (Eds.), *Teaching the Chinese learner: Psychological and pedagogical perspectives* (pp. 47–74). Hong Kong: University of Hong Kong, Comparative Education Research Centre.

Dixon, H. (1999). *The effect of policy on practice: An analysis of teachers' perceptions of school based assessment practice.* Unpublished master's thesis, Massey University, Albany, New Zealand.

Dixon, H., & Williams, R. (2002). Teachers' understanding and use of formative assessment in literacy learning. *New Zealand Annual Review of Education, 12,* 95–110.

Dixon, H., & Williams, R. (2003). Formative assessment and the professional development of teachers: Are we focusing on what is important? *set: Research Information for Teachers,* (2), 35–39.

Education Gazette. (2002). Better assessment likely. *Education Gazette, 81*(6), Available online: http://www.edgazette.govt.nz/articles.php?action=viewandid=6155.

Firestone, W. A., Mayrowetz, D., & Fairman, J. (1998). Performance-based assessment and instructional change: The effects of testing in Maine and Maryland. *Educational Evaluation and Policy Analysis, 20*(2), 95–113.

Fishbein, M., & Ajzen, I. (1975). *Belief, attitude, intention, and behavior: An introduction to theory and research.* Reading, MA: Addison-Wesley.

Garcia, E. (1987, April). *An ethnographic study of teachers' implicit theories on evaluation.* Paper presented at the Annual Meeting of the American Educational Research Association, Washington, DC.

Gilmore, A. (2000). The NEMP Experience: Professional development of teachers through the National Education Monitoring Project. *New Zealand Annual Review of Education, 10,* 141–166.

Gipps, C. V. (1994). *Beyond testing: Towards a theory of educational assessment.* London: Falmer Press.

Gipps, C., Brown, M., McCallum, B., & McAlister, S. (1995). *Intuition or evidence? Teachers and national assessment of seven-year-olds.* Buckingham, UK: Open University Press.

Government of New Zealand. (1998). *Assessment for success in primary schools* (Green Paper). Wellington, New Zealand: Ministry of Education.

Hambleton, R. K., & Slater, S. C. (1997). *Are NAEP executive summary reports understandable to policy makers and educators?* (CSE Technical Report 430). Los Angeles, CA: National Center for Research on Evaluation, Standards, and Student

Testing, Graduate School of Education and Information Studies, University of California, Los Angeles.

Hambrick-Dixon, P. J. (1999, April 19-23). *Meeting the challenges to urban school reform: Assessment portfolios for teachers' professional development.* Paper presented at the Annual Meeting of the American Educational Research Association (AERA), Montreal, QC, Canada.

Hargreaves, A., & Fullan, M. (1998). *What's worth fighting for out there?* New York: Teachers College Press.

Hattie, J. A., Brown, G. T. L., Ward, L., Irving, S. E., & Keegan, P. J. (2006). Formative evaluation of an educational assessment technology innovation: Developers' insights into Assessment Tools for Teaching and Learning (asTTle). *Journal of Multi-Disciplinary Evaluation, 5,* Retrieved 15 February 2007 from http://evaluation.wmich.edu/ JMDE/content/JMDE005content/PDFs_JMDE_005/Formative_Evaluation_of_an_Educa tional_Assessment_Technology_Innovation_Developers_Insights_into_Assessment_Tool s_for_Teaching_and_Learning_asTTle.pdf.

Heaton, J. B. (1975). *Writing English language tests.* London: Longman.

Hill, M. (1999). Assessment in self-managing schools: Primary teachers balancing learning and accountability demands in the 1990s. *New Zealand Journal of Educational Studies, 34*(1), 176–185.

Hill, M. F. (2000.). *Remapping the assessment landscape: Primary teachers reconstructing assessment in self-managing schools.* Unpublished doctoral dissertation, University of Waikato, Hamilton, New Zealand.

Hoyle, R. H. (1995). The structural equation modeling approach: Basic concepts and fundamental issues. In R. H. Hoyle (Ed.), *Structural equation modeling: Concepts, issues, and applications* (pp. 1–15). Thousand Oaks, CA: Sage.

Impara, J. C., Divine, K. P., Bruce, F. A., Liverman, M. R., & Gay, A. (1991). Does interpretive test score information help teachers? *Educational Measurement: Issues and Practice, 10*(4), 16–18.

Kahn, E. A. (2000). A case study of assessment in a grade 10 English course. *The Journal of Educational Research, 93,* 276–286.

Kane, M. T. (2006). Validation. In R. L. Brennan (Ed.), *Educational measurement* (4th ed., pp. 17–64). Westport, CT: Praeger.

Klem, L. (2000). Structural equation modeling. In L. G. Grimm & P. R. Yarnold (Eds.), *Reading and understanding more multivariate statistics* (pp. 227–260). Washington, DC: APA.

Knight, N. (2003). Teacher feedback to students in numeracy lessons: Are students getting good value? *set: Research Information for Teachers,* (3), 40–45.

Marton, F. (1981). Phenomenography – Describing conceptions of the world around us. *Instructional Science, 10,* 177–200.

McMillan, J. H., Myran, S., & Workman, D. (2002). Elementary teachers' classroom assessment and grading practices. *The Journal of Educational Research, 95*(4), 203–213.

Mertler, C. A. (1999, October). *Teachers' (mis)conceptions of classroom test validity and reliability.* Paper presented at the Annual Meeting of the Mid-Western Educational Research Association, Chicago, IL.

Messick, S. (1989). Validity. In R. L. Linn (Ed.), *Educational Measurement* (3rd ed., pp. 13–103). Old Tappan. NJ: MacMillan.

Ministry of Education. (1990). *Tomorrow's standards: The report of the ministerial working party on assessment for better learning*. Wellington, New Zealand: Learning Media.

Ministry of Education. (1994). *Assessment: Policy to practice*. Wellington, New Zealand: Learning Media.

Ministry of Education. (2001). Developing teachers' assessment literacy. *Curriculum Update*, 47, Retrieved 7 November 2007 from http://www.tki.org.nz/r/governance/curric_updates/curr_update47_e.php.

National Research Council. (2001). *Knowing what students know: The science and design of educational assessment*. Washington, DC: National Academy Press.

O'Sullivan, R. G., & Johnson, R. L. (1993, April). *Using performance assessments to measure teachers' competence in classroom assessment*. Paper presented at the Annual Meeting of the American Educational Research Association (AERA), Atlanta, GA.

Pajares, M. F. (1992). Teachers' beliefs and educational research: Cleaning up a messy construct. *Review of Educational Research, 62*, 307–332.

Peddie, R. (2000). *Evaluation of the Assessment for Better Learning professional development programmes: Final Report*. Auckland, New Zealand: Auckland UniServices Limited.

Philippou, G., & Christou, C. (1997). Cypriot and Greek primary teachers' conceptions about mathematical assessment. *Educational Research and Evaluation, 3*(2), 140–159.

Plake, B. S., & Impara, J. C. (1997). Teacher assessment literacy: What do teachers know about assessment? In G. D. Phye (Ed.), *Handbook of classroom assessment: Learning, achievement, and adjustment* (pp. 53–58). San Diego, CA: Academic Press.

Plake, B. S., Impara, J. C., & Fager, J. J. (1993). Assessment competencies of teachers: A national survey. *Educational Measurement: Issues and Practice, 12*(4), 10–12, 39.

Popham, W. J. (2000). The mismeasurement of educational quality. *School Administrator, 57*(11), 12–15.

Quilter, S. M. (1998). *Inservice teachers' assessment literacy and attitudes toward assessment*. Unpublished doctoral dissertation, University of South Carolina, Columbia, SC.

Quilter, S. M., & Chester, C. (1998, October). *Inservice teachers' perceptions of educational assessment*. Paper presented at the Annual Meeting of the Mid-Western Educational Research Association, Chicago.

Rex, L. A., & Nelson, M. C. (2004). How teachers' professional identities position high-stakes test preparation in their classrooms. *Teachers College Record, 106*(6), 1288–1331.

Richardson, V., & Placier, P. (2001). Teacher change. In V. Richardson (Ed.), *Handbook of research on teaching* (4th ed., pp. 905–947). Washington, DC: American Educational Research Association.

Robinson, V. M. J. (1998). Methodology and the research-practice gap. *Educational Researcher, 27*(1), 17–26.

Robinson, V. M. J., & Walker, J. C. (1999). Theoretical privilege and researchers' contribution to educational change. In J. S. Gaffney & B. J. Askew (Eds.), *Stirring the waters: The influence of Marie Clay* (pp. 239–259). Portsmouth, NH: Heinemann.

Saltzgaver, D. (1983). One teacher's dominant conceptions of student assessment. *Curriculum Perspectives, 3*, 15–21.

Schafer, W. D. (1993). Assessment literacy for teachers. *Theory Into Practice, 32*(2), 118–126.

Shepard, L. A. (2001). The role of classroom assessment in teaching and learning. In V. Richardson (Ed.), *Handbook of research on teaching* (4th ed., pp. 1066–1101). Washington, DC: American Educational Research Association.

Shepard, L. A. (2006). Classroom assessment. In R. L. Brennan (Ed.), *Educational Measurement* (pp. 623–646). Westport, CT: Praeger.

Stamp, D. (1987). *Evaluation of the formation and stability of student teacher attitudes to measurement and evaluation practices.* Unpublished doctoral dissertation, Macquarie University, Sydney, Australia.

Stiggins, R. J. (1995). Assessment literacy for the 21st century. *Phi Delta Kappan, 77*(3), 238–245.

Stiggins, R. J. (1998). Confronting the barriers to effective assessment. *School Administrator, 55*(11), 6–9.

Stiggins, R. J. (2001). The unfulfilled promise of classroom assessment. *Educational Measurement: Issues and Practice, 20*(3), 5–15.

Sturrock, F. (1999). *Teacher census: Preliminary report.* Wellington, New Zealand: Ministry of Education, Demographic and Statistical Analysis Unit.

Thompson, A. G. (1992). Teachers' beliefs and conceptions: A synthesis of the research. In D. A. Grouws (Ed.), *Handbook of research on mathematics teaching and learning* (pp. 127–146). New York: MacMillan.

Thompson, B. (2000). Ten commandments of structural equation modeling. In L. G. Grimm & P. R. Yarnold (Eds.), *Reading and understanding More multivariate statistics* (pp. 261–283). Washington, DC: APA.

Timperley, H. (2003). Evidence-based leadership: The use of running records. *New Zealand Journal of Educational Leadership, 18*, 65–76.

Torrance, H., & Pryor, J. (1998). *Investigating formative assessment: Teaching, learning and assessment in the classroom.* Buckingham, UK: Open University Press.

van den Berg, B. (2002). Teachers' meanings regarding educational practice. *Review of Educational Research, 72*, 577–625.

Warren, E., & Nisbet, S. (1999, July). *The relationship between the purported use of assessment techniques and beliefs about the uses of assessment.* Paper presented at the 22nd Annual Conference of the Mathematics Education and Research Group of Australasia (MERGA), Adelaide, Australia.

Webb, N. L. (1992). Assessment of students' knowledge of mathematics: Steps toward a theory. In D. A. Grouws (Ed.), *Handbook of research on mathematics teaching and learning* (pp. 661–683). New York: Macmillan.

Willis, D. (1994). School-based assessment: Underlying ideologies and their implications for teachers and learners. *New Zealand Journal of Educational Studies, 29*(2), 161–174.

Worthen, B. R. (1993). Is your school ready for alternative assessment? *Phi Delta Kappan, 74*(6), 455–456.

AUTHOR NOTE

Gavin Brown is a Senior Lecturer, Research Methodology in the Faculty of Education, University of Auckland, New Zealand. His research interests include conceptions of educational processes, large-scale assessment, and quantitative research methods.

This research was conducted as part of the author's doctoral dissertation in Education at the University of Auckland. The author would like to acknowledge the financial assistance of Auckland UniServices Ltd, the supervision of Professor John Hattie, the assistance of the University of Auckland asTTle team, and the co-operation of hundreds of teachers and trainees.

An earlier version of this chapter was presented at the 2004 IAEA Conference in Philadelphia, Pennsylvania.

Correspondence concerning this chapter should be addressed by email to: gt.brown@auckland.ac.nz

In: Challenging Thinking about Teaching and Learning
Editors: C. M. Rubie-Davies and C. Rawlinson

ISBN: 978-1-60456-744-1
© 2008 Nova Science Publishers, Inc.

Chapter 24

INTERNAL–EXTERNAL LOCUS OF CONTROL BELIEFS AND SELF-PACING IN ELEMENTARY SCHOOL CHILDREN LEARNING A GROSS MOTOR TASK

Elise Timmons Lawton, Richard Hamilton and Mary Rudisill

ABSTRACT

The current study found that students whose internal/external locus of control beliefs matched the context of the learning situation (self- versus experimenter-controlled learning schedule) learned a specific gross motor task more successfully than those whose internal/external locus of control beliefs did not match the learning situation. Results provide construct validity to person–situation interaction and to the internal/external construct from Rotter's social learning theory within the gross motor learning domain. No differences were found between males and females or between participants given self-pacing or experimenter pacing. In terms of instructional implications within the motor learning domain, these results support the creation of learning environments which match the locus of control beliefs of students to maximize learning. In addition, educators should provide environments that foster the development of internal local of control beliefs in their students to maximize those students' potential for achievement.

INTRODUCTION

The internal/external construct, which is also referred to as "locus of control," is one of the most studied variables in psychology and other social sciences (Rotter, 1990). Locus of control was described by Rotter (1966; 1971) as a generalized expectancy which affects how an individual approaches problem solving within a variety of social situations. This generalized expectancy is based either on a belief that reinforcement for behaviour is controlled predominantly by forces inside the individual (internal) or on a belief that reinforcement for behaviour is controlled predominantly by forces outside the individual (external). Examples of "internal locus of control of reinforcement" would be personal effort, persistence, skills, and abilities. Examples of "external locus of control of reinforcement" would be luck, fate, chance, and powerful others. By rewording and restating those beliefs, the importance of reinforcement can be emphasized as follows: Individuals with an internal locus of control believe that use of their own efforts, skills, and abilities will be reinforcing. In contrast, individuals with an external locus of control believe that luck, fate, chance, and powerful others determine when or if their efforts, skills, and abilities will be reinforced.

Within the context of developing effective learning and teaching environments, the construct of locus of control has two specific areas of application. The first is the relationship between the nature of classroom instruction and methods and the locus of control preferences of the individual students within the classroom. A match between methods and preferences may be most beneficial for enhanced learning within the target contexts. If this is the case, then teachers must attempt to tailor their approaches to instruction based on the preferences of the individual students within their classrooms. In contrast to the first area of application, the second area focuses on whether an internal or an external locus of control is the more adaptive preference for enhancing learning within classrooms. That is, will an internal locus of control allow the individual to learn within classrooms which employ student-centred as well as teacher-centred direction and control? If this is the case, then teachers need to embed classroom structures, process, and feedback that facilitate the development of an internal locus of control.

The majority of research has focused primarily on assessing the differential effects of an individual's locus of control on their behaviour rather than assessing the effects of the degree to which relevant environments match an individual's locus of control preferences. Research has found that locus of control is significantly related to academic achievement (cf. Flouri, 2006; Kalechstein & Nowicki, 1997; Martin, Meyer, Nelson, Baldwin, Ting, & Sterling, 2007; Nunn, 1995; Ross & Broh, 2000), health management (Miles, Sawyer, & Kennedy, 1995; Nir & Neumann, 1995), employee productivity, management, and interview success (Gable & Dangello, 1994; Howell & Avolio, 1993; Tay, Ang, & Van Dyne, 2006), effective stress management (Rahim & Psenicka, 1996), and entrepreneurship (Gray, 1992; Langan-Fox & Roth, 1995).

Within the domain of motor learning and sports, only a few studies have integrated locus of control as an individual difference variable and the pattern of results has been somewhat inconsistent. The studies focus more often on the relation between locus of control and choice and less often on the relation of locus of control and performance or achievement. With respect to locus of control and choices in sports, no consistent pattern of relation between these two variables has been found. That is, most studies have found no relation, while a few have found a consistent but weak relation in the expected direction (cf. DiGuiseppe, 1973; Colley, Roberts, & Chips, 1985; Jambor and Rudisill, 1992; Lynn, Phelan, Kiker, 1969). A similar pattern is found within the research on the relation between locus of control and performance in sports. That is, results range from no relation between high performance to a significant relation between high performance and both an internal and external locus of control (cf., Celestino, Tapp & Brumet, 1979; Lufi, Porat, & Tenenbaum, 1986; Morris, Vocarro, & Clarke, 1979; Porat, Lufi, & Tenenbaum 1989). One possible reason for the lack of consistency within this set of studies is the focus on the influence of an individual's personal characteristics on choice or performance separately from the context of that choice or performance.

According to Rotter (1982), within a social learning context, the critical unit of investigation is the interaction between the individual's characteristics and beliefs and the nature of the social learning context or environment. Consequently, if one focuses only on the individual's beliefs about perceived control without taking into consideration the nature of the environment within which the individual is learning, then one is left with an incomplete picture of the potential for change. Given Rotter's social learning theory and the need to focus on the person–situation interaction, one would hypothesize several potential results. First, if some students really believed that their reinforcers were controlled internally, those students would learn better when allowed to control their conditions of learning. Likewise, if other students really believed that the teacher (for example) controlled their reinforcers, one would hypothesize those students would learn better in a teacher-controlled environment. Third, the two inverse conditions would detract from learning. Therefore, one would hypothesize that the congruence or non-congruence between beliefs about perceived control and actual control of learning activities would affect learning.

Although no studies have directly measured these interactive effects, there are some studies which are relevant and do provide some insight into the possible relationship. Klein and Keller (1990) measured the learning outcome of a computer-based lesson in which one group of students controlled the presentation of the lesson and another group of students followed the lesson presentation controlled by the computer program. Although students in both treatment groups performed at about the same level, in both groups the students with internal locus of control beliefs outperformed those with external locus of control beliefs.

Freeman and Miller (1989) assessed a group of workers' job-related performance of and satisfaction with a simulated inspection task. They found no differences on some measures and several small but significant differences on others. Where there were differences, workers with an internal locus of control performed better than those with an external locus of control, and those who were self-paced performed better than those who were machine-paced. There was only one significant interaction effect in performance, and there were no significant differences in job satisfaction either in main effects or interactions.

Finally, in the area of goal setting, a few studies have looked at the relation between locus of control and locus of goal setting (Sandler, Reese, Spencer, & Harpin, 1983; Gagne & Parshall, 1975; Lambert, Moore, & Dixon, 1997). In general, these studies have found that self-set goals improved the performance of individuals with an internal locus of control, while experimenter- or teacher-set goals improved the performance of individuals with an external locus of control. These results suggest that self-paced environments are more conducive to learning for individuals with internal control beliefs while teacher- or other-paced environments are more conducive to learning for individuals with external control beliefs.

In summary, much work has been done over the past several decades using the construct best known as "locus of control". However, the interaction between students' locus of control beliefs and either self-pacing or experimenter-pacing of practice schedules has not been directly investigated. The purpose of the current study was to examine how locus of control beliefs interact with different practice schedules on participants' learning of and performance on a gross motor task. The target task used in this study was learning how to balance on a platform that was placed on a fulcrum (i.e., stabilometer). The task required that participants learn appropriate foot and body placement in order to keep the platform balanced on the fulcrum. The two contrasting practice conditions employed were to either allow the participants to be in charge of the pace of their own practice (self-paced) or having the experimenter in charge of the pace of the participant's practice (experimenter-paced). Based on Rotter's social learning theory, it was predicted that students who had internal locus of control beliefs would learn best in a situation that allowed them to choose their own actions (that is, self-paced). Likewise, it was predicted that students who had external locus of control beliefs would learn best in a situation that was controlled by others (in this case, experimenter-paced).

METHOD

Participants

All of the 261 students in the fourth and fifth grade classes of a suburban elementary school in a large metropolitan area in North America were invited to participate in this research. Of those students, the 142 who returned parental consent forms were allowed to participate. Gender distribution of the participants included 78 females and 64 males, and the participants were primarily of European descent. At the time of the study, these students were nearing the end of the school year; their ages ranged from 9 to 12 years. Students did not receive any extra credit for participating.

Apparatus

This section describes the apparatus used, and includes methodological considerations that were taken into account in the choice of that apparatus. Apparatus included a stabilometer (a balance platform), a pretend platform, a computer with data acquisition instrumentation, two videotapes, three audiotapes, six signs, and eight books.

Stabilometer Equipment

The stabilometer used for this study had been built by modifying a design illustrated by Singer (1968, p. 64) and described by Thomas, Cotton, and Shelley (1974). The 17 x 27 in. (43 x 69 cm) balance platform was ¾-inch plywood resting on and fastened securely to a metal-pipe fulcrum. The sturdy, wooden frame base supported the fulcrum at a height of 6 in. (15 cm) above the floor. At a 19° tip to either side, the platform closed the contact switch on that side of the base. The contact switches were wired to the measuring instrument that recorded sequentially the duration of each OPEN (time-segment the platform was off both switches—that is, both contact switches were open), the duration of each CLOSE (time-segment the platform closed a contact switch), and whether the CLOSE was on the right or left switch.

The top of the balance platform held a pair of footprints and two signs. The footprints, made of sandpaper, marked a stance of 11½ in. (29 cm) centre-to-centre, divided equally over the fulcrum. This stance was an estimated average shoulder-width of the participating students, in order to centre the participants weight over the fulcrum while optimizing force production. In addition to a standardized-width stance, the footprints provided a non-slippery surface that further avoided loss of force and helped the students maintain a consistent foot position. Near the heels of the footprints was a sign stating "KEEP YOUR FEET ON THE FOOTPRINTS," as a constant reminder to the students each time they stepped onto the platform. A sign at toe-level stating "LOOK UP AT TARGET" was another constant reminder to those students who occasionally watched their feet while trying to balance.

Stabilometer Task

Although balancing the stabilometer platform has been described as a difficult task (Carron, 1968; Singer, 1965; Singer, 1968), several factors prompted its choice. First, the stabilometer task is a gross motor task that has been found to be an appropriate task choice for children (Bachman, 1962). Second, the stabilometer has been used in numerous research studies, reportedly more than any other gross motor task (Wade & Newell, 1972). Third, the task itself requires almost no instructions. Fourth, the idea of learning a "balancing game" on a tiny, one-person seesaw, conveyed playfulness and fun, not boredom and stress, and consequently it was hoped that more students would choose to participate. The fifth reason the stabilometer was chosen related integrally to the parameters of social learning theory, because the stabilometer task was novel and ambiguous. The students had no history of reinforcement on which to base any specific expectations as to what the outcome might be, so they had to fall back on generalized expectations. This strengthened the potential that the outcomes could be predicted by whether they held internal or external locus of control beliefs (Strickland, 1989).

Pretend Platform

The pretend platform, a piece of ¾-in. plywood the same size and shape as the balance platform, rested flat on the floor in the instruction-area of the room. A matching pair of sandpaper footprints and two signs mimicked those on the balance platform. The only difference was the wording of the toe-level sign that stated "LOOK UP AT VIDEO." The pretend platform served (a) to maximize the thoroughness of instruction (prior to pretest) and (b) to reduce the time needed to warm up (before the posttest) (cf. Adams, 1987; Carron, 1969).

Signage

In addition to the two signs on the balance platform and the two on the pretend platform, two posters were mounted on the wall. A large poster summarized the schedule in case students wanted a reminder of what to expect next. A smaller poster with a "bull's-eye" target was mounted 6 ft (1.8 m) in front of the stabilometer at about eye level height for the students. This target-poster also bore three statements: "KEEP YOUR EYES ON THIS TARGET," "KEEP YOUR KNEES SLIGHTLY BENT," and "KEEP YOUR FEET ON THE FOOTPRINTS." All signs were designed to limit the amount of verbal communication during the procedure.

Best Strategies

In order to control the participants' strategy-formulation, three "best strategies" were built into the procedure. Each of the statements on the target poster referred to earlier were indexed to one of the three strategies to employ while on the stabilometer. The rationale for the first one (KEEP YOUR EYES ON THIS TARGET) was to keep students from watching their feet and to use vision as feedback for balance skills (McLeod & Hansen, 1989; Singer,

1968; Stones & Kozma, 1987). The second strategy (KEEP YOUR KNEES SLIGHTLY BENT) was to avoid either (a) locked knees or (b) a "squat" position. Biomechanically, the moderate knee bend should offer the greatest stability advantage (Kreighbaum & Barthels, 1990, p. 318). Reasons for the third strategy (KEEP YOUR FEET ON THE FOOTPRINTS) have been discussed earlier within the section on stabilometer equipment. These "best strategies" were designed to minimize the variation of strategies used by the students—narrowing among-student and between-trial differences.

Measuring Equipment

Measurement accuracy was achieved by SuperScope II software, an instrument design environment by GW Instruments, and MacADIOS II data acquisition hardware installed in a space-modified Power Macintosh 6100/60. The instrument was designed to record time segments during pretest, practice, and posttest, including resting intervals. It produced visual wave patterns of OPENS and CLOSES generated by each student attempting to balance the platform. From these waves, OPEN and CLOSE transition points and the direction of the transition could be extracted.

To achieve true self-pacing, the subject had to have complete freedom without being bound by pauses for recording of results or resetting of timers. Therefore, features designed into SuperScope II were as follows. First, the beginning of each trial was initiated by the student; the end of each trial was terminated by the instrument. In other words, each trial was started by the student's first lift-off, so a student who hesitated at the start of a trial was not penalized for that hesitation. Following that, the instrument timer maintained a running summary of trial intervals, and then ceased wave production at the end of each preset interval. That is, it stopped each of the pretest and posttest trials at 15 seconds, the experimenter-paced practice trials at 120 seconds, and the self-paced practice block at the sum total of 360 seconds of "work"—not including time spent "resting". Secondly, in addition to recording trial times, the instrument also recorded duration of each "rest" interval throughout all four portions of the testing procedure—pretest, practice, retention interval, and posttest.

Scripting, Analysis, and Processing Equipment

Data were extracted from the wave form and converted into lists of transition points (with information on whether the board was moving toward or away from the contact switch) using Frontier script (a specialized file of internal computer commands). Further use of Frontier script and Filemaker analyzed the data lists and provided six sets of statistics—mean, standard deviation, maximum, minimum, range, and count.

Videotapes and Audiotapes

A total of two videotapes and three audiotapes (audiotape 1–SP, audiotape 1–EP, and audiotape 2) provided the standardized instructions for the experiment. The "assembly video", which was shown at the opening assembly, introduced students to the project, demonstrated the stabilometer in use, and administered the locus of control instrument. The "demonstration video", which was shown at the very beginning of the testing procedure, introduced students to their pacing, presented more details about the stabilometer and ways to get "a good score," and then led them through a "trial run" using the pretend platform.

Audiotapes 1–SP and 1–EP were played during the one-minute interval between the end of the pretest block and the beginning of the practice block. Each student heard only either

Audiotape 1–SP or 1–EP: Audiotape 1–SP gave practice-block instructions for the self-paced schedule and audiotape 1–EP gave practice-block instructions for the experimenter-paced schedule. Audiotape 2 was played during the 10-minute retention interval and began with the "administration" of the student response poll and ended by directing students through their posttest warm–up on the pretend platform.

Instrumentation

Children's Nowicki-Strickland Internal–External Control Scale

The Children's Nowicki-Strickland Internal–External Control Scale (CNSIE) is one of a life-span series of scales that were designed to assess the construct of internal/external locus of control from childhood throughout the life span (Nowicki, undated). The children's version (Nowicki & Strickland, 1973) was tested on children in Grades 3–12 (Year 4–13 in New Zealand), and is appropriate for use with children from ages 9 through to 18. It is a paper and pencil measure consisting of 40 questions to be answered by marking either the yes or no next to the question. It is scored by giving one point for each answer marked in the external direction, so the higher the score, the higher the degree of externality. The questions describe reinforcement situations across areas such as affiliation, achievement, and dependency.

As reported by Nowicki and Strickland (1973), estimated internal consistency for students in Grades 3, 4, and 5 was $r = .63$, test–retest reliability was .63 for third graders tested six weeks apart, and convergent validity was reported between the CNSIE and several other measures of locus of control. Conversely, the scale showed nonsignificant correlations with variables of gender, social desirability, and intelligence, which indicate its discriminative validity. The children's scale and the other Nowicki–Strickland life-span scales have been used in more than 1,000 research studies (Nowicki, undated).

Out of 260 students completing the CNSIE within the present experiment, 19 sets were deleted because one or more questions were either not answered or both "Yes" and "No" were circled. The remaining 241 scores ranged from 4 (most internal) to 24 (most external). One-third of the students scored 15 and above, and one third scored 11 and below, with a mean score of 13. Cronbach's alpha yielded an inter-item reliability of .6683.

Student Response Poll

The function of the student response poll was to act as a filler activity within the retention interval and to obtain information that may be helpful for future research within this area. Questions focused on perceived levels of fatigue, informal reactions to the stabilometer task, and estimated participation in some types of physical and athletic activities.

Procedure

A consent form for parents and for students was sent home with all fourth- and fifth-grade students. The following week, the students attended a school assembly at which a video depicting the task was shown, and the CNSIE was completed by all students. On this latter test, one third of the students scored 11 or less, one third scored 11 to 15, and one third scored 15 or more. Based on that distribution, students scoring 11 or less were classified as the "internal group" for this study, those scoring 15 or more were classified as the "external group", and those scoring 12–14 were not included in either group and were not included in the study. Neither students nor parents or teachers were told these results. Teachers controlled the order of participation by selecting students from a list that gave no indication of grouping, and each student was tested individually. Upon arrival to the testing session, each student drew a straw to determine whether he or she would follow the self-paced practice schedule or the experimenter-paced practice schedule. The straws were arranged to afford continuous block randomization of all three factors—gender, internal–external locus of control, and pacing—and also some balance in the number of students in each of the eight cells.

A large room had been set aside that allowed complete privacy for one student and the experimenter to be undisturbed during the 35 to 40 minutes required for each testing procedure. Approximate times were as follows:

Demonstration video	8 minutes
Pretest Block	2.25 minutes
Rest and Audio 1–SP or 1–EP	1 minute
Practice Block	6 to 15.5 minutes
Retention Interval	10 minutes
Posttest Block	2.25 minutes

From the demonstration video, students learned their schedule for the procedure, they received information about best practice, and they were led through a "trial run" using the pretend platform. Also, participants were informed that there would be no feedback or communication from the experimenter regarding their performance (i.e., no augmented feedback) until after the research project had been completed. The pretest block consisted of five trials, each 15 seconds in length and separated by 15-second inter-trial intervals (with the student standing near the stabilometer). The practice block included audiotaped instructions and either all self-paced or all experimenter-paced practice trials. The self-paced practice block allowed the student to begin practising, to continue for as short or as long as desired, to stop whenever desired, to rest as short or as long as desired and to begin again as desired. Students were told to continue practising (and resting as desired) until the computer signalled that he or she had practised a total of 6 minutes. Student could sit, stand, or walk around to rest. The experimenter-paced practice block held three trials, each 120 seconds in length and separated by 15-second inter-trial intervals (with the student standing near the stabilometer). Although this was a fairly massed practice schedule, it was chosen to typify practice schedules in physical education classes. The retention block involved students filling out (with the experimenter's help) a questionnaire on students' sport preferences and activities. Before moving on to the posttest, students listened to audiotaped instructions for the posttest and then practised the procedure by stepping on the practice platform. Finally, the students went to the stabilometer to complete the posttest block. The posttest block contained five 15-second trials separated with 15-second inter-trial intervals, the same as the pretest block. Following the fifth posttest trial, the student was thanked and accompanied back to class.

Control of Moderating Procedural Variables

Additional variables were controlled by the design of this study. One of these variables, reinforcement value, is a major factor in Rotter's Social Learning Theory. Two of these variables have been found to affect learning of motor tasks—mental practice and augmented feedback. The fourth, lateral dominance, might be more influential in this task than in some other motor tasks.

Reinforcement Value

There were no promises or even hints of rewards or punishments connected with any phase of this research. Although the task was referred to as a "balancing game" with "rules," there was no mention of competition between participants, or of winners and losers. Students were simply asked to participate in a science project (a term with which they were all familiar).

Lateral Dominance

Of the 105 participating students in either the internal or external group, only 7 were left–handed. In order to control for potential effects of lateral dominance, the video demonstrations were always given with the model facing away from the camera, preserving the correct laterality for students watching the model. In addition, instructions to the students included directions to step on the platform with their "first foot" (after having students recall whether they were right- or left-handed, and designating that as their "first foot"), and rest their "second foot" lightly on the other footprint.

Mental Practice

To eliminate the possibility that some of the students might engage in mental practice, time was tightly structured during the entire 10-minute retention interval in ways that captured and held each student's attention (such as the student poll and the attention-getting books.

Augmented Feedback

According to Magill (1994), performance on the stabilometer could be significantly influenced by knowledge of performance and knowledge of results. Indeed, in a study by Wade and Newell (1972), it was found that despite response-produced feedback available in the stabilometer task (such as the sound and "feel" of the switches as they were touched by the balance platform, or the "feel" of being "balanced or off-balance") participants still performed better with augmented feedback (that is, with knowledge of results) in the Wade and Newell study.

Three techniques were employed in order to control for potential effects of augmented feedback. First, the use of videotapes and audiotapes for instructions eliminated almost all communication between the participants and the researcher. Second, the use of signs and posters continually reminding students of the "rules of the balancing game" again minimized communication and feedback from the researcher. Third, given that the measuring device produced waves and not numbers, students had no way of knowing their "scores".

ANALYSIS OF RESULTS

In addition to a description of the analyses employed within the current study, this section will also discuss how "on balance" was operationalized in the study and the type of gain scores employed in the analysis.

Open and Close

In the literature, "on-balance" frequently has been operationally defined as any time both the left and the right switches were open. It was decided that an OPEN would refer to any time, no matter how controlled or how out-of-control, the student had the balance platform off both switches (and therefore the contacts were open). Paired with that, a CLOSE would refer to any time the balance platform closed either switch.

Residual Gain

According to Manning and DuBois (1962), neither percentage gain nor crude gain provides results that are free of possible contamination by the regression effect in assessing gain from pretest to posttest. Therefore, residual gain, an individual's deviation in standard score units from the score predicted for him or her by means of regression, was used to determine the relative amounts of learning.

Statistical Analysis

Gain score results were analyzed on three levels. The first level was simply to find the three gain scores: crude, percentage, and residual. The second level was a multifactor analysis of variance to determine if there was an interaction between the three independent variables—locus of control, pacing, and gender. The three-factor ANOVA indicated whether these variables were interdependent or whether the main effects of any of these characteristics could be generalized to levels of one or both of the other characteristics. The third level included two t–tests beginning with a single-factor, unpaired t–test to compare scores within each separate dichotomous variable. That was followed by another single-factor, unpaired t–test, which was used to determine the effects of the new variable formed by the "match" "not match" ordering.

RESULTS

Gain Scores

The difference between the sum of OPENS in the five pretest trials and the sum of OPENS in the five posttest trials gave a crude gain score for each student. From these, both percentage gain scores and residual gain scores were calculated. Descriptive statistics for these three different gain scores appear in Table 24.1. Crude gain scores were used to determine whether each individual student had a higher posttest-block score than pretest-block score. All other calculations and comparisons used residual gain scores, the deviation of posttest-block scores from the regression line of posttest-block on pretest-block scores (Manning & DuBois, 1962), in order to control for the regression effect.

Table 24.1. Descriptive Comparison of Three Gain Scores

	Mean	SD	SE	Minimum	Maximum
Crude gain	6.87s	3.55s	.35s	-1.25s	14.99s
Percentage gain	16%	9%	1%	-3%	41%
Residual gain	0	3.55s	.35s	-8.06s	8.03s

Using crude gain scores, it was found that 103 of the students in the internal and the external groups scored higher on their posttest block than on their pretest block, and only two students scored lower on their posttest block than on their pretest block.

Analysis of Variance, Effect Sizes, and Power

Two levels of analysis were performed on the residual gain scores. A multi-factor analysis of variance was employed to determine if there was an interaction between the three independent variables—internal/external locus of control, pacing, and gender (see Table 24.2). The three-factor ANOVA yielded neither main effects nor interaction effects. However, the locus of control/pacing interaction did approach significance $F(1,97) = 6.16$, p $< .015$. Effect sizes were quite small. The largest eta squared was .060 for the interaction of locus of control and pacing; the second largest was .020 for effect of beliefs. The power for the effect of beliefs was only .121 and the power for the interaction of locus of control and pacing was only .447.

Table 24.2. Analysis of Variance Table

	DF	Sum of Sq.	Mean Sq.	F–Value	P–Value
F/M[a]	1	3.24	3.14	.25	.616
Pace[b]	1	7.27	7.27	.59	.446
N/X[c]	1	25.14	25.14	2.03	.158
F/M * pace	1	.64	.64	.05	.821
F/M * N/X	1	.00	.00	.00	.989
Pace * N/X	1	76.43	76.43	6.16	.015
F/M * pace * N/X	1	.01	.01	.00	.972
Residual	97	1,202.58	12.40		

[a]F/M = gender. [b]Pace = self versus experimenter control of practice. [c]N/X = internal versus external locus of control beliefs.

The second level of analysis focused on the issue of congruence between control beliefs and pacing. The three dichotomous variables—internal versus external locus of control of reinforcement, pacing, and gender— were reordered into two person–situation groups. The "match" group included both internal locus of control students on a self-paced practice schedule and external locus of control students on an experimenter-paced practice schedule. The "not-match" group included both experimenter-paced internal and self-paced external locus of control students. The "match" group produced significantly higher residual gain scores than the "not-match" group (mean difference = 1.68 seconds; t (2.481) = 2.48, $p <$ .007) (see Table 24.3).

Table 24.3. Comparison of Single and Grouped Effects, Listed in Order of t-Value

Variable	Count	Group mean	Mean diff.	DF	t-value	P-value
Male	$n = 48$	.146	.269	103	.385	.6495
Female	$n = 57$	-.123				
Experimenter	$n = 53$	.193	.391	103	.562	.2878
Self	$n = 52$	-.197				
Internal	$n = 56$	.441	.944	103	1.365	.0876
External	$n = 49$	-.504				
Match	$n = 53$	.831	1.679	103	2.481	.0074
Not match	$n = 52$	-.847				

Student Response Poll

Students' answers to the Likert questions on the student response poll were reviewed in order to assess the differences between the independent variables or between the "match" and "not match" groups. There were no obvious, large differences, and statistical analysis was not undertaken. A few of the areas that appeared to show some trends were: (a) more females than males and more experimenter-paced than self-paced students expressed feeling tired, and said they were good in sports; (b) more females than males said trying to balance was fun; and (c) equivalent levels of males and females, more internal than external locus of control students, more self-paced than experimenter-paced students, and more "not match" than "match" students said it was hard trying to balance.

With respect to students' participation in physical activities, swimming, bicycle riding, basketball, and jogging or running were the physical activities mentioned with highest hours of weekly participation by the students. Softball, karate, and tae kwan do garnered the least participation. Males reported more hours of participation in physical activities than did females, and internal locus of control students reported higher hours of weekly participation than did students with an external locus of control. Hours of participation in physical activities reported by experimenter-paced and self-paced were almost exactly the same.

DISCUSSION

The purpose of this study was to examine how students who believe in more internal control over their reinforcements would learn following an externally-controlled practice schedule, and its inverse, how students who believe in more external control over their reinforcements would learn following an internally-controlled practice schedule. Based on Rotter's social learning theory, it was predicted that students who believed that they controlled their reinforcements by their own actions would learn best in a situation that allowed them to choose their own actions (that is, self-paced). Likewise, it was predicted that students who believed that their reinforcements were controlled by chance, fate, or powerful others would learn best in a situation that was controlled by chance, fate, or powerful others (in this case, experimenter-paced). The results confirmed these predictions.

If the study had been limited to gender differences, pacing differences, or locus of control differences, then an incomplete assessment of the relation of control beliefs and motor learning would have occurred. The results of the current study clearly indicate the importance of looking at personal characteristics, situational characteristics, and their interaction when trying to understand the influence of motivational beliefs on learning within a motor domain.

Although the literature is mixed on the effect of gender, the lack of significant mean differences between males and females in the current study supports conclusions by Bachman (1962), who studied individuals over the range of 6–26 years of age learning two gross motor tasks (including the stabilometer task). Bachman concluded that differences in both the amount and the rate of learning were not significant. The lack of significant mean differences for pacing supports the results of the study by Goldberger and Gerney (1990) who concluded that both teacher-paced and self-paced practice resulted in adequate levels of learning a motor skill.

Mean differences for the third variable, locus of control, were greater than for the first two variables, yet results were not significant. This supports findings by Celestino et al. (1979) that locus of control was not significantly related to marathon finishers versus non-finishers. It does not support the other result of the study by Celestino et al., that there was a slight but significant relationship between locus of control and finish times of those participants who did finish. Again, the inconsistent pattern of results may reflect the lack of focus on congruence between personal and situational characteristics.

CONCLUSION

In summary, significant differences in learning depended on whether or not the students' generalized locus of control expectations were confirmed or disconfirmed in the learning situation. Results of the current study support the importance of congruence of beliefs and context on learning. From these results, one could conclude that locus of control beliefs are indeed important and predictive when the congruence of the learning situation and the learners' locus of control beliefs is considered.

Limitations

There were two primary limitations, one concerning the composition of the sample, the other concerning the research task. Children in this study were predominantly of European descent, middle to lower-upper class suburban students from 9 to 12 years of age. Results from this current study cannot generalize to individuals from different socioeconomic status, nor to older or younger participants. In addition, since the research task was a specific gross motor task, the results may not generalize to other gross motor tasks, to fine motor tasks, or to academic tasks. There was a minor limitation that also deserves consideration in future research. One male and one female each achieved a 15-second OPEN on one posttest trial. Although this was only one tenth of 1% of all trials, it highlights the potential of a ceiling effect, and any future research should be modified to avoid this possibility.

Another limitation was the lack of a measure of the students' affective responses to the congruence of the learning situation. The current study measured effects, but not the students' feelings. In future research, the student response poll might be expanded to measure students' feelings about the congruence or non-congruence of the learning situation.

Finally, the scope of the present research included only experimenter-paced pre- and posttests. Since there were not an equal number of procedures run with self-paced pre- and posttests, there is no way to determine whether or not this factor biased the results.

Future Research

One goal in future research could be to expand the generalizability of findings in the current study by replication using a larger sample, using participants from differing ethnic backgrounds or differing socioeconomic status, or using older or younger participants. In addition, the use of a similar protocol could be applied to other gross motor tasks, to fine motor tasks, and to academic tasks. The two recommended modifications would be the addition of an affective measure to assess the responses of the participants to the congruity of the person–situation conditions, and a task-design that avoided possible confounding by a ceiling effect.

Another approach to future research might be to expand into the learning of tasks that combine motoric and academic facets such as learning to speak (native language and second language), learning to write, and even learning to read.

In a different vein, research using the measuring equipment created for this study has the potential to provide more detailed analysis of the learning components that come to bear on this particular task (the stabilometer task) than has been afforded by other measuring equipment (Lawton, 1996). Studies using this equipment might, for example, suggest an answer to the question of why the stabilometer task co-ordinates so poorly with other measures of dynamic balance.

Implications for Teachers

Educators could apply results of this study to their own work by considering the importance of the person–situation interaction. Specifically, there are two important implications for instructional planning and evaluation. First, educators should create learning environments which match the locus of control beliefs of their students to maximize learning. For example, for students who possess internal locus of control beliefs, creating self-directed instructional and assessment tasks would be most beneficial. The more that these students are given choices, the greater the match between the instructional methods and their locus of control preferences. In contrast, for students who possess external locus of control preferences, teacher-directed instructional and assessment tasks would be most beneficial. These students should be given clearly specified tasks in which personal choices are minimized. The second instructional implication is that educators should provide environments that foster the development of internal locus of control beliefs in all their students to maximize those students' potential for achievement. At the core of internality is the belief that one has personal control over the consequences to one's behaviours. Employing classroom structures and tasks that are meaningful, self-referenced and self-directed are more likely to help students to develop increased feelings of personal control and internality. Meaningful tasks would draw from students' prior knowledge and experiences so that students would view them as being relevant to their past and future experiences. Self-referenced tasks would involve feedback that is indexed to personal progress and standards. By focusing on personal progress and standards, students will develop heightened perceptions of internal control and internality. Finally, as indicated earlier, self-directed tasks would encourage and require students to make choices about the nature of instructional and assessment tasks in which they are involved within the classroom. This would, again, reinforce students' beliefs of personal control.

REFERENCES

Adams, J. A. (1987). Historical review and appraisal of research on the learning, retention, and transfer of human motor skills. *Psychological Bulletin, 101,* 41–74.

Bachman, J. C. (1962). Motor learning and performance as related to age and sex in two measures of balance coordination. *The Research Quarterly, 32,* 123–137.

Carron, A. V. (1968). Motor performance under stress: Stabilometer. *Research Quarterly, 39,* 463–469.

Carron, A. V. (1969). Performance and learning in a discrete motor task under massed versus distributed practice. *Research Quarterly, 40,* 481–489.

Celestino, R., Tapp, J., & Brumet, M. E. (1979). Locus of control correlates with marathon performance. *Perceptual and Motor Skills, 48,* 1249–1250.

Colley, A., Roberts, N., & Chipps, A. (1985). Sex-role identity, personality and participation in team and individual sports by males and females. *International Journal of Sports Psychology, 16,* 103–112.

DiGiuseppe, R. A. (1973). Internal–external control of reinforcement and participation in team, individual, and intramural sports. *Perceptual and Motor Skills, 36,* 33–34.

Flouri, E. (2006). Parental interest in children's education, children's self-esteem and locus of control, and later educational attainment: Twenty-six year follow-up of the 1970 British Birth Cohort, *British Journal of Educational Psychology, 76*(1), 41–55.

Freeman, M. J., & Miller, D. I. (1989). Effects of locus of control and pacing on performance of and satisfaction with a simulated inspection task. *Perceptual and Motor Skills, 69,* 779–785.

Gable, M., & Dangello, F. (1994). Locus of control, Machiavellianism, and managerial job performance. *Journal of Psychology, 128*(5), 599–608.

Gagne, E., & Parshall, H. (1975). The effects of locus of control and goal setting on persistence at a learning task. *Child Study Journal, 5,* 193–199.

Goldberger, M. & Gerney, P. (1990). Effects of learner use of practice time on skill acquisition of fifth grade children. *Journal of Teaching in Physical Education, 10,* 84–95.

Gray, C. (1992). Enterprise trainees' self construals as entrepreneurs. *International Journal of Personal Construct Psychology, 5*(3), 307–322.

Howell, J., & Avolio, B. (1993). Transformational leadership, transactional leadership, locus of control, and support for innovation: Key predictors of consolidated-business-unit performance. *Journal of Applied Psychology, 78*(6), 891–902.

Jambor, E. A., & Rudisill, M. E. (1992). The relationship between children's locus of control and sport choices. *Journal of Human Movement Studies, 22,* 35–48.

Kalechstein, A., & Nowicki, S. (1997). A meta-analytic examination of the relationship between control expectancies and academic achievement: An 11-year follow-up to Findley & Cooper. *Genetic, Social and General Psychology Monographs, 123*(1), 29–56.

Klein, J. D., & Keller, J. M. (1990). Influence of student ability, locus of control, and type of instructional control on performance and confidence. *Journal of Educational Research, 83*(3), 140–146.

Kreighbaum, E., & Barthels, K. M. (1990). *Biomechanics: A qualitative approach for studying human movement* (3rd ed.). New York: Macmillan.

Lambert, S., Moore, D., & Dixon, R. (1997). *Gymnasts in training: The differential effects of self and coach set goals as a function of locus of control.* Unpublished manuscript, University of Auckland, New Zealand.

Langan-Fox, J., & Roth, S. (1995). Achievement motivation and female entrepreneurs. *Journal of Occupational and Organizational Psychology, 68*(3), 209–218.

Lawton, E. T. (1996). *Computerized recording of the stabilometer task.* Unpublished manuscript.

Lufi, D., Porat, J., & Tenenbaum, G. (1986). Psychological predictors of competitive performance in young gymnasts. *Perceptual and Motor Skills, 63,* 59–64.

Lynn, R. W., Phelan, J. G., & Kiker, V. L. (1969). Beliefs in internal-external control of reinforcement and participation in group and individual sports. *Perceptual and Motor Skills, 29,* 551–553.

Magill, R. A. (1994). The influence of augmented feedback on skill learning depends on characteristics of the skill and the learner. *Quest, 46,* 314–327.

Manning, W. H., & DuBois, P. H. (1962). Correlational methods in research on human learning. *Perceptual and Motor Skills, 15,* 287–321.

Martin, S., Meyer, J., Nelson, L., Baldwin, V., Ting, L., & Sterling, D. (2007). Locus of control, self-control, and family income as predictors of young children's mathematics and science scores. *Perceptual and Motor Skills, 104*(2), 599–610.

McLeod, B., & Hansen, E. (1989). Effects of the eyerobics visual skills training program on static balance performance of male and female subjects. *Perceptual and Motor Skills, 69,* 1123–1126.

Miles, A., Sawyer., & Kennedy, D. (1995). A preliminary study of factors that influence children's sense of competence to manage their asthma. *Journal of Asthma, 32*(6), 437–444.

Morris, A. F., Vaccaro, P., & Clarke, D. H. (1979). Psychological characteristics of age-group competitive swimmers. *Perceptual and motor skills, 48,* 1265–1266.

Nir, Z., & Neumann, L. (1995). Relationship among self-esteem, internal-external locus of control, and weight change after participation in a weight reduction program. *Journal of Clinical Psychology, 51*(4), 482–490.

Nowicki, S., & Strickland, B. R. (1973). A locus of control scale for children. *Journal of Consulting and Clinical Psychology, 40,* 148–154.

Nowicki, S. (n.d.). Unpublished review with extensive bibliography. (Available from Stephen Nowicki, Department of Psychology, Emory University, Atlanta, GA 30322.)

Nunn, G. (1995). Effects of learning styles and strategies intervention upon at-risk middle school students' achievement and locus of control. *Journal of Instructional Psychology, 22*(1), 34–39.

Porat, Y., Lufi, D., & Tenenbaum, G. (1989). Psychological components contribute to select young female gymnasts. *International Journal of Sport Psychology, 20,* 279–286.

Rahim, M., & Psenicka, C. (1996). A structural equations model of stress, locus of control, social support, psychiatric symptoms, and propensity to leave a job. *Journal of Social Psychology, 136*(1) 69–84.

Ross, C., & Broh, B. (2000). The roles of self-esteem and the sense of personal control in the academic achievement process, *Sociology of Education, 73*(4), 270–284.

Rotter, J. B. (1966). Generalized expectancies for internal versus external control of reinforcement. *Psychological Monographs, 80* (Whole No. 609).

Rotter, J. B. (1971). *Clinical psychology* (2nd ed.). Englewood Cliffs, NJ: Prentice-Hall, Inc.

Rotter, J. B. (1982). *The development and applications of social learning theory: Selected papers.* New York: Praeger Publishers.

Rotter, J. B. (1990). Internal versus external control of reinforcement: A case history of a variable. *American Psychologist, 45*(4), 489–493.

Sandler, I., Reese, F., Spencer, L., & Harpin, P. (1983). Person x environment interaction and locus of control: Laboratory, therapy, and classroom studies. In H. M. Lefcourt (Ed.), *Research with the locus of control construct: Vol. 2 Development and social problems* (pp. 198–251). Hillsdale, NJ: Lawrence Erlbaum.

Singer, R. N. (1965). Effect of spectators on athletes and non-athletes performing a gross motor task. *Research Quarterly, 36,* 473–482.

Singer, R. N. (1968). *Motor learning and human performance: An application to physical education skills.* New York: The Macmillan Company.

Stones, M. J., & Kozma, A. (1987). Balance and age in the sighted and blind. *Archives of Physical Medicine and Rehabilitation, 68,* 85–88.

Strickland, B. R. (1989). Internal-external control expectancies: From contingency to creativity. *American Psychologist, 44,* 1–12.

Tay, C., Ang, S., & Van Dyne, L. (2006). Personality, biographical characteristics, and job interview success: A longitudinal study of the meditating effects of interviewing self-efficacy and the moderating effects of internal locus of causality, *Journal of Applied Psychology, 91*(2), 446–454.

Thomas, J. R, Cotten, D., & Shelley, F. (1974). Effects of fulcrum height on stabilometer performance. *Journal of Motor Behavior, 6*(2), 95–100.

Wade, M. G., & Newell, K. M. (1972). Performance criteria for stabilometer learning. *Journal of Motor Behavior, 4,* 231–239.

AUTHOR NOTE

Elise Timmons Lawton is currently completing her PhD in Educational Psychology in the Department of Educational Psychology, University of Houston. Richard Hamilton is a Senior Lecturer in the Faculty of Education, University of Auckland, New Zealand. Mary Rudisill is the Wayne T. Smith Distinguished Professor in the Department of Health and Human Performance, Auburn University, Alabama.

The empirical work for this study was completed in partial fulfilment of the first author's MEd degree.

Correspondence concerning this chapter should be addressed by email to: rj.hamilton@auckland.ac.nz

In: Challenging Thinking about Teaching and Learning   ISBN: 978-1-60456-744-1
Editors: C. M. Rubie-Davies and C. Rawlinson   © 2008 Nova Science Publishers, Inc.

Chapter 25

"You Don't Leave Babies on Their Own": Children's Interests in Early Childhood Education

Helen Hedges

Abstract

A sociocultural approach to curriculum and pedagogy, promoted by New Zealand's early childhood curriculum, Te Whariki, emphasizes pedagogical relationships and interactions between learners and knowledgeable others. Dialogue with an adult or peer maximizes children's learning during participation in play. This chapter analyzes an excerpt of dialogue between a four-year-old child and an adult during research that aimed to explore the place of subject knowledge in early childhood curriculum and pedagogy. This interpretive case study in one kindergarten was underpinned by sociocultural theory and used qualitative data gathering techniques such as participant observation. Findings revealed that children's participation in play-based curriculum experiences provided opportunities for them to express, represent, explore, and extend their interests. These interests may be both responsive to the learning and teaching environment and reflect the social and cultural experiences that they participate in with families and communities. The dialogue is analyzed from three perspectives: sociocultural theory, community of practice, and community of inquiry. These perspectives bring to light the child's interests, experiences, knowledge building, inquiry, and emergent citizenship skills. The chapter also describes some challenges that a focus on children's interests presents for teachers in terms of curriculum and pedagogy.

Introduction

New Zealand's early childhood education curriculum, Te Whariki (Ministry of Education, 1996), has two strong theoretical underpinnings: developmental and sociocultural. Recently, however, it has come to be primarily interpreted as a socioculturally-inclined document. Sociocultural theories of learning have as a fundamental assumption that learning is social in origin and a process of active construction. Much knowledge is gained in social and cultural contexts as a result of interpersonal interactions (Rogoff, 1998, 2003; Valsiner, 1993, 2000; Vygotsky, 1978, 1986). Dahlberg, Moss, and Pence (1999), among others, see relationships and communication as central to children's socially constructed learning. Through meaning-making and dialogue with others and the mediation of cultural tools (e.g., language, books, symbols), children make sense of learning and internalize it in thought. In particular, dialogue in the form of language allows both knowledge construction and the appropriation of complex ideas and cognitive processes. Te Whariki promotes the empowerment of children as learners by viewing them as competent and capable contributors to curriculum co-construction.

Grundy (1994) identifies curriculum as a series of phenomena that are constructed and reconstructed on a moment-by-moment basis during pedagogical relationships. Teachers' curricular decision making is a conscious process that draws on understandings about children, curriculum, pedagogy, theory, philosophy, and context. Pedagogical relationships are therefore likely to be a vital way through which children experience an empowering curriculum. What children learn through these relationships has been investigated and theorized, and linked to outcomes such as literacy and numeracy and implications for teacher knowledge (e.g., see Sammons et al., 2004; Siraj-Blatchford, 2004; Siraj-Blatchford & Sylva, 2004; Siraj-Blatchford, Sylva, Muttock, Gilden, & Bell, 2002). However, while a focus on the teacher's role in listening to children in order to extend their learning has been explicated (Dahlberg & Moss, 2005), the types, nature, and characteristics of pedagogical relationships themselves within early childhood contexts remain largely untheorized. This chapter attempts to theorize children's pedagogical relationships with adults using frameworks and constructs consistent with both the notion of socially constructed learning and the four principles of Te Whariki: relationships, empowerment, family and community, and holistic development. This initial theorising suggests that the advice in Te Whariki for teachers to follow children's interests as a way to weave together planned and evolving curriculum generates significant challenges for teachers.

CHILDREN'S INTERESTS

I undertook a study of teachers', parents', and four-year-old children's beliefs about subject knowledge through the lens of an excursion to Kelly Tarlton's Antarctic Encounter and Underwater World, in Auckland, New Zealand (Hedges, 2002a; Hedges & Cullen, 2005). This interpretive case study was underpinned by sociocultural theory and used qualitative data-gathering techniques such as focus group interviews with children, teachers, and parents (as separate groups), and daily participant observation each morning for seven weeks in one kindergarten. Innovative approaches to incorporating children's participation in research were used (see Hedges, 2002b). In the study, four pedagogical relationships were evident. These relationships occurred between teachers and children, parents and children, among child peers, and between children and the researcher in a teaching role. These highlighted pedagogical approaches that promoted and supported active, collaborative engagement in meaningful, reciprocal dialogic inquiry.

The excursion was planned to extend one child's interest in sea creatures (Hedges, 2004). Preparation for, participation in, and follow-up from the excursion was the focus for the study. However, data from the participant observation provided other interesting findings, one of which is the focus of this chapter. Interests-based curriculum and pedagogy in early childhood is often participative and spontaneous. Findings revealed that children's participation in play-based curriculum experiences provided opportunities for them to express, represent, explore, and extend a range of interests. The findings support that children's interests do not emerge in a vacuum but emanate from children's participation in social and cultural experiences.

As a working definition for the present theorizing, children's interests are considered to be evidence from children's spontaneous play, discussion, inquiry, or investigation that emanates from their social and cultural experiences. These interests may therefore be both responsive to the learning and teaching environment in an early childhood setting and reflect the experiences that they participate in with families and communities. Field notes made during the participant observation revealed that children had a wide range of interests that they wanted to explore through their play. Through this participation, knowledge is constructed and identities as citizens and learners are developed. This knowledge and identity formation is supported by knowledgeable others who know the child or children well.

To illustrate this point, this chapter now focuses on the analysis of a dialogue that occurred between a four-year-old and me as the researcher, as an example of a pedagogical relationship that developed during the seven weeks of the study's field work observation. In the conversational dialogue that follows in full, Jade initiates an interaction that illustrates her interest in and knowledge about participation in culturally valued activities; in particular, caring for babies' well-being. Woven into the dialogue are other conversations about daffodils and peanut butter that rely on memory of earlier interactions between the child and me. Jade shows that she has knowledge of nutrition and bathing routines for babies based on her experience of having younger cousins, knowledge of the world about daffodils (and inquiry about how long they last if picked or kept in the garden), and that she enjoys participating in activities such as learning to read and learning to dance. The dialogue is analyzed from three perspectives: sociocultural theory, community of practice (Wenger, 1998), and community of inquiry (Wells, 1999, 2001a, 2001b). These perspectives highlight in multiple ways the child's interests, experiences, knowledge building, inquiry, emerging identity as a learner, and emergent citizenship skills.

DIALOGUE WITHIN A PEDAGOGICAL RELATIONSHIP

Jade was aged 4 years and 10 months, and had previously demonstrated interests in literacy and family play. The following field notes record the dialogue analyzed in this chapter.

Jade and another four-year-old continue their play from yesterday with the dolls for about an hour. Firstly they are feeding their babies, using spoons and fruit. Jade says her baby needs to eat this before she can have some chocolate. She shows me some bark she has put in the fridge that she is pretending is chocolate. I suggest this is like the story "Eat up your dinner", and they ask me to find it and read it. I bring it to the family corner and read it to them while they finish feeding their babies. Jade soon recognizes the repeated words "nah" and "eat up your dinner" and reads these with me.

They decide their babies need a bath now. I ask them what they need to give their babies a bath. They tell me new clothes, a towel, soap and warm water—not too hot. Jade tells me you have to be careful not to get soap in the baby's eyes, you need to make sure the baby keeps warm, you must hold the baby safely and not leave them alone in the bath. She is going to dress her baby in a ballet skirt after the bath as she is going to ballet. I put some warm water and detergent in the doll's bath and take it onto the Table on the outside deck. I explain that this is special Johnson's [a brand name] baby bath that doesn't make the baby's eyes sting. Jade and Jamie take it in turns to use a wash cloth to bath the doll. Jade is very thorough and knows how to turn the doll over safely to wash its back. She then dries and dresses the doll and goes off to the sandpit.

Soon, she is back. She tells me "She got dirty in the sandpit. I need to give my baby another bath. I rang the ballet teacher and said she didn't want to go today. She goes to ballet and dancing".

Helen: "What's the difference between ballet and dancing?"

Jade: "If you go to dancing you have to dance all time, but I haven't been to ballet so I don't know what you do. When I was about um two and three-quarters, we were going to go to the ballet. But I thought, nah, I thought it would be quite boring. I seen ballet when I was two. I'm holding her head like this to keep her head safe. Can you hold it for me while I come round your side?" I do so and Jade moves to the other side of the bath and turns the doll over. It slips out of the bath.

Helen: "Oh, no!"

Jade: "It's only a doll! Soon she'll get in her ballet clothes again". She notes that on the table beside the bath "Oooh, it's all wet here".

Helen: "Sometimes babies kick and splash water".

Jade: "My friend Anton has a sister Georgia and she just splashes gently. She gets in the big bath now".

Helen: "How old is she?"

Jade: "She's one now and Anton's three".

Jade: "We've got daffodils in our garden. My Mum showed me but I couldn't see them. She said 'Look in the blue pot' and there they were!"

Helen: "Did you recognize they were daffodils because I gave you one a while ago, or because Mum told you?"

Jade: "Mum told me. But we're leaving them in the garden because if you pick them they only last two sleeps".

Helen: "Do they last longer in the garden?"

Jade: "Yes".

Helen: "How long do you think?"

Jade: "I don't know".

Helen: "Will you keep looking at them and let me know?"

Jade: "Haven't you got any in your garden any more?"

Helen: "No".

Jade: "How long did yours last?"

Helen: "I don't know either—that's why I was hoping you could watch yours for me".

I ask her if she remembers the time she made peanut butter for me in the sandpit. She says yes and recalls that some of it dried out quickly in the sun. I ask her if she would like us to make real peanut butter sometime next week. She says yes, but just the Penguins [a small group of girls in the kindergarten] again. Jade notices that the hose is going in the sandpit. She asks me to look after her baby so she can play in the sandpit without her baby getting sandy again. I say that I will and it is responsible of her to leave her baby with someone.

Jade: "Yes, you don't leave babies on their own".

Helen: "Can I feed her for you while you are away?"

Jade: "Yes".

She goes to the sandpit and plays with a group of girls for some time. They all get wet and return for a change of clothes. When I see Jade, I tell her that her baby got tired after I fed her so I put her to bed (I had put the doll in the cot in the family corner). Jade: "Oh, good".

I note that after Jade has changed her clothes, she goes over to the family corner and sees that the doll is in the cot. She then goes away to play elsewhere.

Jade's mother later confirmed that the child had attended a ballet when she was two and that this influenced her decision not to go to ballet classes, and that the children she spoke of were her cousins whom she sees frequently. (Field notes, Oaktree Kindergarten, August 31, 2001)

THEORETICAL ANALYSIS OF THE INTERACTION AND DIALOGUE

Key Concepts of Sociocultural Theory

Vygotsky (1978, 1986) supported that learning should be authentic; that is, it should be relevant to the daily life of a child in a community or culture. As Jordan (2003) notes, "Vygotsky clearly favoured supporting children's learning in the context of their interests" (p. 35). Vygotsky discussed the role of cultural tools in mediating learning and teaching. An example of a cultural tool in the interaction with Jade above is the use of language as the tool of dialogue and thinking, including understanding its written form (the child's recognition of words from the book read to her). This understanding of the written form is important as it supports a positive disposition towards literacy learning. Other key examples of cultural tools in the interaction include: a doll representing and symbolising a baby; sand symbolising peanut butter; and the resources and equipment provided that enabled Jade to demonstrate her expertise in bathing babies.

Another key sociocultural notion is evident: that of intersubjectivity—a shared focus and understanding between people that involves social, emotional, and cognitive interchange. Here the evidence of prior interactions in this pedagogical relationship led to shared understandings about daffodils and representing making peanut butter. In this interaction, the former leads to authentic inquiry and likely future co-construction of knowledge through a genuine question—how long do daffodils stay alive in a garden or in a vase?

Two sociocultural concepts are described as the intended learning outcomes of Te Whariki. Rather than knowledge outcomes, these relate to ways in which "knowledge, skills, and attitudes . . . combine together to form a child's 'working theory' and help the child develop dispositions that encourage learning" (Ministry of Education, 1996. p. 44). A sociocultural perspective of dispositions has been argued recently (Carr & Claxton, 2002; Claxton & Carr, 2004) that has had a major influence on the learning stories assessment practices related to Te Whariki (Carr, 2001a; Ministry of Education, 2004). From this perspective, competent learners are seen to develop positive dispositions for learning linked to the strands of Te Whariki such as curiosity, concentration, persistence, contribution, and communication (Carr, 2001a). Each of these is evident in the interaction analyzed, as are others discussed in the literature such as thinking scientifically (Hedges, 2003), "being nearly five" (Carr, 2001b), or being emergent inquirers (Lindfors, 1999).

The concept of working theories in Te Whariki is most explicit in the strand of "exploration" where the term is used in one of the goals: "[Children] develop working theories for making sense of the natural, social, physical, and material worlds' (Ministry of Education, 1996, p. 82). The concept draws on the work of Claxton (1990) who developed the notion of minitheories based on the idea of implicit theories. Claxton argued that these theories are implicit because much knowledge is tacit; that is, intuitive and intangible. Claxton suggests that implicit theories come largely from three sources: first-hand experience of the physical world, experiences in the social world, and, thirdly, both the explicit and hidden curriculum. Therefore, children's experiences in early childhood settings are likely to inform their working theories as they try to understand the world and reveal themselves in the experiences they choose to participate in. In the interaction described above, Jade reveals a number of working theories about human development and learning and knowledge of the physical and material world.

Another notion consistent with sociocultural theory is that of funds of knowledge. Children's knowledge is based on their unique family and community experiences, encapsulated in the concept of "funds of knowledge" (González, Moll, & Amanti, 2005, Moll, 2000; Moll, Amanti, Neff, & González, 1992). Moll et al. define funds of knowledge as the bodies of knowledge that underlie household functioning, development, and well-being. Examples include economics, such as budgeting, accounting, and loans; repair, such as household appliances, fences, and cars; and arts, such as music, painting, and sculpture (Moll, 2000). Carr (2001a) extended this concept to include broader experiences gained from participation in family and community life, including the occupations of parents. Riojas-Cortez (2001) extended the term to include cultural traits such as parents' language, values, and beliefs; ways of discipline; and the value of education as funds of knowledge sources. My current research extends this analysis to include family members within and beyond the nuclear family and other social and cultural experiences as sources of funds of knowledge (Hedges, 2007). Jade's family and community experiences evident in this interaction are, firstly, having younger cousins. This has enabled her to observe and participate in the care of a baby, with consequent understandings about meal and bathing routines, specifically nutrition, safety, care, and well-being. Secondly, Jade has participated in socially and culturally-valued experiences of dancing, attending ballet, and gardening. She draws on these experiences to make sense of her current learning.

A Learning Community

A focus on learning through participation in a community has led to terms such as "community of learners" (Rogoff, Matusov, & White, 1996), "community of practice"

(Wenger, 1998) and "community of inquiry" (Wells, 1999, 2001a). Rogoff et al.'s (1996) term emphasizes that learning is commonly a collaborative participation in shared experiences. It highlights the intersubjectivity required for meaningful learning and teaching. This chapter now uses Wenger's and Wells' notions of learning community to analyse the interaction with Jade.

Community of Practice

Wenger's (1998) notion sites learning as occurring within observation and participation in the contexts of lived experience that are an integral part of daily human life. In this excerpt, Jade reveals that she has watched a baby being bathed, representing and practising this in the kindergarten setting, and participated in gardening activities. Knowledge in a community of practice is viewed as competence in culturally valued activities. In this excerpt, this includes becoming literate, learning parenting skills in order to be a good citizen, and learning to dance.

Four key elements are present in this concept of learning: meaning, practice, community and identity. They can be defined as follows:

- meaning—experiencing the world and engaging with it creates meaning; learning takes place by talking about those experiences
- practice—learning and talking about shared historical and social activities that are meaningful
- community—a recognition that participation in activities is worth pursuing and results in competence
- identity—a social view of learning has an effect on personal identity within the context of communities participated in.

The four elements are "deeply interconnected and mutually defining" (Wenger, 1998, p. 5). Through negotiating meaning, a community member constructs an identity and sense of belonging in relation to the values and goals of the communities. The elements are all clearly present in the dialogue about bathing babies, learning about daffodils, and participating in dancing and ballet activities.

The community of practice conceptual framework can be viewed as an apprenticeship model as established community members induct others into the ways of the community. This is evident in the way that I ask the children about the equipment they need to bath a baby and query the doll's safety when it slips out of the bath. I am focused on their competence in future parenting skills. It is also evident by Jade wanting to practise the bathing again, understanding that this is necessary if a baby gets dirty. However, such an approach could then also be interpreted as adults asking questions to which children already know the answers, thereby not tapping into children's real interests and inquiries.

In relation to the central focus of this chapter, theorizing pedagogical relationships that arise from teachers working with children's interests and inquiries, a flaw therefore emerges with a community of practice interpretation. The model does not clearly describe how knowledge or assumptions are extended on the initiative of the learner, nor how understandings are challenged and new learning and understandings are co-constructed. For example, in this interaction, the child indicates that she knows the doll is a symbol and challenges me about the doll being not real when it is dropped out of the bath, and we share genuine questions about how long daffodils last in the garden. Further, an emphasis on participation rather than a combination of observation and participation may be critical for young children, as evidenced in the child's lack of interest in attending ballet classes as a result of passively viewing a ballet production at the age of two. While this child is a confident and competent communicator, able to challenge an adult's dialogue, other children may not be so self-assured. Adults may therefore need a different approach to draw out and extend children's understandings. This chapter now, therefore, moves to an alternative conceptual framework in an effort to explain pedagogical relationships.

Community of Inquiry

Human beings appear intrinsically motivated to inquire and to obtain the help of others to go beyond their present understanding. They actively construct and reconstruct knowledge in those pedagogical interactions, intent on understanding the world and their place in it (Lindfors, 1999). Infants, toddlers, and young children observe and talk about things that interest them and try to increase their understanding about them during conversations and interactions with others. This inquiry may be spontaneous and unplanned, and commonly arises out of children taking an interest in everyday experiences and activities in families and communities. Consequently, learning is focused and given meaning by the social and cultural contexts in which it occurs. The disposition to inquire has been linked to the notion of building curriculum on children's interests in learning stories (Carr, 2001a). In learning stories, the notions of inquiry and "taking an interest" are linked to the strand of "well-being" in Te Whariki.

To take a step further and acknowledge the importance of pedagogical relationships in empowering curriculum experiences and children's interests-based learning would be to highlight the integral nature of "learning-and-teaching" (Wells, 2002), a hyphenated term Wells introduces. The term is also consistent with Te Whariki's central metaphor of weaving learning and teaching experiences to form curriculum, and parallels with the Maori term "ako" are also evident, in considering learning and teaching as both a continuum and a concept that operationalizes the knowledge and strengths of teachers and learners. Writing learning-and-teaching stories would also be consistent with the notion of "distributed assessment" (Cowie & Carr, 2004; see also Simmons, Schimanski, McGarva, Cullen, & Haworth, 2005) and acknowledge the centrality of teachers in many of the learning story exemplars (Ministry of Education, 2004).

The concept of a community of inquiry (Wells, 1999, 2001a) arose from researchers observing the importance of children's "real questions" (Wells, 1999, p. 91) and ways in which these questions were responded to by teachers in determining meaningful learning. Acknowledging the cognitive elements of participation is something that Edwards (2005) suggests requires greater acknowledgement in relation to learning within a community.

In this excerpt, the dialogue that the child initiates and the child's questions are the critical leads to the learning and thinking that occurs. Here, the child has returned to earlier learning, understandings, participation, and experience about feeding and bathing babies, growing daffodils, ballet, and dancing. Her growing understandings occur not only through her participation and engagement, but through the inquiry she demonstrates by building on previous knowledge and experiences. Further, when she returns to give the doll another bath, she indicates a lack of interest in learning ballet. Showing an interest in her understandings, the question I ask about the difference between ballet and dancing leads to dialogue that has several concurrent conversations. These indicate her interest and inquiry in several areas of activities she participates in. Engaging with Wells' ideas appears to be fruitful for a focus on children's interests and inquiry.

Wells (2001b) claims that dialogue is "the discourse of knowledge building" (p. 185). While Wells states that knowledge building also takes place through the written mode, the primacy of dialogue between people is fundamental to the concept of inquiry. This claim is consistent with the notion of socially-constructed learning and the importance of reciprocal and responsive relationships highlighted in Te Whariki. Both need emphasis in order to create and sustain dialogue in a community of inquiry. A relationship approach to pedagogy consistent with a sociocultural perspective supports that inquiry learning and co-constructing knowledge are processes of meaning-making (Dahlberg et al., 1999; Dahlberg and Moss, 2005) or negotiating meaning (Wenger, 1998) through intelligent and informed interactions.

Wells' (1999, 2001a) community of inquiry approach suggests teachers and learners explore together issues to which there are no predetermined answers or outcomes. This resonates with a curriculum that emerges from children's interests, which are likely to be broad and varied as the interaction between Jade and myself illustrates. A further implication might be that co-construction (Valsiner, 1993, 2000) may be a promising pedagogical approach within an early childhood community of inquiry (see also Jordan, 2004).

CHALLENGES FOR TEACHERS

Participation in a Community of Inquiry

The models of community of learners, community of practice, and community of inquiry acknowledge the sociocultural origins of knowledge and allow for the flexible and changing agency of participants within the learning and teaching processes. Of these models, the community of inquiry is suggested as being most consistent with the sociocultural view of children as capable and competent. It highlights the role of children's interests and inquiry, encourages teachers to build on children's prior knowledge, and emphasizes both the central role of language as a cultural tool in dialogic inquiry and the intersubjective nature of the reciprocal and responsive relationships highlighted in early childhood pedagogy. Such a model, coupled with a multi-faceted and complex interpretation of the principles of Te Whariki, generates challenges to teachers to provide a curriculum that empowers infants, toddlers, and young children. An empowering curriculum involves relationships, holistic development, and family and community.

An Empowering Curriculum

Young children are likely to have a wide range of interests and inquiries but, because of their age, relatively limited experience and cognitive abilities compared to adults. Therefore a sociocultural approach to curriculum places emphasis on the quality of pedagogical relationships that encourage and extend those interests and inquiries. Firstly, spending time in sustained interactions using active listening and wait time (Walsh & Sattes, 2005) with children can establish their prior knowledge and support their interests. A teacher's role becomes that of listening carefully to children, supporting, extending, and challenging their ideas and thoughts. Teachers may need to look at ways to manage their roles and daily routines to enable such pedagogical interactions to occur.

Assessment in a sociocultural paradigm is dynamic and distributed; that is, children are observed in the process of interacting with people, places, and things over time (Carr, 2001a; Cowie & Carr, 2004; Hatherly & Richardson, 2007). It is not about measuring achievement but about processes of learning, development of dispositions for learning, and co-constructed understandings that empower children and enable them to develop and learn in a holistic manner. Assessment therefore occurs within authentic meaningful experiences and leads to purposeful documentation of children's learning.

Te Whariki's advice to teachers to follow children's interests to create planned and evolving curriculum encourages teachers to regard planning as being responsive to the "here and now" of children's interests and experiences, not just as a future-oriented exercise. Moreover, the boundaries between "planned" and "spontaneous" curriculum become blurred and overlapping rather than polarized. To provide an empowering and responsive curriculum requires teachers to relinquish control of curriculum direction and empower children to lead curriculum (Hill, 2001) and negotiate and co-construct curriculum (Dahlberg & Moss, 2005; Fleet & Robertson, 2004).

Furthermore, partnership with families in children's learning is a strong driver in the philosophy and practice of early childhood education. Yet, a body of literature suggests that implementing partnerships with parents can be problematic and requires maturity coupled with specialist skills and knowledge (see Hedges & Gibbs, 2005). In order to genuinely involve families and communities in children's learning, teachers need to develop authentic ways to get to know children and families besides informal dialogue in the education centre setting and sharing assessment portfolios. Other ways include home visits (see Hensley, 2005) or evening events at the centre that teachers use as an opportunity to focus on families. Another suggestion might be children taking photographs of family and community events to bring to the centre (Feiler, Greenhough, Winter, Salway, & Scanlan, 2006; see also Meade, 2006).

CONCLUSION

Transformation. That is the chief purpose of education—that all who are involved should transform their capacities to act, think, and feel in ways that contribute to the common good and enrich their own individual lives. (Wells, 2001a, p. 1)

As noted earlier, what children learn during early childhood curriculum experiences has been investigated and theorized and linked to outcomes such as literacy and numeracy. The pedagogical relationships that promote these outcomes, and the outcomes of the pedagogical relationships themselves have been investigated less thoroughly. The importance of dialogue and children's real questions in pedagogical interactions points to the usefulness of a community of inquiry as a theoretical framework that may explain aspects of children's interests, as a framework to theorize pedagogical relationships, and as a way to explore these consistent with other sociocultural notions such as intersubjectivity, funds of knowledge, and working theories.

In relation to outcomes, the process outcomes of learning during pedagogical relationships between teachers and children in early childhood education may also be consistent with sociocultural perspectives including funds of knowledge, working theories, and dispositions. These enable children (and teachers) to become empowered as learners, transform their thinking and actions, constructing identities and a sense of belonging in relation to the values and goals of the communities in which they participate. Such ideas about outcomes, coupled with the spontaneous and intuitive approaches to pedagogy in early childhood education, provoke teachers to think differently about pedagogical techniques and approaches to assessment and planning for young children's interests and inquiry-focused learning.

REFERENCES

Carr, M. (2001a). *Assessment in early childhood settings: Learning stories.* London: Paul Chapman.

Carr, M. (2001b). A sociocultural approach to learning orientation in an early childhood setting. *International Journal of Qualitative Studies, 14*(4), 525–542.

Carr, M., & Claxton, G. (2002). Tracking the development of learning dispositions. *Assessment in Education, 9*(1), 9–37.

Claxton, G. (1990). *Teaching to learn: A direction for education.* London: Cassell Educational.

Claxton, G., & Carr, M. (2004). A framework for teaching learning: The dynamics of disposition. *Early Years, 24*(1), 87–97.

Cowie, B., & Carr, M. (2004). The consequences of socio-cultural assessment. In A. Anning, J. Cullen, & M. Fleer (Eds.), *Early childhood education: Society and culture* (pp. 95–106). London: Sage.

Dahlberg, G., & Moss, P. (2005). *Ethics and politics in early childhood education.* London: Routledge Falmer.

Dahlberg, G., Moss, P., & Pence, A. (1999). *Beyond quality in early childhood education and care: Postmodern perspectives.* London: Falmer Press.

Edwards, A. (2005). Let's get beyond community and practice: The many meanings of learning by participating. *The Curriculum Journal, 16*(1), 49–65.

Feiler, A., Greenhough, P., & Winter, J., with Salway, L., & Scanlan, M. (2006). Getting engaged: Possibilities and problems for home-school knowledge exchange. *Educational Review, 58*(4), 451–469.

Fleet, A., & Robertson, J. (2004). *Overlooked curriculum: Seeing everyday possibilities.* Watson, ACT, Australia: Goanna Print.

González, N., Moll, L. C., & Amanti, C. (Eds.). (2005). *Funds of knowledge: Theorizing practices in households, communities and classrooms.* Mahwah, NJ: Lawrence Erlbaum.

Grundy, S. (1994). The curriculum and teaching. In E. Hatton (Ed.), *Understanding teaching: Curriculum and the social context of schooling* (pp. 27–39). Marrickville, NSW, Australia: Harcourt Brace & Co.

Hatherly, A., & Richardson, C. (2007). Making connections—assessment and evaluation revisited. In L. Keesing-Styles & H. Hedges (Eds.), *Theorising early childhood practice: Emerging dialogues* (pp. 51–70). Castle Hill, NSW, Australia: Pademelon Press.

Hedges, H. (2007). *Funds of knowledge in early childhood communities of inquiry.* Unpublished doctoral thesis, Massey University, Palmerston North, New Zealand.

Hedges, H. (2004). A whale of an interest in sea creatures: The learning potential of excursions. *Early Childhood Research and Practice 6*(1). Retrieved June 21, 2004 from http://www.ecrp.uiuc.edu/v6n1/hedges.html

Hedges, H. (2003). Avoiding "magical" thinking in children: The case for teachers' science subject knowledge. *Early Childhood Folio, 7,* 2–7.

Hedges, H. (2002a). *Subject content knowledge in early childhood curriculum and pedagogy.* Unpublished master's thesis, Massey University, Palmerston North, New Zealand.

Hedges, H. (2002b). Beliefs and principles in practice: Ethical research with child participants. *New Zealand Research in Early Childhood Education, 5,* 31–47.

Hedges, H., & Cullen, J. (2005). Subject knowledge in early childhood curriculum and pedagogy: Beliefs and practices. *Contemporary Issues in Early Childhood 6*(1), 66–79.

Hedges, H., & Gibbs, C. J. (2005). Preparation for teacher-parent partnerships: A practical experience with a family. *Journal of Early Childhood Teacher Education, 26*(2), 115–126.

Hensley, M. (2005). Empowering parents of multicultural backgrounds. In N. González, L. C. Moll, & C. Amanti, (Eds.), *Funds of knowledge: Theorizing practices in households, communities and classrooms* (pp. 143–151). Malwah, NJ: Lawrence Erlbaum.

Hill, D. (2001). Passion, power and planning in the early childhood centre. *The First Years: Nga Tau Tuatahi/New Zealand Journal of Infant and Toddler Education, 3*(2), 10–13.

Jordan, B. (2003). *Professional development making a difference for children: Constructing understandings in early childhood centres.* Unpublished doctoral thesis, Massey University, Palmerston North, New Zealand.

Jordan, B. (2004). Scaffolding learning and co-constructing understandings. In A. Anning, J. Cullen, & M. Fleer (Eds.), *Early childhood education: Society and culture* (pp. 31–42). London: Sage.

Lindfors, J. W. (1999). *Children's inquiry: Using language to make sense of the world.* New York: Teachers College Press.

Meade, A. (Ed.). (2006). *Riding the waves: Innovation in early childhood education.* Wellington: New Zealand Council for Educational Research.

Ministry of Education. (1996). *Te Whariki. He whariki matauranga mo nga mokopuna o Aotearoa: Early childhood curriculum.* Wellington, New Zealand: Learning Media.

Ministry of Education. (2004). *Kei tua o te pae: Assessment for learning exemplars.* Wellington, New Zealand: Learning Media.

Moll, L. (2000). Inspired by Vygotsky: Ethnographic experiments in education. In C. D. Lee & P. Smagorinsky (Eds.), *Vygotskian perspectives on literacy research: Constructing meaning through collaborative inquiry* (pp. 256–268). Cambridge: Cambridge University Press.

Moll, L., Amanti, C., Neff, D., & Gonzalez, N. (1992). Funds of knowledge for teaching: Using a qualitative approach to connect homes and classrooms. *Theory into Practice, 31*(2), 132–141.

Riojas-Cortez, M. (2001). Preschoolers' funds of knowledge displayed through sociodramatic play episodes in a bilingual classroom. *Early Childhood Education Journal, 29*(1), 35–40.

Rogoff, B. (1998). Cognition as a collaborative process. In D. Kuhn & R. Siegler (Eds.), *Handbook of child psychology (5th ed.), Vol. 2, Cognition, perception and language* (pp. 679–744). New York: John Wiley.

Rogoff, B. (2003). *The cultural nature of human development.* New York: Oxford University Press.

Rogoff, B., Matusov, E., & White, C. (1996). Models of teaching and learning: Participation in a community of learners. In D. Olson & N. Torrance (Eds.), *The handbook of education and human development: New models of learning, teaching and schooling* (pp. 388–414). Cambridge, MA: Blackwell Publishers.

Sammons, P., Elliott, K., Sylva, K., Melhuish, E., Siraj-Blatchford, I., & Taggart, B. (2004). The impact of pre-school on young children's cognitive attainments at entry to reception. *British Educational Research Journal, 30*(5), 691–712.

Simmons, H., Schimanski, L, McGarva, P., Cullen, J., & Haworth, P. (2005). Teachers researching young children's working theories. *Early Childhood Folio, 8*, 18–22. Wellington: New Zealand Council for Educational Research.

Siraj-Blatchford, I. (2004). Quality teaching in the early years. In A. Anning, J. Cullen, & M. Fleer (Eds.), *Early childhood education: society and culture* (pp. 137–148). London: Sage.

Siraj-Blatchford, I., & Sylva, K. (2004). Researching pedagogy in English pre-schools. *British Educational Research Journal, 30*(5), 713–730.

Siraj-Blatchford, I., Sylva, K., Muttock, S., Gilden, R., & Bell, D. (2002). *Researching effective pedagogy in the early years.* Retrieved June 18, 2003 from http://www.dfes.gov.uk/research/data/uploadfiles/RR356.pdf.

Valsiner, J. (1993). Culture and human development: A co-constructivist perspective. *Annals of theoretical psychology, 10*, 247–298.

Valsiner, J. (2000). *Culture and human development: An introduction.* London: Sage.

Vygotsky, L. S. (1978). *Mind in society: The development of higher psychological processes.* Cambridge, MA: Harvard University Press.

Vygotsky, L. S. (1986). *Thought and language.* Cambridge, MA: MIT Press.

Walsh, J. A., & Sattes, B. D. (2005). *Quality questioning: Research-based practice to engage every learner.* Thousand Oaks, CA: Corwin Press.

Wells, G. (1999). *Dialogic inquiry: Towards a sociocultural practice and theory of education.* New York : Cambridge University Press.

Wells, G. (2001a). The development of a community of inquirers. In G. Wells (Ed.) *Action talk and text: Learning and teaching through inquiry* (pp. 1–22). New York: Teachers College Press.

Wells, G. (2001b). The case for dialogic inquiry. In G. Wells (Ed.) *Action talk and text: Learning and teaching through inquiry* (pp. 171–194). New York: Teachers College Press.

Wells, G. (2002). Inquiry as an orientation for learning, teaching and teacher education. In G. Wells & G. Claxton (Eds.), *Learning for life in the 21st century* (pp. 197–210). Oxford: Blackwell.

Wenger, E. (1998). *Communities of practice: Learning, meaning, and identity.* Cambridge, UK: Cambridge University Press.

AUTHOR NOTE

Helen Hedges is a Senior Lecturer in the Faculty of Education, University of Auckland, New Zealand. Her research and teaching interests involve early childhood curriculum and pedagogy and teachers' professional learning.

The author wishes to thank the supervisors of the project, Joy Cullen and Jenny Boyack. Acknowledgement is made to Massey University College of Education for providing funding for the field work of the study.

An earlier extended version of this chapter was presented as part of a New Zealand symposium entitled "Young children experiencing an empowering early childhood curriculum" at the European Early Childhood Education Research Association conference, Dublin, September 1, 2005.

Correspondence concerning this chapter should be addressed by email to: h.hedges@auckland.ac.nz

In: Challenging Thinking about Teaching and Learning   ISBN: 978-1-60456-744-1
Editors: C. M. Rubie-Davies and C. Rawlinson   © 2008 Nova Science Publishers, Inc.

Chapter 26

QUESTIONING FOR HIGHER ORDER THINKING

Annaline Flint

ABSTRACT

This review of the literature highlights that effective questioning is an art, and reflects the competence of the teacher. Research has shown that most of the questions teachers pose in the classroom are of a managerial nature or are concerned with the recall of factual information. Such questioning is mostly ineffective and can turn students off learning. To make the transition from a transmission mode of delivering information to one that promotes the development of students' creative, critical, and analytical thinking and understanding, teachers need to consciously plan, structure, and implement questions that will provoke higher order thinking. Giving students appropriate wait time to reflect on and think critically about the question being asked without the teacher repeating, rephrasing, or answering it him- or herself will result in improved classroom interactions, more trusting student–teacher relationships and an atmosphere that is conducive to more effective questioning and higher order thinking.

INTRODUCTION

The way a teacher is able to relate to his or her students in a caring and respectful manner is viewed by many as one of the highest ranked characteristics of an outstanding teacher. Paramount to achieving this is the teacher's ability to ask good questions, give appropriate feedback to responses, and to genuinely listen to students. Effective questioning is therefore an art and reflects the competence of the teacher (Carin & Sund, 1971; Morgan & Saxton, 1991; Sanders, 1996).

Research into the use of verbal questioning by Anderson and Burns, 1989; Dantonio, 1990; Graesser and Person, 1994; and Seymour and Osana, 2003 has shown that although teachers verbally ask up to 400 questions a day, presumably with the intention of facilitating the learning process, this skill is not as effective as it could be, and if done incorrectly can turn children off learning (as cited in Vogler, 2005). Since questioning is so pervasive in everyday classroom practice and is most often the means through which deeper thinking is provoked, it is imperative that this aspect of teaching is enhanced and improved in order to achieve the best possible outcomes for students' learning and understanding (Vogler, 2005; Wilen 1991). Hence there is a need to investigate how questions can be planned, structured, and used to provoke higher order thinking in students. This chapter provides a literature review that focuses on four aspects of questioning—the purpose and importance of questioning; the planning, formulation, and use of questions; questioning that provokes higher order thinking; and wait time.

THE PURPOSE AND IMPORTANCE OF QUESTIONING

Many students are reluctant to answer questions or engage in discussion that involves higher order thinking. Barriers such as differences in age, ethnicity, educational opportunities, and personal experiences can affect the confidence with which students interact with each other and with the teacher. Traditional beliefs and attitudes about the role of students in the classroom as passive receivers of information, rather than active participators in discussions and problem solving, is another barrier to achieving higher order cognitive thinking.

Effective use of questioning in teaching is a vital ingredient for fostering good student–teacher interactions, enhancing critical thinking and reasoning, developing student understandings, and thereby promoting student achievement (Mawhinney & Sagan, 2007). In the opinion of Zohar, Degani, and Vaaknin (2001), conditions have to be right before teaching for understanding and higher order thinking can be successful. The importance of effective interactions and interrelations between teacher and student in order to foster self-concept, self-confidence, and self-esteem and to encourage active participation, is well recognized, and, as argued by Mawhinney and Sagan (2007), "higher-level thinking is more likely to occur in the brain of a student who is emotionally secure than in the brain of a student who is scared, upset, anxious, or stressed" (p. 461). The teacher's ability to select and use appropriate questioning techniques and responses are paramount to achieving this. Questions can be used to probe students' thinking and gradually develop their confidence to the point where the teacher can be quite sure that the student will give an appropriate response (Marsh, 1998).

Questioning can be used for the purpose of assessing what students know, as a teaching strategy to encourage students to think more deeply about issues, or as a combination of both of these (Clarke, Timperley, & Hattie, 2003). Research by Hattie (2003) into how teachers can make a difference suggests that expert teachers are those who are able to improve surface and deep learning, influence students' achievement positively, provide relevant and challenging tasks, use a variety of questions, and listen attentively in order to accurately assess students' understanding.

Several ideas are furnished by Morgan and Saxton (1991) and Marsh (1998) as to why questioning is one of the most popular and important modes of teaching. Questioning gives students the opportunity to be actively involved in lessons, to hear the perspectives of others, to improve their perceptions, to express ideas and thoughts, and to explore issues and solve problems while simultaneously benefiting from hearing a variety of explanations from their peers. It enables practitioners to evaluate how well their students have learnt, to diagnose weaknesses, and to make modifications to their practice. However, these results can only be achieved if much thought, effort, and planning goes into effectively formulating and implementing questions.

PLANNING, FORMULATING, AND USING QUESTIONS

The practitioner should be very clear about the context and purpose of the questioning when formulating and using questions. To be most effective, questions should not only meet curriculum goals, but should begin at a point where students feel comfortable to respond (Zevin, 2000). The purpose for questioning should be closely linked to the learning outcomes or intentions that the practitioner has set for the students to achieve. This implies careful advanced planning and formulating of questions that will direct students towards thinking creatively, critically, and analytically and lead them to the expected outcomes (Absolum, 2006). Alton-Lee (2002) argues that questions should be thoroughly planned to "engage students in sustained discourse structured around powerful ideas" (p. 77). This is endorsed by Wilen (2001), who states that teachers need "to plan key questions for guiding discussions to provide direction and structure, increase engagement, and increase the probability that thinking and understanding become discussion outcomes" (p. 28). Teachers need considerable practise to improve their ability to frame worthwhile questions and which pertain to issues necessary to develop students' understanding (Black, Harrison, Lee, Marshall, & William, 2002).

Suggestions for planning, formulating, and asking questions include the use of "advance organizers" or deliberate methods of building on the existing knowledge and experiences of students (Brualdi, 1998). Important, too, is to choose language appropriate to the level of the students and to direct and distribute questions evenly among students. Teachers need to demonstrate suitable pausing and pacing when posing questions to students; they should listen carefully to the responses of students in order to provide effective reinforcement, recognition, and feedback and should provide prompts and probes to elicit deeper thinking and metacognition (Zohar, 2004).

QUESTIONING THAT PROVOKES HIGHER ORDER THINKING

While the key features of higher order thinking cannot be exactly defined, the skills of higher order thinking can be recognized when they arise (Zohar, 2004). This recognition will be enhanced if teachers have a sound understanding of the various cognitive levels, sequencing, and patterns of questions (Vogler, 2005). Characteristics of higher order thinking include cognitive strategies that go beyond the understanding and lower level applications described in the many models or taxonomies which categorize or classify questions. These models or taxonomies describe high-level cognitive questions as those that require complex applications such as thinking critically by reflecting on assumptions underlying actions and considering new ways of looking at and living in the world; analyzing, synthesizing, and evaluating issues; and being able to problem solve (Brualdi, 1998; Morgan and Saxon, 1991). Two models are referred to by Zevin (2000) as closely corresponding with three dimensions of education; namely, the didactic, the reflective, and the affective domains.

The first model that Zevin (2000) cites is Benjamin Bloom's original *Taxonomy of Educational Objectives: Cognitive Domain*, which categorizes cognitive processing by level and is graduated from knowledge or recall at the lowest level through to evaluation at the highest level. In a revised version of Bloom's taxonomy (Anderson & Krathwohl, 2001), limitations in the original taxonomy have been addressed by changing the order of the cognitive processes and featuring a knowledge facts component (Brown, Irving, & Keegan, 2007).

The second model cited by Zevin, J. B. Guilford's *The Structure of Intellect*, categorizes cognitive processing by type and distinguishes between convergent and divergent type thinking (Zevin, 2000). Although both Bloom and Guilford rate memory skills as having lower level difficulty, and skills involving creativity and judgement as being more complex, there are limitations to this categorization because this can vary according to the context in which it is used (Zevin, 2000).

An alternative taxonomy, which Brown et al. (2007) claim resolves such deficiencies, is the Structure of Observed Learning Outcomes (SOLO) taxonomy developed by Biggs and Collis in the 1970s and 1980s. This true hierarchical model involves a five-stage classification system which describes the increasing complexity in a student's understanding and level of abstraction when mastering a task. The SOLO taxonomy enables teachers to vary the level of cognitive challenge provided through questioning and to scaffold students into higher order thinking and metacognition (Chan, Tsui, Chan, & Hong, 2002; Collis & Biggs, 1989; Hattie & Brown, 2004).

While teachers purport that they ask questions which encourage students to engage in higher levels of application, research has shown that very few higher order questions are, in fact, asked and that most questions are to do with the recall of factual information or are managerial in nature (Brualdi, 1998; Wragg & Brown, 2001). Certainly it is necessary to recognize the value and importance of lower level cognitive questions. Wilen (2001) maintains that if students do not possess essential basic knowledge, they do not have anything on which to base and support their views, and their discussions will be unreflective and meaningless. Alton-Lee (2002) believes that higher order questions could sometimes confuse students, particularly if they do not bring the cultural capital of the institution to the activities, and that low level or factual questions are needed to scaffold them to achieve higher order thinking. However, higher level questions are essential for the development of the skills needed by students to be able to solve problems and make decisions; therefore teachers need to make it an important and essential goal to develop students' higher order thinking skills. Teachers should strive to have a good balance of low level and higher level cognitive questions which allow students to move according to their needs from levels at which they feel comfortable, towards increasingly deeper and more complex higher order thinking, understanding, and achievement (Brualdi, 1998).

Zohar (2004) suggests four ways in which teachers can "make the transition from traditional instruction that centres on transmission of information to instruction that sees the development of students' higher-order thinking" (p. 95). First, teachers themselves need to have a variety of thinking skills that they can use on the procedural level and the metacognitive level—the former to solve problems and complete tasks, the latter to articulate and make generalizations about their own thinking processes and describe how, when, and for what purpose they would use these processes. Secondly, teachers need to employ teaching strategies that ensure that students are regularly presented with tasks that require them to use thinking skills. Thirdly, teachers must be able to identify those students who experience difficulty with reasoning and find ways to help and support them, especially low achieving students. There is a belief among some teachers that it is not appropriate for low achieving students to engage in higher order thinking (Zohar et al., 2001). However, Zohar and his colleagues have argued that low achieving students can engage in and benefit from higher order thinking strategies with the necessary support (Zohar et al., 2001). Lastly, teachers have to relinquish the traditional role of being transmitters of knowledge, and embrace being facilitators of student inquiry and problem solving (Zohar, 2004). Part of this role is allowing students ample opportunity and time to deliberate, think critically, and reason before having to answer questions.

WAIT TIME

"Wait time", or "thinking time" as it is sometimes referred to, is a term that is generally understood to mean the time the practitioner waits after a question has been asked. As argued by Dillon, "Silence is a deliberate act by the teacher that encourages thought and response" (as cited in Morgan & Saxon, 1991, p. 82). This sentiment is supported by Zevin (2000), who states that "waiting creates an atmosphere in which contemplation is encouraged and expected" (p. 77). Teachers, on average, allow only one to two seconds of wait time whereas research has shown that at least three to five seconds is the optimum time needed for students to make sense of the question and to process and use the knowledge they have to formulate an answer before responding (Morgan & Saxon, 1991). Often teachers repeat or rephrase their questions, answer the questions themselves, pose another question, or ask a different student to answer. If this becomes the norm, it has been found that students deliberately do not answer questions because they know that the teacher will either provide the answer or ask another question if they wait long enough to answer (Atwood & Wilen, 1991; Clarke et al., 2003).

There are many advantages for both teacher and student when a teacher is able to wait patiently and for a suitable amount of time for students to answer questions: classroom interaction improves, the student–teacher relationship of trust becomes stronger, students have time to consider their responses from different perspectives, teachers ask more varied quality questions, and the atmosphere in the classroom becomes more conducive to more effective questions and higher order thinking. Conversely, too much wait time can have an adverse effect on students and can be perceived as a punishment. The amount of wait time is dependent on factors such as the type and level of question being asked, the students' familiarity with the content, existing knowledge, and ability to answer questions (Carin & Sund, 1971; Morgan & Saxon, 1991; Stahl, 1994). While recall questions can be asked at a faster pace, deeper and more complex questions require longer pauses and sometimes wait time can even be extended from one lesson to the next, thus allowing students to think about their responses for a longer period of time.

CONCLUSION

The notion of effectively using appropriate questioning as a means for provoking higher order thinking in students is something that most, if not all, teachers aspire to. Research has shown that effective interactions and relationships between teacher and students are needed for conditions to be right and for students to feel emotionally secure before teaching for understanding and higher order thinking can be successful (Mawhinney & Sagan, 2007; Zohar et al., 2001).

If teachers are to make the transition from a transmission mode of delivering information to one that promotes the development of students' thinking and understanding, they themselves need to have developed cognitive skills and strategies to engage students in challenging tasks which require them to exercise thinking skills (Hattie, 2003; Zohar, 2004). Careful planning of worthwhile questions by the teacher in order to guide or direct students towards creative, critical and analytical thinking and lead them to the expected outcomes, is therefore vital (Absolum, 2006; Alton-Lee, 2002; Black et al., 2002; Wilen, 2001).

Allowing students the opportunity and the appropriate length of wait time to reflect on and think critically about the question being asked without repeating or rephrasing or even answering it themselves, is a skill that teachers need to master. Teachers who are successful in this will notice improved classroom interactions, more trusting student-teacher relationships, and an atmosphere which is conducive to more effective questioning and higher order thinking (Carin & Sund, 1971; Morgan & Saxon, 1991).

REFERENCES

Absolum, M. (2006). *Clarity in the classroom: Using formative assessment. Building learning-focused relationships.* Auckland, New Zealand: Hodder Education.

Alton-Lee, A. (2003). *Quality teaching for diverse students in schooling: Best evidence synthesis.* Wellington, New Zealand: Ministry of Education.

Atwood, V., & Wilen, W. (1991, March). Wait time and effective social studies instruction: What can research in science education tell us? *Social Education, 55*, 179–181.

Black, P., Harrison, C., Lee, C., Marshall, B., & William, D. (2002). *Working inside the black box: Assessment for learning in the classroom.* London: King's College London, School of Education.

Brown, G., Irving, S., & Keegan, P. (2007). *An introduction to educational assessment, measurement and evaluation: Improving the quality of teacher-based assessment.* Auckland, New Zealand: Pearson Education.

Brualdi, A. C. (1998). Classroom questions. *Practical Assessment, Research and Evaluation, 6*(6). Retrieved October 1, 2007 from http://PAREonline.net/getvn.asp?v=6andn=6

Carin, A., & Sund, R. B. (1971). *Developing questioning techniques: A self-concept approach.* OH: Merrill Publishing Company.

Chan, C., Tsui, M. S., Chan, M. Y., & Hong, J. H. (2002). Applying the structure of the observed learning outcomes (SOLO) taxonomy on student's learning outcomes: an empirical study. *Assessment and Evaluation in Higher Education, 27*(6), 511–527.

Clarke, S., Timperley, H., & Hattie, J. (2003). *Unlocking formative assessment: Practical strategies for enhancing students' learning in the primary and intermediate classroom.* Auckland, New Zealand: Hodder Moa Beckett.

Collis, K., & Biggs, J. (1986). Using the SOLO taxonomy. *SET (2),* Item 4.

Hattie, J. (2003, October). *Teachers make a difference: What is the research evidence?* Paper presented at the Australian Council of Educational Research Annual Conference on Building Teacher Quality, Melbourne, Australia.

Hattie, J., & Brown, G. (2004). *Cognitive processes in asTTle: The SOLO taxonomy.* asTTle Technical Report No. 43, University of Auckland/Ministry of Education.

Marsh, C. (1998). *Teaching studies of society and environment,* (2nd ed.). Sydney, Australia: Prentice Hall.

Mawhinney, T., and Sagan, L. (2007). The power of personal relationships. *Phi Delta Kappan. 88*(6) 460–464.

Morgan, N., and Saxon, J. (1991). *Teaching, questioning and learning.* London: Routledge.

Sanders, N. (1996). *Classroom Questions: What kinds?* New York: Harper & Row.

Stahl, R. J. (1994). Using "think-time" and "waiting time" skilfully in the classroom. *ERIC Digest*, ED370885 1994-05-00.

Vogler, K. (2005 Nov/Dec). Improve your verbal questioning. *The Clearing House, 79*(2) 98–103. ProQuest Education Journals.

Wilen, W. (1991). *Questioning skills, for teachers: What research says to the teacher,* (3rd. ed.). West Haven, CT: NEA Professional Library.

Wilen, W. (2001, Jan/Feb). Exploring myths about teacher questioning in the social studies classroom. *Social Studies, 92*(1), 26–34.

Wragg, E. C., & Brown, G. (2001). *Questioning in the primary school.* London: Routledge Falmer.

Zevin, J. (2000). S*ocial studies for the twenty-first century: Methods and materials for teaching in the middle and secondary schools (2nd ed.).* New York: Lawrence Erlbaum.

Zohar, A. (2004). *Higher order thinking in science classrooms: Students' learning and teachers' professional development.* London: Kluwer Academic Publishers.

Zohar, A., Degani, A., & Vaaknin, E. (2001). Teachers' beliefs about low-achieving students and higher order thinking. *Teacher and Teacher Education, 17,* 469–485.

AUTHOR NOTE

Annaline Flint is a Lecturer in the Faculty of Education, University of Auckland, New Zealand.

Correspondence concerning this chapter should be addressed by email to: a.flint@auckland.ac.nz

In: Challenging Thinking about Teaching and Learning   ISBN: 978-1-60456-744-1
Editors: C. M. Rubie-Davies and C. Rawlinson   © 2008 Nova Science Publishers, Inc.

Chapter 27

INQUIRY-BASED PROFESSIONAL DEVELOPMENT: THE PRACTICE OF STUDYING ONESELF IN PRACTICE

Deidre M. Le Fevre

ABSTRACT

This case study examines the experiences and learning of two teacher participants who used video records of their own practice as a tool for studying learning and teaching within a larger inquiry-based professional development community. The two teachers in the study became more informed regarding the experiences and understandings of students in their classrooms. They perceived that this more in-depth understanding of their students informed them in their subsequent pedagogical decision making. Key processes identified in this inquiry approach to professional development include: making practice accessible for teachers to examine, grounding talk about practice, and teachers' gaining new perspectives on their own classroom learning and teaching. Implications regarding the facilitation of this professional development work include the importance of balancing a safe yet challenging learning environment for professional development.

INTRODUCTION

This study examines an approach to professional development in which teachers view and discuss video records of their own classrooms. It examines how teachers investigate their practices of learning and teaching and what this affords them in terms of future classroom practice. This work represents an inquiry stance (Cochrane-Smith & Lytle, 1999) for teacher professional development. Inquiry-based professional development locates the construction of knowledge about teaching in the classroom and in the life of the teacher, thus enabling teachers to address issues that they themselves identify as significant (Cochran-Smith & Lytle, 1999; Hammerness et al., 2005). It does not come without challenges, however; for example, identifying a significant and appropriate focus for inquiry can be difficult for teachers (Nelson & Slavit, 2007). Theoretically, inquiry is effective when teachers make meaning out of their own questions that are situated in learning and teaching. In practice, however, inquiry can result in teachers investigating ideas that are not necessarily central or significant. The facilitator of such inquiry-based professional development then faces the agenda-setting dilemma—that is, the tension between allowing teachers to set their own focus for inquiry and influencing the focus of inquiry as the facilitator (Le Fevre & Richardson, 2002). Keeping in mind these challenges, the intention of inquiry-based professional development is for teachers to be active investigators of their own practice, setting their own agendas for investigation based on problems of practice that are of immediate concern to them as practitioners (Borko, 2004).

VIDEO AS A TOOL FOR INQUIRY-BASED PROFESSIONAL DEVELOPMENT

Inquiry that is grounded in data representing actual classroom practice is a crucial element in successful inquiry-based professional development, and video recordings of classrooms are a key source of such data. Several different types of video have been used in teacher professional development; however this study focuses on the use of video records of practice—in other words, unscripted, unedited video recordings of a teacher's own classroom practice as a source of data for inquiry (Le Fevre, 2004a; Sherin & Han, 2004). A unique characteristic of video records of practice is their potential to enable teachers to see themselves in action, thus making their practice accessible to themselves (Louden, Wallace, & Groves, 2001; Rosebery & Warren, 1998). The video camera can capture and reveal aspects of classroom life that a teacher does not have the opportunity to notice in the midst of teaching (DiSchino, 1998; Jaworski, 1989; Le Fevre, 2004a; Le Fevre, 2004b). The purpose of using video in the professional development initiative studied here is not to provide an image of exemplary practice—in other words, a model for teachers to approximate as a desired form of pedagogy—but rather to provide a medium through which teachers can investigate their own knowledge, beliefs, practices, and questions about classroom practice. This use of video as a tool for inquiry-based learning is not typical. Video is often used as an exemplar of practice with the intention of having viewers understand a particular point of view, resource, curriculum, or pedagogy. The content of such video is typically edited and includes voice-over narration. Video records of one's own practice, on the other hand, are raw, unedited short clips of actual classroom practice. The use of video records of one's own practice in this way has sometimes been referred to as video clubs (see, for example, Sherin & Han, 2004; Sherin & van Es, 2005, Tochon, 1999). In examining the use of video records of practice, it is critical to consider the supporting pedagogy in which it is embedded, the nature of knowledge that teachers gain, how this relates to their practice, and future implications for professional development.

THE CURRENT STUDY

The focus of interest is what happens when teachers view video clips of their own practice in an ongoing collaborative professional development community and how this informs future practice.

The Professional Development Context

The inquiry-based professional learning community discussed in this chapter was part of a larger professional development programme aimed at improving outcomes in science and mathematics for students from diverse ethnic and cultural backgrounds. The overall programme was intensive (25 teachers and 3 professional development facilitators), lasted for three years, and comprised biweekly two-hour sessions and an annual week-long summer seminar. The current study was undertaken from the tenth month of the first year to the end of the third year, and focused on a specific aspect of the larger programme; that is, on an inquiry-based video-sharing group. The video-sharing group comprised eight primary teachers and one professional development facilitator. The group's goal was for ongoing collaboration focused on critically examining practice with a view to improving outcomes for students with diverse needs (Toole & Seashore Louis, 2002), with a specific focus on science and mathematics. The professional learning community met and shared video recordings of their own teaching throughout the second and third years of the overall programme. Participation in the group and the sharing of videos was voluntary and involved the teachers selecting a short segment of their classroom practice (5–8 minutes previously viewed by them) about which they had a question or concern to pose to the group, as a basis for inquiry and discussion. The question was posed before the group viewed the video. In this way, the teacher was responsible for selecting the aspect of their practice that the group would focus on. Teachers might, for example, focus on understanding a particular student's contribution to a discussion, how they as the teacher interpreted that student's contribution, and what they did with the contribution. The group of eight (plus the facilitator) would view the video and discussion would ensue around the question or focus of the teacher whose video has been viewed. This professional learning community had an experienced professional developer who facilitated all video viewing sessions and ensured that there was a high level of resources available. It was based in a large urban area with a diverse student population. The group was selected for this study for the window it might provide into the possible but not necessarily the typical activities and outcomes of an inquiry-based professional learning community

METHODOLOGY

Borko (2004) highlights the importance of examining all key elements of a professional development system; for example, the programme, the teachers who are learners in the system, the facilitators who guide the participants as they construct new knowledge, and the contexts in which the professional development occurs. The researcher in the current study was a non-participant observer in this professional learning community for just over two years and paid attention to all four of the key elements. The case study presented here focused on two teacher participants (Mia and Kim), the context (the video-sharing professional learning community), and the facilitator (Ana). Mia and Kim were primary teachers who were selected randomly from the group of eight teachers. Mia and Kim were studied because of their willingness to have the researcher carry out follow-up interviews and observations in their classrooms. The researcher wrote field notes and collected artefacts (e.g., the videotaped material) during 14 of the video sharing sessions (12 biweekly sessions and two summer sessions over the course of two years). Additional data comprised videotapes and transcripts of 8 sessions that the researcher did not attend. This second set of data consisted of videos of the professional learning community viewing their own video records of practice. This gave data for 22 sessions in total, all of which were analyzed, either from the data obtained from direct researcher observation or from video recordings and transcripts of the other 8 sessions, to understand what teachers do as they view video records of their own practice. The researcher also conducted individual semi-structured interviews with the two teacher participants on three occasions throughout the professional development (six interviews). The purpose of these interviews was to elicit participant perceptions of what they learned through viewing video records of their own practice within the professional development community, and how this informed their subsequent classroom practice. Two classroom observations were also made in both Mia and Kim's classrooms. Five interviews were conducted with the facilitator (throughout the two-year period) to elicit the facilitator's perceptions of the purposes and processes of the inquiry-based video sharing professional learning community. All quotations come from interview data, while description of the events is based on observations, artefacts, and transcripts of video-sharing sessions.

FINDINGS AND DISCUSSION

Teachers engaged in three key processes while viewing and discussing video records of their own classrooms: (a) making practice accessible; (b) grounding the talk about practice; and (c) gaining new perspectives. Findings regarding how these processes informed the teachers' future classroom practice are followed by a discussion of the implications for future professional development initiatives.

Making Practice Accessible

The complexity and pace of teaching and its position within a culture of privacy and isolation often results in teaching that is not readily accessible to observe (Lortie, 1975). The tasks of teaching are often too complex and rapid to register, let alone to access and examine (Hammerness et.al. 2005; Le Fevre, 2004a). Eckart and Gibson (1993) conclude that teachers "are more likely to change their classroom behaviours if they are aware of the need for improvement by observing their own performances" (p. 291). In the current study, Mia discussed the opportunity to see herself and her students in action:

> I get to see what I am doing. What my students are doing . . . or not doing. How am I listening? Who am I looking at? For example there is research about teachers talking to

boys more in mathematics and you don't realize [you do] this until you see a video of your own class.

Kim explained:

> Video enables me to identify greater understanding in the kids' conversation than I realized at the time. . . . It makes me think that I don't listen as well as I might, and so the video allows me to be a better listener when I'm separated from that situation, and it allows me to know that some of my kids know things that I didn't think they did when I finished the lesson.

Video records of practice can enable one to "revisit a moment" in a way that is not otherwise possible. In other words, it can provide an opportunity to witness one's own teaching in action. The video camera can reveal aspects of practice that there is not time to notice in the midst of actual practice. As Ana, the professional development facilitator, observed:

> Video is a way of "stopping time". You don't have the luxury of "stepping back" and saying "OK it's time for reflection now" while in the middle of teaching 30 kids.

It is rare for teachers to have the opportunity to observe colleagues and to share ideas and perceptions. However, as Kim explained, "Video captures the moment so that other people can be in the moment and you can discuss it from a common point".

Grounding the Talk about Practice

Videotape records of practice have the potential to be grounding in the way talk about practice can be embedded in actual practice—rather than talking about practice in an abstract way, participants can identify and describe what they are seeing and hearing and refer to this in their discussion of ideas, and in this way, talk is grounded in actual classroom practice. Ana, the professional development facilitator, explained:

> I've never been very successful at getting people to talk from abstractions to the concrete. . . . I just don't do that any more but just show them the stuff and then generate responses in what is seen. So those kinds of conversations then become very grounded in something substantial if you start with the actual video of practice.

Creating professional development opportunities that are grounded in elements and artefacts of actual classroom practice can promote an inquiry stance that informs future practice (Ball & Cohen, 1999). Ana continued:

> Teachers come saying I want to see how to do something. . . . I don't want to have an abstract conversation about what's going on here you know . . . show me what somebody else does. You know it's a window in on their profession in the way that doctors have in making the rounds or something like that and I personally think it's very valuable for that if set up appropriately.

Kim discussed her experience as a participant:

> For the first time we could really struggle over what they were seeing and we could have real conversations that were grounded by a common point, I mean a common image of practice. I mean it wasn't just talking theory, it was talking about something real and using the evidence from the videotape to talk about and show things.

And Mia said:

> For me it gave real concrete faces that show the complexity, that honour the complexity of teaching and provides a place that we can really go in and study it in a detailed way. There is a visual picture so that you can hang things on it . . . so you can actually go back and say "Where in the video do you see images of kids that look like they are in engaged?" so you can actually get a handle by what they mean by those words.

Video records of practice have potential to function as a shared common experience of practice for teachers. Video can be shared or common to the extent that multiple people can access it, either viewing collaboratively or independently. The "sharedness" refers to the way the same representation of practice can be viewed by several people. It is uncommon to share access to the same teaching in real-life situations. This is in part because of the complicated logistics of having a group of teachers present in the same classroom together. Significant, too, is the effect the presence of such a group might have on the integrity and authenticity of the situation of practice. Video has been critiqued as never being able to promote a shared understanding of practice on the basis that sometimes there is just too much information for viewers to digest and integrate (Seel & Winn, 1997). However, the fact that each person can be expected to see something different, and to make different interpretations as they view from different perspectives, can be an asset for learning teaching. As such, video might be used as a basis for calibrating knowledge and grounding talk about practice. The concept of "calibration" is perhaps key here; the video record of practice can serve as a common referent around which people can talk (Weick, 1995), thus making visible different perspectives and understandings of the observed practice.

Gaining New Perspectives

As Kim and Mia shared video records of their teaching practice with their colleagues, they jointly constructed new understandings and interpretations of their practice. The different lens that individual participants brought to the collective group provided the foundations for "seeing the previously unseeable"—for seeing in new ways and from new perspectives.

Both Mia and Kim spoke of the power of having the perspectives of others when viewing and discussing video records of their own classroom practice. Mia said: "I end up understanding something that has transpired in more depth, this comes from having other peoples' perspectives". Kim also referred to the learning implications of access to other perspectives in saying, "I think that you get blind and you can't see your own style, even if you are looking at it yourself, you can't always see it". Mia also discussed how video helped her to both review and question her perspective and to identify misinterpretations. She said:

> With the video I can hear it and depending on the videographer I can also see things I wouldn't otherwise see. So it gives me a lot of information about what is going on. When you are in front of the class you know you don't see it all, or hear it all, but with video you can see what was going on in the class that you couldn't see at the time. It gives me the opportunity to go back and really find out what happened. It gives me more concrete impressions because it is easy to misinterpret things and have a different impression at the end of the lesson of what I thought was going on when I've been in the middle of it.

Kim described how her discussions about video gave her a perspective that allowed her to see more of what was happening in the classroom situation. She commented:

> For me when I watch the tape things in my classroom are sometimes going better than I perhaps think, when I step back out of the role of making things happen I am able to see that things are happening.

Kim was cognisant of the different perspectives she had on her teaching and the different values she was able to place on it when viewing it on video retrospectively, in contrast to being in the midst of it. She talked about video enabling her to clarify her perspective on her practice and to identify misconceptions which result from being in the thick of the teaching moment. She referred to video as providing her with the "opportunity to see what I am doing". For example:

> I realize that when I am watching it, I can remember how I was feeling in the moment . . . feeling confusion or feeling whatever feeling I was having at the specific moment. With Kari [student] who was very confused, I was feeling personally confused with what she was trying to say. [I was] feeling concerned about "Oh I am losing all these kids", and having all of that to juggle, and then in watching the video realizing that what was happening was quality, it was quality discourse. Kids don't always have to be looking and sitting up straight and looking in that direction to be getting something out of it.

Mia discussed how video enabled her to gain a different perspective on her practice to that which she leaves the classroom with. She talked of the "Oh my gosh did you hear that?" experiences she had in terms of seeing and hearing things in the video that she missed within the pace and demands of being in the actual moment of teaching.

This particular use of video provided them with a way to step back from the frenetic pace of classroom practice to gain a retrospective perspective on the action of the classroom. This then contributed towards a richer self-perspective and also provided a platform for accessing the perspectives of others.

Informing Future Pedagogical Moves

Mia and Kim each discussed their learning in terms of becoming more informed about the experiences of their students and therefore what made sense in terms of future pedagogical and content-related decisions in their practice. Video clips informed Mia in terms of her future pedagogical moves with respect to (a) following student thinking; (b) making assessment decisions; and (c) constructing a map for her teaching.

Mia "replayed" her teaching and gained access to seeing her students in ways that were not accessible to her in the midst of the teaching. This capacity to repeatedly view video records of the class after the fact afforded Mia rich opportunities to follow student thinking. In discussing how the video clips helped her to hear, see, and observe in her classroom, Mia referred to her students and said: "The power of being able to follow their ideas is very important to me". She talked about what it would be like if she could not use video in this way.

> I don't think that I could know where the kids are at in the same way without video, it would be my interpretation a whole lot more. I wouldn't be able to get a hold of their questions so well, I mean I have questions but they are my questions and not necessarily theirs. Watching the video helps me plan where to go from here.

Mia used video in her assessment processes. She said that the video data provided her with increased understanding in making judgements regarding student thinking, understandings, and interactions.

> Video gives me a chance to hear what they say and it is a way of evaluating and assessing what they know. You know, are they participating and speculating and what ideas do they have? It gives me a chance to see this, so this is how I know what question to pose and what steps to take next. So in many ways it is an evaluation tool for me and it is also giving me ideas on what to follow up on and do next.

Mia also regarded the video as providing her with a basis for constructing a map for teaching. She gained access to information regarding where her students were in their learning and used this to help her position them and herself in the bigger picture of where she would like them to go from there. Mia's engagement in viewing video records of her practice gave her a retrospective view on the class that then informed her prospective moves. She said:

> It helps me see and hear, if you are really trying to get somewhere you need a map, otherwise if it goes all over the map then nobody knows anything more about anything. So I need to focus the [classroom] conversation and I want the focus to come from the children and what they are saying. To be able to adjust this focus I really need the video to be able to see what they are saying. Without the video I do a lot more speculating and guessing myself without necessarily really getting where I want to.

Video assisted Mia in learning how to respond with more understanding to the thinking of her students. It also functioned as a platform from which she learned how to construct coherence and direction out of the myriad ways the students might go. Both of these were critical features of an improvement in Mia's teaching as she was able to change her practice to being more encompassing of students while also getting more deeply into subject content. Video records provided a way to manage the tension between responding to different student ideas while also navigating a cohesive path through the content.

Kim talked in terms of what might be referred to as learning a more "generalized way of knowing teaching" or theory building. Kim said:

> I think I use my video more, not as an instructional . . . not to determine next steps for instruction, more to deepen my understandings of next steps for instruction.

Kim talked about her learning being generalized from thinking about a specific student in her video to considering broader questions about her practice. When teachers play a participatory role in the creation and use of knowledge in the field, they are empowered to trust their own ability to construct knowledge, to be meaning-makers, and to improve their practice (Glesne, 1991).

Kim shared how she could generalize what she learnt to other contexts. For example:

> Through Greg [student in her class] I learned more about this kind of confusion that kids have, so then in future work with kids I have more thoughts about it. I have more understanding about it and what kinds of questions will untangle that. I get new ways to look at things and that often transfers to other stuff. It is not just "Ok, now I know how to deal with a kid who is having trouble with putting ten blocks together." I have talked about it with somebody, so next time a different kind of confusion about any other math concept comes up I can use that experience. . . it fuels my other work. I don't specifically Figure out what to do with Greg, it is more I Figure out what to do as a whole with confusion, but focusing on Greg allows me to Figure that out in a more structured way.

Mia's and Kim's perspectives on their learning suggests that inquiring into practice represented in video records of practice has the potential both to inform specific acts in practice and to promote theory building or a move toward a more generalized knowledge about learning and teaching.

New Challenges for Inquiry-Based Professional Development Initiatives

The use of video records of practice as discussed in this chapter departs from traditional approaches to professional development and so introduces new challenges for teachers and professional developers. There is a need to focus resources and attention on suitable facilitation strategies for this work. This is accompanied by the need to rethink the traditional time frames in which teacher development work has often been undertaken, rethinking the one-off, one-day deal and considering the provision of ongoing initiatives (Borko, 2004).

Making one's actions and beliefs visible to others is a risky endeavour. It is not a typical part of the culture of teaching for teachers to share their teaching, let alone to expose it in such a raw form as an unedited video recording of classroom practice. One takes the risk of being harshly critiqued and exposed in doing this. An important issue requiring attention in future professional development initiatives is therefore the provision of a safe and supportive environment within which to share video records. Both Kim and Mia talked of the preparation and planning needed for an environment to be set up in which teachers were willing to share video of their own practice with colleagues. Kim said:

> The thing is that Ana [the professional development facilitator] has done so much work to get people to the place where we are able to share video. I mean this is two years of work, the end of last year was the first time that we showed our video.

Kim talked about the act of showing video clips of one's classroom practice to others as being "a lot to share". Mia also spoke to this in her comment that "the whole idea of being videotaped is a big one, there is a lot that goes before being able to do this". Both Mia and

Kim referred extensively to the critical importance of establishing a learning community so that, first, people were willing to share their video footage and second, productive conversations could take place around the viewing of those videos.

The presence of a "judgemental voice" can have a negative effect on the provision of a safe and supportive environment in which to share video footage of one's own practice. Observations of sessions indicate an absence of judgemental comments made about practice, and interviews with both the professional developer and participants suggest that this is an intentional move that is overt and known to be a part of the culture and discourse practices of the learning community. For example, Kim said:

> Unless it is done with people who know how to facilitate teachers' talking about video it is not, I mean I think it is detrimental. And what I mean by that is no one wants to show their video and be told all the things that they might have done, all the missed opportunities.

Kim believed that the professional development facilitator of the group "has intentionally done something here, she didn't start the first week, we went slowly, slowly, slowly". Kim talked about building trust and a safe environment in terms of learning ways to watch and talk about video:

> I think building trust is the biggest issue involve. The trust part has to be first. I think it is a combination of building trust and learning how to watch it. I mean, you build trust by knowing how to watch it, learning how to watch it is part of the building trust process and it is a tricky one because how you do it has to be modelled in a way. But you know if you show your video and someone is saying "You should have done or said this to so and so" and, "I think this was a missed opportunity", you will never want to watch it. I mean, you would be horrified. You really have to reframe how people look at what they are going to get from this and I think it is really a retraining of a deep conditioning that teachers have had.

Kim described the setting up an explicit and publicly articulated agenda for the viewing of video clips, and the facilitator's role in this. She provided the following example:

> We had a set of guidelines of how discourse occurs in this group. We don't give advice, we don't ask questions disguised as advice, you know, "Have you thought of this?" (laughter). Just being given those guidelines [means] people don't talk until they Figure out what is the way to talk in this group. For me personally my experience has been that this culture makes a difference.

Both Kim and Mia talked about the importance of having a guiding framework for discussing the video records. They suggested that it should provide some balance between a predetermined and directed conversation and the completely open and non-focused conversation that might otherwise ensue. Kim gave an example:

> People are not sure how to look at the video but if you say . . . "In this video I want you to watch what the teacher is doing to get the kids to Figure out unknown words", and so that they are focused on that and it is not just free form where the viewers are left to pursue their own judgements because you have framed it in such a way that it wouldn't be.

Observations of video sharing sessions and interviews with the professional developer provided further evidence that the professional developer introduced facilitation processes specifically designed to support the teachers' work. Effectively mediated discourse requires skilled facilitation which has important implications for professional development practices.

CONCLUSION

When this professional learning community engaged in the work of viewing video clips of their own practice with colleagues, they developed new insights into their own practice. These insights informed their future pedagogical moves. Findings from this research indicate that using video records of one's self for professional development, while requiring large amounts of trust, has potential as an effective professional development strategy and can be an effective tool for promoting data-based inquiry into practice.

Mia and Kim each articulated different purposes for their work with video. Mia predominantly referred to video records as an educative tool helping her to make informed decisions regarding next steps in her teaching practice. She referred to the processes of it helping her to assess student thinking and to thus make informed choices about next steps in practice. On the other hand, Kim predominantly considered her learning from video to be of a more generalized nature. There appears to be overlap in their perspectives in what they do, the contextual conditions they identify a being important, the learning they articulate as being achieved, and the ways in which they learn through viewing and discussing videotape of their own practice with others. This suggests that a facilitated discourse around the viewing of video records of one's own practice has the potential to function both to inform specific acts in practice and to promote a more generalized knowledge about teaching. Furthermore, it is apparent that this new approach to professional development requires careful facilitation to enable the provision of a safe yet challenging learning environment for classroom teachers.

This is a single case study and the findings should be interpreted accordingly. Future research might further examine the role of the professional developer to a greater degree. Crucial too will be a deeper understanding of the influences of this professional development work on classroom practice. Ultimately, the challenge is to undertake research that enables identification of the effect of professional development initiatives of this nature on student learning outcomes.

REFERENCES

Ball, D., & Cohen, D. (1999). Developing practice, developing practitioners: Toward a practice-based theory of professional education. In L. D. Hammond & G. Sykes (Eds.), *Teaching as the learning profession: Handbook of policy and practice* (pp. 3–32). San Francisco: Jossey-Bass.

Borko, H. (2004). Professional development and teacher learning: Mapping the terrain. *Educational Researcher, 33*(8), 3–15.

Cochran-Smith, M., & Lytle, S. L. (1999). Relationships of knowledge and practice: Teacher learning in communities. *Review of Research in Education, 24,* 249–306).

DiSchino, M. (1998). Why do bees sting and why do they die afterward? In A. Rosebery & B. Warren (Eds.), *Boats, balloons, and classroom video* (pp. 109–133). Portsmouth, NH: Heinemann.

Eckart, J. A., & Gibson, S. L. (1993). Using camcorders to improve teaching. *The Clearing House, 66*(5), 288–292.

Glesne, C. E. (1991). Yet another role? The teacher as researcher. *Action in Teacher Education, 13*(1), 7–11.

Hammerness, K., Darling-Hammond, L., Bransford, J., Berliner, D. C., Cochran-Smith, M., McDonald, M., et al. (2005). How teachers learn and develop. In L. Darling-Hammond & J. Bransford (Eds.), *Preparing teachers for a changing world* (pp. 358–389). San Francisco: Jossey-Bass.

Jaworski, B. (1989). *Using classroom videotape to develop your teaching.* Milton Keynes, UK: Open University, Centre for Mathematics Education.

Le Fevre, D. (2004a). Designing for teacher learning: Video-based curriculum design. In J. Brophy (Ed.), *Advances for research on teaching: Using video in teacher education* (Vol. 10, pp. 235–258). London: Elsevier.

Le Fevre, D. (2004b). Video-based multimedia teacher learning. *The International Principal, 8*(2).

Le Fevre, D. M., & Richardson, V. (2002). Staff development in early reading intervention programs: The facilitator. *Journal of Teaching and Teacher Education, 18*(4).

Louden, W., Wallace, J., & Groves, R. (2001). Spinning a web (case) around professional standards: Capturing the complexity of science teaching. *Research in Science Education, 31*, 227–244.

Nelson, T. H., & Slavit, D. (2007). Collaborative inquiry among science and mathematics teachers in the USA: Professional learning experiences through cross-grade, cross-discipline dialogue. *Journal of In-service Education, 33*(1), 23–39.

Rosebery, A. S., & Warren, B. (Eds.). (1998). *Boats, balloons, and classroom video: Science teaching as inquiry.* Portsmouth, NH: Heinmann.

Seel, N. M., & Winn, W. D. (1997). Research on media and learning: Distributed cognition and semiotics. In R. D. Tennyson, F. Schott, N. Seel, & S. Dijkstra (Eds.), *Instructional Design: International perspectives* (pp. 293–326). Mahwah, NJ: Lawrence Erlbaum.

Sherin, M., & Han, S. Y. (2004). Teacher learning in the context of a video club. *Teaching and Teacher Education, 20*(2), 163–183.

Sherin, M. G., & van Es, E. A. (2005). Using video to support teachers' ability to notice classroom interactions. *Journal of Technology and Teacher Education, 13*(3), 475–491.

Tochon, F. V. (1999). Video study groups for education, professional development, and change. Madison, WI: Atwood.

Toole, J. C., & Seashore Louis, K. S. (2002). The role of professional learning communities in international education. In K. Leithwood and P. Hallinger (Eds.), *Second international handbook of educational leadership and administration* (pp. 245–279). Dordrecht Netherlands: Kluwer Academic.

van Es, E., & Sherin, M. (2002). Learning to notice: Scaffolding new teachers' interpretations of classroom interactions. *Journal of Technology and Teacher Education, 10*(4), 571–596

Weick, K. E. (1995). *Sensemaking in organizations.* Thousand Oaks, CA: Sage Publications.

AUTHOR NOTE

Deidre M. Le Fevre is a Senior Lecturer in the Faculty of Education, University of Auckland, New Zealand.

Correspondence concerning this chapter should be addressed by email to: d.lefevre@auckland.ac.nz

In: Challenging Thinking about Teaching and Learning   ISBN: 978-1-60456-744-1
Editors: C. M. Rubie-Davies and C. Rawlinson   © 2008 Nova Science Publishers, Inc.

Chapter 28

IT'S NOT AN "EITHER/OR": PASTORAL CARE AND ACADEMIC ACHIEVEMENT IN SECONDARY SCHOOLS

Margaret Agee and Pauline Dickinson

ABSTRACT

The world through which adolescents navigate their pathway to adulthood in New Zealand presents them with complex challenges; young people frequently experience pressures that are not well understood by adults. Despite teachers' commitment to the promotion of academic achievement, significant barriers to students' learning may include factors related to their well-being and readiness to learn that need to be identified and addressed. The role and importance of pastoral care seem, however, to have been discounted in the current efforts to promote academic achievement. Recent local as well as international research indicates that caring relationships between teachers and students, the promotion of resilience, psychosocial interventions, and counselling need to be given greater acknowledgement as integral to supporting the academic mission of schools and the well-being of students.

INTRODUCTION

Ask any teacher and you will hear the litany of mental health concerns that arise daily and at critical times during the school year. The kids who are misbehaving, the ones who seem emotionally upset, the ones who are victims of physical and sexual abuse, the ones who can't get along with others, those who have difficulty adjusting to school requirements, and more. .Anyone who has spent time in schools can itemise the multifaceted mental health and psychosocial concerns that warrant attention. The question for all of us is: How should our society's schools address these matters? (Alderman and Taylor, 2004, p. 1)

The relationship between academic development and the pastoral care of students finds its origins in age-old practices that include the mentoring aspect of teacher–student relationships, and the concept of educating the whole person. Vocational and educational guidance systems were formalized during the early-mid twentieth century in Britain, North America, and New Zealand (Hermansson & Webb, 1993; Jones, Stefflre, & Stewart, 1970; Lytton & Craft, 1968). In fact, school counsellors and guidance networks had been established in New Zealand secondary schools (Crowe, 2006) well before educational philosophers such as Noddings (1984) and Gilligan (1982) were advocating for the promotion of caring relationships and an ethic of care in educational practice. Currently, specific Ministry of Education policy guidelines can be identified as underscoring the need for effective pastoral care systems.

Under the National Educational Goals (NEGS) and the National Administration Guidelines (NAGS), boards of trustees and teachers in New Zealand are mandated to enhance learning and achievement by promoting and supporting the well-being of young people in their schools (Ministry of Education, 2005). Particularly relevant are the following educational priorities: NEG 1: "The highest standards of achievement through programmes which enable all students to realize their full potential as individuals"; and NEG 2: "Equality of educational opportunity for all New Zealanders, by identifying and removing barriers to achievement". Pastoral care systems, including guidance and counselling, play a key part in the attainment of such goals by addressing students' psychosocial and developmental needs, including building coping skills and resilience and providing therapeutic support and crisis intervention (Agee, 1997).

Boards of trustees are also specifically required to "provide a safe physical and emotional environment for students" (NAG 5i). Emotional safety

> can be interpreted as freedom from such things as harassment of all forms, including bullying and violence, emotional, physical and sexual abuse, and from discrimination such as racism and sexism. It can be seen as the maintenance of a caring and supportive environment in which students are enabled to develop effective communication, conflict resolution and communication skills with their peers and with staff. (Agee, 1997, p. 21)

While school managers are responsible for the maintenance of a safe environment, ensuring that this requirement is fulfilled depends upon an effective and adequately resourced guidance and pastoral care system within each school. In recent years, however, pastoral care, guidance and counselling seem to have become marginalized in educational policy and practice within New Zealand. Inconsistencies have become apparent between official mandates and the ways in which they are interpreted and implemented in practice.

FROM VALUED PARTNER TO THE POOR RELATION

State-funded educational and vocational guidance services in New Zealand have been provided in the local community since the early part of the twentieth century, established in the era of planned social policy and the welfare state (Winterbourn, 1974). The appointment of the first guidance counsellors in the early 1960s marked the beginning of formally established pastoral care systems in secondary schools (Hermansson & Webb, 1993). By the late 1970s, at least one counsellor had been appointed to most state secondary schools. Guidance networks, in which counsellors often played leading roles, had also been developed in a number of schools. In addition to counsellors, key staff members included deans, form teachers, careers advisors, guidance teachers, and senior managers (Hermansson & Webb, 1993). Pastoral care and guidance systems were regarded as integral to secondary schooling (Miller, Manthei, & Gilmore, 1993), and the established counsellor/student ratio was 1:500.

Although their remedial–adjustive function was emphasized at first, a developmental approach became valued, serving the wide ranging needs of all students (Hermansson & Webb, 1993) "not merely as the amelioration of trauma or the prevention of mistakes but rather the maximum development of the individual" (Jones et al., 1970, p. 4). As pastoral care systems in schools continued to evolve, counsellors not only worked with individual students, but also developed and implemented many programmes to meet student, staff, and parent needs. Working from a developmental perspective, they took on a range of roles that were documented in a series of research reports (e.g. Baker, 1985; Brammer, 1982; Cox, 2002; Manthei, 1999; McDiarmid, 1981; Miller et al., 1993; Post Primary Teachers' Association, 2004).

The impact of monetarist policies of the 1980s, however, resulted in a reduction of responsibility on the part of the state for welfare support (Koopman-Boyden, 1990). Ensuing changes have had particularly detrimental consequences for pastoral care and counselling in schools. In this environment of self-managing schools, in which economic considerations and managerial control have claimed the foreground, the value of caregiving, associated as it is with trust, co-operation, community, and caring, has been undermined (Codd, 1999). Types of work that are not always easily definable and measurable, and that cannot be assessed in terms of commodities, have been discounted, and the invisibility of caring has been normalized. As Anderson and Nairn (2005) have contended, "conditions which undermine care and caring work may breed less and less care, an outcome which would undoubtedly be costly at all levels" (p. 216).

With the introduction of the National Certificate of Educational Achievement (New Zealand's main national educational qualification for senior secondary school students), increased workloads have also lessened teachers' availability and energy for pastoral care roles. Although a New Zealand study by Cox (2002) found that most schools have pastoral care programmes, some of exceptional quality, problems with inadequate staffing, funding, and time tend to undermine their effectiveness. Under such conditions, in which the atmosphere is increasingly competitive, the curriculum is overloaded, and there is less time and emphasis on caring for the individual, "students receive negative messages about how they are valued"; students and staff alike can feel alienated and uncared for, reducing motivation and impeding students' learning (Cooper, 2004, p. 21).

In preservice training for teachers, pastoral care is squeezed out by other curriculum-related instruction and pedagogy. Training for the wide range of staff involved in pastoral care is primarily undertaken in-house by counsellors and senior managers within each school (Cox, 2002). If teachers do not go out into schools equipped with foundational knowledge and understanding for this dimension of their work, is it any wonder that some lack commitment or confidence for the task? A principal interviewed for a recent study expressed his sadness at teachers' perceptions of form teaching as simply an administrative role, peripheral to their "real" work (Pritchard, 2007).

Additionally, perusal of recent programmes for principals' and senior managers' training events and conferences reveals that in these contexts little, if any, attention is being paid to topics related to pastoral care or adolescent mental health, in face of other priorities. Yet the understanding and commitment of principals and senior managers are vital to the effectiveness of pastoral care programmes in schools (Cox, 2002). Thus both in professional education and within schools, it seems that academic goals are promoted independently of, or even seemingly in opposition to, the pastoral care needs of students.

School guidance counsellors' positions have also been undermined in recent years, despite the demanding nature of their roles and the statutory requirement under the Education Act 1989 that guidance and counselling are provided to young people who are subject to suspension and stand-down (Ludbrook, 2003). Under the educational management reforms that were instituted almost 20 years ago (Ministry of Education, 1988; Picot, 1988), specific resourcing provisions for guidance in schools and the tagging of school counsellor positions were removed (Crowe, 2006). The regional support systems for specialist areas formerly provided by the Department of Education were disestablished, and funding provisions for the training of guidance counsellors were maintained but at a reduced level. No official definition of the role of guidance counsellors can be found in current Ministry of Education documents, and as schools have had autonomy over counsellors' employment conditions and job descriptions, wide variations are evident in the nature of their responsibilities. These depend on a number of factors including the understanding and appreciation that school management has of counselling and the guidance counsellor's role (Crowe, 2006).

Although the New Zealand Association of Counsellors has assisted school managers and boards of trustees with the development of the School Guidance Counsellor Appointment Kit (New Zealand Association of Counsellors, 2003), counsellors currently have to negotiate their own roles and responsibilities themselves. The Post Primary Teachers' Association's submission to the Ministry of Education Staffing Review Group reported that schools were experiencing pressures "to transfer guidance time into administration and curriculum" at a time when "schools are facing greater demands on the guidance professionals" (Ministry of Education, 2001, p. 16). As a result, although in many schools counsellors are valued and the role is well understood, many also find themselves in a very vulnerable position (Post Primary Teachers' Association, 2004), and observation indicates their circumstances within a school can change dramatically with a change of principal.

A survey of school counsellors conducted by Manthei (1999), which elicited responses from 212 practitioners, revealed that working conditions had changed during the 1990s, and counsellors reported that:

> their workload had expanded, resources they could call on for support and expertise had deteriorated, the time they have to do their work was inadequate, the atmosphere in the school itself was often critical and unhelpful, and the job had become considerably more difficult. (p. 45)

Under these conditions, guidance, counselling, and pastoral care become an adjunct rather than core to the educational mission of the school. Yet in the words of one school counsellor:

> Many of our clients represent a virtual layer cake of social, educational, personal, family and psychiatric misfortune. Many are in the "too hard basket" for many agencies who give up because of no-shows and lack of co-operation. Schools don't have a choice. School counsellors have to be there for these clients. (Manthei, 1997, pp. 31–32)

It seems that the resources allocated to pastoral care, guidance, and counselling systems in schools have been eroded and the service provision undermined at the very time in which the needs of young people are arguably greater than ever before.

STRESS IN THE LIVES OF YOUNG PEOPLE

Young people attending New Zealand secondary schools find themselves navigating their ways through increasingly diverse worlds. Rapid social, economic, and technological changes continue to have profound effects on society and on the settings of home, school, and community in which adolescents interact. Significant trends that influence young people's well-being include earlier physical maturity, changing labour markets, increased levels of psychosocial health concerns, and fluid family structures, with families forming and reforming at an increasing rate (Hanna, 1999). Our country's more culturally diverse population, and the increasing influence of globalization, new cultural and economic imperatives, and cyber-technologies also increase the complexity of young people's worlds, affecting their identity development and processes of learning (Luke, 2000). This is a strikingly different environment from the one in which many of the adults in young people's lives grew up.

In addition, groups of students with particular pastoral care needs now include many more sojourner, immigrant, and refugee youngsters (Everts, 2003, 2004). Concerns about the pastoral care needs of international students led the Ministry of Education to develop a code of practice for working with this group in particular (Ministry of Education, 2002).

Each adolescent's process of negotiating normative cognitive and psychosocial changes holds potential for both growth and vulnerability (Geldard & Geldard, 1999; Irwin & Vaughan, 1988). Most young people are able to find their way through the predictable changes and challenges of adolescence, emerging relatively unscathed (Adolescent Health Research Group, 2003). The lives of a number of young people, however, are complicated by circumstances beyond their control or by risky behaviour such as binge drinking, drink driving, drug abuse, and unsafe sexual activity (Adolescent Health Research Group, 2003). Converging with normative developmental transitions, non-normative experiences involving change and loss can present challenges that compromise young people's well-being by causing intense stress (Eccles, 1999; Furlong, 2002; Ge, Conger, & Elder, 2001; Green, 1999; Simmons, Burgeson, Carlton-Ford, & Blyth, 1987). Such experiences include bereavement, family separation, divorce or relocation, broken relationships, emotional, physical or sexual abuse, cultural alienation and bullying. It is widely acknowledged, both nationally and internationally, that the lives of approximately one in five young people are adversely affected by trauma arising from abuse, crisis events including sudden death or violence, or family conflict and disruption (Adolescent Health Research Group, 2003; Beautrais, 2000; New Zealand Health Information Service, 2001; World Health Organisation, 2004).

These challenges for adolescents are reflected in many encounters that occur daily in our schools. When working with students, teachers and counsellors often find that seemingly straightforward presenting problems may in reality represent complex situations. Difficult family circumstances can contribute to problems with lateness to school, truancy, studying, and completing homework. Parental aspirations may be a problem for a young person trying to develop realistic vocational goals. A history of loss and grief, trauma, or abuse may be acted out in the classroom in the form of withdrawal or overt misbehaviour such as defiance and non-compliance. Aggression towards peers may be a symptom of domestic violence in the home, or of grief-related anger and confusion following parental separation, divorce or another significant loss such as the break-up of the student's first romantic relationship.

Experiencing sequential change has been found to be more manageable than changes that occur simultaneously. Just one of the situations described above may stretch any adolescent's coping capacity, but a convergence or pileup of stressful life-change events can intensify mental health distress for adolescents. This is likely to result in academic disengagement and a decline in school performance, lower self-esteem and less functional interpersonal relationships within a school community (Balk, 1996; Larson & Ham, 1993; Simmons et al., 1987).

Gossens and Marcoen (1999) have argued that young people are better able to manage important issues in their lives if they are afforded the time they need to process them. Furthermore, an arena of comfort has been identified as significant for young people: when they feel comfortable in some aspects of their lives, then other areas of discomfort can be tolerated and managed, whereas if there is discomfort in all major areas of their lives, they are less able to cope successfully (Gossens and Marcoen, 1999; Simmons et al., 1987). Often help is needed to enable them to find or create that arena of comfort.

Despite ample research and practice-based evidence related to the stressors in young people's lives, the effect of these pressures on their well-being, including their academic progress, does not appear to be uniformly well-understood. Researchers and counsellors find that young people's distress in response to change commonly seems to remain unacknowledged, underestimated, or discounted, and is, therefore, often socially disenfranchised and unsupported (e.g., Corr & Balk, 1996; Dickinson, 2000; Lenhardt, 1997). It seems that large numbers of young people who have directly experienced trauma may go unrecognized as having been affected, and therefore may not be provided with appropriate support (Saltzman, Steinberg, Layne, Aisenberg, & Pynoos, 2001). Adverse, sequential consequences that could follow a traumatic event or the death of a loved one affecting a family include "financial hardship, family estrangement, dissolution or displacement, and adolescent assumption of adult responsibilities" (Saltzman et al., p. 49). The personal consequences for such young people commonly include a decline in academic performance and disengagement from school that may be temporary or may result in the abandonment of their studies (Ridling, 1995; Silva, 1999).

Disturbingly, reports from young people who have experienced change, loss, and grief in their lives suggest that while some teachers can be helpful and supportive, others are somewhat indifferent, making little effort to acknowledge that their students are experiencing difficulties (Dickinson, 2000). One young person who had lost all her grandparents in four years at secondary school described seeing her school counsellor for support. The counsellor then met with her six teachers to explain the student's situation, which was affecting her capacity to concentrate on her school work. Of these teachers, only one was able to provide caring support:

> One teacher was good. She used to come up to me and go "How are you feeling today?" She would check if I understood the work but she didn't put any pressure on me. (Kim, aged 16, p. 69)

The others were described as being insistent that completing school work was the student's priority, and lacked empathy or understanding, thereby intensifying the pressure she was under and exacerbating her distress and inability to perform. Their cajoling was counter-productive: the student ended up hating and dropping her favourite subject in which she had done well previously. She required a great deal more support from the school counsellor to cope with the complications that the teachers' responses created.

Another student in the same study (Dickinson, 2000), who had moved from a small, supportive, rural secondary school to a larger, more impersonal urban school, described her feelings of isolation and sadness, saying:

> The teachers here, they don't really care about students. They just care about marks.
> (Natalie, aged 17, p. 69)

It is well accepted that a student's capacity to learn will be impaired by such influences as drug or alcohol use, lack of sleep, poor nutrition, or poor general health. Less obvious are the hidden, emotionally-related barriers to learning associated with the kinds of events and circumstances described above. Saltzman and his colleagues (2001) have voiced international concern about the need to acknowledge the detrimental consequences associated with traumatic life events for young people's learning and achievement, given that "promoting academic excellence in public education constitutes one of our nation's most important missions in the coming years" (p. 49). More effective support could be provided for students if teachers understood the ways in which students' emotional states can affect their capacity to function within the classroom.

GETTING THE MESSAGE ACROSS: THE IMPORTANCE OF EMOTIONAL WELL-BEING

The struggles students experience with school work when under stress can be explained by recent research regarding the way in which the brain operates under different conditions. Investigations have revealed that students need to experience positive emotions in order to learn effectively (Weare & Gray, 2003). Conversely, when a student is experiencing considerable stress, the brain reverts to more primitive survival needs. The sense of stress can be the result of personal or environmental threat, such as witnessing violence or being bullied, or within the classroom environment, having to struggle unduly with a task set by a teacher. Emotions such as sadness and anger can block learning, while feeling safe, feeling valued, and experiencing a sense of belonging are more likely to promote learning (Weare & Gray, 2003). When powerful, distressing emotions are evoked, they occupy cognitive time and space, leaving little capacity for engagement with other tasks; basically, students are not able to think clearly (Elias, Zins, Weissberg, Frey, Greenberg, Haynes, et al., 1997).

A recent review of a range of educational studies has indicated that the achievement of academic goals is complemented by, rather than in conflict with, a focus on emotional well-being (Weare, 2000). The cross-national study Health Behaviour in School-Age Children (World Health Organisation, 2004) has indicated that when young people are satisfied with school, they are better motivated and are therefore able to achieve more, according to their ability level, than their unsatisfied peers. Among the factors associated with satisfaction with school are having a sense of belonging; being treated fairly by teachers; perceiving school rules as fair; and experiencing teachers as showing a personal interest in them. These establish an environment that supports rather than inhibits academic achievement, which in turn enhances students' satisfaction with school.

There is an interesting correspondence between these factors and those that contribute to building resilience and protecting young people's well-being. These include strong supportive and positive connections with significant adults, either their parents or other important non-parental adults such as teachers and school counsellors, as well as feeling connected to school through a sense of belonging, being valued, and feeling safe and secure (Resnick, Bearman, Blum, Bauman, Harris, Jones, et al., 1997). The experience of being cared for has also been identified as a significant factor in people's capacity to learn (Noddings, 1984). Such caring can be experienced by students through a teacher's attitudes, manner, and interest in them as people as well as through evidence of the teacher's desire to promote their well-being, including their academic progress (Dickinson, 2000; Hawk, Cowley, Hill, & Sutherland, 2002; Khaleghian, 2003).

For populations that often seem disenfranchised in traditional educational settings, the teacher–student relationship can be critical in helping students from these groups perform well academically. It is interesting that in their analysis of the results of three separate studies involving Maori and Pacific Island students, Hawk and her colleagues (2002) found that the quality of the teacher–student relationship emerged as critically important in enabling them to succeed as learners, transcending the relative weighting the students gave to the teacher's ethnicity. Characterizing these relationships were the interpersonal qualities of empathy, caring, and respect. Teachers also showed commitment to students' academic well-being in the form of extra efforts to reward and encourage, passion to enthuse and motivate, patience and perseverance, and belief in students' ability. When teachers model the attitudes, inter-personal relationships, and classroom behaviour they want from their students, such as consideration for others, consistency and congruence, expecting and demonstrating a strong work ethic, and so on, "it is probable that effective teacher/student relationships are conducive to learning for most students from all socio-economic groups" (Hawk et al., 2002, p. 49). As one student in Dickinson's (2000) research advised teachers:

> First of all they need to be themselves, that is best, more real. They should be careful and observe everything, be patient, be more calm, and observe people in their class and see who is acting how and what kind of needs they have. They need to try and talk to the person and get to know them. They should be concerned because that is their profession. (Helen, aged 15, p. 79)

It therefore seems evident that "one of the most fundamental reforms needed in secondary or high school education is to make schools into better communities of caring and support for young people" (Hargreaves, Earl, & Ryan, 1996, p. 77). Such communities are created when there is commitment to developing an environment that supports not only academic, but also social and emotional learning, and when resources are provided to enable this ideal to be realized in practice.

CONCLUSION

Effective systems of pastoral care and support for young people are integral to successful programmes of teaching and learning. They are therefore essential to the core business of our schools. Rather than marginalizing guidance and counselling and reducing the resources for pastoral care, their significance in supporting the academic mission of schools needs renewed acknowledgement, in light of the evidence from both research and practice.

There is increasing recognition both nationally and internationally that the multifaceted academic, psychological, and social needs of students can best be met by whole-school approaches, based on an ecological perspective that includes families, schools and their communities (Dickinson, Neilson, & Agee, 2004; Patton, Glover, Bond, Butler, Godfrey, Di Pietro, et al., 2000; Wyn, Cahill, Holdsworth, Rowling, & Carson, 2000). Several components have been identified as critical to the implementation of a whole-school approach to promoting and supporting well-being (Alderman & Taylor, 2004; Bennett & Coggan, 1999; Hazell, O'Neill, Vincent, Robson, & Greenhalgh, 2004; UCLA School Mental Health Project, 2004; Weare, 2000). A pre-existing, positive school ethos and commitment to pastoral care and student well-being is fundamental and has significant implications for principals and school managers who, through the very nature of their positions, set the tone of their schools. In addition, leadership and responsibility for pastoral care needs to come from within the school, from principals, senior managers, and guidance counsellors, rather than from outside providers (Hazell et al., 2004).

School counselling and guidance staff are skilled professionals who are ideally positioned to provide an important leadership role within their schools, including managing the interface between school and community (Keys & Bemak, 1997). Fostering partnerships between schools, families, support services, and their wider communities can support students' academic, personal, social, and vocational development (Walsh, Howard, & Buckley, 1999). The transitions that young people make between these settings influence the course of their development, including their academic progress, either supporting it or impeding it.

Facilitating social support and smooth transitions is integral to building both resilience and effective pastoral care systems (UCLA School Mental Health Project, 2004). Positive informal as well as formal encounters among students and teachers contribute to building a supportive atmosphere in which people feel acknowledged and emotionally safe (Education Review Office, 2000). Welcoming and supporting staff, students, and families at school every day both enhance and reflect a positive school environment (UCLA School Mental Health Project, 2004).

Roeser, Eccles, and Sameroff (2000) have referred to the important role of school-based initiatives to enhance a range of outcomes. In their view:

> Schools in the twenty-first century will need to continue to focus on a dual mission: (a) providing classroom and school environments that address the developmental needs of all students; and (b) providing a 'hub' for additional support services needed to ensure that high-risk students get on track academically toward a successful future. (p. 465)

Thus, within the context of an effective pastoral care system, teachers at the "front line" are able to monitor and support the well-being of students in day-to-day interactions and developmentally-oriented programmes, while school counsellors and other guidance personnel are able to address the needs of significant numbers of students who require particular assistance and therapeutic intervention. More than ever, therefore, the Ministry of Education needs to take responsibility for ensuring that guidance counsellors in secondary schools are adequately resourced and supported to meet the challenges they encounter.

A successful whole-school approach also involves a high level of participation in school life by staff and students (Bennett & Coggan, 1999; Patton et al., 2000; Wyn et al., 2000). This is particularly so when schools have a strong sense of community, all staff members are engaged, communication is open, and participatory decision-making processes involve staff and students. This sense of community develops through the creation of an atmosphere that encourages mutual support and caring within the school, as well as through promoting the well-being and resilience of staff so that they can do more to promote the well-being and resilience of students. In this context, professional development for all school staff can enhance their knowledge, understanding, and skills so they are able to play their parts effectively within the pastoral care system (Hazell et al., 2004; UCLA School Mental Health Project, 2004).

Underpinning this approach is a need for planning, consultation, and appropriate resource allocation within each school (Bennett & Coggan, 1999; Patton et al., 2000; Wyn et al., 2000). An overarching framework that is well understood and collaboratively created supports the ongoing development of initiatives related to student and staff well-being.

Finally, research also indicates that a valuable aspect of the whole-school approach is the creation of opportunities for staff to critique the culture of their school, their pedagogical practices and the ways in which they relate to young people (Hazell et al., 2004). The open style of communication identified above helps facilitate productive reflection, including a receptive attitude to feed back and a desire to improve the quality of experience of teaching, learning and pastoral care within the school.

It is not an "either/or": there is an integral relationship between academic achievement and the pastoral care of young people. Time and resources allocated to pastoral care will reap benefits for young people and for schools as communities. Schools are in a unique position to be both educational and therapeutic communities that advance young people's cognitive development and academic success, as well as contributing to the mental, emotional, social, spiritual, and physical well-being of young people.

REFERENCES

Adolescent Health Research Group. (2003). *New Zealand youth: A profile of their health and wellbeing.* Auckland, New Zealand: University of Auckland.

Agee, M. N. (1997). Privacy and the school counsellor. *Access: Critical Perspectives on Cultural and Policy Studies in Education, 16*(1), 20–36.

Alderman, H., & Taylor, L. (2004). *Mental health in schools: Reflections on the past, present and future—from the perspective of the Center for Mental Health in Schools at UCLA.* Los Angeles: Department of Psychology, UCLA.

Anderson, V., & Nairn, K. (2005). Commentary: Teaching and mothering: Reflections on the dual role. *New Zealand Journal of Educational Studies, 40*(1), 211–220.

Baker, C. (1985). What does the counsellor do all day? A self-analysis. *New Zealand Counselling and Guidance Association Journal, 7*(1), 57–62.

Balk, D. E. (1996). Models for understanding adolescent coping with bereavement. *Death Studies, 20,* 367–387.

Beautrais, A. (2000). Risk factors for suicide and attempted suicide among young people. *Australia and New Zealand Journal of Psychiatry, 34,* 420–436.

Bennett, S., & Coggan, C. (1999). *A comprehensive evaluation of the Mentally Healthy Schools initiative.* Auckland: Injury Prevention Research Centre, University of Auckland.

Brammer, L. M. (1982). *New Zealand school guidance counsellors: Their training and work.* Wellington, New Zealand: New Zealand Council for Educational Research.

Codd, J. (1999). Educational reform, accountability and the culture of distrust. *New Zealand Journal of Educational Studies, 34*(1), 45–53.

Cooper, B. (2004). Empathy, interaction and caring: Teachers' roles in a constrained environment. *Pastoral Care in Education, 22*(3), 12–21.

Corr, C. A., & Balk, D. E. (Eds.) (1996). *Handbook of adolescent death and bereavement.* New York: Springer.

Cox, R. (2002). *Report on New Zealand Secondary Schools Pastoral Care Survey.* Auckland, New Zealand: Project K Trust.

Crowe, A. (2006). Guidance and counselling in New Zealand secondary schools: Exploring the issues. *New Zealand Journal of Counselling, 26*(3), 16–25.

Dickinson, P. (2000). *Change, loss and grief in school communities: Supporting the needs of young people.* Unpublished master's dissertation, University of Auckland, Auckland, New Zealand.

Dickinson, P., Neilson, G., and Agee, M. (2004). The sustainability of mentally healthy schools initiatives: Insights from the experiences of a co-educational secondary school in Aotearoa/New Zealand. *International Journal of Mental Health Promotion, 6*(2), 34–39.

Eccles, J. (1999). The development of children ages 6 to 14. *The future of children when school is out, 9*(2), 30–44.

Education Review Office. (2000, Autumn). *Safe students in safe schools* (Vol. 2). Wellington, New Zealand: Author.

Elias, M., Zins, J., Weissberg, R., Frey, K., Greenberg, M., Haynes, N., et al. (1997). *Promoting social and emotional learning.* Alexandria, VA: ASCD.

Everts, J. F. (2003). The Peer Support Programme and pastoral care of overseas born students. *New Zealand Journal of Counselling, 24*(2), 40–68.

Everts, J. F. (2004). The pastoral needs of international students in New Zealand secondary schools. *New Zealand Journal of Counselling, 25*(2), 54–73.

Furlong, A. (2002). *Youth transitions and health: A literature review.* Glasgow: University of Glasgow, UK.

Ge, X., Conger, R. D., & Elder, G. H. (2001). The relation between puberty and psychological distress in adolescent boys. *Journal of Research on Adolescence, 11*(1), 49–70.

Geldard, K., & Geldard, D. (1999). *Counselling adolescents: The proactive approach.* London: Sage.

Gilligan, C. (1982). *In a different voice: Psychological theory and women's development.* Cambridge, MA: Harvard University Press.

Gossens, L., & Marcoen, A. (1999). Relationships during adolescence: Constructive vs. negative themes and relational dissatisfaction. *Journal of Adolescence, 22*, 65–79.

Green, E. (1999). *Transitions from childhood to youth and adulthood. A supplement to the wellbeing of British Columbia's children and youth.* Vancouver, Canada: First Call: the BC Child and Youth Advocacy Coalition.

Hanna, D. (1999). Social policies: A youth development approach. *Public Sector, 22*(3), 12–14.

Hargreaves, A., Earl, L., & Ryan, J. (1996). *Schooling for change.* London: Falmer Press.

Hawk, K., Cowley, E. T., Hill, J., & Sutherland, S. (2002). The importance of the teacher/student relationship for Maori and Pasifika students. *Set, 3*, 44–49.

Hazell, T., O'Neill, D., Vincent, K., Robson, T., & Greenhalgh, S. (2004). *MindMatters evaluation: Schools case study.* Newcastle, NSW, Australia: Hunter Institute of Mental Health.

Hermansson, G., & Webb, S. (1993). Guidance and counselling in New Zealand: Weathering a decade of transformation. *The International Journal for the Advancement of Counselling, 16*(3), 213–227.

Irwin, C. E., & Vaughan, E. (1988). The psychosocial context of adolescent development. *Journal of Adolescent Health Care, 9*, 11–19.

Jones, A. J., Stefflre, B., & Stewart, N. R. (Eds.). (1970). *Principles of guidance* (6th ed.). New York: McGraw-Hill.

Keys, S. G., & Bemak, F. (1997). School-family-community linked services: A school counseling role for changing times. *The School Counselor, 44*, 255–263.

Khaleghian, E. (2003). School counsellors and the ethics of care. *New Zealand Journal of Counselling, 24*(2), 1–10.

Koopman-Boyden, P. (1990). Social policy: has there been one? In M. Holland & J. Boston (Eds.), *The fourth Labour government: Politics and policy in New Zealand* (2nd ed., pp. 213–231). Auckland, New Zealand: Oxford University Press.

Larson, R. W., & Ham, M. (1993). Stress and "storm and stress" in early adolescence: The relationship of negative events with dysphoric affect. *Developmental Psychology, 29*(1), 130–140.

Lenhardt, A-M. (1997). Disenfranchised grief/hidden sorrow: Implications for the school counselor. *The School Counselor, 44*(4), 264–270.

Ludbrook, R. (2003). *The counsellor and the law.* Hamilton: New Zealand Association of Counsellors.

Luke, A. (2000). The jig is up: An alternative history of psychology or why current concepts of identity and development are part of the problem rather than part of the solution. *New Zealand Association of Counsellors Newsletter, 20*(3), 12–18, 23–26.

Lytton, H., & Craft, M. (Eds.). (1968). *Guidance and counselling in British schools: A discussion of current issues.* Whitstable: Edward Arnold.

Manthei, R. J. (1999). School counselling in New Zealand. *New Zealand Journal of Counselling, 20*(1), 24–46.

Manthei, B. (1997). School counselling: Client issues, training and support. *New Zealand Association of Counsellors Newsletter, 18*(1), 31–34.

McDiarmid, J. K. (1981). The guidance counsellor's role: Consensus and conflict. *PPTA Journal, Term, 3*, 28–30.

Miller, J., Manthei, R., & Gilmore, A. (1993). School counsellors and guidance networks: Roles revisited. *New Zealand Journal of Educational Studies, 28*(2), 105–124.

Ministry of Education (2005). *Making a bigger difference for all students: Schooling strategy 2005–2010.* Wellington, New Zealand: Author.

Ministry of Education (2002). *Code of practice for the pastoral care of international students.* Wellington, New Zealand: Author.

Ministry of Education. (2001). *Report of the School Staffing Review Group.* Wellington, New Zealand: Author.

Ministry of Education (1988). *Tomorrow's schools: The reform of education administration in New Zealand.* Wellington, New Zealand: Author.

New Zealand Association of Counsellors. (2003). *School guidance counsellor appointment kit.* Hamilton, New Zealand: Author.

New Zealand Health Information Service. (2001). *Health statistics.* Wellington, New Zealand Health Information Service.

Noddings, N. (1984). *Caring: A feminine approach to ethics and moral education.* Berkeley, CA: University of California Press.

Patton, G., Glover, S., Bond, L., Butler, H., Godfrey, C., Di Pietro, G., et al. (2000). The Gatehouse Project: A systematic approach to mental health promotion in secondary schools. *Australian and New Zealand Journal of Psychiatry, 34,* 586–593.

Picot, B. (1988). *Administering for excellence: Report of the Taskforce to Review Educational Administration.* Wellington, New Zealand: Ministry of Education.

Post Primary Teachers' Association. (2004, June). *PPTA survey of guidance counsellors.* Wellington, New Zealand: Author.

Pritchard, F. (2007). *Principal and counsellor perceptions of the role of the secondary school guidance counsellor.* Unpublished master's dissertation, University of Auckland, Auckland, New Zealand.

Resnick, M. D., Bearman, P. S., Blum, R. W., Bauman, K. E., Harris, K. M., Jones, J. et al. (1997). Protecting adolescents from harm: Findings from the national longitudinal study on adolescent health. *Journal of the American Academy of Child and Adolescent Psychiatry, 278,* 823–832.

Ridling, L. (1995). Traumatic death in secondary schools. *New Zealand Journal of Counselling, 17*(1), 8–16.

Roeser, R. W., Eccles, J. S., & Sameroff, A. J. (2000). School as a context of early adolescents' academic and social-emotional development: A summary of research findings. *The Elementary School Journal, 100*(5), 443–549.

Saltzman, W. R., Steinberg, A. M., Layne, C. M., Aisenberg, E., & Pynoos, R. S. (2001). A developmental approach to school-based treatment of adolescents exposed to trauma and traumatic loss. *Journal of Child and Adolescent Group Therapy, 11*(2/3), 43–56.

Silva, G. (1999). *Helping young people survive the suicide of a school friend: A study of the effects of school postvention strategies on middle adolescent students who have lost a friend to suicide.* Unpublished master's dissertation, University of Auckland.

Simmons, R., Burgeson, R., Carlton-Ford, S., & Blyth, D. (1987). The impact of cumulative change in early adolescence. *Child Development, 58,* 1220–1234.

UCLA School Mental Health Project. (2004). Addressing barriers to learning. *UCLA Mental Health in Schools Center: Training and technical assistance, 9,* 1–12.

Walsh, M. E., Howard, K. A., & Buckley, M. A. (1999). School counselors in school-community partnerships: Opportunities and challenges. *Professional School Counseling*, *2*(5), 349–356.

Weare, K. (2000). *Promoting mental, emotional and social health: A whole school approach.* London: Routledge.

Weare, K., & Gray, G. (2003). *What works in developing children's emotional and social competence and wellbeing.* Southampton, UK: The Health Education Unit: Research and Graduate School of Education, University of Southampton.

Winterbourn, R. (1974). *Guidance services in New Zealand education.* Wellington: New Zealand Council for Educational Research.

World Health Organisation. (2004). *Young people's health in context: Health behavior in school-aged children (HBSC) study: International report from the 2001/2002 survey.* Geneva: World Health Organisation.

Wyn, J., Cahill, H., Holdsworth, R., Rowling, L., & Carson, S. (2000). MindMatters, a whole-school approach promoting mental health and wellbeing. *Australian and New Zealand Journal of Psychiatry*, *34*, 594–601.

AUTHOR NOTE

Margaret Agee is a Senior Lecturer in the Faculty of Education, University of Auckland, New Zealand, and co-ordinator of counsellor education.

Pauline Dickinson is a Senior Tutor in the Faculty of Education, University of Auckland, a Senior Evaluation Researcher and Evaluation Team Leader, SHORE, Massey University, and a counsellor in a secondary school in New Zealand.

Correspondence concerning this chapter should be addressed by email to: m.agee@auckland.ac.nz

INDEX

B

C

D

E

F

J

K

L

M

T

U

V

W

Y